Sport Management

Now available in a fully revised and updated sixth edition, *Sport Management: Principles and Applications* tells you everything you need to know about the contemporary sport industry.

Covering both the professional and nonprofit sectors, and with more international material than any other introductory sport management textbook, it focuses on core management principles and their application in a sporting context, highlighting the unique challenges of a career in sport management. The book contains useful features throughout, including conceptual overviews, guides to further reading, links to important websites, study questions, and up-to-date case studies showing how theory works in the real world. It covers every core area of management, including:

- Strategic planning
- Human resource management
- Leadership and governance
- Marketing and sponsorship
- Sport and the media
- Sport policy
- Sport law

The sixth edition includes expanded coverage of key contemporary issues, including integrity and corruption, digital business and technology, and legal issues and risk management.

With useful ancillary material for instructors, including slides and case diagnostic exercises, this is an ideal textbook for first- and second-year students in sport management degree programs and for business students seeking an overview of applied sport management principles.

Russell Hoye is Dean of Allied Health, Human Services and Sport at La Trobe University, Australia, and Adjunct Professor in the School of Human Kinetics at the University of Ottawa, Canada. He is also Director of La Trobe Sport. His research interests are in corporate governance, public policy, volunteer management, and the impact of sport on individuals and society. Russ is a member of the editorial boards for *Sport Management Review*, *International Journal of Sport Policy and Politics*, and *Journal of Global Sport*

Management; the Editor of the Sport Management Series for Routledge; and a graduate of the Australian Institute of Company Directors. He has previously served as Pro Vice-Chancellor of Research Development, Director of the Sport, Exercise and Rehabilitation Research Focus Area, Inaugural Director of the Centre for Sport and Social Impact at La Trobe University, and is a past president of the Sport Management Association of Australia and New Zealand (SMAANZ).

Katie Misener is Associate Professor in the Department of Recreation and Leisure Studies, Faculty of Health, at the University of Waterloo, Canada. Her primary research focuses on the capacity and social impact of nonprofit community sport organizations, with a particular focus on how capacity can be enhanced to support sport service delivery and foster social engagement through sport. Her current research examines the broader social impact of community sport organizations through their social responsibility efforts and the development of social capital among sport volunteers. Through community-engaged research, she has worked with organizations such as the Waterloo Soccer Club, Sport Information Research Centre (SIRC), Parks and Recreation Ontario, OutSport Toronto, World Vision Canada, Oakville Rangers, YMCA of Greater Toronto, and Ringette Canada.

Michael L. Naraine is Assistant Professor in the Department of Sport Management at Brock University, Canada. His primary research expertise is concentrated on digital sport management and marketing, including examining conventional (e.g. TV) and emergent (e.g. social media, AI, blockchain) tech and its impact on sport stakeholders. Michael's additional research expertise extends to sport event management and sport organization theory. He has been published in some of the leading sport management journals, including the *Journal of Sport Management*, *Sport Management Review*, *European Sport Management Quarterly*, *International Journal of Sport Communication*, and *International Journal of Sport Management and Marketing*, and consults with various sport organizations, including the Canadian Olympic Committee and the Geelong Cats Football Club.

Catherine Ordway is Assistant Professor of Sports Management at the University of Canberra, Australia. Catherine lectures in sports integrity, ethics and law, and leadership in sport. She is an international expert in the field of integrity in sport and has specialized in anti-doping policy for 20 years. Catherine is also a sports lawyer, acting for the Australian Olympic Committee in a legal capacity in the lead-up to the Sydney 2000 Olympic Games, and has extensive experience in international anti-doping administration, consulting on projects including the Rio 2016 Olympic Games Bid, the Budapest 2024 Olympic Games Bid, and the Gold Coast 2018 Commonwealth Games. Catherine is a member of the UN Office on Drugs and Crime (UNODC) Anti-Corruption Academics Initiative and the Education for Justice expert group, developing the Gender Ethics Module.

Sport Management Series

Series Editor: Russell Hoye, La Trobe University, Australia

This **Sport Management Series** has been providing a range of texts for core subjects in undergraduate sport business and management courses around the world for more than ten years. These textbooks are considered essential resources for academics, students, and managers seeking an international perspective on the management of the complex world of sport.

Many millions of people around the globe are employed in sport organizations in areas as diverse as event management, broadcasting, venue management, marketing, professional sport, community and collegiate sport, and coaching as well as in allied industries such as sporting equipment manufacturing, sporting footwear and apparel, and retail.

At the elite level, sport has moved from being an amateur pastime to one of the world's most significant industries. The growth and professionalization of sport has driven changes in the consumption and production of sport and in the management of sporting organizations at all levels.

Managing sport organizations at the start of the 21st century involves the application of techniques and strategies evident in leading business, government, and nonprofit organizations. This series explains these concepts and applies them to the diverse global sport industry.

To support their use by academics, each text is supported by current case studies, targeted study questions, further reading lists, links to relevant web-based resources, and supplementary online materials such as case study questions and classroom presentation aids.

Available in this series:

Sport Management
Principles and Applications (Fourth edition)
Russell Hoye, Aaron C.T. Smith, Matthew Nicholson and Bob Stewart

Sport and the Media
Managing the Nexus (Second edition)
Matthew Nicholson, Anthony Kerr and Merryn Sherwood

Sport Management
Principles and Applications (Fifth edition)
Russell Hoye, Aaron C.T. Smith, Matthew Nicholson and Bob Stewart

Sport Management
Principles and Applications (Sixth edition)
Russell Hoye, Katie Misener, Michael Naraine, and Catherine Ordway

For more information about this series, please visit: www.routledge.com/Sport-Management-Series/book-series/SMS

Sport Management
Principles and Applications

SIXTH EDITION

Russell Hoye, Katie Misener,
Michael L. Naraine, and
Catherine Ordway

 Routledge
Taylor & Francis Group

LONDON AND NEW YORK

Cover image: © Shutterstock

Sixth edition published 2022
by Routledge
4 Park Square, Milton Park, Abingdon, Oxon, OX14 4RN

and by Routledge
605 Third Avenue, New York, NY 10158

Routledge is an imprint of the Taylor & Francis Group, an informa business

© 2022 Russell Hoye, Katie Misener, Michael L. Naraine, and Catherine Ordway

The right of Russell Hoye, Katie Misener, Michael L. Naraine, and Catherine Ordway to be identified as authors of this work has been asserted in accordance with sections 77 and 78 of the Copyright, Designs and Patents Act 1988.

First edition published by Butterworth-Heinenmann, an imprint of Elsevier 2005
Fifth edition published by Routledge 2018

British Library Cataloguing-in-Publication Data
A catalogue record for this book is available from the British Library

Library of Congress Cataloging-in-Publication Data
Names: Hoye, Russell, 1966– author. | Misener, Katie, author. | Naraine,
    Michael L., 1987– author. | Ordway, Catherine, author.
Title: Sport management : principles and applications / Russell Hoye, Katie
    Misener, Michael Naraine and Catherine Ordway.
Description: Sixth Edition. | New York : Routledge, 2022. | Series: Sport
    Management Series | "First edition published by Elsevier 2005. Fifth edition
    published by Routledge 2018"—T.p. verso. | Includes bibliographical
    references and index.
Identifiers: LCCN 2021050789 | ISBN 9781032109664 (Hardback) |
    ISBN 9781032109640 (Paperback) | ISBN 9781003217947 (eBook)
Subjects: LCSH: Sports administration.
Classification: LCC GV713 .S6775 2022 | DDC 796.06/9—dc23/
    eng/20211109
LC record available at https://lccn.loc.gov/2021050789

ISBN: 978-1-032-10966-4 (hbk)
ISBN: 978-1-032-10964-0 (pbk)
ISBN: 978-1-003-21794-7 (ebk)

DOI: 10.4324/9781003217947

Typeset in Berling and Futura
by Apex CoVantage, LLC

Access the Support Material: www.routledge.com/9781032109640

Contents

Figures

Images

Tables

In practice examples

Case studies

Preface

This sixth edition features three new authors: Katie Misener and Mike Naraine, both from Canada, and Catherine Ordway, one of Australia's leading sports lawyers. The chapter on legal issues was also supported by Björn Hessert, from the Universität Zürich. This enhanced international expertise and perspectives are reflected in the broad range of in practice examples and detailed case studies provided in this new edition covering sport organizations and issues from around the globe.

The feedback we have received from academics using the book for their courses asked us to add coverage of legal issues and risk management and the ever-changing impact of digital technology on sport. In order to do so and maintain the suitability of the textbook to support a single introductory course for sport students, we have added a new chapter on legal issues and transformed the chapter on sport and media to cover digital technology. To make room for this new content and to address other feedback, we have omitted the chapter on finance that appeared in previous editions and weaved the concepts of performance management into the strategic management chapter.

We recognize that many instructors, lecturers, and course leaders have used the various iterations of this textbook in core courses over many years, and we wanted to maintain the basic structure but update the case materials, examples, and current issues while maintaining as much as possible the existing framework of the book. As with previous editions, the book is divided into two parts. Part one provides a concise analysis of the evolution of sport; the unique features of sport and sport management; the current drivers of change in the sport industry; and the role of government policy and agencies, nonprofit organizations, and the professional sectors of sport. Part two covers core management principles and their application in sport, highlighting the unique features of how sport is managed compared to other industrial sectors, with chapters on sport governance, legal issues and risk management, strategic management, organizational design, human resource management, leadership, organizational culture, sport marketing, and sport media and digital technology.

The success of the previous five editions of this textbook points to a continued need for *Sport Management: Principles and Applications* to fill the gap for an introductory text in sport management that provides a balance between management theory and the analysis of the highly dynamic context of the global sport industry. The textbook continues to be adopted by many educational institutions across Australia, Canada, New Zealand, the United Kingdom, Europe, and increasingly other countries as a core undergraduate textbook, as well as being reprinted in five other languages. Our intention with this new edition is not to replace the core introductory texts on management theory or to ignore the increasing volume of books that examine various elements of the global sport industry. Our aim continues to be the provision of a textbook that includes sufficient conceptual detail for undergraduate students to grasp the essentials of management while highlighting the unique aspects of how management is applied to sport across the globe.

The book provides a comprehensive introduction to the principles of management and their practical application to sport organizations operating at the community, state/provincial, national, and professional levels. The book is primarily written for first- and second-year university students studying sport management courses and students who wish to research the nonprofit, government, and commercial dimensions of sport. It is especially suitable for students studying sport management within business-focused courses, as well as students seeking an overview of sport management principles within human movement, sport development, sport science, or physical education courses.

To assist lecturers and instructors, all chapters include an overview, a set of objectives, a summary, a set of review questions for students to use to test their comprehension, discussion questions for tutors and instructors to use for in-class or online discussion, suggestions for further reading, and a list of relevant websites for further information. Chapters 2 through 13 each contain three substantial examples (dubbed "In Practice") that help illustrate concepts and accepted practice at the community, state/provincial, national, and international levels of sport. As with previous editions, the majority of these have been completely rewritten with new examples and the remainder extensively revised with updated information.

We have also written detailed new case studies for Chapters 2 to 13 which can be used by lecturers and instructors for classroom discussion or assessment. For those academics who prescribe the book as essential reading for students, a comprehensive website is available that contains an updated set of PowerPoint slides that summarize each chapter as well as teaching notes to accompany each of the case studies to guide instructors in their use for in-class activities or assessment tasks.

We would like to thank our colleagues and students for their valuable comments on the previous editions of the book and the insightful anonymous reviews provided on those editions. We are indebted to our Commissioning Editor Simon Whitmore for his belief in us to deliver a quality book. We acknowledge and thank our respective partners and families for their support and patience while we developed this new edition.

Russell Hoye
Katie Misener
Michael L. Naraine
Catherine Ordway

PART I

The sport management environment

CHAPTER 1

Sport management

OVERVIEW

This chapter provides a brief review of the development of sport into a major sector of economic and social activity and outlines the importance of sport management as a field of study and employment. It explains the unique nature of sport and the drivers of change that affect how sport is produced and consumed. A model that explains the public, nonprofit, and professional elements of sport is presented, along with a brief description of the salient aspects of the management context for sport organizations. The chapter also serves as an introduction to the remaining sections of the book, highlighting the importance of each of the topics.

DOI: 10.4324/9781003217947-2

After completing this chapter, the reader should be able to:

- Describe the unique features of sport;
- Understand the environment in which sport organizations operate;
- Describe the three sectors of the sport industry; and
- Explain how sport management is different to other fields of management study.

WHAT IS SPORT MANAGEMENT?

Sport employs many millions of people around the globe, is played or watched by the majority of the world's population, and, at the elite or professional level, has moved from being an amateur pastime to a significant industry. The growth and professionalization of sport has driven changes in the consumption, production, and management of sporting events and organizations at all levels of sport. Countries with emerging economies such as Qatar, hosts of the 2022 World Cup for football, or Mexico, partnering with Canada and the United States to host the 2026 World Cup, as well as advanced economic powerhouses such as France (host of the 2024 Summer Olympic Games) and Italy (host of the 2026 Winter Olympic Games), increasingly see sport as a vehicle for driving investment in infrastructure; for promoting their country to the world to stimulate trade, tourism, and investment; and for fostering national pride amongst their citizens.

Managing contemporary sport organizations involves the application of techniques and strategies evident in the majority of modern business, government, and nonprofit organizations. Sport managers engage in strategic planning and performance management, manage large numbers of paid and voluntary human resources, deal with media rights contracts worth billions of dollars, and manage the development and welfare of elite athletes who sometimes earn 100 times the average working wage. Sport managers also work within a highly integrated global network of international sports federations, national sport organizations, government agencies, media corporations, sponsors, and community organizations that are subject to a myriad of regulations, government policies, and complex decision-making frameworks.

Students seeking a career as a sport manager need to develop an understanding of the special features of sport and its allied industries; the environment in which sport organizations operate; and the types of sport organizations that operate in the public, nonprofit, and professional sectors of the sport industry. The remainder of the chapter is devoted to a discussion of these points and highlights the unique aspects of sport organization management.

UNIQUE FEATURES OF SPORT

Smith and Stewart (2010) provided a list of ten unique features of sport which can assist us to understand why the management of sport organizations requires the application of specific management techniques. A unique feature of sport is the phenomenon of people developing irrational passions for sporting teams, competitions, or athletes. Sport has a symbolic significance in relation to performance outcomes, success, and celebrating achievement that does not occur in other areas of economic and social activity. Sport managers must learn to harness these passions by appealing to people's desire to buy tickets for events, become a member of a club, donate time to help run a voluntary association, or purchase sporting merchandise. They must also learn to apply clear business logic and management techniques to the maintenance of traditions and connections to the nostalgic aspects of sport consumption and engagement.

There are also marked differences between sport organizations and other businesses in how they evaluate performance. Private or publicly listed companies exist to make profits and increase wealth of shareholders or owners, whereas in sport, other imperatives such as winning championships, delivering services to stakeholders and members, or meeting community service obligations may take precedence over financial outcomes. Sport managers need to be cognizant of these multiple organizational outcomes while at the same time being responsible financial managers to ensure they have the requisite resources to support their organization's strategic objectives.

Competitive balance is also a unique feature of the interdependent nature of relationships between sporting organizations that compete on the field but cooperate off the field to ensure the long-term viability of both clubs and their league. In most business environments the aim is to secure the largest market share, defeat all competitors, and secure a monopoly. In sport leagues, clubs and teams need the opposition to remain in business, so they must cooperate to share revenues and playing talent and regulate themselves to maximize the level of uncertainty in the outcome of games between them so that fans' interest will be maintained. In some ways, such behaviour could be construed as anti-competitive, but governments support such actions due to the unique aspects of sport.

The sport product, when it takes the form of a game or contest, is also of variable quality. While game outcomes are generally uncertain, one team might dominate, which will diminish the attractiveness of the game. The perception of those watching the game might be that the quality has also diminished as a result, particularly if it is your team that loses! The variable quality of sport therefore makes it hard to guarantee quality in the marketplace relative to providers of other consumer products such as mobile phones, cars, or other general household goods.

Sport also enjoys a high degree of product or brand loyalty, with fans unlikely to change the team or club they support or to switch sporting codes because of a poor match result or the standard of officiating. Consumers of household products have a huge range to choose from and will readily switch brands for reasons of price or quality, whereas sporting competitions and their teams are hard to substitute. This advantage is also a negative, as sporting codes that wish to expand market share find it difficult to attract new fans from other codes due to their familiarity with the customs and traditions of their existing sport affiliation.

Sport engenders unique behaviours in people, such as emulating their sporting heroes in play, wearing the uniform of their favourite player, or purchasing the products that sporting celebrities endorse. This vicarious identification with the skills, abilities, and lifestyles of sports people can be used by sport managers and allied industries to influence the purchasing decisions of individuals who follow sport.

Sport fans also exhibit a high degree of optimism, at times insisting that their team, despite a string of bad losses, is only a week, game, or lucky break away from winning the next championship. It could also be argued that the owners or managers of sport franchises exhibit a high degree of optimism by touting their star recruits or new coach as the path to delivering them on-field success.

Sporting organizations, argued Smith and Stewart (2010), are relatively reluctant to adopt new technologies unless they are related to sports science or data analytics, where on-field performance improvements are possible and, indeed, highly desirable. In this regard, sport organizations can be considered conservative and tied to traditions and behaviours, more so than other organizations.

The final unique aspect of sport is its limited availability. In other industries, organizations can increase production to meet demand, but in sport, clubs are limited by season length and the number of scheduled games. This constrains their ability to maximize revenue through ticket sales and associated income. The implication for sport managers is that they must understand the nature of their business, the level of demand for their product and services (whatever form that may take), and the appropriate time to deliver them.

Collectively, these unique features of sport create some challenges for managers of sport organizations and events. It is important to understand the effects of these features on the management approaches and strategies used by sport managers; the next section explains how these unique features of sport influence the operating environment for sport organizations and their managers.

SPORT MANAGEMENT ENVIRONMENT

Globalization has been a major force in driving change in the ways sport is produced and consumed. The enhanced integration of the world's economies has enabled communication to occur between producers and consumers at greater speed and variety, and sport has been one sector to reap the benefits. Consumers of elite sport events and competitions such as the Olympic Games; World Cups for rugby, cricket, and football; English Premier League Football; the National Basketball Association (NBA); and Grand Slam tournaments for tennis and golf enjoy unprecedented access through mainstream and social media. Aside from actually attending the events live at a stadium or venue, fans can view these events through free-to-air and pay or cable television on flat-screen TVs or mobile devices; listen to them on radio and via the internet; read and hear about game analyses and their favourite players and teams through newspapers and magazines in both print and digital editions as well as podcasts; receive progress scores, commentary, or vision on their mobile phones or tablets through websites or social media platforms such as Twitter, Facebook, or dedicated apps; and sign up for special deals and information through online subscriptions using their email address or preferred social media platform. The global sport marketplace is very crowded, and sport managers seeking to carve out a niche need to understand the global environment in which they must operate. Thus, one of the themes of this book is the impact of globalization on the ways sport is produced, consumed, and managed.

Most national governments view sport as a vehicle for nationalism, economic development, or social development. As such, they consider it their role to enact policies and legislation to support, control, or regulate the activities of sport organizations. Most national governments support elite training institutes to assist in developing athletes for national and international competition, provide funding to national sporting organizations to deliver high performance and community-level programs, support sport organizations to bid for major events, and facilitate the building of major stadia. In return for this support, governments can influence sports to recruit more mass participants, provide services to discrete sectors of the community, have sports enact policies on alcohol and drug use or gambling, and support general health promotion messages. Governments also regulate the activities of sport organizations through legislation or licensing in areas such as industrial relations, anti-discrimination, taxation, and corporate governance. A further theme in the book is the impact that government policy, funding, and regulation can have on the way sport is produced, consumed, and managed.

The management of sport organizations has undergone a relatively rapid period of professionalization since the 1980s. The general expansion of the global sports industry and commercialization of sport events and competitions, combined with the introduction of paid staff into voluntary governance structures and the growing number of people who now earn a living managing sport organizations or playing sport, has forced sport organizations and their managers to become more professional. This is reflected in the increased number of university sport management courses, the requirement to have business skills as well as industry-specific knowledge or experience to be successful in sport management, the growth of professional and academic associations devoted to sport management, and the variety of professionals and specialists that sport managers must deal with in the course of their careers. Sport managers will work with accountants, lawyers, human resource managers, taxation specialists, government policy advisors, project management personnel, architects, market researchers, and media specialists, not to mention sports agents, sports scientists, coaches, officials, and volunteers. The ensuing chapters of the book will highlight the ongoing professionalization of sport management as an academic discipline and a career.

The final theme of the book is the notion that changes in sport management frequently result from developments in technology. Changes in telecommunications have already been highlighted, but further changes in digital technology are evident in areas such as performance-enhancing drugs, communication technology, data analytics focused on both on-field and off-field elements, coaching and high-performance techniques, sports venues, sport betting and wagering, and sporting equipment. These changes have forced sport managers to develop policies about their use, to protect intellectual property with a marketable value, and generally adapt their operations to incorporate their use for achieving organizational objectives. Sport managers need to understand the potential of technological development but also the likely impact on the future operations of their organizations.

THREE SECTORS OF SPORT

To make sense of the many organizations that are involved in sport management and how these organizations may form partnerships, influence each others' operations, and conduct business, it is useful to see sport as comprising three distinct sectors. The first is the state or public sector, which includes national, state/provincial, regional, and local governments and

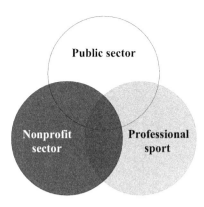

FIGURE 1.1 Three-sector model of sport

specialist agencies that develop sport policy, provide funding to other sectors, and support specialist roles such as elite athlete development or drug control. The second is the non-profit or voluntary sector, made up of community-based clubs, governing associations, and international sport organizations that provide competition and participation opportunities, regulate and manage sporting codes, and organize major championship events. The third sector is professional or commercial sport organizations, comprising professional leagues and their member teams, as well as allied organizations such as sporting apparel and equipment manufacturers, media companies, major stadia operators, and event managers.

These three sectors do not operate in isolation, and in many cases, there is significant overlap. For example, the state is intimately involved in providing funding to nonprofit sport organizations for sport development and elite athlete programs, and in return, nonprofit sport organizations provide the general community with sporting opportunities as well as developing athletes, coaches, officials, and administrators to sustain sporting participation. The state is also involved in commercial sport, supporting the building of major stadia and other sporting venues to provide spaces for professional sport to be played, providing a regulatory and legal framework for professional sport to take place, and supporting manufacturing and event organizations to do business. The nonprofit sport sector supports professional sport by providing playing talent for leagues, as well as developing the coaches, officials, and administrators to facilitate elite competitions. Indeed, in some cases, the sport league itself will consist of member teams which are technically nonprofit entities, even though they support a pool of professional managers and players. In return, the professional sport sector markets sport for spectators and participants and in some cases provides substantial funds from TV broadcast rights revenue. Figure 1.1 illustrates the three sectors and the intersections where these relationships take place.

WHAT IS DIFFERENT ABOUT SPORT MANAGEMENT?

Sport managers utilize management techniques and theories that are similar to managers of other organizations, such as hospitals, government departments, banks, mining companies, car manufacturers, and welfare agencies. However, there are some aspects of governance, legal issues and risk management, strategic management, organizational structure, human resource management, leadership, organizational culture, marketing, and media that are unique to the management of sport organizations.

Governance

Organizational governance involves the exercise of decision-making power within organizations and provides the system by which the elements of organizations are controlled and directed. Governance is a particularly important element of managing sport organizations, many of whom are controlled by elected groups of volunteers, as it deals with issues of policy and direction for the enhancement of organizational performance rather than day-to-day operational management decision-making. Appropriate governance systems help ensure that elected decision-makers and paid staff seek to deliver outcomes for the benefit of the organization and its members and that the means used to attain these outcomes are effectively monitored. As many sport managers work in an environment where they must report to a governing board, it is important that they understand the principles of good governance and how these are applied in sport organizations.

Legal issues and risk management

Sport organizations have the authority to decide on internal matters on their own without state interference, a unique aspect of sports' autonomy. At a national level, sports can be governed by a federated (European) or a private ownership (American) model. In both systems, the sport governing body can implement sports rules and regulations and apply and enforce them against the people under its authority. However, all decisions and regulations of sport organizations must comply with general law provisions. Sport organizations have an interest in the protection of the integrity of sport and have implemented rules and regulations aiming at preventing all forms of corruption in sport, including doping and match-fixing. The latter pose major threats to the fairness, equality, and unpredictability of sports competitions. It is important for sport managers to understand that athletes and other participants are subject to stringent sports regulations that impose limits on their personal and professional lives but that such rules and regulations serve to protect not only the values and ethics of sport but also the honest athletes who believe in those values of fair and equal sports competitions.

Strategic management

Strategic management involves the analysis of an organization's position in the competitive environment, the determination of its direction and goals, the selection of an appropriate strategy, and the leveraging of its distinctive assets. The success of any sport organization may largely depend on the quality of its strategic decisions. It could be argued that nonprofit sport organizations have been slow to embrace the concepts associated with strategic management because sport is inherently turbulent, with on-field performance and tactics tending to dominate and distract sport managers from the choices they need to make in the office and boardroom. In a competitive market, sport managers must drive their own futures by undertaking meaningful market analyses, establishing a clear direction, and crafting strategy that matches opportunities. An understanding of strategic management principles and how these can be applied in the specific industry context of sport are essential for future sport managers.

Organizational structure

An organization's structure is important because it defines where staff and volunteers "fit in" with each other in terms of work tasks, decision-making procedures, the need for collaboration, levels of responsibility, and reporting mechanisms. Finding the right structure for a sport organization involves balancing the need to formalize procedures while fostering innovation and creativity and ensuring adequate control of employee and volunteer activities without unduly affecting people's motivation and attitudes to work. In the complex world of sport, clarifying reporting and communication lines between multiple groups of internal and external stakeholders while trying to reduce unnecessary and costly layers of management is also an important aspect of managing an organization's structure. The relatively unique mix of paid staff and volunteers in the sport industry adds a layer of complexity to managing the structure of many sport organizations.

Human resource management

Human resource management, in mainstream business or sport organizations, is essentially about ensuring an effective and satisfied workforce. However, the sheer size of some sport organizations, as well as the difficulties in managing a mix of volunteers and paid staff in the sport industry, make human resource management a complex issue for sport managers. Successful sport leagues, clubs, associations, retailers, and venues rely on good human resources, both on and off the field. Human resource management cannot be divorced from other key management tools, such as strategic planning or managing organizational culture and structure, and is a further element that students of sport management need to understand to be effective practitioners.

Leadership

Managers at the helm of sport organizations need to be able to influence others to follow their visions; empower individuals to feel part of a team working for a common goal; and be adept at working with leaders of other sport organizations to forge alliances, deal with conflicts, or coordinate common business or development projects. The sport industry thrives on organizations having leaders who are able to collaborate effectively with other organizations to run a professional league; work with governing bodies of sport; and coordinate the efforts of government agencies, international and national sport organizations, and other groups to deliver large-scale sport events. Sport management students wishing to work in leadership roles need to understand the ways in which leadership skills can be developed and how these principles can be applied.

Organizational culture

Organizational culture consists of the assumptions, norms, and values held by individuals and groups within an organization, which impact the activities and goals in the workplace and in many ways influence how employees work. Organizational culture is related to organizational performance, excellence, employee commitment, cooperation, efficiency, job performance, and decision-making. However, how organizational culture can be defined, diagnosed, and changed is subject to much debate in the business and academic world. Due to the strong traditions of sporting endeavour and behaviour, managers of sport organizations, particularly those such as professional sport franchises or traditional sports, must be cognizant of the power of organizational culture as both an inhibitor and driver of performance. Understanding how to identify, describe, analyse, and ultimately influence the culture of a sport organization is an important element in the education of sport managers.

Sport marketing

Sport marketing is the application of marketing concepts to sport products and services and the marketing of non-sports products through an association with sport. Like other forms of marketing, sport marketing seeks to fulfil the needs and wants of consumers. It achieves this by providing sport services and sport-related products to consumers. However, sport marketing is unlike conventional marketing in that it also has the ability to encourage the consumption of non-sport products and services by association. It is important to understand that sport marketing means the marketing of sport as well as the use of sport as a tool to market other products and services.

Sport media and digital technology

The relationship between sport and the media is the defining commercial connection for both industries at the beginning of the 21st century, and at the elite and professional levels, sport is becoming increasingly dependent on the media for its commercial success. Managers of professional or commercial sport organizations and events need an understanding of the advancements in digital technology that will support their business goals, the implications of media diversity and convergence, the importance of media rights, and the restrictions that government policy and regulation have on media's relationship with sport in some jurisdictions. The explosion in the use of social media platforms by consumers demands that sport managers know how to use these platforms to communicate, engage, and ultimately influence consumer decisions in relation to their product, service, or brand.

SUMMARY

Sport has a number of unique features:

- people develop irrational passions;
- there are differences in judging performance;
- relationships between sporting organizations are interdependent;
- there exists anti-competitive behaviour;
- sport product (a game or contest) is of variable quality;
- it enjoys a high degree of product or brand loyalty;
- it engenders vicarious identification;
- sport fans exhibit a high degree of optimism;
- sport organizations are relatively reluctant to adopt new technology; and
- sport often has a limited supply.

Several environmental factors influence the way sport organizations operate, namely globalization, government policy, professionalization, and technological developments. The sport industry can be defined as comprising three distinct but interrelated industries: the state or public sector, the nonprofit or voluntary sector, and the professional or commercial sector. These sectors do not operate in isolation and often engage in a range of collaborative projects, funding arrangements, joint commercial ventures, and other business relationships.

There are some aspects of governance, legal issues and risk management, strategic management, organizational structure, human resource management, leadership, organizational culture, marketing, and media that are unique to the management of sport organizations. The remainder of the book explores the three sectors of the sport industry and examines each of these core management issues in more detail.

REVIEW QUESTIONS

1 Define sport management.

2 What are the unique features of sport that interest you the most?

3 Describe the main elements of the environment that affect sport organizations.

4 What sort of relationships might develop between sport organizations in the public and nonprofit sectors?

5 What sort of relationships might develop between sport organizations in the public and professional sport sectors?

6 What sort of relationships might develop between sport organizations in the professional and nonprofit sectors?

7 Explain the major differences between managing a sport organization and a commercial manufacturing firm.

8 Why does the sport industry need specialist managers with tertiary sport management qualifications?

9 Identify one organization from each of the public, nonprofit, and professional sport sectors. Compare how the environmental factors discussed in this chapter can affect their operation.

10 Discuss whether the special features of sport discussed in this chapter apply to all levels of sport by comparing the operation of professional sports league, an elite government sport institute, and a community sport club.

DISCUSSION QUESTIONS

1 Why do governments support sport through the use of taxpayer money to build facilities and stadia in order to host major sport events?

2 Why have some professional sports, such as the English Premier League football competition or the NBA, become more successful than others?

3 What are some of the unique attributes of sport that have attracted you (as a student) to study this field?

4 Is sport still as popular as a leisure or active recreation activity as, say, 20 years ago? Why or why not?

5 What might be some of the emerging challenges that sport managers will have to face in the next decade?

FURTHER READING

Hoye, R., & Parent, M. (Eds.). (2017). *Handbook of sport management.* London: Sage.
Jarvie, G. (2013). *Sport culture and society: An introduction* (2nd ed.). London: Routledge.
Mackintosh, C. (2021). *Foundations of sport development.* London: Routledge.
Shilbury, D., & Ferkins, L. (Eds.). (2020). *Routledge handbook of sport governance.* London: Routledge.

RELEVANT WEBSITES

The following websites are useful starting points for general information on the teaching programs and research communities focussed on the management of sport:

African Sport Management Association at asma-online.com
Asian Association for Sport Management (AASM) at asiansportmanagement.com
European Association for Sport Management (EASM) at www.easm.net
North American Society for Sport Management (NASSM) at www.nassm.org
Sport Management Association of Australia and New Zealand (SMAANZ) at www.smaanz.org
World Association for Sport Management at www.wasmorg.com

CHAPTER 2

Sport policy

OVERVIEW

This chapter examines the role and impact of sport policies enacted by governments and their national or state/provincial agencies on the development of sport systems and practices. It explores why governments seek to intervene in the operations of sport organizations and the different forms such intervention can take, such as assisting and promoting participation in sport, improving levels of elite performance, using sport to drive economic activity through sport infrastructure development and major events, and also attempting to control and regulate sport. Throughout the chapter, incidents

DOI: 10.4324/9781003217947-3

and cases are used to illustrate both the concepts and theories that underpin sport policy and the implications for sport organizations and their leaders that arise from this intervention.

After completing this chapter, the reader should be able to:

- Explain the role and purpose of government in relation to sport;
- Distinguish between nations – and their governments – that operate from different ideological perspectives, which are first socialist, second reformist, third neoliberal, and finally conservative;
- Explain how each of these ideologies impact the way governments go about assisting sport on one hand and regulating it on the other; and
- Critically compare and contrast strategies that aim to improve elite sport systems and standards with those that aim to build the participation base of sport.

THE ROLE OF GOVERNMENT

Government, by which we mean the structures and systems that govern, rule, and control societies, is pivotal in shaping the economic structure of nations and setting their social and cultural "tone". The government sector – or public sector, as it is sometimes called – includes all levels of government – federal, state/provincial, and local. These three levels intervene in the economy by collecting and spending tax revenue and by establishing and enforcing laws, rules, and other regulations. The government sector undertakes this intervention because society has deemed that the provision of some goods and services is better handled by the imposition of government than by market decisions involving the interaction of independent buyers and sellers. Government decisions thus impact the allocation of a nation's scarce resources, which means that it can, in line with its policies and goals, and hopefully with the interests of the broader community front and centre, either expand or contract a particular industry and the products and jobs it creates. Sport is one such industry.

Government and its agencies provide a complex array of sport facilities and services. Many sport stadia throughout the world were initially financed by government funds and, while subsequently controlled and operated by independent operators, are now subject to government legislation and policy guidelines (John & Sheard, 1997). In most western nations, the central government has funded both the establishment of training centres for elite athletes and their ongoing operation. As a result, many thousands of coaches, sport scientists, and sport facility managers are now on the government payroll.

The world's leading sport policy scholar, Barrie Houlihan (2017, p. 183), encapsulated the contemporary relationship between government and sport:

> Without government support organised sport at both the domestic and international levels would decline dramatically and in some sports almost cease to exist.

Even those highly commercial sports such as American football, Formula 1, professional road cycling, golf and soccer would be altered dramatically if the public policies that support them were withdrawn. The importance of public policy in relation to community sport and most Olympic sports is far more evident. In many countries it is the state that provides most of the facilities for community sport either through local government or through educational institutions. The state is often heavily involved in supporting the preparations of elite Olympic athletes through the funding of specialist training centres, subsidising the cost of living of athletes and providing specialist support services such as coaching, medical care and sports science research. While the highly commercial sports and events which receive substantial broadcasting and sponsorship income may not depend on direct state financial support they depend for their commercial success on a wide range of supportive public policies.

WHY SHOULD GOVERNMENTS ENGAGE WITH SPORT?

Sport, especially in Western nations, is highly valued by government, even though many people – even those with significant political clout – consider it a frivolous use of valuable time. It is often seen as superficial, fleeting, anti-intellectual, and trivial (Stebbins, 2007). Sport was summarized by the 1960s US sport broadcaster Howard Cosell as the "toy department of life". So, is there really a place for government involvement in sport, or is it there only because it feels obligated and that it is the right thing to do?

The idea that sport can be used to build nations is something in which governments have a strong investment. Governments have responsibility for creating the commercial and cultural space where people can build not only strong families, neighbourhoods, communities, and workplaces but also healthy ones. Nearly all modern nations allocate a special space for sport, since sport is seen to be a practice that delivers a multitude of individual and social benefits. This is the case in Cuba, North Korea, and China as much as it is in the United States, Great Britain, and Germany. This is why, from a global perspective, governments have constructed infrastructure to service sport's needs and have provided substantial funding to assist sport organizations in delivering services to members. The benefits and social utility that governments believe arise from the sport experience include the following.

First, sport is supposed to contribute to the wellbeing of society by providing the context in which appropriate values, attitudes, and behaviours are learnt and perpetuated. It is claimed that sport participation allows young people to better fit into mainstream cultural and behavioural patterns of society. In this way, it contributes to the stability, maintenance, and perpetuation of established society.

Second, sport is seen as character building, a principle that was the cornerstone of the British public school education system during the Victorian and Edwardian era. Not only does sport build "character"; it also inculcates values which support and reinforce the central beliefs of modern industrial societies. These beliefs and attitudes are the ones that industrial society holds so dear to its heart and the ones that drive the progress of these societies (Coakley et al., 2009). So, what exactly are these values? First and foremost, they include a strong belief in the idea that success comes through hard work, self-discipline, and lots of initiative. They also include a respect for authority and adherence to rules and laws. Finally, they include all those traits and dispositions that make for a compliant and diligent workforce, which include leadership, hierarchy, cooperative behaviour, and the desire for success and goal achievement. These are exactly the sort of traits a modern 21st-century nation wants from its citizens, since they enable a fully functioning commercial system, and a strong sense of civic pride, to flourish. Moreover, these are the exact same values that characterized the newly industrialized 19th-century societies and strengthened their commitment to the "Protestant work ethic", which is precisely what enabled them to progress out of feudalism. And sport is seen to be the ideal practice for building these values (Rigauer, 1981).

Governments also recognize that sport has many other functions that can strengthen the bonds between disparate communities and build a healthier and stronger society. For instance, sport participation is increasingly viewed as a mechanism for the dissipation of stress and management of tension. Additionally, sport is seen as a socially approved outlet for otherwise unacceptable behaviour and attitudes. For example, mass spectator sports can channel hostile emotions into socially useful activities. Aggression can, therefore, be cathartically released by crowds of spectators cheering the players and jeering the umpires. Sport can also increase levels of excitement, which means participants use sport to actually increase tension and stress as an antidote to the routines of their work life and household chores (Coakley, 2009).

Governments also understand that discipline and commitment are just one side of a productive community and that in order to sustain reasonable levels of mental health, there needs to be a means of escape from the restricted and bureaucratic world of contemporary work. Recreational sport is the perfect release, and wilderness sports like bushwalking, snow skiing, and bicycle touring reflect this urge to balance the automated banality of urban life. They provide peak experiences by taking people out of their comfort zones and removing them from the safe realities of everyday life. Sport consequently becomes a "sacred" time full of excitement, exhilaration, and sometimes peace (Stebbins, 2007). With the recognition that sport delivers healthy bodies and fresh minds, most governments around the world are enamoured with the idea that sports have the capacity to build better societies. This is certainly evident in the following example of how the Victorian state government, in one of the major states in Australia, supports the sport sector.

In Practice 2.1 Victorian state government support for sport

The Victorian state government in Australia has a very comprehensive suite of policies related to sport that are largely reflected in its strategic framework for the sport and recreation industry for 2017 to 2021. The framework makes explicit reference to the many benefits that sport and recreation provide for the Victorian community – health and wellbeing, social connections, economic growth and employment outcomes, and cultural benefits.

Deciding how to influence, control, or work with the sport and active recreation industry must be done in the context of a number of challenges identified in the framework:

- Growing population
- Ageing population
- Changing lifestyles and expectations
- Meeting physical activity targets
- Increasing female participation in sport
- Broader and more inclusive participation
- Meeting sport and recreation needs in growth corridors
- Land availability in inner city and established suburbs
- Building rural and regional opportunities
- Maintaining Victoria's competitive edge in sport and events
- Future-proofing sport and recreation
- Strengthening system resilience and capacity
- A changing high-performance system

The Victorian government vision is to make Victorians more active, or at least have an increased proportion of Victorians participating in sport and active recreation. But the government recognizes that whatever policy decisions it makes it has to address some bigger-picture issues such as the changing population of the state of Victoria (set to double in 40 years), an ageing population, greater diversity in languages and cultural backgrounds, the relatively low rate of people who meet the minimum prescribed level of weekly activity, and the need for better research and data analysis in relation to sport and active recreation participation, as well as better governance and integrity controls in sport.

The government also has to work with system made up of 16,000 community sport clubs involving 580,000 volunteers, 9500 community sport facilities, 44 major state facilities supporting high-performance sport events, 30 professional teams playing in national competitions, more than 90 major sport events supported by government funding, and a state institute of sport.

The government's sport policy intersects with a myriad of other policy areas of government, including:

- Aboriginal Victorians
- Active transport
- Biodiversity
- Climate change
- Crime prevention
- Disability
- Diversity
- Education
- Equity

- Family violence
- Infrastructure
- Local government
- Mental health
- Multicultural
- Older Victorians
- Parks and reserves
- Planning
- Preventative health
- Regional development
- Roads and paths
- Social cohesion
- Suburban development
- Tourism
- Tracks and trails
- Trade and investment
- Visitor economy
- Women
- Young Victorians

One of the responses of government within the sport and active recreation framework is to provide targeted financial support in the form of grants to various other agencies and groups involved in the sport and recreation sector. Some examples include:

- Significant Sporting Events Program – helps sporting, community, and event organizations deliver significant sporting events in Victoria.
- Emergency Sporting Equipment Grants Program – provides assistance to grassroots sport and active recreation clubs and organizations to replace essential sporting or equipment, including first aid equipment that has been lost or destroyed as a consequence of fire, flood, significant storm event, theft, or criminal damage
- Community Motorsport Program – motorsport investment program that provides grant opportunities through two funding categories – developing club capacity, increasing engagement, and building participation outcomes in motorsports and providing funding to upgrade motorsport racing infrastructure and equipment that assists clubs in delivering increased participation opportunities.
- World Game Facilities Fund – assists local football (soccer) clubs and organizations to upgrade existing or develop new facilities across metropolitan Melbourne and regional Victoria.
- Community Sport Sector Short-Term Survival Package – provides grants to support the operational viability of community sport and active recreation organizations impacted by the coronavirus (COVID-19) pandemic.
- Community Cricket Program – a state-wide competitive investment program that provides a range of grant opportunities across two funding streams.

- Local Sports Infrastructure Fund – a state-wide competitive program that provides a range of grant opportunities across five funding streams.
- Change Our Game Women in Sports Broadcasting Program – designed to give women who are interested in sports media and broadcasting the knowledge and skills to progress their careers in this industry.
- Change Our Game Community Activation Grants Program – funds one-off community-level events that celebrate the role of women and girls in sport and active recreation.
- Change Our Game Scholarship Program – provides funding to assist women to access professional learning and development opportunities to enhance skills in sport and recreation leadership and management.
- Athlete Pathway Grants Program – provides grants to improve Victorian athlete development pathways from the community to national representation level. Support is available to assist with costs of travel for high-performance athletes to represent Victoria and emerging athletes travelling to train or compete at events that contribute to their development within their sporting pathway. Assistance is also available for officials' and coaches' travel.
- Aboriginal Sport Participation Grant Program – provides grants to assist Aboriginal Victorians to participate in Aboriginal sporting carnivals and buy sports uniforms and equipment, as well as funding for travel and accommodation expenses for athletes to compete in state and national competitions.
- Country Football and Netball Program – provides funding to assist regional football and netball clubs, associations, and umpiring organizations to upgrade and develop facilities in rural, regional, and outer metropolitan locations.
- Together More Active – provides grants that assist organizations in the sport and active recreation sector with initiatives that increase inclusive participation and enhance sector capability.

Source: Sport and Recreation Victoria policy "Active Victoria; A strategic framework for sport and recreation in Victoria 2017–2021" at https://sport.vic.gov.au/__data/assets/pdf_file/0018/55602/download.pdf and their grant schemes via their website at https://sport.vic.gov.au/grants-and-funding/our-grants

REASONS FOR GOVERNMENT INTERVENTION

Governments have always intervened in the affairs of society for the fundamental reason that it enables them to set the nation's economic and political direction. More specifically, governments believe they can improve the wellbeing of society through various interventions (Braithwaite & Drahos, 2000). For example, providing rail and road infrastructure can improve transport systems and thereby increase the levels of overall efficiency in industry and commerce. Similarly, funding the establishment of schools, universities, and hospitals can go a long way to not only improving the educational abilities of its citizens but also enhancing their capacity to work more productively and more vigorously participate in the cultural and commercial affairs of the nation. The same sort of logic underpins governments' goal of having fit and healthy people that can defend the nation's sovereignty in times of war and generate international kudos and prestige through the success of its elite athletes.

At the same time, governments may wish to more directly control the behaviour of their citizens by establishing laws that prohibit things like industry pollution and anti-competitive behaviour by businesses and various forms of discrimination and anti-social behaviour of individuals. The aim here is to reduce the negative "market externalities" (Braithwaite, 2008, p. 27). In this context, the state has a history of regulating sport to ensure the safety of its participants. One of the best examples is motor racing, where the risk of injury is very high, and externally imposed regulations are essential to ensure a lower chance of sustaining acute injury.

Thus, because of sport's potential to deliver significant social benefits, there are a number of sound reasons for governments wanting to invest in it. However, government resources and taxpayer funds are always scarce, and sport is one of many institutions that want to claim part of the government budget. As a result, sport assistance cannot always be guaranteed, and it must compete with defence, health, policing, social welfare, and education. Additionally, in capitalist economies, at least, sport has also traditionally been seen as outside the scope of government responsibility on the grounds that it is far removed from commerce and more in the territory of volunteer amateurs. However, it is not that difficult to mount a case for government intervention in sport. For example, it is not difficult to argue that not only will society be better off with more sport facilities and services, but that without state support, the resources invested in sport will be far less than optimal.

Market failure and the supply of sport services

In capitalist nations like Australia, Canada, Great Britain, New Zealand, and the United States, resources are in the main allocated in markets through the interaction of demand, supply, and prices. However, there are often cases where markets do not operate in the best interests of the community or nation. This is known as market failure (Grattton & Taylor, 2000). Market failure can occur when the full benefits of markets are not realized because of an under-supply of socially desirable products or, alternatively, an over-supply of less desirable products. Market failure and under-supply arise in situations where there are significant external or social benefits in addition to private benefits. Private benefits are the value consumers obtain from the immediate purchase of a good or service and are measured by the prices people are prepared to pay for the experience. In sport, private benefits arise from a number of activities and practices. They include attending a major sport event, working out at a gymnasium, playing indoor cricket, or spending time at a snow resort. Social benefits, on the other hand, consist of the additional value communities obtain from the production of a good or service. These social benefits are over and above the private benefits. In those cases where social benefits can be identified, society would be better served by allocating additional resources to those activities. However, private

TABLE 2.1 Social benefits of sport development	
Arising from active participation	*Arising from elite athlete successes*
Improvement in community health and productivity	Tribal identification and belonging
Fall in medical costs	Social cohesion
Reduction in juvenile crime rate	Civic and national pride
Development of "character" and sense of "fair play"	International recognition and prestige
Building of social capital, social cohesion, and civic engagement	Economic development and tourism

Source: Adapted from Stewart, Nicholson, Smith, and Westerbeek (2004)

investors will not usually do this because of a lack of profit incentive. Consequently, it will be left to government to fill the breach and use taxpayers' money to fund additional sporting infrastructure and services.

In other words, since sport provides significant social benefits, it deserves state support to ensure that the welfare of the whole community is maximized. According to the proponents of sport assistance, social benefits can arise from both active participation and spectator sport. In the case of active participation, the benefits include improved community health, a fall in medical costs, a reduction in the crime rate, the inculcation of discipline and character, the development of ethical standards through the emulation of sporting heroes, greater civic engagement, and the building of social capital. Research into social capital building suggests that sport not only expands social networks but also produces safer neighbourhoods and stronger communities (Productivity Commission, 2003). Moreover, the social benefits linked to social capital are extended when sport groups and clubs look outward and encompass people across diverse social cleavages. This bridging or inclusive social capital can be contrasted with bonding social capital, which characterizes sport groups and clubs with a narrow ethnic, social, or occupational base (Putnam, 2000, p. 22). Either way, sport is seen to be a great builder of social capital.

In the case of elite and spectator sports, the social benefits include tribal identification with a team or club, social cohesion, a sense of civic and national pride, international recognition and prestige, economic development, and the attraction of out-of-town visitors and tourist dollars (Gratton & Taylor, 1991). When these social benefits are aggregated, the results are quite extensive, as can be seen in Table 2.1. At the same time, they are often difficult to quantify, and in some cases, the evidence to support the claimed benefit is soft and flimsy.

Sport as a public good

A case can also be made for the state's involvement in sport on the grounds that sport is often a public or collective good (Li, Hofacre, & Mahony, 2001). Public goods are those goods where one person's consumption does not prevent another person's consumption of the same good. For example, a decision to visit a beach, or identify with a winning team or athlete, will not prevent others from doing the same. Indeed, the experience may be enhanced by others being in proximity. This is the non-rival feature of the good. Public goods are also goods where, in their purest form, no one can be prevented from consuming the good. Again, a visit to the beach and identifying with a winning team meet this criterion. This is the non-excludable feature of the good. Public goods can provide substantial benefits throughout the whole of society and are usually not rationed through high prices. However, they are not attractive to private investors since there is no assurance that all users will pay the cost of providing the benefit. As the number of so-called free riders increases, there is a shrinking incentive for private operators to enter the public good market. In this instance, it is argued that government should provide for this higher demand by increasing its funding to ensure an appropriate infrastructure and level of service.

Sport equity and inclusiveness

Finally, it can be argued that government should be funding sport on equity grounds. For example, if the whole community benefits from being fit and healthy, then no one should be excluded because of low income or lack of facilities. In these cases, the optimal community benefit can only be realized if everyone has access to appropriate sport and recreation services to help them improve their health and fitness, enhance their self-image, and build the community's social capital. In order to improve accessibility and ensure equality of opportunity, governments can establish their own low-cost sport facilities, subsidize existing sport activity providers, and design targeted programs for disadvantaged groups.

This raises the question of just how much assistance government should provide to sport to ensure ease of access, equality of participation, and a diversity of experiences. Local and city governments have a long tradition of using taxpayer money to build sport facilities for the use of their constituents. One of the more innovative and ambitious national policies has been the creation of the Irish National Sport Campus, explained in this next example.

In Practice 2.2 Sport Ireland Campus

The Sport Ireland Campus is a unique project developed by the Irish government over the last two decades. Facilities developed to date have largely been in line with the 2004 Development Control Plan (also known as the Master Plan) for the campus. The 477-acre campus in the western suburbs of Dublin is home to 27 sporting organizations and office accommodation for Sport Ireland as well as other national governing bodies for sport.

The campus provides world-class training facilities to support elite athletes in preparing for competition. As a secondary objective, it also provides facilities and programs targeting broader-based participation among the general public, where usage levels are increasing, reflecting both increased participation in the existing swimming, diving, and gymnastics programs and the introduction of new athletics and multi-sport offerings. The guiding principles to govern access to facilities, including pricing strategy, strike a balance between:

- Priority access across the year for high-performing athletes;
- Promotion of participation by communities to maximize the use of facilities;
- Contribution of the users of facilities to the running costs; and
- Minimizing the level of subsidy.

In 2021, the major facilities located on the campus included:

- National Indoor Arena
- National Gymnastics Training Centre
- National Aquatic Centre and Competition Pools
- National Indoor Training Centre
- National Indoor Athletic Training Centre
- National Indoor Covered Pitches
- Conference Centre
- National Horse Sport Arena
- Fitness Centre
- Multi Sport Synthetic and Turf Pitches
- National Modern Pentathlon Centre
- Cross Country Track and Trails
- National Indoor Arena Private Gym
- Cyclocross Skills Zone
- Hockey Pitch
- National Dryland Diving Centre

Project Ireland 2040, the National Development Plan (NDP) 2018–2027, reiterated the government's commitment to the continued development of the Sport Ireland National Sports Campus. €42 million in capital funding has been committed for the period 2018–2021, and Phase 2 of the National Indoor Arena and the National Velodrome and Badminton Centre are highlighted as priorities for delivery in the early years of this policy.

This unique campus represents a long-term commitment by the national government to develop the elite sport infrastructure and associated programs required to support the major sports in which Ireland competes internationally while also servicing the local demand for sport facilities in the western suburbs of Dublin.

Source: Sport Ireland Campus website at www.sportirelandcampus.ie

EXTENT AND FORM OF GOVERNMENT INTERVENTION

In general, there is a broad array of arrangements by which governments can fund, develop, and deliver sport facilities and programs. At one extreme, governments can distance themselves from sport development by claiming that sport is a private matter for individuals and communities and is, therefore, best left to the market and voluntary sectors to run. This arrangement was a primary feature of Australian sport until the 1970s when the national government resolved to fund sport facilities and programs (Stewart et al., 2004). In the United States, the national government has also adopted an arm's-length approach to sport and has left the funding and development of sport to the market, schools, and university sectors (Chalip, Johnson, & Stachura, 1996).

As noted previously, governments can intervene in sport in all sorts of ways. The extent of the intervention and the form it takes are strongly influenced by the ideology, values, and overall philosophy of governments and their agencies (Gardiner, Parrish, & Siekman, 2009). There are a number of different ideologies to choose from, but when implemented, they become difficult to completely erase at a later time.

The first ideology is conservatism. A conservative ideology values tradition and customary ways of doing things. Conservative governments have a tendency to regulate the social lives of people and, therefore, want to censor works of art and literature they find offensive. They also want to control the distribution of legal drugs like alcohol and generally act to protect people from themselves. On the other hand, they believe that business should be left to its own devices, where the combination of individual self-interest, the profit motive, and market forces will ensure a favourable outcome. However, because conservative governments believe a strong private sector is the key to progress, they are prepared to assist and protect industry when the need arises. While they recognize sport as an integral part of the social life of most people, they do not want to assist or protect it since it is not part of the world of business. Indeed, for many conservatives, it is another world altogether that should be best kept at a distance from business. This sport world is underpinned by the belief that sport fulfils its function best when it is done for its own sake, played by amateurs, managed by volunteers, and generally left to look after its own affairs.

The second ideology is reformism or, as it is also known, welfare statism or social democracy. Reformism is primarily concerned with social justice and equity. While reformists recognize the necessity of a strong private sector, they believe it cannot be trusted to deliver fair and equitable outcomes. It, therefore, needs to be strictly managed. This could take the form of additional government-owned enterprises or tight regulations on business behaviour. Reformists share the conservative view that assistance and protection may be necessary in the public interest. Unlike conservatives, though, reformists believe primarily in social development, which not only means legislating for social freedom but also for social justice. Income redistribution to disadvantaged groups is important and is done by ensuring that wealthy individuals and corporations are taxed most heavily. State spending is also crucial to reformists, since it is used to stimulate the economy when demand and spending are low. Reformist governments tend to be more centralist and aim to use this centralized power to engineer positive social outcomes. Reformists consequently see sport as a tool for social development and aim to make sport more accessible to the whole community. In these cases, programs are established to cater to the needs of minority groups like the Indigenous, the disabled, migrants who speak another language, and women. In short, reformist government policy focuses more on community and less on elite sport development.

The third ideology is neoliberalism. Neoliberals believe that society is at its most healthy when people can run their daily lives without the chronic intrusion of the state.

The rule of law is important, but beyond that, people should be free to choose how they organize their social lives, and businesses should be free to organize their commercial lives as they see fit. Neoliberals see little value in government-owned enterprises and argue that the privatization of government services produces greater efficiency and higher-quality outcomes. Moreover, deregulated industries are seen to run better than tightly controlled ones. In short, neoliberals believe government should not engage directly in most economic activity but rather provide only base-level infrastructure and legislative guidelines within which private business can thrive. Within this philosophy, sport is valued as an important social institution but should not be strictly controlled. However, neoliberals also believe sport can be used as a vehicle for nation building and economic development and should be supported in these instances. This produces a sport policy that tends to focus on elite sport at the expense of community sport.

The final ideology is socialism. Socialists believe that a combination of privately owned and unregulated markets will produce severe levels of inequality and alienation. As a result, capitalist modes of production and distribution need to be replaced by strong governments where resource allocation is centrally controlled. Like neoliberals, socialists agree that sport is an important social institution but, unlike neoliberals, go on to assert that sport should be controlled from the centre to ensure a fair spread of clubs and facilities throughout society. To this end, a socialist system of sport development will be driven by a central bureaucracy that sets the sport agenda. In this type of setting, governments provide most of the funds and resources by which to develop sport at both the community and elite levels.

Each of these four ideologies not only contains quite different assumptions about the proper role of government but also different ideas about what sport can do to improve the welfare of society. As a result, each ideology will produce different sport development outcomes, and the ideology often overrides the claims of interest groups like sport scientists, coaches, and officials. The four ideologies described provide a simplified typology, and in practice, governments will often take bits and pieces of each ideology when forming their position on a particular sport issue or problem. At the same time, most governments will be characterized by more of one and less of another ideology. Table 2.2 outlines the different ideologies and indicates how they can shape a government's views on sport development, regulation, and assistance.

TABLE 2.2 Links between political ideology and sport development

Ideological type	Features	Implications for sport development
Conservatism	Private ownership of business Regulation of social practices	Arm's-length association with sport. Sport is seen as a private activity that grows out of the community and is managed by the volunteer sector
Reformism	Mixed economy Regulation of both social and economic affairs	Direct involvement in sport facility construction and community sport participation

Ideological type	Features	Implications for sport development
Neo-liberalism	Emphasis on the market Deregulation of industry	Most resources go to the elite end of sport development and its commercial outcomes
Socialism	Limited scope for the market Central planning Bureaucratic control over resource allocation	Direct involvement in all aspects of sport development. Often tightly regulated. Both community and elite sport are resourced

REGULATION AND CONTROL

There are also many situations where the state may want to regulate and control the provision of sport activities and limit the resources devoted to some activities (Baldwin, Cave, & Lodge, 2012). For example, it may be necessary to enact laws and rules that safeguard public order when a large number of people are spectators of or are playing in a sport event. In most countries, there are laws that clearly define the parameters within which sport grounds are to be constructed. These laws will cover things like design specifications, the provision for seating, the number of entry and exit points, and fire prevention facilities (Frosdick & Walley, 1997). There may also be rules that govern the behaviour of spectators. Most commonly, these laws will relate to the consumption of alcohol and disorderly and violent behaviour (Greenfield & Osborn, 2001).

One of the most highly regulated activities is horse-racing. It is not just a case of ensuring the animals are treated humanely but also of making sure the gaming and gambling practices that surround the sport are tightly controlled so that corrupt practices are minimized. There are many cases around the world where horses have not been allowed to run on their merits. This can involve doping activities where stimulants will be given to horses to make them run quicker and depressants administered to make them go slower. In both instances, the aim is to undermine the betting market and through the use of inside information to back the horse that has been advantaged and avoid the horse that has been slowed. Similar incidents are now happening more frequently in a number of professional team sports around the world (Muller, Lammert, & Hovemann, 2012). Crime syndicates and bookmakers have bribed sport officials, players, and even referees to provide confidential information on the game, deliberately play poorly, and make decisions that favour one team and not another. Two recent cases involved Italy's premier football competition and the Pakistan cricket team. In each instance, government action was immediately taken to more strictly regulate the competitions.

Another form of regulation involves the media in general, and TV in particular. In both Australia and England, there are anti-siphoning rules that effectively give free-to-air television stations privileged access to major sport events at the expense of pay and cable television providers (Brown &Walsh, 1999). This means that a major sport event like the Australian Football League (AFL) Grand Final must initially be offered to free-to-air stations before being offered to pay TV stations or streaming services. This is done on the grounds that a sport of national significance should be made as widely available as possible. In Australia, pay TV subscriptions cover less than 35% of all households, and it is consequently argued that it is inequitable to give exclusive rights to a pay TV station only.

In Practice 2.3 Child safety

The last 20 years have seen an increased focus on ensuring the safety and welfare of participants, especially children, in sport, an issue taken on by many national governments around the world. The Child Protection in Sport Unit (CPSU) is part of the National Society for the Prevention of Cruelty to Children (NSPCC) and is funded by Sport England, Sport Northern Ireland, Sport Wales, and UK Sport. The CPSU was founded in 2001 in response to a series of high-profile cases of abuse of young athletes in the United Kingdom. Its aim is to help improve safeguarding and child protection practices within sport organizations to ensure all children and young people are safe while participating in sport.

The unit plays a strategic role in the landscape of sport in the United Kingdom. It works directly with UK sport councils, national governing bodies (NGBs), active partnerships (APs – previously known as county sports partnerships), and other organizations. It supports organizations to implement and maintain safeguarding practices, to minimize the risk of abuse, and to ensure that sport stays safe and enjoyable for all those involved. The CPSU assists sporting organizations in developing and embedding safeguarding policies and procedures, creating a safe and inclusive environment for all participants, staff, and volunteers by:

- supporting sports organizations to follow a set of standards for safeguarding children in sport;
- guiding sports organizations through a framework process to ensure standards are embedded across their work;
- providing expert safeguarding and child protection advice to national governing bodies, active partnerships, clubs, coaches, and parents;
- developing and delivering sports-specific training, resources, and guidance; and
- commissioning and supporting research into a range of issues, developing understanding and an evidence base for work.

The CPSU plays the lead role in helping sports organizations to develop and implement their responses, policies and procedures, systems, and structures for safeguarding. Since 2001, it has worked with sport and statutory agencies to ensure that all children, regardless of their level of participation in sport or where they participate, have a safe and enjoyable experience. It supports organizations to:

- recognize their responsibility to protect children and young people left in their care;
- recognize their responsibility to pass on any concerns about children's welfare or protection in their families or communities to a statutory agency;
- develop strategies and standards to protect children and young people;

- identify and respond to adults who are a threat to children and young people; and
- develop safeguarding knowledge and skills among all staff and volunteers.

Source: The Child Protection in Sport Unit (CPSU) at www.thecpsu.org.uk

SUMMARY

Governments have the capacity to significantly shape the structure and scope of sport through a number of mechanisms. First, they can construct sport facilities; second, they can fund the day-to-day operations of sporting associations and clubs; third, they can deliver sport programs to the community directly; fourth, they can establish training facilities for elite athletes to assist their ongoing development; and finally, they can control the operation of sport by introducing various laws, regulations, and rules that shape the delivery of sport events, programs, and services (Hylton, Bramham, Jackson, & Nesti, 2001). However, the scale of government support, and the form it takes, will vary between nations depending on the dominant political ideology and the overall cultural importance of sport to society. In some cases, governments will directly control and manage sport, while at the other end of the political spectrum, governments will step back from the sport system and encourage the commercial and volunteer sectors to take up the slack.

At this point in time, the evidence suggests that governments have a pivotal role to play in supporting both the community participation and elite-sport ends of the sport development continuum. The establishment of sports infrastructure and facilities and the funding of sport programs enables greater levels of community participation, creates all sorts of health and social benefits, improves international sport performance, and enhances a country's international status and prestige. It now seems as if some governments believe "too much sport is never enough".

REVIEW QUESTIONS

1 Why should the state want to intervene in sport?

2 Apart from the state, what other social forces contribute to sport development?

3 Explain how the state may contribute to sport development.

4 How might local investment in sport stadia assist local development and job creation?

5 What can the state do to increase the level of sport participation and sport club membership?

6 What can the state do to increase the level of elite sport performance?

7 Would sport development be best left to the voluntary and commercial sectors?

8 Is there any evidence that a centralized model of elite sport development is any more effective than a market-based sport development model?

9 How might the state go about increasing the scale of sport participation at the community or "grassroots" level?

10 Why do governments choose to regulate some aspects of sport?

DISCUSSION QUESTIONS

1 What should be the role of government in relation to community sport? What about in relation to elite sport?

2 In what areas of society are government assistance and regulation most evident, and why?

3 How can governments shape the structure and conduct of the sports sector, and why do they now have such an influential role to play?

4 What strategies can government initiate to improve elite sport systems and standards?

5 How might government go about building the participation base of sport?

FURTHER READING

Coakley, J., et al. (2009). *Sport in society*. Sydney: McGraw Hill.

Delaney, K., & Eckstein, R. (2003). *Public dollars, private stadiums: The battle over building sports stadiums*. New Brunswick: Rutgers University Press.

Green, M., & Houlihan, B. (2005). *Elite sport development*. London and Houlihan: Routledge.

Houlihan, B. (2017). Sport policy and politics. In R. Hoye & M. M. Parent (Eds.), *Handbook of sport management* (pp. 183–200). London: Sage.

Hoye, R., Nicholson, M., & Houlihan, B. (2010). *Sport and policy*. Oxford: Elsevier Butterworth-Heinemann.

Nicholson, M., Hoye, R., & Houlihan, B. (Eds.). (2011). *Participation in sport: International policy perspectives*. London: Routledge.

Stebbins, R. (2007). *Serious leisure*. New Brunswick: Transactions Publications.

Stiglitz. (2000). *Economics of the public sector* (3rd ed.). New York: W.W. Norton.

RELEVANT WEBSITES

Sport Australia at www.sportaus.gov.au

Sport England at www.sportengland.org

Sport New Zealand at www.sportnz.org.nz

Sport Scotland at www.sportscotland.org.uk

Sport Wales at www.sport.wales

CASE STUDY 2.1

Sport 2030 and the high-performance strategy for Australia

Australian governments have released a succession of national sport policy statements since 1983, and the focus of the many iterations over the last four decades has been the pursuit of greater participation in sport and physical activity as well as enhanced performances in elite sport. The driving force behind these policies has been a consistent belief in the benefits that sport provides for individuals, communities, and the nation – all front and centre in the introductory remarks of the Chair of Sport Australia in the current national sport policy, Sport 2030:

> Sport matters a great deal to our country. It's part of our DNA. We're a proud sporting country, we love to see Australians mix it with the best on the world stage, and our long and illustrious record of success is admired around the world. Our love of sport is a great asset to our country. Sport motivates young Australians to be active, producing on the whole better results at school and providing the early foundation of skills and habits that help them remain healthy and active throughout life. Sport promotes social inclusion and cohesion, and teaches vital lifelong personal qualities of character, resilience and teamwork, as well as the life lessons gained by both winning and losing. There's nothing like sport as a force for social change and good. The awe-inspiring rise in women's sport and para-sport in the past decade has changed community perceptions and led broader societal changes. Sport matters economically to our country. It delivers some $83 billion of benefits to Australia each year – a return of $7 for every dollar invested, and our national brand in sport supports indirectly many other industries such as food exports and tourism.

Sport 2030 sets a bold vision for "Australia to be the world's most active and healthy nation, known for our integrity and sporting success". It sets out the following goals to be achieved by 2030:

- We have a diverse and inclusive sport and physical activity sector that supports more Australians to be more active more often, creating a stronger and healthier Australia where as many people as possible see and feel the benefits of sport and physical activity through every stage of their lives;
- Future generations will be more physically active and better prepared with the skills and knowledge to live healthy, active lives;
- Sport and physical activity organisations are connected into other sectors such as health, education and infrastructure to tackle challenges such as physical inactivity and leverage sport for social benefits;
- Barriers will be reduced, allowing greater access to sporting facilities and infrastructure for all Australians no matter where they live;

- Our high-performance system will be focused around sports, teams and athletes and ensuring they have world-leading technology, practices, systems and people to enable them to achieve lasting podium success;
- There will be greater collaboration across the sport sector and with partner organisations, including various levels of Government. The best governance systems will better position our sports for a changing world, enabling them to focus their energy, time and revenue on driving international performance, strengthening the pathways system, creating greater commercial opportunities and increasing participation rates among more Australians;
- Australian sport can identify, address, and proactively deter threats to sport integrity allowing fans and participants to have faith that our sport is safe and fair; and
- The Australian sports industry leads the world in many areas – including integrity, inclusion, innovation, research, physical literacy and technology.

Australia's national sport plan has four key priority areas which will, when fully implemented, create a platform for sporting success through to 2030 and beyond. The priorities are:

- Build a more active Australia – More Australians, more active, more often;
- Achieving sporting excellence – National pride, inspiration and motivation through international sporting success;
- Safeguarding the integrity of sport – A fair, safe and strong sport sector free from corruption; and
- Strengthening Australia's sport industry – A thriving Australian sport and recreation industry.

Sitting under the priority areas are five target outcomes that will:

- Improve the physical health of Australians – through the benefits of sport and physical activity, including reduced risk of chronic conditions.
- Improve the mental health of Australians – through the recognized mental health benefits of sport and physical activity, including the improved management of mental illness and greater social connectedness.
- Grow personal development – from taking up a new challenge, to setting a new personal goal or striving for the podium, being active can help everyone endeavour to be their best self.
- Strengthen our communities – by harnessing the social benefits of sport including through improved cohesion and reduced isolation; and
- Grow Australia's economy – building on the already significant contribution of sport to the Australian economy.

Cynical observers of sport policy would suggest that these grand goals are very difficult to accurately measure, and, if they were to be objectively measured, it would be even harder to ascribe the achievement of the goals to specific actions undertaken by Sport

Australia. On page 11 of Sport 2030, the policy clearly positions Sport Australia "as the primary agency for sport promotion, programs and investment . . . and the critical link between sports policy and practice". The remainder of the Sport 2030 policy explains how these goals will be achieved as well as making a commitment to establish specific targets and program guidelines to ensure delivery of the policy. The policy makes these specific statements about targets on pages 65 and 66 in relation to the four priority areas:

- PARTICIPATION – By 2030, 15% more Australians participating in at least 150 minutes of moderate to vigorous activity each week.
- HIGH PERFORMANCE – Sport Australia will develop a measurement of sporting excellence and success in line with Sport 2030.
- INTEGRITY – The Australian Government will develop specific monitoring and reporting arrangements in response to the Wood Review.
- INDUSTRY – The Australian Government will monitor and report on economic and employment growth across the wider sport and physical activity sectors.

Following the release of Sport 2030, Sport Australia developed the National High Performance Sport Strategy 2024 to address the second of these four priorities – to achieve sporting excellence. The background statement to the strategy explains what the focus is and who is involved with this strategy:

> The National High Performance Sport Strategy 2024 (NHPSS) focuses on Olympic, Paralympic and Commonwealth Games outcomes. The NHPSS is a joint strategy of National Sporting Organisations (NSO), the National Institute Network (NIN)1 and other system partners. The NHPSS is a first, positioning Australia's HP Institutes/Academies and athletes under a national framework, strengthening its dealings with governments, communities, academic institutions, industry and the private sector, moving towards a common goal of National Pride and Inspiration through International Sporting Success.

The focus of the NHPSS is creating greater alignment between all the elements that contribute to a high-performance sport system in order to support athletes, coaches, and sport organizations. The NHPSS sets out three success factors and performance criteria for each:

1 Podium Success – Australians consistently winning medals at major international events – measured by Number of medals and medallists at Olympics, Paralympics and Commonwealth Games and at International Championships.
2 Pride and Inspiration – Our sporting champions are a positive influence on the community – measured by the level of positive sentiment from sporting results, athlete conduct and engagement within the community.
3 World-leading System – Our high performance sports system is recognized as world leading – measured by Sports' progress against a performance monitoring framework and the National Institute Network achieving strategic priorities.

In order to generate the more integrated and effective high-performance system for Australia, the NHPSS sets out seven guiding principles for how the system will operate:

1 A National High Performance Sport Strategy, developed by the AIS in partnership with the State and Territory Institutes/Academies of Sport (SIS/SAS) and in consultation with sport, will inform the Federal and State and Territory governments' investment in this strategy.
2 Sports have ownership for leading, developing and implementing their high performance plans to support the National High Performance Sport Strategy.
3 System partners within the HP Sport System will strive to provide a nationally consistent minimum level of resources to categorised athletes.
4 The AIS will lead and enable a united, collaborative high performance system that supports Australian athletes to achieve international success.
5 The SIS/SAS will support identified sports to develop and deliver high performance pathways for categorised athletes within their jurisdiction and available resources.
6 The SIS/SAS and State and Territory Agencies of Recreation and Sports (STARS) will work in collaboration with sport to align support for athlete pathways in their jurisdiction that facilitate progression/development of athletes to categorised status.
7 Decision making by system partners will be collaborative, informed and transparent.

The NHPSS also sets out the core operational roles and responsibilities for all the national high-performance system partners under those principles.

1 Sports are responsible for developing their HP plans in collaboration with the AIS and consultation with relevant stakeholders.
2 The AIS is responsible for leading the National HP Sports planning and resource allocation process to ensure it meets the objectives for the National High Performance Sport Strategy in a timely manner.
3 National Institute Network members are responsible to develop a transparent, accountable and sustainable joint funding and investment model that will inform the respective governments (Australian and State/Territory) underpinning investment in the National High Performance Sport System and sports' plans.
4 Sports are responsible for leading the alignment of the National Institute Network and other system partner support to implement their high performance athlete pathway strategy and programs that support the objectives of the NHPSS.
5 The National Institute Network, under the leadership of the Australian Institute of Sport, will be responsible to deliver world-leading performance support services to be positioned as the preferred provider to sports and athletes.

6   National Institute Network members are individually responsible for confirming their jurisdictional level of investment in each sport's HP plans.

7   Resources from a National Institute Network member may be invested at their discretion to support additional performance or capability enhancing initiatives complementary to Sports' National HP plans.

CASE STUDY QUESTIONS:

1   On page 11 of Sport 2030, a number of claims are made about the influence Sport Australia will have on the sport and physical activity sectors. Do you think this is possible given the current scale and budget of Sport Australia?

2   Is there good evidence for all the claims made by the Chair of Sport Australia in their introduction to Sport 2030?

3   The NHPSS makes no mention of professional sport that is arguably more visible and regularly consumed by Australians than the Olympics, Paralympics, Commonwealth Games, and International Championships. Why might that be the case?

4   The NHPSS is the plan to deliver on the promise of Sport 2030. Do you think this plan addresses the core issues with Australia's high-performance sport system that are discussed at length in Sport 2030?

Sources: Sport 2030 found via the Sport Australia website at www.sportaus.gov.au/national-sportplan/home and the National High Performance Sport Strategy 2024, also found via the Sport Australia website at www.sportaus.gov.au/__data/assets/pdf_file/0003/717501/National-HP-Sport-Strategy-2024_FINAL.pdf

CASE STUDY 2.2

Irish National Sport Policy 2018–2027

The current national sport policy for Ireland covering the period 2018 to 2027 sets out a vision for Irish sport and contains 57 specific policy actions to be undertaken by government in relation to sport. The rationale for the development of a national policy is the accepted notion that sport contributes to health and wellbeing, social and community development, economic activity, educational performance, and life-long learning.

The policy makes it clear that the national government must work with all the relevant stakeholders in sport in order to deliver the comprehensive sport policy actions:

- National Governing Bodies – NGBs organise, promote and facilitate opportunities for participation in sport and physical activity in both recreational and competitive forms. They train and deploy coaches, officials and administrators, organise representative level sport, provide opportunities and pathways leading from local sports to national and international competition, deliver critical national sports programmes in areas such as the safeguarding of children in sport, and organise and host international sporting events. They are the delivery agents for the rollout of many essential programmes and will remain to the forefront in the Government's policy and practice in sport and physical activity.
- Local Sports Partnerships – the LSP network plays a similarly vital role and has been tasked, in particular, with increasing participation levels in sport and physical activity, especially among those sectors of society that are currently underrepresented in sport. Their capacity to remove barriers and ensure that opportunities for participation in sport are progressive, innovative and fully inclusive at a local level is a unique and valuable strength. A key priority of the LSPs is to continue to support a sustainable level of development within the local sport infrastructure, through support to clubs, groups, coaches and volunteers. The Government will continue to invest in the network of LSPs to ensure the consistent and sustainable delivery of sport and physical activity at a local level.
- Representative Sporting Organisations – play a vitally important strategic, operational and advocacy role for Irish sport at all levels. Their wide-ranging national and international perspective and expertise on issues affecting sport is a particularly valuable input to sports policy development. It is expected that the key bodies concerned – the Federation of Irish Sport, the Olympic Council of Ireland, Paralympics Ireland, Ireland Active and the CARA Centre among others – will contribute significantly to the effective implementation of this policy.

The major policy areas include participation, sports facilities (including a focus on the Sport Ireland Campus covered earlier in this chapter), high performance, building capacity in the sport system, sport in a cross-cultural and international context, and integrity in sport. The policy also explains how it will be funded and how it will be monitored and reviewed.

While there is not time to examine every aspect of this 108-page policy, the section on integrity of sport highlights the complexity of developing a comprehensive policy that will have a material impact. The policy sets the context for why integrity in sport is important:

> Integrity and trust lie at the heart of people's expectation of sport. In their absence, sport is diminished and devalued. At every level, from the club member to the player to the spectator, people want to believe that fairness

and authenticity prevail. Those competing in or watching sport should have no doubt that it is being conducted on a level playing field. Competition in sport provides enthralling experiences that are rightly to be cherished. An attitude and approach to sport that is built on a "win at all cost" mentality is completely unacceptable. Mutual respect amongst all those involved in sport, from coaches to competitors to spectators, is the bedrock of fair competition in sport and we are fully entitled to demand that. Nowhere is that respect more absent than doping in sport, which can never be tolerated and must be fought relentlessly.

The policy calls out anti-doping, match fixing, and corruption as three aspects of integrity that require specific action by the national government. In relation to anti-doping, the government committed to examining the potential for establishing an independent anti-doping agency and, in relation to match-fixing, committed to potentially signing up to the Council of Europe Convention on the Manipulation of Sports Competitions. Neither action statement makes firm commitments, and they point to a long-term horizon for implementation, and thus any real impact in the short term on addressing the issues they flag in their statement on the importance of integrity in sport.

In comparison, the policy actions in relation to sport facilities are much more convincing. The policy sets the context for why investing in sport facilities is important:

> Over the past 20 years, Ireland's stock of sports facilities at local, regional and national level has been substantially improved with the help of Government support under the Sports Capital and Local Authority Swimming Pool Programmes, as well as through investment in the Sport Ireland National Sports Campus, Croke Park, Aviva Stadium, Thomond Park, Páirc Uí Chaoimh and other sporting arenas. This investment is helping to ensure quality sporting experiences for all adults and children regularly participating in sport, as well as assisting Ireland's top sports persons to compete successfully at the highest levels. The investment is contributing to the health and wellbeing of the nation as well as to social and economic development in Ireland.

In relation to sport facilities, the policy commits to eight specific actions.

1 We will commit to run the Sports Capital Programme in each year of this policy, to fund facilities targeting increased participation and improved participation experiences throughout the population. The scoring system and assessment process for the Sports Capital Programme will be reviewed to ensure that the programme is achieving objectives in line with this National Sports Policy.
2 We will conduct periodic Value for Money Reviews of the Sports Capital Programme with the first one to commence in 2019. Recommendations of the reviews will be reflected in subsequent investment programmes.

3   We will periodically conduct a nation-wide audit of sports facilities (whether publicly or privately owned), with the first such audit to be completed within 2 years of the publication of this policy. These audits will guide decisions regarding the sport capital projects to be prioritised for public funding and we will also consult with NGBs in relation to any further actions required. Local Authorities will conduct the audit at a local level, as part of their role in implementing their Local Sports Plans. As part of the audit we will work with relevant stakeholders to develop and maintain a fully-accessible, comprehensive and up-to-date national database of sports facilities which will also be translated into a web-based portal to serve the needs of the public.

4   We will establish a new Large Scale Sport Infrastructure Fund to support projects where the Exchequer investment will exceed the maximum amount available under the Sports Capital Programme.

5   We will work closely with relevant Government Departments, Local Authorities, sporting bodies and other stakeholders to agree a coherent national strategy for swimming. As part of this, we will review swimming pool provision to identify where gaps exist and how these can be met.

6   We will work with relevant stakeholders to explore the merits of a new programme of current sports funding under a targeted scheme to support schools on a sustainable basis in defraying reasonable costs (such as necessary transport and facility hire) incurred in delivering the aquatics strand of the PE curriculum.

7   We will encourage Local Authorities to promote and facilitate more sharing of facilities locally, especially where capacity is available at off-peak times during the day, in the evening or during holiday periods in the case of educational establishments. This will involve working closely with clubs and sporting bodies, schools and colleges, leisure facility providers and others. As part of the Local Sport Plans, Local Authorities will also lead on other collaborative initiatives to improve access locally e.g. Local Authorities and LSPs will combine to see how recreational areas can be utilised more fully by local communities for sport and physical activity e.g. for parkruns.

8   We will aim to secure a new stream of annual funding for a targeted sports scheme to subvent Local Authorities in the operation of loss-making facilities where these have a key role in increasing participation, as well as to support programmes to increase active participation.

CASE STUDY QUESTIONS

1   Download the National Sports Policy and review the scope of the document. What advantages and disadvantages are there for having such a wide-ranging suite of policy actions?

2   The ten-year timeframe is unusual for a national sport policy. Why is a ten-year timeframe important in this context?

3   The policy requires significant investment over a long period. Does section 10 adequately explain how this will be funded?

4   How important will partners be in achieving these policy actions? Please explain with an example.

Source: National Sports Policy 2018–2027 found at https://assets.gov.ie/15979/04e0f52 cee5f47ee9c01003cf559e98d.pdf

CHAPTER 3

Nonprofit sport

OVERVIEW

This chapter examines the role of the nonprofit sector in the provision of sport participation and consumption opportunities and explores the reasons the nonprofit sector plays such a large part in the delivery of sport participation opportunities. The scope of the nonprofit sector's involvement in sport around the world is examined, with a particular emphasis on the role of volunteers in administration, officiating, and coaching and the role of nonprofit sport organizations in facilitating people's enjoyment of sport as active participants, supporters, or consumers. The chapter also provides a

DOI: 10.4324/9781003217947-4

summary of the relationship between nonprofit sport organizations and the state and with commercial providers.

After completing this chapter, the reader should be able to:

- Describe the scope of the nonprofit sector's involvement in sport;
- Understand the differences in the roles performed by the state and nonprofit sport organizations;
- Understand the ways in which nonprofit sport organizations provide sport partici- pation and consumption opportunities around the world;
- Understand some of the challenges facing the nonprofit sector in delivering these opportunities; and
- Understand the field of sport development versus sport *for* development.

INTRODUCTION

The model presented in Chapter 1 presents the sport industry as comprising three distinct but overlapping sectors: the state or public sector, the commercial or professional sport sector, and the nonprofit or voluntary sector. This chapter focuses on the nonprofit or voluntary sec- tor of the model: the various sport organizations that would be classified as nonprofit. Many terms have been used to refer to nonprofit organizations that operate in a variety of indus- try sectors and countries around the world. These terms include voluntary, not-for-profit, non-government, community, club-based, associations, co-operatives, friendly societies, civil society, and the third sector. For our purposes, we have chosen to use the term nonprofit organizations to describe those organizations that are institutionally separate from the state, do not return profits to owners, are self-governing, have a significant element of voluntary contribution, and are formally incorporated as separate legal entities.

The nonprofit sport sector comprises organizations that are markedly different from state organizations discussed in Chapter 2 and also profit-seeking organizations, which are discussed in Chapter 4. Nonprofit organizations vary in size, focus, and capability and include groups as diverse as community associations, chambers of commerce, private schools, charitable trusts and foundations, religious groups, welfare agencies, and sporting organizations. Nonprofit orga- nizations are a major part of many industries in health services, education, housing, welfare, culture, and sport. Describing these organizations as nonprofit does not mean they run at a financial loss or do not generate a surplus of revenue over costs; the term nonprofit refers merely to the fact they do not exist for the primary purpose of making profits to reward their owners.

NONPROFIT SECTOR AND SOCIETY

Nonprofit organizations exist to develop communities, meet the needs of identifiable and discrete groups in those communities, and work for the benefit of public good rather than wealth creation for individuals. Nonprofit organizations have evolved to fill gaps in the provision of services such as welfare assistance that are not provided by the state or market sector and are driven largely by the efforts of volunteers, with the occasional support of paid staff.

Nonprofit organizations enable individuals to contribute their talent, energy, and time to engaging in group activities and causes that are not otherwise provided by the public or private sectors. Nonprofit organizations are self-determining; in general, they are governed by volunteers; run on the time and money contributed by volunteers; and enable volunteers to contribute to enhancing their local, regional, national, and global communities in ways that volunteers have chosen. For example, the *2018 General Social Survey: Giving, Volunteering and Participating* showed over 24 million Canadians volunteered in 2018, donating approximately 5 billion volunteer hours to the 86,000 various nonprofit organizations and charities in Canada. Similar rates of involvement are found in other westernized, developed economies and illustrate that the nonprofit sector represents a major part of the economic activity of many nations and plays a pivotal role in encouraging people to engage in social, religious, charitable, philanthropic, and sport-related activities.

Nonprofit organizations usually focus on delivering services to very specific population groups or within defined geographic areas. Many of them provide services to targeted groups, and only a few focus solely on providing services to members. The variety of activities carried out by nonprofit organizations is very broad and ranges from providing sporting opportunities to funding hospital and medical services. As a result, the revenue sources, cost base, numbers of paid staff and volunteers, and sophistication of management systems also vary markedly between nonprofit organizations.

The nonprofit sector is not without its problems. Larger organizations such as independent schools, colleges, and hospitals receive the majority of funding, and almost half the funding for most nonprofit organizations comes from government. The resourcing of nonprofit organizations in some sectors continues to be inadequate as they struggle to keep up with demand, particularly organizations providing welfare, housing, or other general charitable services. By far the biggest problem facing nonprofit organizations is the inability to fulfil their missions due to problems securing adequate numbers of volunteers, finding board members, and attracting enough sustainable funding (Cuskelly, 2017). As governments around the world seek to decrease their costs and devolve responsibility for service delivery to the private and nonprofit sectors without adequately funding such delivery, nonprofit organizations will find it increasingly difficult to operate.

In Practice 3.1 Volunteers in Australia

In Australia, statistics on volunteering are gathered by the Australian Bureau of Statistics through the national census and general social surveys. The most recently published report on volunteers in Australia was produced in 2019 using the results from the General Social Survey. The highlights from the report about volunteering trends were:

- In 2019, approximately 6 million Australians or about 33% of people aged 15 years and older did volunteer work. They devoted close to 600 million hours each year to their volunteer activities.

- The volunteer rate in 2019 (28.8%) was lower than that recorded in 2010 (36.2%) for Australians aged 18 years and over, with the decline most evident for women, whose rate decreased from 38.1% in 2010 to 28.1% in 2019.
- Women are more likely to have volunteered for more than 10 years (43.0% of female volunteers compared to 32.9% of males).
- People aged 40–54 years are more likely to volunteer (36.2%) than other age groups. Volunteering rates for other age groups are: 15–24 (28.8%), 25–29 (25.7%), 55–69 (29%), and 70 years or more (24.5%).
- The most common types of organizations for which people volunteered were those relating to sport and physical recreation (39.1% of volunteers), religious groups (23.3%), and education and training (21.8%).
- The rate of volunteering is higher in regional areas than capital cities and lower for people with a disability.
- People from culturally and linguistically diverse communities are more likely to volunteer informally in their community rather than formally through an organization.
- Older people are more likely to volunteer in welfare, community, and health settings.
- Volunteering is associated with higher levels of post-secondary education.
- Men are more likely than women to volunteer for sport and physical recreation – 47.5% and 30.5%, respectively.

Source: Volunteering Australia (2021). Key Volunteering Statistics at.volunteeringaustralia.org/wp-content/uploads/VA-Key-Statistics_2020.01.pdf

NONPROFIT SECTOR AND SPORT

The International Classification of Nonprofit Organizations (ICNPO) has a designated category for sports and recreation organizations. This category includes three broad groups: (1) sports, including amateur sport, training, fitness and sport facilities, and sport competition and events; (2) recreation and social clubs such as country clubs, playground associations, touring clubs, and leisure clubs; and (3) service clubs such as Lions, Rotary, Kiwanis, and Apex clubs. Of particular interest are those organizations that operate on a nonprofit basis in sport, including professional service organizations, industry lobby groups, sport event organizations, and sport governing bodies.

Nonprofit professional service organizations operate in sport in similar ways to professional associations like accrediting medical boards or associations for lawyers and accountants. These organizations assist in setting standards of practice in their respective industries, provide professional accreditation for qualified members, and offer professional development opportunities through conferences, seminars, or training programs. They operate in a business-like fashion, but the aim is to return surpluses to members through improved service delivery rather than creating wealth for owners.

In Australia, the Australian Council for Health, Physical Education and Recreation (ACHPER) is a national professional association representing people who work in the areas of health education, physical education, recreation, sport, dance, community fitness, or movement sciences. The roles of ACHPER include advocating for the promotion and provision of sport opportunities, providing professional development programs for teachers, and accrediting and training people wanting to become community fitness instructors. Similar groups operate in Canada (Canadian Association for Health, Physical Education, Recreation and Dance), the United States (American Alliance for Health, Physical Education and Dance), the United Kingdom (British Institute of Sports Administration), and New Zealand (Physical Education New Zealand).

A number of industry lobby groups, representing the interests of nonprofit sport organizations, also operate throughout the world. A leading example is the Central Council of Physical Recreation (CCPR) in the United Kingdom, the representative body for national sports organizations. It acts as the independent umbrella organization for national governing and representative bodies of sport and recreation in the United Kingdom to promote their interests to government and other players in the sport industry.

Some of the largest and most influential sport event organizations in the world operate on a nonprofit basis, including the International Olympic Committee (IOC) and the Commonwealth Games Federation (CGF). The IOC was founded in 1894 by Baron Pierre de Coubertin and is an independent nonprofit organization that serves as the umbrella organization of the Olympic Movement. The IOC's primary role is to supervise the organization of the summer and winter Olympic Games.

The IOC has come under much criticism in recent years for poor governance practices, corruption allegations against some officials, and not doing enough to share the proceeds of Olympic Games with those nations in most need. In reaction, the IOC has greatly improved its reporting to member organizations, providing far greater transparency for how revenues are distributed to national Olympic committees and through a variety of sport development programs around the globe.

Similar to the IOC, the role of the CGF is to facilitate a major games event every four years, but it also provides education assistance for sports development throughout the 53 Commonwealth countries. There are more Commonwealth Games Associations (CGAs) (72) than countries (53) because some countries, like the United Kingdom, have more than one CGA (Scotland, England, Northern Ireland, Wales, Isle of Man, Jersey, and Guernsey) that all compete in the Games as separate nations (www.commonwealth-games.com). Both the IOC and CGF fund their operations through contributions from governments that host the games and the sale of international broadcasting rights, corporate sponsorship, ticket sales, licensing, and merchandising sales.

There is also a range of specialist nonprofit organizations that focus on discrete community groups. Foremost among these is the International Paralympic Committee (IPC), which is the international representative organization of elite sports for athletes with disabilities. The IPC organizes, supervises, and coordinates the Paralympic Games and other multi-disability sports competitions at the elite level (www.paralympic.org). Other similar nonprofit organizations include the Cerebral Palsy International Sports and Recreation Association and the International Blind Sport Federation, which facilitate major events for athletes.

Our focus for the remainder of the chapter is on those nonprofit sport organizations that provide sporting competition or event participation opportunities for their members and other members of the public – sport governing bodies and sports clubs. In countries such as

Australia, the United Kingdom, Canada, New Zealand, Hong Kong, and other others with club-based sporting systems, almost all sporting teams and competitions are organized by nonprofit sport organizations. These organizations take many forms. They include small local clubs that may field a few teams in a local football competition; regional associations that coordinate competitions between clubs; and state or provincial organizations that not only facilitate competitions but also manage coach development, talent identification, volunteer training, marketing, and sponsorship. They also comprise national sporting organizations that regulate the rules of competition in a country, coordinate national championships between state or provincial teams, manage elite athlete programs, employ development officers to conduct clinics, and undertake many other tasks that facilitate participation in sport. Finally, there are international sports federations that coordinate the development of sport across the globe and facilitate rule changes and liaison between countries on issues like international competitions.

The common element amongst all these sport organizations is their nonprofit focus – they exist to facilitate sporting opportunities for their members, who may be individual athletes, coaches, officials or administrators, clubs, associations, or other sport organizations. They are also interdependent, relying on each other to provide playing talent; information to access competitions; resources for coach, official, and player development; and funding to support their activities. It is important to note that volunteers are at the heart of these organizations, playing significant roles in service delivery and decision-making at all levels of nonprofit sport organizations. At the same time, though, many of the larger nonprofit sport organizations contain a significant number of paid staff who support their ongoing administration and service delivery to member associations and clubs.

GOVERNING BODIES OF SPORT

Sport clubs compete against other clubs in competition structures provided by regional or state/provincial sporting organizations. State-based teams compete in competitions facilitated by national sporting organizations, and nations compete in leagues or events provided by international federations of sport, such as the Fédération Internationale de Football Association (FIFA), or major competition organizations such as the International Olympic Committee or the Commonwealth Games Association. These organizations are known as governing bodies for sport that have the responsibility for the management, administration, and development of a sport on a global, national, state/provincial, or regional level.

The structure of World Netball typifies the relationships between these various governing bodies of sport. The members of World Netball comprise 76 national associations from five regions: Africa, Asia, Americas, Europe, and Oceania. World Netball is the world governing organization responsible for setting the rules for netball, running international competitions, promoting good management in the regions, striving to seek Olympic accreditation for netball, and increasing participation levels around the globe.

Netball Australia, one of the members of World Netball in the Oceania region, governs the sport of netball played by 1.2 million men, women, and children who participate through a variety of programs delivered by eight state/provincial associations. They in turn have a total of more than 550 affiliated associations. Each of the state/provincial associations has a delegate to the national board who, along with the staff of Netball Australia, is responsible for communicating rule changes from World Netball to their members, managing a national competition, promoting good management in the state/provincial organizations, increasing participation nationally, and bidding to host world events.

One of the largest members of Netball Australia, Netball Victoria, has 68,000 registered members who compete in 180 affiliated associations, organized into seven regions across the state. Netball Victoria's role differs markedly from Netball Australia and World Netball, with responsibility for coach, official, and player development; managing state competitions; promoting good management in the clubs; providing insurance coverage for players; assisting in facility development; trying to increase participation in the state; bidding to host national events; and managing two teams in the national competition. Finally, netball clubs field teams, find coaches and players, manage volunteers, and conduct fundraising and may own and operate a facility.

It is important to remember that these sport governing organizations are volunteer based, with volunteers involved in decisions at every level from clubs to international federations. As will be discussed in Chapter 5, nonprofit sport organizations do not operate as top-down power hierarchies, with clubs always abiding by regional directives, or national governing bodies agreeing with international policy initiatives. Communication and agreement can be difficult between these organizations, which may have competing priorities and localized issues. A spirit of cooperation and negotiation is required to make the nonprofit sport system operate effectively. The simple exertion of authority in a traditional organizational hierarchy is not appropriate for most nonprofit sport organizations.

THE SPORTS CLUB ENVIRONMENT

At the centre of sport development in countries such as Canada, New Zealand, Australia, and the United Kingdom is the local or community sports club. It is worth taking some time to reflect on the role of the sports club, how volunteers and staff work in the club environment, and how clubs contribute to sport development.

The most striking thing about local sport clubs is their diversity. Sport clubs have many functions, structures, resources, values, and ideologies, and they provide an enormous range of participation opportunities for people to be involved in sport. Most clubs provide activity in a single sport and have as their focus enjoyment in sport rather than competitive success. They operate with minimum staffing, structures, income, and expenditure and often rely on a small group of paid or unpaid individuals to organize and administer club activities. The majority of club income comes from membership payments, so they tend to operate fairly autonomously. The vast majority of sport clubs rely almost exclusively on volunteers to govern, administer, and manage their organizations and to provide coaching, officiating, and general assistance with training, match-day functions, and fundraising.

Administrators

Administrators who fill roles as elected or appointed committee members have the responsibility for the overall guidance, direction, and supervision of the organization. The management committee of a sports club is generally responsible for:

- Conducting long-term planning for the future of the club
- Developing policy and procedures for club activities
- Managing external relations with other sport organizations, local governments, or sponsors
- Managing financial resources and legal issues on behalf of the club
- Carrying out recommendations put forward by members
- Communicating to members on current issues or developments
- Evaluating the performance of officials, employees (if any), and other service providers
- Ensuring adequate records are kept for future transfer of responsibilities to new committee members
- Acting as role models for other club members

While governance will be covered in detail in Chapter 5, it is important to note here that the ability of clubs to carry out these tasks effectively will vary according to their resources, culture, and quality of people willing to be involved. The important administrative roles within local sports club are the chairperson or president, secretary, treasurer, and volunteer coordinator. Other committee roles might involve responsibility for coaching, officiating, representative teams, match-day arrangements, fundraising, or marketing.

The chairperson or president should be the one to set the agenda for how a committee operates, work to develop the strategic direction of the club, chair committee meetings, and coordinate the work of other members of the committee. Club secretaries are the administrative link between members, the committee, and other organizations and have responsibility for managing correspondence, records, and information about club activities. The treasurer has responsibility for preparing the annual budget; monitoring expenditure and revenue; planning for future financial needs; and managing operational issues such as petty cash, payments, and banking. The position of volunteer coordinator involves the development of systems and procedures to manage volunteers such as planning, recruitment, training, and recognition.

Coaches

Coaches working in the sport club system may be unpaid or paid, depending on the nature of the sport and the resources of individual clubs. The role of the coach is central to developing athlete's skills and knowledge and helping them learn tactics for success and enjoy their sport. Coaches also act as important role models for players and athletes.

Most sports provide a structured training and accreditation scheme for coaches to develop their skills and experience to coach at local, state/provincial, national, or international levels. In Australia, for example, the National Coaching Council established a three-tier National Coaching Accreditation Scheme (NCAS) in 1978 that has been the basic model for coach development and accreditation since that time. Coaches could undertake a Level 1 introductory course, Level 2 intermediate course, and Level 3 advanced courses in coaching. NCAS training programs comprised three elements: (1) coaching principles that cover fundamentals of coaching and athletic performance; (2) sport-specific coaching that covers the skills, techniques, strategies, and scientific approaches to a particular sport; and (3) coaching practice where coaches engage in practical coaching and application of coaching principles. This model was revised in 2017, with the national scheme replaced with more bespoke coach accreditation and development frameworks, something we examine in detail in Case Study 3.2.

Officials

Sports officials include those people who act as referees, umpires, judges, scorers, or time-keepers to officiate over games or events. The majority of officials are unpaid, but some sports such as Australian rules football, basketball, and some other football codes pay officials at all levels, enabling some to earn a substantial salary from full-time officiating. Other sports such as netball, softball, or tennis rarely pay officials unless they are at the state or national championship level. Sports officials are critical to facilitating people's involvement in sport but are the hardest positions to fill within the nonprofit sport system since they absorb a lot of time and often have low status.

All sports provide a structured training and accreditation scheme for officials in much the same way as coaches to develop their skills and experience at local, state/provincial, national, or international levels. The Australian National Officiating Accreditation Scheme (NOAS) was established in 1994, modelled on the NCAS, but does not prescribe formal levels of officiating, as these vary greatly between sporting codes. The NOAS aims to develop and implement programs that improve the quality, quantity, leadership, and status of sports officiating in Australia through training programs that comprise three elements: (1) general principles of officiating and event management; (2) sport-specific technical rules, interpretations, reporting, and specific roles; and (3) practice at officiating and applying the officiating principles.

General volunteers

Sports clubs also depend on people to perform roles in fundraising, managing representative teams, helping with match-day arrangements such as car parking or stewarding, or helping to market the club. The majority of general volunteers have an existing link to a sports club through being a parent of a child who plays at the club, having some other family connection, or having friends and work colleagues involved in the club.

It is clear that volunteers make an enormous contribution as coaches, officials, and administrators in order to facilitate people's involvement in sport. However, there are some worrying signs that such voluntary involvement may be on the wane in some age cohorts of the population and that in order to sustain current levels of involvement in sport, the management of sport volunteers needs to improve.

GOVERNMENT INTERVENTION

The substantial funds allocated to nonprofit sport organizations by governments to support their activities in areas of mass participation or elite performance has meant that governments have tried various means to influence the way in which the nonprofit sector of sport operates. Examples of these early attempts include the Australian Sports Commission Volunteer Management Program and the policy of Sport England to have national organizations develop "whole of sport" plans. These are briefly reviewed in the following to highlight the increasingly interdependent nature of government and sport organizations in seeking improvements in nonprofit sport.

The Australian Sports Commission (ASC) developed the Volunteer Involvement Program in 1994 in partnership with the Australian Society of Sports Administrators, the Confederation of Australian Sport, and state departments of sport and recreation. The program aimed to improve the operation of nonprofit sport clubs and associations by providing a series of publications on sport club administration. In 2000, the Volunteer Management Program (VMP) and the Club and Association Management Program (CAMP) resources were published, and the ASC encouraged all clubs to join a club development network and engage in strategic planning and other management techniques.

Another example is the policy developed by Sport England to require national sport organizations to develop "whole of sport" plans. In 2003, Sport England identified 30 priority sports based on their capability to contribute to Sport England's vision of an active and successful sporting nation and worked with the national sport organizations to develop and implement these plans. The plans were designed to outline how a sport from grassroots right to the elite level will attract and keep participants and improve their sporting experiences. The plans were intended to drive decisions by Sport England to provide funding to national organizations based on clearly articulated ideas of the resources they need to develop their sport. The plans were also intended to provide for measurable performance results and assist Sport England in evaluating the benefits that accrue from funding nonprofit sport organizations.

The Clubmark program developed by Sport England is indicative of an approach many governments have taken toward trying to enhance the capacity of the nonprofit sport sector at the community club level. Because approximately 60% of young people in England belong to a sports club outside of school (where government can influence delivery standards via the education system), the government sought to improve the standard of service delivery that young people receive from community sport clubs by creating Clubmark, a cross-sport quality accreditation for clubs with junior sections run by Sport England. The main purpose of Clubmark was to encourage sport clubs to seek accreditation as a Clubmark club. National governing bodies of sport and county sport partnerships (CSPs) award a Clubmark to proven high-quality clubs. The national scheme was in place from 2002 until 2019 and led to the accreditation of many thousands of clubs in the Clubmark scheme.

Clubmark accreditation was awarded to clubs that complied with minimum operating standards in four areas: the playing program, duty of care and child protection, sports equity and ethics, and club management. Clubs working towards accreditation could receive support and advice from their NGB and other partners such as county sports partnerships. Circumstances vary between clubs and sports, but the process of accreditation was the same. The benefits of implementing a single, national standard for sport club operations gives sports clubs of all types structure and direction, specifically in areas such as:

- Club development – The foundation for any club is its youth structure. By encouraging and attracting young members, it is building a strong future.

- Increased membership – Addressing issues like equity and child protection gives parents confidence when choosing a club for their children.
- Developing coaches and volunteers – As part of Clubmark, clubs receive help in developing the skills of those involved in their organization.
- Raised profile – Once Clubmark accredited, clubs are listed on a national database and in other directories to help them attract new members and grow.

The Clubmark program was intended to provide sports clubs a framework for volunteer management as well as a series of templates that they could adapt for their specific circumstances. Clubmark was superseded in 2019 with the creation of ClubMatters, a new Sport England program, funded by the National Lottery, that provides free resources, support, guidance, and workshops to sport clubs and associations (sportenglandclubmatters. com). The ClubMatters program includes a large variety of digital resources, workshops, online tutorials, podcasts, templates, and learning resources designed to upskill the volunteer workforce managing sport organizations.

These examples of the volunteer involvement program, volunteer management program, requirements for sport plans, club quality programs, and variants have all been intended to improve the skill base and professionalism of people working within sport clubs and associations. They are usually very resource-intensive to create and require a consistent investment in time and resources from national agencies to have a material impact on the quality of sport club operations. One particularly ambitious, high-profile approach that was designed to leverage the impact of London hosting the 2012 Olympic Games to leave a legacy of increased volunteering is explored in our next In Practice: Sport England's Sport Makers initiative.

In Practice 3.2 Sport England Sport Makers

One of the more ambitious government intervention programs aimed at influencing the direction and capacity of the nonprofit sport sector was the Sport Makers program, an initiative tied to the legacy of the London 2012 Olympic Games. According to the Sport England website before the 2012 Games, the intention was for the Sport Makers program would recruit, train, and deploy 50,000 new sports volunteers aged 16 years and over to organize and lead community sporting activities across England. The program was designed to grow the volunteer base, who would have:

> A positive and inspiring introduction to the world of sport volunteering via a series of workshops delivered locally through a training provider and in conjunction with a county sports partnership. We anticipate that many volunteers will continue to give of their time, further increasing sport participation long after the 2012 Games are held in the UK. These Sport Makers will organise and support hundreds of thousands of new hours of grassroots sport, creating new opportunities across the country. While doing so, they will bring the Olympic and

Paralympic values to life in every community. Sport Makers will be fully inclusive and target participants including people who have a disability, both males and females and participants from BME groups

(Sport England, 2011).

The Sport Makers program was originally scheduled to run from April 2011 until September 2013, with a budget of £4 million drawn from National Lottery Funding, with approximately half delivered via county sport partnerships. The outcomes were planned to include (Sport England, 2011):

- 50,000 new Sport Makers recruited and invited to an orientation workshop delivered locally through a CSP and by an inspirational trainer.
- 40,000 Sport Makers are provided with deployment opportunities to increase participation for a minimum of 10 hours each by their CSP. Of those deployed, we anticipate 20,000 will continue to volunteer in sport beyond these 10 hours
- Olympic and Paralympic values are brought to life for the Sport Makers through their orientation workshop so that they feel part of the Olympic movement and role model these values in raising participation
- As a result of their deployment, thousands of new opportunities for people aged sixteen and over to participate will be created.

This ambitious program involved the British Olympic Association, London Organising Committee of the Olympic Games, national governing bodies, county sports partnerships, local authority sports development teams, local governments, and a range of national and county/sub-regional voluntary partners.

A review published in March 2013 (Nichols et al.) concluded that while it had assisted the work of county sports partnerships, it had failed to meet its original targets. A further review published in 2014 by CFE Research (Adamson & Spong, 2014) found that about 25% of people who registered to be a Sport Maker failed to attend any workshops or undertake any activities and that Sport Makers tended to recruit people they already knew to participate in sport activities. They also found that overall, Sport Makers themselves benefitted from being involved in the program. Such a centralized, target-driven approach highlights the complexities of achieving significant sustainable change in volunteering rates within the nonprofit sport sector where partnerships and collaboration across all the stakeholders involved in delivering sport are required.

Source: Sport England. (2011). *Sport Makers factsheet*. London, UK: Sport England; Nichols, G., Ferguson, G., Grix, J., & Griffiths, J. (2013). *Sport Makers: Developing good practice in volunteer and sports development*. University of Sheffield; Adamson, J., & Spong, S. (2014). *Sport Makers evaluation*. London: CFE Research.

ISSUES FOR THE NONPROFIT SPORT SECTOR

A range of challenges exists for the nonprofit sport sector around the globe. Foremost among these is the dependence on volunteers to sustain the sports system in areas such as coaching, administering, and officiating. As highlighted earlier in this chapter, there is evidence to suggest that the rate of volunteerism is declining for roles such as officiating and administration in sport. Governments and nonprofit sport organizations will need to address this issue if their mutually dependent goals of increasing participation in organized sport are to be achieved.

The increasingly litigious nature of society and the associated increase in costs of insurance for nonprofit sport organizations directly affects the cost of participation. In Australia, fewer insurers are providing insurance cover for sporting organizations, and insurance premium prices have risen significantly in recent years. Public liability insurance is vital to run sport events and programs, and these costs are passed onto participants for no additional benefits, which raises the question of whether people can afford to keep playing sport in traditional nonprofit systems.

A further issue for nonprofit sport organizations is the trend away from participating in traditional sports, organized through clubs and associations, to a more informal pattern of participation. Some people are unwilling to commit to a season of sporting involvement and are seeking ways to engage in sport and physical activity on a more casual basis, either through short-term commercial providers or with friends in spontaneous or pick-up sports. The increase in options available to young people to spend their discretionary leisure dollars, euros, or pounds has also presented challenges for nonprofit sport organizations to market themselves as an attractive option.

As highlighted earlier, nonprofit organizations, including nonprofit sport organizations, face significant capacity problems. They are often constrained by the size of their facilities or venues and may struggle to attract enough quality people to manage the operations of their organization. They are also constrained by the interdependent nature of sport – they require other clubs, teams, and organizations to provide competition – so they need to work cooperatively with other nonprofit sport organizations to expand their "product".

The very nature of nonprofit sport organizations requires adherence to frequently cumbersome consultative decision-making processes, often across large geographic areas and with widely dispersed and disparate groups of stakeholders. The additional complexity of the governance and management requirements of these organizations presents its own set of challenges in terms of making timely decisions, reacting to market trends, being innovative, or seeking agreement on significant organizational changes.

THE RISE OF SPORT FOR DEVELOPMENT

One area of nonprofit activity related to sport has been the enormous growth of the field of sport for development. In contrast to sport development (the player development pathways and structures for the delivery of sport), sport for development is the use of sport to deliver other non-sport outcomes for individuals or communities. One of the more widely cited definitions of sport for development is:

> the use of sport to exert a positive influence on public health, the socialisation of children, youths and adults, the social inclusion of the disadvantaged, the economic development of regions and states, and on fostering intercultural exchange and conflict resolution.
>
> (Lyras & Welty Peachey, 2011, p. 311)

In the most recent comprehensive review of sport for development, Schulenkorf, Sherry, and Rowe (2016, p. 22) stated that

> As a consequence of growing political and institutional support, the number of sport-based projects aimed at contributing to positive development in these areas has been constantly increasing . . . the popularity of SFD stems from its ability to capture or "hook" a large number of people – particularly those interested in sport and physical activity – and use the momentum in and around sport as a strategic vehicle to communicate, implement, and achieve nonsport development goals.

The sport for development field is dominated by work in Africa, Asia, and Latin America, where sport is used as a focal point to attract participants to programs aimed at youth development, tackling poverty, increasing retention rates in education programs, or overcoming social disadvantage. Programs are supported by individual philanthropists, corporations, governments, charitable organizations, and international and national sport federations, and sport for development is an increasing area for employment and volunteering for people skilled in sport management as well as community development, international relations, or social work. This area will increasingly become a significant employer of sport management graduates as well as a focal point for voluntary efforts of people seeking to facilitate community outcomes associated with sport activities or programs.

In Practice 3.3 City in the Community

A contemporary example of sport for development in action is the work of the charitable arm of the Melbourne City Football Club – City in the Community, established in 2010 in Melbourne, Australia. Part of the City Football Foundation operated by the clubs' owner, Manchester City Football Club, the foundation's activities in Australia use the power of football to address five social issues: social inclusion, health, education, unemployment, and crime prevention. The various instances of its community outreach program have engaged with more than 500,000 young people to promote health, education, and leadership development and create safe community spaces.

By using football as the hook to engage with young people suffering disadvantage, the City in the Community program delivers a number of bespoke social support programs supported by foundation or third-party funding from health agencies or other charitable foundations. Some examples of their programs include:

- Young leader training to develop employment-seeking skills and public speaking confidence to assist young people in becoming leaders in their own local communities while also developing their football skills
- I Speak Football – a social inclusion program that invites newly arrived migrants to meet and talk about a common interest in football, helping them develop their language skills and connect with others in their new communities.
- CALD Carers – a project funded by the Victorian Health Promotion Foundation aimed at getting culturally and linguistically diverse carers active and connecting them with the club.
- Walking Football – a program for older adults aimed at keeping them active and playing football.
- Disability programs, including Powerchair Football and Blind Football supported by the Westpac Foundation.
- Free school holiday programs for groups unable to afford attending fee-paying programs.

The City in the Community suite of programs is designed to address specific social or health issues, and the power of the sport of football and the brand power of the Melbourne City Football Club facilitate the engagement of individuals in these programs – sport for development in action, in every sense of the word.

SUMMARY

Nonprofit organizations were defined as those organizations that are institutionally separate from the state, do not return profits to owners, are self-governing, have a significant element of voluntary contribution, and are formally incorporated. Nonprofit organizations exist to develop communities, meet the needs of identifiable and discrete groups in those communities, and work for the benefit of public good rather than wealth creation for individuals. The majority of nonprofit organizations are driven largely by the efforts of volunteers rather than paid staff.

Sport organizations that operate on a nonprofit basis include professional service organizations, industry lobby groups, sport event organizations, and sport governing bodies. By far the greatest number of nonprofit sport organizations are those that provide sporting competition or event participation opportunities for their members and other members of the public – sport governing bodies and sports clubs. The common element amongst all these sport organizations is their nonprofit focus – they exist to facilitate sporting opportunities for their members, who may be individual athletes, coaches, officials or administrators, clubs, associations, or other sport organizations. They are also interdependent, relying on each other to provide playing talent; information to access competitions; resources for coach, official, and player development; and funding to support their activities.

Sport governing bodies and clubs rely almost exclusively on volunteers to govern, administer, and manage their organizations and to provide coaching, officiating, and general assistance with training, events, and fundraising. The substantial funds allocated to nonprofit sport organizations by governments to support their activities in areas of mass participation or elite performance have meant that governments are increasingly trying to influence the way in which the nonprofit sector of sport operates. Finally, a number of challenges exist for the nonprofit sport sector, including the dependence on volunteers to sustain the sports system, the increasingly litigious nature of society, and the associated increase in costs of insurance for nonprofit sport organizations. There is also a trend away from participating in traditional sports, significant capacity problems, and the additional complexity of the governance and management requirements of these organizations.

REVIEW QUESTIONS

1　What is the role of the nonprofit sector in relation to sport?

2　What are the unique aspects of nonprofit sport organizations that set them apart from profit-oriented or privately owned sport organizations?

3　Describe the role of a local community sport club.

4　Explain how the state and the nonprofit sector may contribute to sport development.

5　In what ways are volunteers important to the delivery of sport?

6　What are some of the challenges faced by nonprofit sporting clubs in relation to their volunteer workforce?

7　Explain the role of a national governing body for a sport.

8　Why does the government attempt to intervene in the management of nonprofit sport organizations? Explain how governments do this in your own country.

9　How can nonprofit sport organizations reduce the costs to participants?

10　Explain how nonprofit sport organizations have to work cooperatively with each other but still compete on the playing field.

DISCUSSION QUESTIONS

1　Why is sport an attractive vehicle to assist delivery of other development programs aimed at overcoming social disadvantage?

2　How could sport change its delivery model to better recruit and retain volunteers?

3　Should sport continue to rely on volunteers to support its delivery, or should we move to a more user-pays model with more paid employees delivering sport?

4　What other sport for development programs have you seen in action? What makes them succeed (or not)?

5　Why is it important for sport organizations to remain self determining?

FURTHER READING

Cuskelly, G. (2017). Volunteer management. In R. Hoye & M. M. Parent (Eds.), *Handbook of sport management* (pp. 442–462). London: Sage.

Hoye, R., Cuskelly, G., Auld, C., Kappelides, P., & Misener, K. (2020). *Sport volunteering*. London: Routledge.

May, T., Harris, S., & Collins, M. (2013). Implementing community sport policy: Understanding the variety of voluntary club types and their attitudes to policy. *International Journal of Sport Policy and Politics*, 5(3), 397–419.

Misener, K., & Doherty, A. (2013). Understanding capacity through the processes and outcomes of interorganizational relationships in nonprofit community sport organizations. *Sport Management Review*, 16(2), 135–147.

Schulenkorf, N., Sherry, E., & Rowe, K. (2016). Sport for development: An integrated literature review. *Journal of Sport Management*, 30, 22–39.

RELEVANT WEBSITES

The following websites are useful starting points for further information on nonprofit sport organizations:

Sport Australia at www.sportaus.gov.au

Sport New Zealand at sportnz.org.nz

Sport Canada at canada.ca/en/services/culture/sport.html

Sport for Development Foundation at sportanddev.org

Sport England at sportengland.org

Sport Scotland at sportscotland.org.uk

CASE STUDY 3.1

Sport Scotland's Clubs and Communities Framework

This case study explores the program created by Sport Scotland, the national sport agency for Scotland, to help build the capability and capacity of the many (largely) nonprofit sport organizations within the Scottish sport system – the Clubs and Communities Framework. The overall focus of the program is to help the people of Scotland get the best out of their sport system.

The Clubs and Communities Framework is designed to guide the development of club and community organizations. It provides a common reference for those working on building the capability and capacity of club and community organizations to improve the sporting system. The framework is primarily aimed at professional staff to help them support local leaders, coaches, volunteers, and/or employees but can equally be used by clubs themselves. The framework asks sport organizations to self assess whether they undertake actions under six priority areas: three enabler pillars of people, places, and profile, along with three quality pillars that organizations should be able to demonstrate – organized, sustainable, and connected.

For people, the framework asks whether organizations:

- take a planned and inclusive approach to the engagement, development, and retention of their volunteers and/or employees;
- have a committee/board with the knowledge, skills, and behaviours to lead;
- have coaches/deliverers with the knowledge, skills, and behaviours to meet the needs of those taking part;
- have volunteers and/or employees with the knowledge, skills, and behaviours to fulfil their role;
- empower and support young people as leaders; and
- value and celebrate the contribution of volunteers and/or employees.

For places, the framework asks whether organizations:

- engage with and understand the place needs of those taking part and the wider community;
- are creative and willing to work with others to ensure their place needs are met in a sustainable way;
- take a planned and realistic approach to places that are fully aligned to their overall development plan; and
- ensure their places are accessible and appropriate for those taking part as well as the wider community.

For profile, the framework asks whether organizations:

- understand their audiences and communicate through the right channels at the right time;
- work with partners to help promote their activities;
- communicate their vision, purpose, activities, and the impact they have on their community;
- provide accessible information about the activities they offer;
- demonstrate their diversity and inclusion of under-represented groups; and
- identify and share learning and best practices.

For organized, the framework asks whether organizations:

- have an appropriate legal structure that suits their needs;
- comply with standards of good governance to mitigate risk;
- ensure everyone is clear on their role and responsibility and that this is adhered to;
- ensure the wellbeing, safety, and protection of all;

- develop and deliver on a clear vision and purpose;
- take a planned approach to the development of their activities;
- are inclusive and open to everyone in their community and aim to attract under-represented groups;
- are clear on how their work fits within and contributes to their wider community;
- have sound financial management processes in place; and
- are focused on the quality of the activities they offer.

For sustainable, the framework asks whether organizations:

- identify what sustainability looks like for them;
- have a sound financial model as part of an effective business model;
- plan for succession in key roles, such as committee/board members, coaches, volunteers, and/or employees;
- are clear about the support available to them and how to access it;
- are ready for investment from external sources to help achieve their aspirations;
- seek to understand the needs of all those taking part and the needs of the wider community;
- are clear on the difference they expect their activities to make to those taking part and the wider community; and
- continuously reflect on their work and embed a cycle of improvement to all their activities.

For connected, the framework asks whether organizations:

- welcome people and bring the community together;
- offer pathways to help people take part and progress in sport;
- provide recreational opportunities for people to take part; and
- work closely in partnership with other sporting and non-sporting organizations to achieve common goals.

The framework points organizations to a range of digital resources that will help them answer the questions and develop action steps to address any shortcomings.

   Source: The material for this case study is based on the contents of the Sport Scotland website, which can be found at sportscotland.org.uk

CASE STUDY QUESTIONS

1   Visit the Sport Scotland website: https://sportscotland.org.uk/media/4828/clubs-and-communities-framework.pdf and review page 4, where the variety of organizations are listed that form part of the Scottish Sport System. Would the framework be easier to adopt for some organizations than others?

2   What are the potential barriers to organizations using the framework?

3   If Sport Scotland wants all organizations to get better, should it mandate each organization adopt the framework? What are the advantages and disadvantages of that strategy?

4   What alternative approaches could be used by Sport Scotland to improve the experience of people wanting to be involved in sport in Scotland?

CASE STUDY 3.2

How to improve coaching quality

This case study explores the evolution of the National Coaching Accreditation Scheme in Australia over the last 40 years to illustrate the changing nature of the nonprofit sport sector and the influence of national sport agencies on their activities.

The Australian Coaching Council Ltd (ACC) is a not-for-profit organization aimed at providing support for national sporting organizations (NSOs) to develop, implement, and coordinate coaching and officiating policy and coach and official development programs.

In 1979, representatives of the Canadian National Coaching Certification Program (NCCP) provided the Australian Coaching Council Inc. with the information and expertise needed to establish the National Coaching Accreditation Scheme. Over time, the NCCP has been recognized as a world leader in coach education and is currently the largest adult continuing education program in Canada.

The focus of the Australian Coaching Council was to develop, implement, and co-ordinate coaching policy and coaching development programs on a national basis in co-operation with national sporting organizations. The ACC in partnership with the various national sporting organizations administered the NCAS until 1991, when the Australian Coaching Council's NCAS administrative functions were incorporated into the Australian Sports Commission (now Sport Australia). According to the ACC website, at the time of this change, the ACC had accredited 81,076 coaches by the middle of 1991.

The accreditation of NSO coaches via the NCAS was mandated by the ASC as compulsory from 1991, which ensured compliance with the model. From 2001, this was not a mandatory requirement, and NSOs gradually began to develop and operate their own respective coach accreditation frameworks. As NSOs increasingly operated independently of the ACC, the relevance of the NCAS declined. In 2017, the NCAS ceased to be directly supported by Sport Australia.

After almost 40 years, the control of coach accreditation evolved from a partnership between the ACC and respective NSOs where coaches undertook generic learning modules from the ACC supplemented by sport-specific learning modules to a system where NSOs control the curriculum and accreditation process for their coaches. In response, in 2018, the ACC was reconstituted as the representative administrative body for the NCAS and those NSOs who wished to continue with the NCAS as the accreditation program for their respective sports.

In 2020, the ACC produced a proposal for a revised, contemporary NCAS that would provide external quality assurance to NSOs programs as well as facilitating access of registered coaches to a national community of coaches. This proposal grew out of an assumption that there remained a need for independent quality assurance of NSO coaching courses and that assistance was needed with the design and development of courses (including course outcomes, delivery methods, and assessment of coaches). The ACC proposed it would focus on three key roles:

1   Influencing and leading on ideas and modern thinking about coaching.
2   Working with NSOs and other relevant organizations to develop quality coach education programs.
3   Providing a quality assurance framework through a national coaching accreditation scheme.

The core principles of the Australian Coaching Council are:

1   Provide national and international thought leadership: Constantly challenging and testing prevailing orthodoxies surrounding all aspects of coaching at all levels. Promote and develop coaching and officiating throughout Australia, ensuring the sustainability and longevity of each sport.
2   Embed a collaborative approach in all aspects of the ACC's work through extensive collaboration with NSOs.
3   Facilitate sharing between sports.
4   Provide coaching and coach development resources that fill knowledge gaps and complement the work of NSOs.
5   Promote inclusive, diverse learning experiences for coaches and coach developers.
6   Manage a responsive national coaching accreditation scheme to provide an option to NSOs for the external recognition and quality control of their coaching programs.
    a   NSOs may submit some or all their courses for accreditation under the NCAS.
    b   Courses submitted to the ACC are reviewed against agreed-upon quality criteria.
7   Work with sport to develop continuous improvement strategies in systematic planning and strategy implementation in the areas of coaching and coach development.

8 Broaden the profile, priority, and standing of coaching and officiating within the sporting and general communities.

9 Build cooperation and collaboration with a wide range of external stakeholders, including government, the education sector, and others in the pursuit of enhancing coaching and officiating development strategies, programs, and resources.

10 Promote activities that improve the welfare of sport participants and their coaches and that maintain the integrity of sport.

Source: The Australian Coaching Council website at australiancoachingcouncil.com and the ACC document Coaching in the 2020s: The National Coaching Strategic Framework *developed by the Australian Coaching Council, also available from their website.*

CASE STUDY QUESTIONS

1 Why is it important to the ACC that it provide quality assurance to coaching programs offered by NSOs?

2 What are the advantages and disadvantages of having a national sport agency like Sport Australia mandating nonprofit groups like NSOs adopt the NCAS as the framework for their sport-specific coaching program?

3 Why does it seem the ACC is struggling to argue for its relevance as an important nonprofit sport organization to the national sport agency, Sport Australia?

4 Should coach development and accreditation be left to individual, self-determining sports rather than being overseen by the ACC?

CHAPTER 4

Professional sport

OVERVIEW

This chapter examines the key features of professional sport organizations and provides examples of the unique features of professional sport leagues, teams, and athletes. The chapter does not examine local, state/provincial, or national sport organizations; rather, it concentrates on elite, professional sport organizations and their goals of business development and revenue generation and how they fit within the sport industry at large.

DOI: 10.4324/9781003217947-5

After completing this chapter, the reader should be able to:

- Identify various professional sport entities throughout the global sport industry;
- Understand and explain the complexity of professional sport organizations and their use of corporate strategies and structures to deliver their products and services; and
- Understand and explain the roles of players, agents, sponsors, leagues, and teams/clubs in professional sport.

WHAT IS PROFESSIONAL SPORT?

Unlike local, grassroots sport, where goals are often developed around increasing participation and strengthening the community, professional sport, wherever it is played, is about elite, high-performance competitions that capture large audiences and generate revenue. Professional sport around the world is, by far, the most visible element of the sport industry. There are multiple, dedicated channels and streams to professional sport on radio and television, as well as programs dedicated to these entities on podcasts and streaming services (e.g., Netflix, Amazon Prime). Although community sport might receive some traditional or digital media coverage, the large amount of coverage of professional sport is quite significant and emphasizes its place in the sport industry. What also emphasizes its importance is the fact that professional sport can be found all over the world. From Buenos Aires, Argentina, to Mumbai, India, to Melbourne, Australia, professional sport can be readily found in large, cathedral-esque stadia (La Bombonera, Wankhede Stadium, and Melbourne Cricket Ground), played by athletes who often earn millions of pesos, rupees, and dollars. It is because of this high visibility that professional athletes are also considered cultural celebrities adored by fans, young and old, and inspire youth to participate in community sport. So, in this respect, sport at the local, regional, state/provincial, and national levels can serve as an important feeder system to develop athletes who will professionalize and compete at the highest, most visible stage. Thus, professional sport can be considered the peak of the sport industry, supported by sport entities at the grassroots, community levels beneath it, achieving high levels of revenue generation and cultural significance in society. However, professional sport can also be criticized for its ability to be a greedy commercial animal, demanding financial, cultural, and social resources to sustain its structure and place within the sector and society at large.

Professional sport can be thought to comprise three tiers: premier, minor, and developing (O'Reilly, Séguin, Abeza, & Naraine, 2022). Premier professional sport consists of those leagues, teams, and clubs at the highest levels of sport competition in their country of operation, or even internationally. Prominent examples would include the National Basketball Association, Major League Baseball (MLB), and National Hockey League (NHL) in North America; Volleyball Bundesliga, the Blast T20, and Netball Superleague in Europe; and Nippon Professional Baseball, Chinese Basketball Association, and Indian

Premier League in Asia. Certainly, this is not an exhaustive list of premier professional sport leagues, but these examples provide an important range of the types of professional sport entities that would fall in this category.

One of the most important aspects of premier professional sport is the sport of football. Football codes differ from country to country and, in some cases, within a country. As premier professional sport has developed worldwide, there is consensus within the industry that, to avoid confusion, soccer or association football is referred to as global football, while other forms could be qualified by their sporting country (e.g., American football, Australian football). With that in mind, there are several key premier professional sport entities in football around the world that require further discovery.

In North America, the National Football League has emerged as the preeminent professional league for American football in this region, a sport sometimes referred to as gridiron football. The NFL consists of 32 teams, all located in the United States of America, but routinely hosts exhibition and regular-season matches in Canada (i.e., Toronto), Mexico (i.e., Mexico City), England (i.e., London), and Australia (i.e., Sydney), with future plans for games in Germany. While professional gridiron football is not as common in other parts of the globe, it dominates news headlines from large urban centres that house teams to small, rural regions that admire the competition from afar. Part of the history of gridiron football in the United States originates in the late nineteenth century, when American universities would play one another on an ad hoc basis for pride and prestige, events that would slowly grow and develop amongst locals and media outlets. Eventually, the sport was codified but also professionalized as university students graduated from their respective institutions, creating a new league that connected the East, Mid-West, South, and Pacific regions of the United States. Today, the NFL continues to captivate audiences with major plots and subplots each week in the form of winners and losers, injuries and transgressions, trades and free agency signings, and coach and front office executive hiring and firing. In turn, the particular premier professional sport has created a weekly, episodic-like system, allowing fans to plan their consumption of matches and other content that surrounds their favourite athletes and teams. It is this constancy and consistency which have built an important foundation for premier professional sport's popularity, ingraining sport into the cultural fabric of society.

While the NFL does have a footprint across the pond, a different type of premier professional football in Europe dominates the professional sport landscape. Whether it's the English Premier League (EPL), La Liga, Ligue 1, Bundesliga, or Serie A, global football has no shortage of premier opportunities for which elite athletes can compete and which fans can support and engage in consumption behaviours. These premier entities are highly lucrative, with athletes from all over the world migrating to Western Europe to compete (Frick, 2009) and financial institutions investing in these professional clubs. Table 4.1 lists *Forbes* magazine's estimation of the value of global football teams in Europe in 2021. The list demonstrates that many of these teams are significant corporate entities that have risen in value over time due to excellent annual revenues. In the previous edition of this book, many of these teams' values maxed out around the $2B USD mark, levels that are now the new floor, with the max value creeping closer to $5B USD. Furthermore, what has helped these clubs raise their valuations over time has been the rise of professional women's sport offerings. Clubs like Chelsea, Paris Saint-Germain, and Arsenal all boast women's sides,

TABLE 4.1 Professional global football teams with highest valuations in 2021

Team	Country	Value (US$)	5-year change in value
Barcelona	Spain	4,760,000,000	34%
Real Madrid	Spain	4,750,000,000	30%
Bayern Munich	Germany	4,210,000,000	57%
Manchester United	England	4,200,000,000	27%
Liverpool	England	4,100,000,000	165%
Manchester City	England	4,000,000,000	108%
Chelsea	England	3,200,000,000	93%
Arsenal	England	2,800,000,000	39%
Paris Saint-Germain	France	2,500,000,000	207%

Source: www.forbes.com

providing another touchpoint for consumers who cheer for their favourite club or community to latch onto and support simultaneously.

The final example of premier professional football in the sport sector can be found down under. In Australia, premier professional football has four major codes: Australian football, also known as "footy", rugby league, rugby union, and, of course, global football. The Australian Football League is the wealthiest and most popular professional sport organization in Australia, with annual club/team revenues ranging from $45M AUD on the low end to $100M AUD on the high end. Much of the AFL's revenues are attributable to sponsorship and broadcast rights (see Chapters 12 and 13). However, the AFL's reach, while national, tends to favour the southern and western parts of the country (i.e., Victoria, South Australia, and Western Australia). In New South Wales and Queensland, the National Rugby League (NRL) boasts a much stronger following. This unique intra-country divide with premier football codes is demarcated by a cultural phenomenon known as the "Barassi Line", which separates the AFL-favouring states from the NRL-favouring states (Fujak & Frawley, 2013). Rounding out the premier football entities in Australia are the Super Rugby league and the A-League, both of which involve teams in Australia and across the Tasman Sea in New Zealand.

In Practice 4.1 Just win, baby?

The NFL is a powerhouse not just by North American standards but by global standards. It is, by all accounts, the most popular and profitable sporting league in the world. The marquee event for the NFL, the Super Bowl, is one of the most-watched events, not just sport related, in the world. In fact, during the COVID-19 pandemic-plagued 2020–2021 season, the Super Bowl between the Tampa Bay Buccaneers and Kansas City Chiefs amassed over 90 million viewers in 130 countries. At its core, the NFL is made up of 32 teams across two conferences. Of those 32 teams, 24 were ranked in the *Forbes* top 50 most valuable sporting teams of 2021:

- Dallas Cowboys (1)
- New England Patriots (8)
- New York Giants (9)
- Los Angeles Rams (13)
- San Francisco 49ers (15)
- New York Jets (17)
- Chicago Bears (18)
- Washington Football Team (19)
- Philadelphia Eagles (21)
- Houston Texans (23)
- Denver Broncos (25)
- Las Vegas Raiders (29)
- Seattle Seahawks (29)
- Green Bay Packers (31)
- Pittsburgh Steelers (32)
- Baltimore Ravens (33)
- Minnesota Vikings (34)
- Miami Dolphins (35)
- Atlanta Falcons (36)
- Indianapolis Colts (32)
- Los Angeles Chargers (41)
- Carolina Panthers (42)
- Kansas City Chiefs (43)
- New Orleans Saints (46)
- Jacksonville Jaguars (47)
- Cleveland Browns (50)

The Arizona Cardinals, Tampa Bay Buccaneers, Tennessee Titans, Buffalo Bills, Cincinnati Bengals, and the Detroit Lions missed out on making the top 50 in 2021, but nearly half of the world's most valuable sporting teams are in the NFL. In the #1 spot, the Dallas Cowboys have an estimated value of $5.7B USD, while the Cleveland Browns were in 50th position with an estimated value of $2.35B USD. In a previous edition of this book, the focus was on the Dallas Cowboys. The Cowboys have significant international notoriety, given their high-profile owner and general manager, Jerry Jones, and their Super Bowl success in the early 1990s, and are often ranked #1 or #2 on *Forbes* team valuation list. But there's another team in the NFL worth exploring: the Las Vegas Raiders. The Raiders have quite the history; born in Oakland, California, in 1960, a 10% share of the team was sold for $18,000 USD in 1966 to Al Davis, who then proceeded to buy out other owners, taking sole control of the team a decade later. Davis was quite the charismatic owner, coining the phrase, "just win, baby", emblematic of the team's focus on winning, despite notoriously rough, dirty, and illegal tactics on the field of play. After winning the Super Bowl in 1976 and 1980, Davis turned his attention to capitalizing on the team's winning ways, relocating the team to Los Angeles, a major urban market. The team's "bad boy" image followed along as well, and the Raiders gained mainstream recognition, with rap artists donning the silver-and-black team paraphernalia. After a stadium dispute, the team would eventually relocate back to Oakland in 1995, staying there until 2019 when, again, the ownership group, this time led by Al Davis' son, Mark, decided to relocate to Las Vegas, Nevada. Like their move to Los Angeles, the team believed that there could be greater value with a new billion-dollar stadium in Las Vegas. The appreciation of the new stadium is one of the major reasons the teams' franchise valuation has increased 117% in the last five years. So, even though the team credo might be "just win, baby", winning often leads to new opportunities to capitalize and generate more revenues for the club, and the real credo might be "just move, baby".

Sources: Las Vegas Raiders website at www.raiders.com; Forbes website at www.forbes.com; ESPN website at www.espn.com

While entities in the premier typology are the default for many fans and learners when considering professional sport, there are two other tiers that sit beneath it that are important to discuss: minor and developing. Minor professional sport consists of high-level competition, but in training or preparation for the premier levels. In this capacity, minor professional sport operates as an important feeder system to premier teams and clubs with which they might be affiliated. For instance, consider the American Hockey League (AHL) in North America. The AHL is designated as the minor professional ice hockey league with direct links to the NHL. So, while the Vegas Golden Knights play in the NHL, they can develop athletes and coaches at their AHL affiliate, the Henderson Silver Knights. Minor leagues are known throughout the world, too. Consider the global football structure in England. While the EPL sits atop the structure, there exists the English Football League Championship, League One, and League Two beneath it. In this system, teams are unique and not necessarily affiliated with other clubs, but it still serves to maximize the delivery of professional sport to the masses in English city centres and rural areas who have a passion for global football. Some of the other well-known minor leagues are Minor League Baseball and the NBA G-League. In Australia, the Victorian Football League occupies a similar space, serving as the de facto minor league to the AFL. However, the developing tier of professional sport is much more widespread internationally.

There are many different types of sport and corporate bodies looking to take advantage by creating new teams and targeting elite athletes. In Canada, while the Toronto Raptors play in the NBA, the Canadian Elite Basketball League was recently established with more domestic opportunities for professional basketball players. Similarly, the Canadian Football League offers more opportunity for fans in Canada to consume gridiron football.

TABLE 4.2 Selection of women's professional sport leagues

Name	Country	Sport	Year founded
WNBA	United States	Basketball	1996
NWSL	United States	Global Football	2012
NWHL	United States	Ice Hockey	2015
NFP	United States	Softball	2004
WSL	England	Global Football	2011
WBBL	Australia	Cricket	2015
AFLW	Australia	Australian Football	2017
NRLW	Australia	Rugby League	2018
W-League	Australia	Global Football	2008
Damehåndboldligaen	Denmark	Handball	1936

Certainly, there are a wealth of developing professional sport leagues and teams, whether they have been recently established or have been operating for decades, even centuries! What separates the minor and developing professional sport entities from the premier category is the amount of exposure and commercial interest injected into the system. Premier sport leagues often include billion-dollar broadcast deals, long-term sponsorship agreements, and thousands of fans attending matches. Minor and developing sport entities tend to exist on a much smaller scale: athlete salaries are lower; broadcast deals are less lucrative or nonexistent; and revenues are more dependent on ticket sales, concessions, and merchandise, as opposed to large sponsorship deals (that are unlikely to come).

It should also be noted that, recently, there has been a considerable rise in the number of professional women's sport properties. While leagues such as the Women's National Basketball Association have existed for some time, others have begun to pop up in different parts of the world. Table 4.2 provides some of the more prominent leagues that have entered the mainstream in the professional sport landscape.

In the first chapter of this book, you were introduced to the three-sector model of sport: public, nonprofit, and private. In Chapters 2 and 3, the public and nonprofit sectors were examined, while this fourth chapter examines professional sport. It would be a mistake, however, to assume that the terms private and professional are synonymous in the context of sport organizations and their operations. Rather, in this chapter, we are examining those sport organizations in which competitive commercial revenue is used to sustain their operations, as opposed to organizations that are funded by the state or almost exclusively through membership fees or subscriptions. It is important to recognize that many of the organizations featured in this chapter are nonprofit and are not privately owned.

Professional sport organizations have two important features that define them. First, they share a scale of operations (particularly commercial and financial) that means they exist at the apex of the sport industry, and second, all the players or athletes are "professionals" – sport is their job, and they are paid to train and play full time. Sports in which the players or athletes are required to find additional employment to supplement their income cannot be considered professional. While some employment does take place in premier, minor, and developing leagues, athletes can also compete in various tournaments or circuits.

SPORT CIRCUITS

In addition to professional leagues that have defined structures with regular seasons, play-offs, and off-season periods, professional sport also exists in the form of sport circuits. Circuits are like a travelling roadshow, where the entire event occurs in a one-off location and then rotates to another location thereafter. Consider Formula 1 (F1) racing, an elite form of professional motorsport. F1 operates on the basis of rotations, with races in different cities around the world given their seasonality (e.g., summer). For instance, the Australian Grand Prix, held at the Albert Park street course in Melbourne, typically takes place in March as the sweltering Australian heat tempers and transitions towards autumn. Conversely, the Canadian Grand Prix, held in Montréal, Quebec, takes place in June (i.e., summer), which would be the midst of Australian winter. F1 races are typically held in the same place for a longer term, but it has started to expand its offering to new, unique places like Abu Dhabi, United Arab Emirates (circa 2009), and Sochi, Russia (circa 2014). In fact, F1 is expected to host new races in Jeddah, Saudi Arabia, in 2021, and Miami, United States, in 2022. While COVID-19 has put a damper on attendance levels, adopting a sport circuit model allows F1 to offer its product globally and encourage more fans to consume the sport. It also provides an opportunity for drivers and teams to experience new places and dynamic environments instead of being tied down to a repetitive home-and-away–type schedule.

The locations of events or tournaments that are part of national or global sport circuits are determined on the basis of cities or countries bidding for the rights to host an event, traditional affiliations with venues such as Wimbledon for the annual All England Tennis Tournament, or the rights of qualifying teams to host the event in their own venue. In the case of the Champions League, a major global football tournament in Europe, teams that qualify for the tournament are entitled to host their home games (performance-based flexibility), while in tennis, the Australian Open, the US Open, the French Open, and Wimbledon are the only marquee events (no flexibility) that are based in venues with long-term hosting rights. In other circuits, such as the World Rally Championship (WRC), the location of the events on the yearly calendar can change as cities and nations bid for the rights to host rounds. From 2014 to 2017, the WRC held a round in the European nation of Poland, which had only hosted two rounds in the previous 35 years. Similarly, Cyprus, Greece, and Turkey hosted rounds at various times between 2000–2014 but not in the 2017 season. Bidding for these types of events can often be very competitive, as cities and nations seek to secure the prestige, status, tourism profile, and potential economic benefits that are associated with hosting popular global sport circuits.

There are also global sport circuits in which participation in the event is dependent almost entirely on money, which situates them at the peak of the professional sport apex. The International Cycling Union (UCI) governs the UCI World Tour, a global cycling circuit featuring some of the most well-known events like the Tour de France, Giro D'Italia, and La Vuelta a España. Competing in this global circuit requires significant investment, covering coaching, training, bicycle and other equipment costs (including research and development), and travel. Thus, competitors in the UCI World Tour group up and scale operations under one team, one banner. These groups are known as UCI WorldTeams and are driven by large corporate sponsorships, including major brands like Movistar, the European telecommunications brand, and Emirates, the Middle Eastern airliner. To participate in the UCI World Tour, WorldTeams must pay a registration fee of approximately €100,000 and then €8,500 per race. Relatedly, prize purses are tiered based on the World Tour event and where the rider places. So, even though a rider might finish with a personal best time at the Tour de France, their eighth-place finish would only yield their team €1,000. So, to compete in the UCI World Tour, a significant financial investment must be made up front and on a consistent basis to maintain operations and participation in the competition.

In Practice 4.2 Women's Tennis Association

Founded in 1973, the Women's Tennis Association (WTA) is the peak body for women's professional tennis; its membership consists of more than 2500 players who represent almost 100 nations. In 2019, these players competed for $179 million USD in prize money across 55 events and four Grand Slams (Wimbledon, US Open, French Open, and Australian Open), staged in 28 countries. Unlike sporting circuits such as F1, which have multiple races that the same drivers and constructors compete in, the WTA essentially consists of a series of sporting circuits based on level of prize money and player ability/ranking, with the Grand Slam, WTA Finals and Elite Trophy, and premier mandatory events serving as the most well known to tennis fans.

Grand Slam

Each year, the four Grand Slam events are held; the Australian Open takes place in January, the French Open (May–June), Wimbledon (July) and the US Open (August–September). Each of these Grand Slams is conducted over a two-week period. Normally, 104 of the top-ranked female tennis players in the world compete for the title, in addition to 24 players who qualify for the tournament by winning a qualifying tournament in the weeks leading up to the event or who are given wild cards by the tournament organizers. Wimbledon, the French Open, and the US Open all started towards the end of the nineteenth century, with the Australian Open first played in 1905. The so called "open era" of tennis began in 1968 when professionals were allowed to compete with amateurs in the Grand Slam events. In terms of the operations of the global tennis circuit, there is extremely limited flexibility in the location or scheduling of the four Grand Slams and no capacity for nations or cities to bid to host a Grand Slam as there is in other sports. For instance, while the Australian Open is played in Melbourne, there is the potential for the event to move, given it is the Open for Australasia. Similarly, the United States Tennis Association governs where the US Open is played, and the event was not always played in Queens, New York (its first incarnation was in Rhode Island!).

WTA Finals and WTA Elite Trophy

The WTA Finals are held in Shenzhen, China, while the WTA Elite Trophy is held in the last week of the season in Zhuhai (China). In 2019, the prize money for the WTA Finals was $14 million USD, making it the most lucrative event after the four Grand Slam events. Throughout the year, players compete in WTA tournaments and Grand Slam events, earning ranking points as they do so. The top eight players in the world qualify for the WTA Finals, which is played as a round-robin event with two groups of four players. Unlike the Grand Slams, the WTA Finals have been played in a variety of countries since they were launched in 1972; prior to Shenzhen, the Finals were played in Singapore from 2014–2018; Istanbul, Turkey, from 2011–2013; Doha, Qatar, from 2008–2010; Madrid, Spain, from 2006–2007; and Los Angeles, United States, from 2002–2005. The location of the WTA Finals is awarded through a competitive bidding process, which was most recently won by Shenzhen for the period of 2019 to 2028 inclusive.

Premier Mandatory

In the 2019, the WTA calendar also featured events beyond the Grand Slams, known as "premier mandatory". These tournaments consist of Indian Wells (USA), Miami (USA), Madrid (Spain), and Beijing (China). In comparison to the Australian Open Grand Slam, which offered more than $49 million USD in prize money, these four premier mandatory events have total prize pools north of $4 million USD (i.e. less than the WTA Finals). While these events have lower prize amounts, the WTA has begun to award winners similar amounts to their male counterparts winning the same tournament on the men's side. The WTA is obliged to provide all of the top ten ranked women's players in the world for these events, as well as all players who qualify by ranking for acceptance into the main draw. In this way, the WTA and the event organizers are able to ensure that the premier mandatory events are a success for tournament organizers, drawing in large attendance figures and significant sponsorship and media attention. If seven or fewer of the top-ranked players play in the premier mandatory events, the WTA pays the tournament $500,000 USD in compensation. Although the premier mandatory events were cancelled in 2020 due to COVID-19, they are sure to remerge in 2021 and beyond.

Sources: WTA website at www.wtatennis.com

ATHLETE MANAGEMENT

As professional sport can exist at different levels (i.e., premier, minor, and developing) and with different models (e.g., sport circuits), the number of opportunities for athletes has also significantly increased. Many athletes from all parts of the globe work towards professionalizing in their sport and often migrate to countries where they offer premier leagues and teams (e.g., the NFL in the United States, the AFL in Australia). The growth that these leagues have experienced with the number and quality of athletes has also led to rising player salaries and the rise of "sport stars". Elite, high-profile professional athletes have commanded significant off-field/off-court/off-ice commercial opportunities, creating an industry focused on athlete management, representing talent in contract negotiations in return for a share or percentage of their income. In the modern era, athlete management is such an important part of the professionalization of sport that it has produced major talent representation firms.

One of the most prominent athlete management companies is the International Management Group (IMG), which was formed in the 1960s and employs in excess of 3000 staff in more than 25 countries. What began exclusively as an athlete management business evolved into a complex commercial operation that includes media production, consulting, and athlete development divisions. Golfer Arnold Palmer, winner of the US Masters golf tournament in 1958, 1960, 1962, and 1964; the US Open in 1960; and the British Open in 1961 and 1962, was the first athlete in the world to be branded by Mark McCormack, the creator of IMG. Back in the 1960s, the "brand-name" principle by which Palmer and McCormack approached sport was the first attempt to transform the business activities of leading athletes. Sport and business were previously related, but the scale of their operation was unique. The level of vertical and horizontal integration was essential to what became known as "sportsbiz" (Boyle & Haynes, 2000). The sportsbiz landscape put athletes, their teams, leagues, media, and sponsors into a dynamic circle that could unearth more business opportunities for all stakeholders involved, especially athletes. Agencies like IMG work proactively to secure contracts and agreement for athletes and other aspects of the sportsbiz circle. For IMG specifically, today, it is part of a larger entity known as Endeavor, a publicly traded firm that owns and operates two sport circuits (Ultimate Fighting Championship mixed-martial arts promotion and the Professional Bull Riders competition), as well as other leagues, media, and sport and entertainment representation elements (among others).

Another example is Octagon, a global sport marketing company that competes directly with Endeavor's IMG. Sitting within another publicly traded company, Interpublic Group of Companies, Octagon represents and promotes more than 800 athletes in 35 different sports across the world. Octagon provides a broad range of services for the athletes it manages, including the following:

- Contract negotiations
- Marketing initiatives and endorsements
- Public relations and charity involvement

- Financial planning
- Media management
- Property development
- Speaking engagements

Octagon claims that it generates annual marketing revenues of in excess of $300 million USD by maximizing its athletes' off-field corporate relationships. The company is able to accrue such large revenues due to its personalized approach to marketing for each of its athletes. Octagon represents some of the most well-known sport stars, including Giannis Antetokounmpo in the NBA, Elena Della Donne in the WNBA, Leon Draisaitl in the NHL, and Karolína Plíšková in the WTA. While Octagon and IMG are two of the larger firms, there are many smaller and medium-sized athlete representation firms, such as Newport Sport Management in Canada, JSW Sports in India, and Elevation Sports Agency in Australia.

Athletes competing in individual sports such as tennis and golf are logical targets for agents and representation firms; however, athletes in team sports are often as valuable, if not more so, particularly because they play often (weekly or more regularly) and, in many cases, across very long seasons. For instance, while a tennis athlete may compete in the grand slams, premier mandatory, and other events, the total number would still be well below the 162 regular-season game schedule in MLB and even less than the 82 regular-season game schedule in the NBA and NHL. Thus, sport stars in these team sports have the ability to attract significant media and endorsement agreements, such as Fernando Tatis Jr. of the San Diego Padres, Sabrina Ionescu of the New York Liberty, and Nathan McKinnon of the Colorado Avalanche. This increased attention is also extraordinarily valuable for the teams for whom these athletes belong, helping to bring fans to the game, secure broadcast contracts or sponsorship deals, increase merchandise and licensing sales, and generally improve the financial worth of the organization. Thus, an athlete's commercial potential can be calculated in individual earnings (through the team or an agent) but also in terms of club or league growth.

Professional sport stars are highly paid. Importantly, their salaries are relative to revenue of the clubs, leagues, tournaments, and events in which they partake. In fact, in some professional sports with strong player unions or associations, the level of remuneration for players is set as a percentage of league revenue. Table 4.3 provides an estimate of the highest-paid football players in the world in 2021. Their annual earnings are indicative of their on-field worth and the significant investment made by their respective teams, as well as their commercial worth off the field. Consider Cristiano Ronaldo, who is second on the list. Ronaldo's annual earnings of approximately $120 million USD can be broken down into his salary to play for Juventus and his endorsement deals off the pitch, the latter of which accounts for $50 million of his total earnings that year. The importance of those commercial opportunities is also impacting women's professional athlete earnings. Naomi Osaka, one of the top tennis players in the WTA, earned $5 million from winning Grand Slams and tournaments in 2021 but received $55 million from endorsing various products.

TABLE 4.3 Football players with highest earnings in 2021

Player	Football type	Team	Annual earnings (in USD)
Lionel Messi	Global football	Barcelona	130,000,000
Cristiano Ronaldo	Global football	Juventus	120,000,000
Dak Prescott	American football	Dallas Cowboys	107,500,000
Neymar	Global football	Paris Saint-Germain	95,000,000
Tom Brady	American football	Tampa Bay Buccaneers	76,000,000
Patrick Mahomes	American football	Kansas City Chiefs	54,500,000
David Bakhtiari	American football	Green Bay Packers	48,500,000
Ronnie Stanley	American football	Baltimore Ravens	47,500,000
Joey Bosa	American football	Los Angeles Chargers	44,000,000
Jalen Ramsey	American football	Los Angeles Rams	43,500,000

Source: www.forbes.com

In Practice 4.3 Jumpman, Jumpman!

Michael Jordan is one of the greatest, if not the greatest, male basketball players of all time, winning six NBA championships with the Chicago Bulls between 1991–1993 and 1996–1998, including the Finals MVP in each of those championship years, five League MVP awards, and ten league scoring titles. Jordan retired from basketball after his third NBA championship in 1993 in an attempt to play professional baseball, then retired again after his sixth championship in 1998, prior to returning briefly for a two-year career with the Washington Wizards. Jordan also won two gold medals with Team USA at the 1984 and 1992 Olympic Games, the first time as a collegiate athlete playing for the University of North Carolina and the second time as part of the celebrated "Dream Team" that included Magic Johnson and Larry Bird. Continuing his influence on basketball in retirement, Jordan is now the majority owner of the Charlotte Hornets. His most significant influence, however, might not be his exploits on the court but rather his relationship with Nike, which began in 1984 and has been an extraordinary commercial success.

Famous for its iconic swoosh logo, Nike is a global sportswear brand with a mission to "bring inspiration and innovation to every athlete in the world" (it notes that if you have a body, you are an athlete, meaning that this inspiration and innovation extends to everyone living on planet Earth). Although the company creates products for a variety of sports and activities, in its 2019 annual report, Nike reported that it focused its business in six key sectors: running, basketball, global football, men's and women's training, sportswear (sport-inspired lifestyle products), and "the Jordan brand". The Jordan brand has predominantly focused on basketball using Michael Jordan's jumpman trademark, though the brand has also begun to enter other sport spaces like global football (through its Paris Saint-Germain sponsorship), American football, and baseball.

The basketball offerings include the "Jordan Brand", which "designs, distributes and licenses athletic and casual footwear, apparel and accessories predominantly focussed on Basketball using the Jumpman trademark". In 2019, Nike's revenue was $37.2B USD, with the wholesale revenues for the Jordan brand equating to nearly $3B USD.

In its 1984 annual report, a year in which its revenue was $919 million USD and it initially signed Michael Jordan, Nike wrote that "extensive promotional programs, tailored for each sport, are aimed at having athletes wear Nike products. Shoes and equipment are provided to outstanding athletes and teams, athletes are hired as consultants, and product endorsements are obtained from leading professional athletes". Upon signing Jordan, Nike made the first "Air Jordan" basketball shoes, which reportedly made the company $70 million USD in their first two months on the market. Since then, Nike has employed a very successful strategy of using athletes to endorse its products, although the scale of its operations in this area grew exponentially during the 1990s and into the twenty-first century. According to the 2019 annual report, cash payments due to athletes, teams, and leagues as part of endorsement contracts were scheduled for $1.3B USD in 2020, $1.27B USD in 2021, and $1.3B USD in 2022. One of the reasons this figure is so high is the incredible roster of sport stars on Nike's payroll, including several athletes on the *Forbes* 2021 list of highest-earning athletes:

- Cristiano Ronaldo
- LeBron James
- Neymar
- Kevin Durant
- Naomi Osaka
- Russell Westbrook
- Giannis Antetokounmpo

Both Ronaldo and James have followed in Jordan's footsteps, as they both signed "lifetime" endorsement deals with Nike, a marker of their on-field success, global popularity, and media saturation. However, while they and others (e.g., Kevin Durant, Giannis Antetokounmpo) have their own shoe lines, athletes like Russell Westbrook are specifically denoted as Jordan brand athletes and don the jumpman logo on their shoes, clothes, and other sport accessories.

Sources: Nike website at www.nike.com, Forbes website at www.forbes.com

OWNERSHIP STRUCTURES

One of the most important defining features of professional sport is the varying ownership structures that exist (Cousens & Slack, 2005). Unlike community sport, which often does not have a single "owner", professional sport teams can be owned by a single person or a group. For instance, in the NFL, teams follow this model of ownership, with teams privately owned by wealthy individuals and their families. Prominent examples include the Pegula family for the Buffalo Bills, the Hunt family for the Kansas City Chiefs, and the Rooney family for the Pittsburgh Steelers. There are similar trends across other North American sport leagues, but one other important feature is the involvement of media and corporate entities in ownership. In the NBA and NHL, an entity known as Maple Leaf Sports and Entertainment (MLSE) operates the Toronto Raptors and Toronto Maple Leafs, and MLSE itself is majority owned by two major Canadian telecommunications giants (Rogers and Bell). In MLB, the Toronto Blue Jays are also owned by Rogers Communications, but the Atlanta Braves are likewise owned by a media conglomerate known as Liberty Media. While it was a much more prominent trend in the 1990s and early 2000s, corporate entities see professional sport team ownership as a way to vertically integrate their products and services. So, when a customer signs up for a Rogers cellular phone plan, they can watch the Toronto Blue Jays on a Rogers-owned sports station broadcasting to mobile devices and consume exclusive team content through their Rogers service, resulting in the company reaping revenues at every stage of the fan's journey.

In Europe, the commercialization and privatization of sport teams and clubs, especially those in global football, happened over the course of generations, transferring from local communities to the highest bidder. In some cases, teams eventually experienced incorporation and became commodities that could be bought and sold on stock exchanges. A prominent example of this is Juventus Football Club, one of the most popular teams in Italy, which is listed on the Borsa Italiana (i.e., Milan Stock Exchange). In another case, Manchester United is primarily owned by a wealthy family (the Glazers) but is also a publicly traded entity on the NASDAQ stock exchange in the United States. More recently, Europe has experienced a rise of foreign ownership. In the EPL, foreign ownership is quite high and is slowly edging closer to nearly 50% of teams in the league. There are also a handful of clubs in France, Italy, Spain, and Belgium that are foreign owned, with investors predominantly from China, though there are major investments from the Middle East also occurring.

In Australia, professional club ownership takes on a different model. Although AFL clubs, for example, have annual revenues near the $100 million AUD mark, they are non-profit organizations – all revenues generated are used on club operations (e.g. to pay players and staff, maintain facilities, or promote the club). No funds earned by AFL clubs are paid out to owners or shareholders, which sets it apart from its peers abroad.

Professional sports utilize different ownership models in order to regulate and manage their businesses effectively. Some of the models have strong historical traditions (e.g. NFL), while others have been selected or adapted for their utility (e.g. EPL). One of the key distinctions between professional sport teams and leagues is that they can be considered "profit maximizers" and "win maximizers". Profit-maximizing teams, such as those in the major American professional sport leagues, are typically owned by individuals or businesses who seek to maximize the financial return on investment. In some sports, however, such as English, Scottish, and Australian football and cricket (Quirk & Fort, 1992), the need to win is a greater priority than the need to make a profit. In fact, in some instances, win-maximizing teams will place the club in financial jeopardy, particularly by purchasing players they cannot afford.

Whether teams are win maximizing or profit maximizing, they must cooperate with each other at some level to ensure that fans, sponsors, and the media remain interested and involved with the sport. Sport leagues that are dominated by one or two teams are often perceived to be less attractive to fans than leagues in which the result of games is uncertain. There is, however, a long history of leagues in which strong rivalries have maintained interest in the game (Los Angeles Lakers versus Boston Celtics in the NBA and Carlton FC versus Collingwood FC in the AFL, for example), although often the teams that are part of the rivalry benefit at the expense of teams that perform poorly. A league that is not dominated by only a couple of teams and in which there is an uncertainty of outcome (of a game or season) is said to have "competitive balance" (Quirk & Fort, 1992). Leagues across the world have instituted a range of measures to try to achieve competitive balance, which is often elusive. Perhaps the most obvious and publicized measure is the draft system that operates in the NFL, NBA, MLB, NHL, and AFL. The draft allows the league to allocate higher draft preferences (the best athletes on offer) to poorer-performing teams in order to equalize the playing talent across the league and create more competitive games.

SUMMARY

This chapter has presented an overview of professional sport, its tiers, and key elements of its landscape. There has been significant change in professional sport over the last 50 years and new trends in the last decade itself impacting the commercialization and revenue generation that characterizes this form of sport. Consequently, the rise of the sportsbiz has facilitated the emergence of new sectors (e.g. athlete management) and approaches to commercialization (e.g., foreign ownership) and continues to promote the growth and longevity of the professional sport model. Further, professional sport does not refrain from adopting trends that suit the needs of its fans, media, and sponsors, such as sport circuits that promote the sport product on a rotational, ongoing basis.

REVIEW QUESTIONS

1 What is the role of professional sport in the sport industry landscape?

2 Explain the rationale behind a company sponsoring a professional sport club, league, or athlete.

3 What are the differences between the three tiers of professional sport?

4 Identify a premier professional sport league and examine its operations. What are the special features of that league that attract fans?

5   Choose a premier professional sport team or club and examine its value over the last 5, 10, and 20 years. Has their value increased or decreased? Why?

6   Choose a sport which uses a sport circuit model. Imagine that the city you live in is going to bid for the right to host an event in that circuit and create a list of potential benefits – think about features such as the economy, environment, transportation, public services, and housing.

7   Select two men's and two women's athletes. Are they sports stars? Justify your reasoning.

8   How do athlete management agencies help athletes?

9   Create a list of the top five paid sportspeople in your country. What does the list tell you about the popularity of sport?

10   Choose a sporting league of the world and identify whether it should be classified as "win maximizing" or "profit maximizing". Provide a rationale for your answer that includes a commentary on the ownership of teams in the league.

DISCUSSION QUESTIONS

1   How can the increasing number of social and digital media opportunities aid or inhibit minor and developing professional sport leagues and teams? Is digital media the answer for non-traditional sports to challenge dominant sports, football codes especially, for growth, popularity, and profit?

2   Some sport circuits have been criticized because of the amount of money that cities and nations have to pay to gain entry or access to the circuit. Are these circuits worth the money that cities and nations invest, and what criteria might be used to make such a determination?

3   Who are the dominant stakeholders in the sportsbiz circle? Are there any stakeholders missing from the circle not mentioned in this chapter? How does the sportsbiz circle of the 2020s compare to that of the 2000s?

4   As the commercialization and privatization of professional sport continue, there is an abundance of wealth distributed to various leagues, teams, and clubs around the world. But does that wealth flow equitably to athletes? Are all athletes compensated fairly for their services?

5   Many of the world's highest-profile football teams (e.g., NFL, EPL) are owned by some of the richest people in the world. Why do these people want to invest in sport, and what are the implications of having a collection of the world's richest people owning sport teams, which are often concentrated in a selection of high-profile leagues?

FURTHER READING

Cousens, L., & Slack, T. (2005). Field-level change: The case of North American major league professional sport. *Journal of Sport Management*, *19*(1), 13–42.

Downward, P., Frick, B., Humphreys, B. R., Pawlowski, T., Ruseski, J. E., & Soebbing, B. P. (2020). *The Sage handbook of sports economics*. Sage. http://dx.doi.org/10.4135/9781526470447

Fielding, L, Miller, L., & Brown, J. (1999). Harlem Globetrotters International, inc. *Journal of Sport Management*, *13*(1), 45–77.

Foster, G., O'Reilly, N., & Dávila, A. (2016). *Sports business management: Decision making around the globe*. London: Routledge.

Frick, B. (2009). Globalization and factor mobility: The impact of the "Bosman-ruling" on player migration in professional soccer. *Journal of Sports Economics*, *10*, 88–106. https://doi.org/10.1177%2F1527002508327399

Fujak, H., & Frawley, S. (2013). The Barassi line: Quantifying Australia's great sporting divide. *Sporting Traditions*, *30*, 93–109.

MacIntosh, E. W., Bravo, G. A., & Li, M. (2020). *International sport management*. Champaign, IL: Human Kinetics.

O'Reilly, N., Séguin, B., Abeza, G., & Naraine, M. L. (2022). *Canadian sport marketing*. Champaign, IL: Human Kinetics.

Shilbury, D., & Ferkins, K. (2019). *Routledge handbook of sport governance*. London: Routledge.

Shropshire, K. (1995). *The sports franchise game*. Philadelphia: University of Pennsylvania Press.

RELEVANT WEBSITES

North America
National Football League at http:// www.nfl.com
National Basketball Association at http:// www.nba.com
Women's National Basketball Association at http://www.wnba.com
Major League Baseball at http:// www.mlb.com
Major League Soccer at http://www.mlssoccer.com
National Women's Soccer League at http://www.nwslsoccer.com
Minor League Baseball at http://www.milb.com
National Hockey League at http:// www.nhl.com
Canadian Football League at http://www.cfl.ca
Professional Golfers' Association at http:// www.pga.com
Ladies Professional Golf Association at http:// www.lpga.com

Australia and New Zealand
Australian Football League at http:// www.afl.com.au
Cricket Australia at http://www.cricket.com.au
National Rugby League at http:// www.nrl.com
Super Rugby at http://super.rugby
A-League at http://www.a-league.com.au

Great Britain
English Premier League at http:// www.premierleague.com
British Rugby League at www.superleague.co.uk/
Netball Superleague at https://www.netballsl.com/

Asia
J-League at https://www.jleague.jp/en/index.html
Japanese Sumo Association at http:// www.sumo.or.jp/en/
Korean Baseball Organization at http://eng.koreabaseball.com/

Europe
European Champions League at http:// www.uefa.com/
Serie A (Italy) at http://www.legaseriea.it
La Liga at http://www.lfp.es/en
Bundesliga (Germany) at http:// www.bundesliga.de
Ladies European (golf) Tour at https://ladieseuropeantour.com/

Global
Olympics at http:// www.olympic.org
World Cup at http:// www.fifa.com
America's Cup at http:// www.americascup.com
Formula One at http:// www.formula1.com
Ultimate Fighting Championship at http://www.ufc.com
World Surf League at https://www.worldsurfleague.com/
Association of Tennis Professionals (men) at https://www.atptour.com/
Women's Tennis Association at http://www.wtatennis.com/
World Rally Championship at https://www.wrc.com/en/

CASE STUDY 4.1

Taking cricket to new heights: the Indian Premier League

With a growing number of professional sport leagues sprouting up in the last two decades, there is arguably no greater success story than the Indian Premier League (IPL). The league was launched on 18 April, 2008, as the domestic Twenty20 competition for cricketers in India, governed by the Board of Control for Cricket in India (BCCI). The principal strategy that drove and continues to underpin the IPL is the commercial opportunity that Twenty20 has brought to the global cricket landscape. As traditional cricket fans – those who were fans of the longer, test form of the game – age, a new, younger generation of fans has emerged, yearning for a shorter, more intensive frenzy of activity. Concurrently, the lucrative nature of broadcasting professional sport has fuelled multiple Twenty20 leagues around the world, including the Big Bash League in Australia, the Caribbean Premier League in the West Indies, and, of course, the IPL in India. Specifically, with the latter, the IPL has generated enormous financial commitments from Indian sport broadcaster Star Sports (part of the Walt Disney Entertainment empire) and global sponsors (e.g.,

Vivo, Mondelez, Amazon) and has captured the imagination of cricket fans eager to see the world's biggest stars in action. But its success, a decade and a half later, required a bold strategy and unique business model.

The current IPL competition is composed of eight franchises representing different cities or regions in India: Chennai Super Kings, Delhi Capitals, Kolkata Knight Riders, Mumbai Indians, Punjab Kings, Rajasthan Royals, Royal Challengers Bangalore, and Sunrisers Hyderabad. Back in 2008, eight franchises were awarded to various media groups and business entrepreneurs, netting over $700M USD for the BCCI. Some of those entrepreneurs included Bollywood movie stars Preity Zinta and Shah Rukh Khan, as well as business moguls Mukesh Ambani and Sajjan Jindal. What helped accelerate the rise of the IPL was its international stardom. Instead of just operating with Indian athletes, the IPL allowed imports from major cricket-playing nations, including Australia, England, New Zealand, Sri Lanka, South Africa, the West Indies, and even rival Pakistan. Structured as a tournament, the IPL involves 60 matches in total, 56 regular matches, 3 qualifying matches, and the final. To date, the Mumbai Indians have won the most titles, with five, with winning teams earning a $2.8M USD prize to be distributed amongst the players and a golden trophy to commemorate the victory.

Strategically, the IPL represents the first serious attempt to globalize cricket with a short-format that is conducive to media broadcasting across free-to-air, pay television, internet, and mobile. Typically, a Twenty20 match takes about three hours, which, while that is more than global football matches, is in line with other batted sports like baseball, and less than the five days required for test cricket. Twenty20 was first tested in England back in 2003, with other one-off iterations in Australia and Pakistan. By 2007, there was a formalized international competition, marking the arrival of domestic leagues, including the IPL. With the Indian market enthralled with cricket, the shorter format was ripe for domestic television viewership – capturing the audience's attention but for a more direct, purposeful period. Initially, domestic and international television rights for the IPL were sold to Sony Entertainment Television and World Sport Group for just over a billion USD for ten years. At the time, the agreement was a big bet for Sony – it was making a long-term investment in a property that was not properly tested. But the results were staggering. Sony's MAX station (where matches were televised) became the most-watched station in India, and advertising revenue was in the hundreds of millions each season. In 2017, rival Star Sports secured the global rights to the IPL, with a whopping five-year, $2.55-billion USD contract.

Franchise owners were also making a significant investment without a clear return guaranteed. The Mumbai Indians ownership group, led by Mukesh Ambani and his conglomerate, Reliance India Ltd., carried the most expensive franchise fee, estimated at $111.9M USD, and then required millions more to build the team's infrastructure and secure talent, the latter on an annual, recurring basis. However, the league raises substantial revenues from broadcast and sponsorships. In 2020, even with the COVID-19–plagued year, the IPL generated north of $500M USD to be split amongst the eight teams. This high figure is driven by the broadcast contract, as well as the title sponsorship with Vivo, a Chinese smartphone manufacturer, which pays $61.7M USD per year for the right to associate with the property. On top of this, teams yield revenue from gate receipts and concessions, as well as local sponsorships and arrangements. For instance, Mumbai was recently featured in a Netflix docuseries about the team, its trials and tribulations, and an upfront view of the business operations and management of the team. Thus, the IPL business model allows each franchise to share revenues but also keep what it earns individually.

Part of the IPL business model proposition is the availability of high-quality talent imported for a 60-match, compact two-to-three month schedule. The IPL uses an auction system where each franchise, prior to the beginning of the season, bids for top players. Auction-style selection is unique; teams have salary caps by which they must abide and a set number of import and domestic roster spots and can bid on available talent each year as it becomes available. The auction is exactly how it sounds: each team sits at a table with the executives and management team and determines whether a player is worth bidding on, except, unlike in a traditional professional sport model, where a team negotiates individually with a player, the cost for each player could be artificially driven up in the moment as teams go back and forth on a player up for auction. Notably, some of the top bids have amassed over $2M USD, including Chris Morris with the Rajasthan Royals in 2021 and Pat Cummins with the Kolkata Knight Riders in 2020, both of whom are imports (from South Africa and Australia, respectively). The IPL bidding process has been a brilliant piece of marketing and attracted enormous media publicity. Additionally, the IPL has introduced marketing elements from other professional sports, including cheerleaders, Bollywood choreographed dancing, pyrotechnics, and vivid uniforms.

The key to understanding the IPL's ongoing strategy is to appreciate the economic background that allowed it to come about. India's government introduced its first major wave of economic liberalism in the mid-1990s. One of the key moves was the de-regulation of the state-owned telecommunications monopoly, which suddenly allowed private companies to bid for the rights to deliver specific telecommunication services. As it turned out, telecommunications for the vast Indian marketplace proved lucrative, expanding into broadcasting and entertainment. The limitation with all telecommunications, however, is content. It is this fact which has underwritten the IPL's business model. The BCCI, as the owner of the IPL, has effectively duplicated the Indian government's success with commercial deregulation. Selling off its content in the form of broadcasting rights and franchises, the BCCI has secured billions of dollars and a sustainable revenue stream. In addition, it has revenues from commissions on the player auctions and sponsorship rights, although two-thirds of the television rights and sponsorship fees are to be shared with the franchisees.

As a global, commercial entity, the IPL has a favourable mix of potential global audiences, international talent, and a television-friendly playing format packed with entertainment and action. The business model is its most powerful asset, commanding the attention of corporate sponsors and broadcasters. The gambles have mainly been associated with a number of key uncertainties. For example, playing talent could be unavailable, there could be clashes with national cricket boards fearful of damage to their traditional test commitments, the probability of escalating player salaries, the extended length of the competition, and even the possibility of match-fixing. The IPL seems to look sustainable – but is it? Now a decade and a half later and facing a global health pandemic, the IPL will have its broadcast rights deal expire in the next few years, and sponsors might rethink their expenditures given the economic uncertainty. So, the question is, will the IPL continue its rapid pace? Is its business model sustainable coming out of the pandemic, or are changes needed? With international travel being severely limited and revenues being impacted through gate receipts, it is plausible that Australian, West Indian, New Zealand, and English nationals are unable to fly in for the IPL season. Furthermore, with more and more domestic Twenty20 leagues propping up, import talent may begin to decrease, and the international prospect of the IPL may lose its allure.

CASE STUDY QUESTIONS

1   Consider the IPL's business model and discuss the strategy that underpins it.

2   Consider cricket in your country. How well does the IPL do with fans in your country, and is there enough room on the competitive global sporting map for this major sporting league?

3   Consider the product itself and how it matches the opportunities in the market-place for short, fast-paced, television-friendly sport. Purely on the basis of the product, do you think that the league will continue to prosper?

CASE STUDY 4.2

The king and queen of the court: LeBron James and Serena Williams

This case explores two of the most prominent athletes in world sport, LeBron James and Serena Williams, one from a team sport, basketball, and the other an individual competitor in tennis. The sportsbiz concept referred to in the chapter explains how professional sport is more than just sport and provides opportunities for athletes to emerge with their own commercial interests. James and Williams, both of whom have a large global reach, have not only accumulated significant personal wealth for themselves but have also delivered significant benefits to others in the sportsbiz landscape. It is, in effect, a win-win situation where everyone benefits from the stardom of the athletes.

LeBron James is a professional basketball player who plays for the Los Angeles Lakers in the NBA. The NBA consists of 30 teams, 29 of which are located in the United States of America and 1 of which is located in Canada. The NBA is split into the Eastern and Western conferences, and each conference is split further into three divisions. James and the Lakers play in the Pacific division of the Western conference. James has won four NBA championships, two with the Miami Heat, one with the Cleveland Cavaliers, and his most recent victory with the Los Angeles Lakers in 2020. He has also amassed four NBA most valuable player awards for the regular season and has been named most valuable player for all four of the championships he has won. In 2018, James became an unrestricted free agent, which led him to being courted by a range of teams in the NBA. Unlike his first stint as an unrestricted free agent, where James worked with ESPN to produce a television special entitled, "The Decision", airing his official announcement to join another team (i.e., the Miami Heat), James was more subdued the second time around. After leaving his hometown team for South Beach in 2010, there was a lot of criticism from fans, media, and even the team owner, Dan Gilbert, who wrote an open letter about James' cowardice and betrayal. In a twist, James became a free agent in 2014 and chose to go back to Cleveland, delivering a championship to the city in 2016. But after some roster shuffling, James was disgruntled and opted for free agency. His athlete management group, Klutch Sports, indicated that James wanting to go to Miami was about winning championships, going back to Cleveland was about fulfilling his promise to his home team, and his decision to sign in Los Angeles was about freedom and choice.

James' achievements on the court for the Cavaliers, Heat, and Lakers have resulted in a significant global public profile, media coverage, product endorsements, personal sponsorships, and a range of business ventures. His contract with the Lakers is a reported four-year deal with over $150 million USD. According to *Forbes*, James is the fifth highest-earning athlete in world sport at $96.5 million USD, behind Conor McGregor, Lionel Messi, Cristiano Ronaldo, and Dak Prescott. Off the court, LeBron has deals with major firms such as Nike, Coca-Cola, McDonalds, Samsung, Intel, and KIA Motors. At the end of 2015, it was reported that James and Nike had signed a lifetime endorsement agreement, and it was speculated that this was worth more than $30 million USD per year. Additionally, James was able to find financial success on the silver screen, appearing in a 2015 movie, *Trainwreck*, starring comedian Amy Schumer, and himself starring in 2021's *Space Jam: A New Legacy*.

James' off-court endorsements can in part be explained by his significant social media presence but also the interaction between himself, the Lakers, the NBA, and Nike in the James sportsbiz circle. In 2016, it was estimated that a LeBron James tweet on Twitter was worth $165,000 USD. In 2017, the following figures were evident on Facebook and Twitter, which indicate why LeBron James is such an important commercial property for the NBA, Lakers, and Nike, the reaches of which are unable to compete with James on social media:

* James has 49.7 million followers on Twitter (@KingJames), the 26th most popular Twitter handle in the world, 25 million page likes on Facebook, and 88.9 million followers on Instagram

- The NBA has 33.5 million followers on Twitter (@NBA), 39 million page likes on Facebook, and 57.1 million followers on Instagram
- Nike has 8.5 million followers on Twitter (@Nike), 35 million page likes on Facebook, and 156 million followers on Instagram
- The Lakers have 9.9 million followers on Twitter (@Lakers), 21 million page likes on Facebook, and 16.7 million followers on Instagram

Serena Williams, a fellow American, is also a professional athlete. She is a tennis player who predominantly enters singles competitions and is widely recognized as one of the greatest tennis players of all time. She rose to prominence at the turn of the millennium, winning the 1999 US Open Grand Slam and beating world number-one-ranked Martina Hingis. In 2003, she achieved the "Serena Slam", holding the Grand Slam titles to all four events at the time. After dominating the early 2000s, Williams was hit with a string of injuries that set her back for a few years. However, she mounted a comeback and by 2010 was dominating again. In 2012, she achieved the Career Golden Slam, having won every Grand Slam on the WTA tour and Olympic gold in women's tennis singles (after already having a Career Golden Slam for doubles with her sister, Venus). Her dominance continued, with her holding the number-one ranking in women's tennis for a full calendar year in 2014 and completing another Serena Slam in 2015. While there are other top tennis players on the men's and women's sides, Williams' longevity at the top is notable and significant.

The impressiveness of Williams' athletic career arguably culminated in 2017 when, after winning the Australian Open Grand Slam for the seventh time in her career, she announced she was 20 weeks pregnant. After giving birth to her daughter, Alexis Olympia Ohanian Jr., in September that year, Williams began to train and re-entered play at the Grand Slams in 2018. Although she has not won a Grand Slam since 2017, she has won several smaller tournaments and remains a top-ten-ranked player. Although there is often a healthy debate about the greatest tennis player of all time, even her peers, like Roger Federer, have been quite vocal about her dominance and place atop the tennis world.

Serena Williams' gift on the court is also matched by her influence off the court, her sportsbiz circle. At the beginning of her career, Williams wore Puma, the famed European sportswear company, but quickly switched to Nike in 2004 after her slew of Grand Slam victories in 2002 (French Open, Wimbledon, US Open) and 2003 (Australian Open, Wimbledon). Her initial endorsement deal with Nike was $40 million USD over five years, but she has been a member of Team Nike since then. She has also used Wilson racquets and endorses other brands such as Gatorade, Pepsi, Beats by Dre, Chase Bank (USA), and Delta Airlines. In 2015, Williams endorsed Aston Martin, the luxury car company, being named "Chief Sports Officer", a creative but non-formal role within the automaker. Her off-court influence is also highlighted by her entry into fashion and glamour. In 2009, Williams launched a signature handbag and jewellery collection that was sold on television shopping networks and, in 2018, unveiled a new clothing line entitled Serena. Adopting a more sustainable approach to business, Williams added S by Serena, an environmentally conscious line of clothing for a range of body types and sizes, valuing inclusivity in apparel.

However, Williams is also widely regarded for her activism, supporting equality movements (e.g. Black Lives Matter) and equal pay for men and women in tennis (and other industries). She has also been a vocal supporter for the LGBTQ community, calling out other players for insensitive and homophobic remarks. In her advocacy for gender equality, Williams has also recently announced her investment in a new women's professional sport team, Angel City FC, alongside notable actors, media figures, businesswomen, and former elite global football athletes.

In 2021, *Forbes* ranked Williams as the 28rd highest-paid athlete in the world, with $1.5 million USD in salary/winnings and $40 million USD in endorsements. Unlike LeBron James, who is represented by Klutch Sports, Williams is represented by WME-IMG, one of the athlete management divisions of the larger sport management entity Endeavor. Aside from the sponsorship endorsements mentioned earlier, Williams also features in advertisements for AB InBev (e.g., Budweiser, Stella Artois), AT&T (telecommunications), and Bumble (dating application). Williams has a modest social media following, with 10.7 million followers on Twitter, 7 million page likes on Facebook, and 13.2 million followers on Instagram.

CASE STUDY QUESTIONS

1 How do James' and Williams' sportsbiz circles compare, and how are they similar?

2 What explains the difference in the money earned via endorsements by James and Williams?

3 What is the relative importance of James and Williams to their respective sports in terms of the sportsbiz circle concept?

4 Both James and Williams have created charitable foundations. How much are their foundations built around service to the community, and how much is about enhancing their public image and/or personal brand?

Sources: NBA website at www.nba.com, ESPN website at www.espn.com, Sports Illustrated website at www.si.com, LeBron James website at www.lebronjames.com, Serena Williams website at www.serenawilliams.com, Forbes website at www.forbes.com, WTA website at www.wtatennis.com

PART II

Sport management principles

CHAPTER 5

Sport governance

OVERVIEW

This chapter reviews the core concepts of organizational governance, explores the unique features of how sport organizations are governed, and summarizes the key research findings on the governance of sport organizations. The chapter also provides a summary of principles for governance within community, state, national, and professional sport organizations, including a section on ethical conduct of directors.

After completing this chapter, the reader should be able to:

- Identify the unique characteristics of organizational governance for corporate and nonprofit sport organizations;
- Differentiate the various theories of governance relevant to sport organizations;

DOI: 10.4324/9781003217947-7

- Understand and explain the role of boards, staff, volunteers, members, and stake-holder groups in governing sport organizations;
- Understand some of the challenges facing managers and volunteers involved in the governance of sport organizations;
- Have an appreciation of the importance of ethics in relation to sport governance; and
- Identify and understand the drivers of change in governance systems within sport organizations.

WHAT IS GOVERNANCE?

Organizational governance is concerned with the exercise of power within organizations and provides the system by which the elements of organizations are controlled and directed. Governance is necessary for all groups – nation states, corporate entities, societies, associations, and sport organizations – to function properly and effectively. An organizational governance system not only provides a framework within which the business of organizations is directed and controlled but also "helps to provide a degree of confidence that is necessary for the proper functioning of a market economy" (OECD, 2004, p. 11). Governance deals with issues of policy and direction for the enhancement of organizational performance rather than day-to-day operational management decision-making.

The importance of governance and its implied influence on organizational performance was highlighted by Tricker (1984, p. 7) when he noted, "if management is about running business, governance is about seeing that it is run properly". Sport Australia, in its latest release of its sport governance principles, defines governance as "the system by which organisations are directed and controlled. It is the way in which expectations are made clear and the culture of the organization is modelled" (Sport Australia, 2020, p. 5). Good organizational governance should ensure that the board and management seek to deliver outcomes for the benefit of the organization and its members and that the means used to attain these outcomes are effectively monitored.

Governing sport well has been a perennial challenge for many years. A 1997 report to the Australian Standing Committee on Recreation and Sport (SCORS) identified a major concern amongst the sporting community, which was the "perceived lack of effectiveness at board and council level in national and state sporting organizations" (SCORS Working Party on Management Improvement, 1997, p. 10). Since the mid-1990s, national sport agencies in the United Kingdom, New Zealand, and Canada have also identified improving governance of sport organizations as a strategic priority and continue to invest in governance guidelines, reviews, and assistance to improve governance practices in sport. Failures in the governance of national sport organizations, together with reviews of professional sport governance, continue to highlight the importance of developing, implementing, and regulating sound governance practices in both amateur and professional sport organizations.

CORPORATE AND NONPROFIT GOVERNANCE

The literature on organizational governance can be divided into two broad areas: (1) corporate governance that deals with the governance of profit-seeking companies and corporations that focuses on protecting and enhancing shareholder value and (2) nonprofit governance that is concerned with the governance of voluntary-based organizations that seek to provide a community service or facilitate the involvement of individuals in social, artistic, or sporting activities.

Studies of corporate governance have covered "concepts, theories and practices of boards and their directors, and the relationships between boards and shareholders, top management, regulators and auditors, and other stakeholders" (Tricker, 1993, p. 2). The literature in this field focuses on the two primary roles of the board in first ensuring conformance by management and second enhancing organizational performance. Conformance deals with the processes of supervision and monitoring of the work of managers by the board and ensuring that adequate accountability measures are in place to protect the interests of shareholders. Enhancing organizational performance focuses on the development of strategy and policy to create the direction and context within which managers will work.

The unique characteristics of nonprofit organizations demand a governance framework different to that of the corporate firm. Nonprofit organizations exist for different reasons than do profit-seeking entities and generally involve a greater number of stakeholders in their decision-making structures and processes. The relationships between decision-makers – the governance framework – will, therefore, be different to that found in the corporate world. The management processes employed to carry out the tasks of the organizations might well be similar, but a fundamental difference between nonprofit and corporate organizations is found in their governance frameworks.

While many sports organizations such as major sporting goods manufacturers, athlete management companies, retail companies, and venues can be classed as profit-seeking, the majority of sport organizations that provide participation and competition opportunities are nonprofit. These organizations include large clubs, regional associations or leagues, state or provincial governing bodies, and national sport organizations.

IS THERE A THEORY OF SPORT GOVERNANCE?

Clarke (2004) was one of the first to provide an overview of the development of theories of corporate governance, with McLeod (2020) also providing a more contemporary summary. Some of the important theories applied to the study of organizational governance include agency theory, stewardship theory, institutional theory, resource dependence theory, network theory, and stakeholder theory. In this section, we shall examine each of them in turn and assess how relevant they are to understanding the governance of sport organizations.

Agency theory proposes that shareholders' interests should prevail in decisions concerning the operation of an organization. Managers (agents) who have been appointed to run the organization should be subject to extensive checks and balances to reduce the potential for mismanagement or misconduct that threatens shareholders' interests. This has been the predominant theoretical approach to the study of corporate governance and has focused on exploring the best ways to maximize corporate control of managerial actions, information for shareholders, and labour in order to provide some assurance that managers will seek outcomes that maximize shareholder wealth and reduce risk. In relation to corporations operating in the sport industry that have individual, institutional, and government shareholders, this theory helps explain how governance systems work. For the majority of nonprofit sport organizations, which have diverse stakeholders who do not have a financial share in the organization (aside from annual membership fees), agency theory has limited application.

Stewardship theory takes the opposite view to agency theory and proposes that rather than assuming managers seek to act as individual agents to maximize their own interests over those of shareholders, they are motivated by other concepts such as a need for achievement, responsibility, recognition, and respect for authority. Thus, stewardship theory argues that managers' and shareholders' interests are actually aligned and that managers (agents) will act in the best interests of shareholders. This theoretical view can also be applied to sport corporations such as Nike, FoxSports, or a listed professional football club franchise. The application of either agency or stewardship theory is dependent on the actions of the managers (who choose to act as agents or stewards) and the view of shareholders (who create either an agent or stewardship relationship through their conscious choice of governance framework). Stewardship theory is arguably more applicable than agency theory to the study of nonprofit sport organizations where managers may have a connection to the sport as an ex-player, coach, or club official and, therefore, have a deeper sense of commitment to the organization and be more likely to act as stewards.

Agency and stewardship theories focus on the internal monitoring issues of governance. Three theories that seek to explain how organizations relate to external organizations and acquire scarce resources are institutional theory, resource dependence theory, and network theory. Institutional theory argues that the governance frameworks adopted by organizations are the result of adhering to external pressures of what is deemed acceptable business practice, including legal requirements for incorporation. Such pressures reflect wider societal concerns for proper governance systems to be employed. Further, if all organizations of a similar type and size seek to conform to these pressures, they are likely to adopt very similar governance frameworks, a situation know as institutional isomorphism. Evidence of this is apparent throughout club-based sporting systems such as in Canada, Australia, New Zealand, and the United Kingdom, where most national and state or provincial sporting organizations operate under remarkably similar governance frameworks.

Resource dependence theory proposes that in order to understand the behaviour of organizations, we must understand how they relate to their environment. Organizations paradoxically seek stability and certainty in their resource exchanges by entering into interorganizational arrangements, which require some loss of flexibility and autonomy in exchange for gaining control over other organizations. These interorganizational arrangements take the form of mergers, joint ventures, cooptation (the inclusion of outsiders in the leadership and decision-making processes of an organization), growth, political involvement, or restricting the distribution of information (Pfeffer & Salancik, 1978). Such arrangements have an impact on the governance structure adopted, the degree to which stakeholders are involved in decision-making, and the transparency of decision-making.

A final theory that attempts to explain elements of governance based on how organizations relate to external organizations is network theory. Network theory posits that organizations enter into socially binding contracts to deliver services in addition to purely legal contracts. Such arrangements create a degree of interdependency between organizations and facilitate the development of informal communication and the flow of resources between organizations. This is particularly true of sport organizations that, for example, rely on personal contacts to facilitate the success of major events by securing support from high-profile athletes, using volunteers in large numbers from other sports organizations, and depending on government support for stadia development of event bidding. Network theory can help explain how governance structures and processes, particularly concerning the boards of sports organizations, evolve to facilitate such informal arrangements.

These three theories emphasize the need to examine governance in terms of the external pressures that organizations face and the strategies, structures, and processes they put in place to manage them. Such an approach offers a more realistic view of how and why organizations have a particular governance framework than agency and stewardship theories.

Stakeholder theory provides another perspective for examining the relationship between organizations and their stakeholders. It argues for conceptualizing a corporation as a series of relationships and responsibilities which the governance framework must account for. This has important implications for corporations acting as good corporate citizens and particularly for sport organizations that need to manage a myriad of relationships with sponsors, funding agencies, members, affiliated organizations, staff, board members, venues, government agencies, and suppliers.

Much of the writing and research on organizational governance has been based on corporations rather than nonprofit entities. Applying a particular theory to the study of sport organizations must be done with regard to the type and industry context of the sport organization being studied. Sport organizations and their governance frameworks have diverse elements that prevent the development of an overarching theory of sport governance. The value of the theories presented here is that each of them can be used to illuminate the governance assumptions, processes, structures, and outcomes for sport organizations.

GOVERNANCE STRUCTURAL ELEMENTS

The governance elements of a corporate or profit-seeking sport organization are the same for any general business operation. These elements can include paid staff, including a CEO who may or may not have voting rights on a board, a board of directors representing the interests of many shareholders (in the case of a publicly listed company), or directors who are direct partners in the business. The real differences in governance elements can be found in volunteer sport organizations.

A simple governance structure of Volunteer Sport Organizations (VSOs) is depicted in Figure 5.1 and comprises five elements: members, volunteers, salaried staff, a council, and a board. Normally, members meet as a council (usually once per year at an annual general

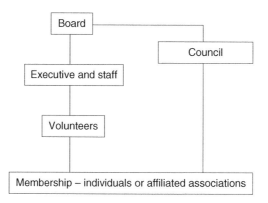

FIGURE 5.1 Typical governance structure of a voluntary sport organization

meeting) to elect or appoint individuals to a board. If the organization is large enough, the board may choose to employ an executive and other paid staff to carry out the tasks of the organization. Together with a pool of volunteers, these employees deliver services to organizational members. The board acts as the main decision-making body for the organization, and therefore the quality of its activities is vital to the success of the organization.

Members of a VSO can be individual players or athletes, or, in some cases, members are classified as other affiliated organizations, such as a club that competes in a league provided by a regional sports association. Members can also be commercial facility providers such as basketball, squash, or indoor soccer stadia. The membership council comprises those people or organizations that are registered members and may be allocated voting rights according to membership status. The board comprises individuals who have been elected, appointed, or invited to represent the interests of various membership categories, geographic regions, or sporting disciplines in decision-making. The senior paid staff member, often designated the CEO, is employed by and reports directly to the board. Other paid staff are appointed by the CEO to assist in performing various organizational tasks. These staff must work with a variety of volunteers in sport to deliver essential services such as coaching, player and official development, marketing, sport development, and event delivery. Finally, a wide range of stakeholders such as sponsors, funding agencies, members, affiliated organizations, staff, board members, venues, government agencies, and suppliers must be consulted and managed in order for the organization to operate optimally.

The majority of national and state or provincial sport organizations that provide participation and competition opportunities in club-based sporting systems are governed voluntarily by elected office bearers, who fill positions on either committees or boards. Most of these VSOs operate under a federated delegate system, with club representatives forming regional boards, regional representatives forming state or provincial boards, and state or provincial representatives forming national boards.

This traditional governance structure has been criticized for being unwieldy and cumbersome, slow to react to changes in market conditions, subject to potentially damaging politics or power plays between delegates, and imposing significant constraints on organizations wishing to change. On the other hand, the majority of sports organizations still use this model today and value its ability to ensure members have a say in decision-making, the transparency of decisions, and the autonomy granted to organizations at every level of the system. Practice 5.1 explains a typical governance structure of a large national sport governing organization and its range of responsibilities.

In Practice 5.1 Swim England

The Amateur Swimming Association (ASA) was the first governing body of swimming to be established in the world (1869) and has evolved to become Swim England, the English national governing body for swimming, diving, water polo, open water, and synchronized swimming. Their 2020 vision is "A Nation Swimming", and their mission is to create a happier, healthier, and more successful nation through swimming.

Swim England supports over 1100 affiliated swimming clubs through a national/regional/sub-regional structure. It endeavours to ensure every athlete – whatever their age or level of experience – belongs to a club that provides the best possible support and environment. It organizes competitions throughout England, from the grassroots to elite level, including the highly successful Age Group and Youth Championships that attract more than 1600 young swimmers aged 11–17 and the ASA Nationals. A particular focus of Swim England during the COVID-19 pandemic during 2020 to 2022 was producing club toolkits to help them navigate operational issues and provide financial assistance and guidance for hosting COVID-19-safe swimming activities and events.

The Swim England website (www.swimming.org/swimengland) states that the English talent program is a world-leading, seamless pathway that puts in place performance opportunities for swimmers to develop their skills and potential. The ASA operates a Learn to Swim award scheme based on the National Plan for Teaching Swimming. Over 2 million certificates and badges are issued to children all over the world under this scheme. Swimming is the number-one participation sport in England, with over 20 million people swimming every year, and Swim England is dedicated to giving more people more opportunities to swim for health and for fun.

It should be noted that Swim England is not a provider of swimming facilities; therefore, it acts as a catalyst and facilitator to ensure suitable facilities, with appropriate access and programs, are provided to meet the needs of the community and aquatic clubs. Swim England operates comprehensive certification and education programs for teachers, coaches, and officials. It has pioneered work on the UK Coaching Framework and is developing e-learning programs, all of which are helping to drive up quality and "raise the bar" to ensure Swim England has an appropriately skilled workforce for the whole swimming industry.

Swim England's strategy for 2017–2021 was superseded by a shorter-term strategy for 2020 to 2021 to deal with impact of the COVID pandemic and the reduced financial capacity of Swim England. It set out six strategic goals, summarized as:

1 Supporting members and clubs.
2 Sport development by increasing awareness of swimming, ensuring access to diverse participants, and providing an inclusive talent pathway.

3   Retaining and attracting talented volunteers and employees and providing quality training for the aquatics industry.

4   Facilitating learn-to-swim programs to provide the opportunity for everyone to enjoy swimming.

5   Provide expert advice to the aquatics industry for infrastructure development.

6   Streamline business process to be more sustainable.

Swim England's success is dependent on many people across the organization, both staff and volunteers, working together to deliver services at the right standard. Good governance is essential in monitoring and supporting the performance of individuals and member clubs and associations in that endeavour. The Swim England Board is made up of representatives from across the sport and physical activity sector, as well as backgrounds in law, human resources, and finance. This group meets six times per year to ensure that Swim England is working to the highest standards for all those involved in swimming and aquatics.

Source: The Swim England website at www.swimming.org/swimengland

STRATEGIC ROLE OF THE BOARD

Ferkins and Shilbury (2012) were the first to articulate the meaning of a strategically capable nonprofit sport board, identifying four key elements based on a study of New Zealand NSOs. First, the need to have capable people who can think longer term or "big picture", who can make decisions impartially, and who collectively have a mix of complementary skills and knowledge of the sport. Second, a frame of reference or being able to set a very clear vision and mission for the organization and the requisite skills to monitor progress toward a strategic direction or set of goals. Third, facilitative board processes such as a board agenda focused on strategy, genuine shared leadership between the CEO and board members, and an annual work plan for the board. Finally, the existence of facilitative regional relationships, where regional affiliate organizations work cooperatively with the NSO, with genuine board-to-board relationships.

Ferkins and Shilbury (2015) later articulated six factors and their relationships in influencing the strategic capability of sport boards: meaningful contributions of volunteer board members, the extent of a board's operational knowledge, boards integrating affiliated bodies into the governance of an overall sport organization, boards maintaining monitoring and control function, boards co-leading in strategy development; and integration of that strategy into its processes. They argued that these six factors all need to be present for boards to be strategic and that these factors are interdependent. While untested to date, this emerging theory provides a useful framework in which to examine governance practices, relationships, and impacts on sport organization outcomes. For more detail on the strategic role of the board, Ferkins (2020) provides an excellent summary of the key questions of why boards should be involved in strategy, how boards should get involved, and who should be central to strategy.

BOARD–STAFF RELATIONSHIPS

The gradual introduction of professional staff into VSOs over the last 20 years has created the need for volunteers and paid staff to work together at all levels, including the board table. This has led to some degree of uncertainty about what roles should be performed by each group and the extent to which staff and volunteers should be involved in strategic planning, policy development, performance evaluation, and resource acquisition. The potential for tension between these groups as they negotiate their respective roles has been well established, as has the ongoing desire of volunteers to maintain a degree of involvement in decision-making while at the same time utilizing the expertise of paid staff to assist them in running their organizations. This, then, is the crux of board–staff relationships: What areas do volunteers maintain control over, and which do paid staff control?

Hoye and Cuskelly (2003) found that VSO boards perform better if a degree of trust exists between the board and staff and board leadership is shared amongst a dominant coalition of the board chair, executive, and a small group of senior board members. As mentioned earlier, the executive controls the flow of information to board members, and so the quality, frequency, and accuracy of this information are vital to their ability to make decisions. Ensuring the board and executive work together effectively enhances this information flow and, therefore, the performance of the board.

More recently, research has focused on one of the major criticisms often directed toward the boards of nonprofit sport organizations – their inability to be strategic (Shilbury & Ferkins, 2011; Ferkins & Shilbury, 2012, 2015). Using three case studies of New Zealand NSOs, Shilbury and Ferkins (2011, p. 110) illustrated the ongoing challenges of largely volunteer-led boards dealing with the increasingly complex commercialization of the operations of NSOs, specifically the "delicate balance between volunteer involvement and professional management by paid staff". This first paper reaffirmed the increasing centrality of the paid CEO and staff in shaping the strategic direction of NSOs but, importantly, "demonstrated that the traditional expectations of volunteers might be at risk" (Shilbury & Ferkins, 2011, p. 124). The increasing requirements for nonprofit boards to be strategic increase the time commitment and competency required of volunteer board members, an issue through which Shilbury and Ferkins (2011, p. 124) suggest "that the traditional volunteer sport board director might be at risk, which may serve to undermine the role that sport has traditionally played in the community for the community".

PRINCIPLES OF GOOD ORGANIZATIONAL GOVERNANCE

The notion of good organizational governance extends beyond ideas of monitoring to ensure conformance and developing to improve performance discussed earlier in this chapter. Henry and Lee (2004) provide a list of seven key principles for good organizational governance in sport organizations that still resonate almost 20 years later:

1   Transparency – ensuring the organization has clear procedures for resource allocation, reporting, and decision-making.

2   Accountability – sports organizations need to be accountable to all their stakeholders.

3   Democracy – all stakeholder groups should be able to be represented in the governance structure.

4   Responsibility – the board has to be responsible for the organization and demonstrate ethical stewardship in carrying out that responsibility.

5   Equity – all stakeholder groups should be treated equitably.

6   Efficiency – process improvements should be undertaken to ensure the organization is making the best use of its resources.

7   Effectiveness – the board should establish and monitor measures of performance in a strategic manner.

This list of principles is not exhaustive, but it does give us a clear indication of the philosophical approach organizations should adopt in designing and implementing an appropriate governance framework. It may be somewhat surprising to find that even some of the more high-profile sport organizations in the world struggle to implement good governance standards.

Corporate governance of English Premier League football clubs has come under increasing scrutiny in recent years. The Premier League (PL) is the flagship of the game's governing body in England, the Football Association (FA). The FA is in turn under the control of a European governing body, the Union of European Football Associations (UEFA), which in turn is a member of the world's governing body, the Federation of International Football Associations. The regulatory system for Premier League clubs comprises four elements: (1) regulation by the football authorities, (2) regulation through the legal system in terms of company law, consumer law, labour law, and competition law; (3) regulation by a code of corporate governance developed by the Premier League; and (4) shareholder activism and stakeholder participation. The football authorities (namely FA and UEFA) have developed criteria such as a "fit and proper person" test aimed at improving the quality of individuals appointed or elected to govern Premier League clubs and the development of a code of corporate governance that provides guidelines for good governance. These actions are largely designed to ameliorate the effects of poor financial management within the Premier League clubs (since 1992, 50% of PL clubs have been in hands of administrators or insolvent) and to improve the sustainability of cubs that are promoted or relegated between the FA leagues. The Football Governance Research Centre (FGRC) noted that the PL clubs that regularly compete in the UEFA Champions' League hold a distinct financial advantage over other PL clubs. As a consequence, the governing body of the PL must be cognizant of the more powerful clubs and their potential to influence decision-making at the board table.

The English legal system requires PL clubs to fulfil a number of obligations for communicating with shareholders, consultation with fans, the use of customer charters, and dialogue with supporters' trusts. The FGRC noted that while the majority of PL clubs do an adequate job in this area, there was room for improvement. In addition, PL clubs that are listed public companies must follow a combined code that sets out principles for the activities of directors, director's remuneration, accountability and audit requirements, and relations with shareholders and institutional shareholders. The FGRC found that while PL clubs are moving towards having more independent directors, they fall short compared to other listed companies.

There are now more than 70 supporters' trusts for clubs in the FA, and about 60% of PL clubs have a supporter's trust. The trusts fulfil an important governance role, with 25% of PL clubs having a trust representative on their board. This representation means that committed fans have the chance to participate in decision-making at the highest level with regard to the future of their club and in return support the club in sport development, marketing, and fundraising activities.

While there are signs that PL clubs have generally accepted good governance practices and abide by the majority of codes of conduct and principles for good governance, they do fall down in certain areas of governance practice. These include the lack of performance evaluation of individual directors or the overall board in a small number of clubs and a significant portion of clubs failing to adopt standard strategic planning practices. While the English PL enjoys an enormous global profile as a leading football competition, the governance of the member clubs does not reach such exalted heights.

These failures in football governance are also evident in other countries; Hamil, Morrow, Idle, Rossi, and Faccendini (2010) documented the failings in governance that have plagued Italian football in recent years, noting

> there is a clear and transparent system of regulatory oversight for the Italian football industry . . . [and a licensing system that] . . . suggests a high standard of club governance should exist [but] there is a very serious gap between theory and practice, a gap which has had significant consequences for the health of the Italian football industry.
>
> (p. 379)

They argue that inappropriate ownership and governance structures among football clubs have led to a series of problems that have dogged Italian soccer over the last three decades, including betting scandals, doping, false passports, bribery and match-fixing, and violence. They cite the problem of clubs being controlled by familial networks with little separation of ownership and control (one of the central tenets of effective governance) as a central cause of these problems. Hamil et al. (2010, p. 388) also noted that "what emerges in football are networks consisting of powerful individuals connected with clubs, governing bodies, political parties and the media, which are in prominent positions to influence decision-making within football and the business of football". The legacy of a lack of competitive balance in the Italian league and the growing disparity of resources that exists between mid-tier clubs and those few large clubs that play in the lucrative UEFA Champions League also compounds the problem. They concluded that Italian football should adopt "modern regulation – including sanctions for misdemeanours – and clear guidelines for strong governance" (Hamil et al., 2010, p. 404).

In Practice 5.2 Wipeouts and barrelling: governance of surfing

Surfing Australia is a National Sporting Organisation that was formed in 1963 to establish, guide and promote the development of surfing in Australia. Surfing Australia is the representative body on the International Surfing Association (ISA) of which there are 86 member countries and is recognised by Sport Australia, the Australian Olympic Committee and is a member of the Water Safety Council of Australia.

The objectives of Surfing Australia are many and varied:

1 provide for the conduct, encouragement, promotion and administration of surfriding throughout Australia;

2 ensure the maintenance and enhancement of the company, its members and surfriding, its standards, quality and reputation for the benefit of the members and surfriding;

3 at all times promote mutual trust and confidence between the Company and the Members in pursuit of these Objects;

4 affiliate and otherwise liaise with the International Surfing Company, in the pursuit of these objects and the objects of surfriding;

5 recognise surfing values and the implications on surfing in recreational and natural resource planning and management;

6 at all times act on behalf of and in the interest of the Members and surfriding;

7 represent the interests of its Members and of surfriding generally in any appropriate forum in Australia and internationally;

8 actively support the preservation and conservation of the environment, and join with or affiliate with bodies or organisations concerned with the conservation and preservation of the environment;

9 Conduct national competitions and arrange for the conduct of national championships and the selection of national teams and squads and create rules and regulations for the conduct of these.

10 Develop young surfers to compete successfully at an international level and must maintain the high profile and success of Australian surfers internationally.

11 To establish and operate a hall of fame for the preservation, storage and exhibition of information and objects illustrating and relating to the sport of surfing.

12 Do all things which are necessary incidental or conducive to further the interests of Surfing Australia.

Surfing Australia is a Limited Company, with members consisting of six state associations (Victoria, New South Wales, Queensland, Western Australia, South Australia and Tasmania), along with affiliated surf clubs, and individual and life members. The Board of Surfing Australia comprises five appointed state delegates and between two and four independent directors. At the end of 2021, former seven times world champion, Layne Beachley AO, was the long serving Chair of Surfing Australia, having held that role since 2015.

The role of the board is to act in the interests of all the members of Surfing Australia specifically to:

- govern the sport of surfing in Australia in accordance with the objects of the Company;
- determine major strategic directions of the Company;
- review the Company's performance in achieving its pre-determined aims, objectives and policies;
- manage the financial performance of the Company; and
- manage international responsibilities.

Source: Surfing Australia website at www.surfingaustralia.com and the Surfing Australia Limited Constitution available at its website.

BOARD PERFORMANCE

Board performance has been found to be related to the use of appropriate structures, processes, and strategic planning; the role of the paid executive; whether the board undertakes training or development work; personal motivations of board members; and the influence of a cyclical pattern in the life cycle of boards. How to measure board performance, however, is a subject of ongoing debate. Herman and Renz (1997, 1998, 2000) support the use of a social constructionist approach to measure board performance based on the work of Berger and Luckmann (1967). Their view is that the collective judgements of those individuals directly involved with the board can provide the best idea of its performance. A widely used scale, the Self Assessment for Nonprofit Governing Boards Scale (Slesinger, 1991), uses this approach and provides sporting and other nonprofit organizations with an effective way to gauge board performance.

Aspects of board activity that are evaluated using a scale of this type include the working relationship between board and CEO, working relationships between board and staff, CEO selection and review processes, financial management, conduct of board and committee meetings, board mission statement and review of the mission, strategic planning, matching operational programs to the mission and monitoring program performance, risk management, new board member selection and training, and marketing and public relations. The performance of the board in undertaking these activities is then rated by board members, executives, and the chair of the board. While this approach is open to criticisms of self reporting bias, the fact that the whole group makes judgements on performance and then compares perceptions is an aid to board development and improvement.

The evaluation of individual board member performance is more problematic. Research into the human resource management practices related to board members shows that smaller sports organizations may struggle to find board members, while larger sports have an element of prestige attached to them, so the problem is the opposite – how to engage in succession planning within a democratic electoral process. Very few board members are inducted, trained, provided with professional development opportunities, and evaluated at all with regard to their role and the role of the board, a potentially serious problem for nonprofit sport organizations given the significant responsibilities with which board members and board chairs are charged.

DRIVERS OF CHANGE IN GOVERNANCE

VSOs are increasingly under pressure from funding agencies to improve the delivery of their core programs and services. Funding agencies recognize that sports' capacity for this delivery depends to a large extent on sport organizations being appropriately governed and as a result have implemented a range of measures to improve the governance of VSOs. For example, Sport Australia has a dedicated program of management improvement for NSOs that provides advice on governance issues, funding to undertake reviews of governance structures, and information on governance principles and processes. Sport England has negotiated detailed strategic plans with NSOs to improve the delivery and coordination between regional sport organizations.

The threat of litigation against sport organizations, their members, or their board members has forced sport organizations to address issues such as risk management, fiduciary compliance, incorporation, directors' liability insurance, and board training and evaluation. The heightened awareness of the implications of governance failure due to several much-publicized corporate cases of impropriety worldwide has also forced sport organizations to improve their governance systems. Legislative changes to address issues of equity and diversity are additional pressures sports organizations must face, and their governance systems, particularly membership criteria, voting rights, and provision of information, must change accordingly.

The threat of competition in the marketplace also has forced sports organizations to become more commercial and business-focused, primarily through employing paid staff. Large clubs and regional sports associations that in the mid-1990s were exclusively run by volunteers are increasingly investing in paid staff to manage the increased compliance demands from government and their members and customers. As discussed earlier, the employment of paid staff changes the governance structures, the decision-making processes, and the level of control exerted by volunteers. Maintaining governance structures devised decades ago creates many problems for sports organizations.

Arguably the most influential change agent in the governance of NSOs in countries such as Australia, New Zealand, and the United Kingdom has been their respective national governments seeking to directly influence the governance of sport organizations via the imposition of performance targets as part of funding agreements between elite sport agencies and national governing bodies, direct interventions to reshape and professionalize governance systems in sport, and indirectly influencing strategy and governance priorities through funding support. Olympic and Commonwealth Games sports largely dependent on government funding for their high-performance programs in each of these countries seem to have responded to these influences, whereas the professional sport codes (i.e. cricket, football codes, golf, and tennis) have not. A systematic review of all previous research on the application of good governance principles by Parent and Hoye (2018, p. 21) demonstrated that

> despite an increase in interest in research associated with good governance principles and guidelines in sport, there is a clear need for both the international sport community and researchers to develop an agreed set of governance principles and language relevant for international, national, provincial/state and local level sport governance organisations. This may be unrealistic given the multitude of stakeholders involved, such as the International Olympic Committee, IFs and numerous national (sport) agencies, as well as the different legal and cultural contexts between national sport systems; but, this lack of coherence will limit the ability of both sport organisations to improve their governance and researchers to understand which principles and guidelines are central to improved governance performance in sport organisations.

In Practice 5.3 Governance reform in sport

Sport Australia has attempted to improve governance standards amongst Australian NSOs for more than two decades. During the period 2013 to 2015, the then-Australian Sports Commission released updated governance guidelines for NSOs and worked directly with some of them to facilitate change. These reform efforts focused on issues such as:

- Board chair elected by the board, not the members;
- Performance evaluation processes for boards;
- Corporate rather than association structures;
- Establishment of key board committees, including nominations, audit, and risk; and
- Board diversity and skill mix.

They pointed to four key drivers that were shaping why they were becoming increasingly interventionist with the governance of NSOs (ASC, 2016, p. 2):

- the growing importance of integrity, safety, and duty of care responsibilities;
- increasingly lucrative commercial broadcast and media deals for the larger professional sports, which are placing smaller sports at a growing competitive disadvantage in the sports marketplace;
- a challenging and highly competitive sports sponsorship market, causing sponsors to focus increasingly on those sports with large broadcast audiences; and
- national economic pressures, which mean that sports cannot rely on increased government funding to bridge the revenue gap to remain competitive.

Their most recent attempt to influence governance practices came in mid-2015 when they released a "white paper" for discussion throughout the Australian sport industry. The white paper focused on three themes:

- Voting structures and appropriately delineated roles of members, boards, and management;
- How the collection of member registration fees is best managed; and
- The need for sports to continuously evolve their governance for improved performance.

By focusing on these themes, the ASC was attempting to improve alignment within NSOs with federated structures, improve the revenue streams of NSOs, focus boards on more strategic matters, and clean up inconsistent voting rights within NSOs. In response to the feedback they received from sport organizations through a detailed consultation process, the ASC focused on the lack of trust evident within sport, stating (ASC, 2016, p. 3) that:

> It is also clear to the ASC that many Australian sports are held back today from realising their full potential by a lack of trust between key stakeholders. Sometimes this manifests itself in a lack of trust between the national Board and state Boards, sometimes it is between state Boards themselves. Trust cannot be mandated by an external party in documentary governance principles, it has to be built and earned over time by behaviours between stakeholders in a sport; particularly by the demonstration, and receipt in return, of respect. It is true, however, that organisational structures and governance processes can enhance or diminish trust.

In 2020, Sport Australia (the renamed ASC) released a new set of Sport Governance Principles, this time developed for use by sport organizations at all levels, including clubs, rather than previous iterations focused on NSOs. This new version included nine principles:

1 The spirit of the game – values-driven culture and behaviours
2 The team – aligned sport through collaborative governance
3 The gameplan – a clear vision that informs strategy
4 The players – a diverse board to enable considered decision-making
5 The rulebook – documents that outline duties, powers, roles, and responsibilities
6 The playbook – board processes which ensure accountability and transparency
7 The defence – a system which protects the organization
8 The best and fairest – a system for ensuring integrity
9 The scorecard – embedded systems of internal review to foster continuous improvement

It is hard to determine whether these successive iterations of good governance principles have dramatically improved the quality of governance undertaken by Australian NSOs. What is clear is the Australian government, through the national sport agency, has been working to improve the governance of sport for more than two decades by providing guidelines, principles (sometimes mandatory for funded NSOs), direct support to undertake governance reviews, and direct intervention with some sports when in desperate need of governance reform.

Source: The archived Australian Sports Commission website at www.ausport.gov.au and ASC (2016), *Governance Reform in Sport.* Canberra: Australian Sports Commission, along with the most recent version of the Sport Australia Governance Principles on www.sportaus.gov.au

ETHICS

The ethical conduct of directors on sport organizations has come under increased scrutiny in recent years as sport is beset with challenges around high-profile cases of drug use in sport, scandals about the bidding process for awarding hosting rights for sport events to host cities, and failures in oversight of management teams. As noted eatlier, one of the more damning pieces of research was completed by Hamil et al. (2010, p. 379), who documented the many failings in governance that have plagued Italian football through the 2000s, noting that while

> there is a clear and transparent system of regulatory oversight for the Italian football industry . . . [and a licensing system that] . . . suggests a high standard of club governance should exist . . . there is a very serious gap between theory and practice.

Their paper identified an exhaustive list of problems that have plagued Italian soccer between 1980 and 2010, including betting scandals, doping, falsification of passports, bribery and match-fixing, and violence – all of which they concluded is largely a result of inappropriate ownership and governance structures among football clubs.

Geeraert, Alm, and Groll (2014) provided a telling analysis of the quality of governance within the 35 Olympic sport governing bodies and highlighted a number of problems, including a lack of accountability arrangements and transparency in the distribution of funding to members, a lack of independent ethics committees overseeing the conduct of these organizations, a lack of athlete participation in governance, inequitable gender representation on governing boards, and a lack of term limits for board members that concentrates power with incumbents.

As highlighted with In Practice 5.1, government agencies such as Sport Australia have acted by imposing tighter restrictions on term limits for directors, auditing standards for sport organizations, using nominations committees for appointment of directors, and enforcing good practice around declarations of interest for directors who may benefit from sitting on a board by having a register of such conflicts. One of the more meaningful requirements is to ensure all directors are independent. The Sport Australia principles require directors not be elected to represent any group, not be employed by the organization, not hold any other material office within the organizational structure, and not have material interests in being a director. Sport Australia also requires NSOs, and their directors, to sign up to all Sport Australia integrity measures on anti-doping, protocols for sport science, and match-fixing as well as publishing annual reports consistent with the Corporations Act requirements.

SUMMARY

Organizational governance has been described as the exercise of power within organizations and provides the system by which the elements of organizations are controlled and directed. Good organizational governance should ensure that the board and management seek to deliver outcomes for the benefit of the organization and its members and that the means used to attain these outcomes are effectively monitored.

A distinction is made between corporate governance that deals with the governance of profit-seeking companies and corporations that focus on protecting and enhancing shareholder value and nonprofit governance that is concerned with the governance of voluntary-based organizations that seek to provide a community service or facilitate the involvement of individuals in social, artistic, or sporting activities.

Sport organizations and their governance frameworks have diverse elements that prevent the development of an overarching theory of sport governance. A number of theoretical perspectives, namely agency theory, stewardship theory, institutional theory, resource dependence theory, network theory, and stakeholder theory, can be used to illuminate parts of the governance assumptions, processes, structures, and outcomes for sport organizations.

The traditional governance structure for VSOs outlined earlier has been criticized for being unwieldy and cumbersome, slow to react to changes in market conditions, subject to potentially damaging politics or power plays between delegates, and imposing significant constraints on organizations wishing to change. On the other hand, the majority of sports organizations still use this model today and value its ability to ensure members have a say in decision-making, the transparency of decisions, and the autonomy granted to organizations at every level of the system.

VSO boards perform better if a degree of trust exists between the board and staff and board leadership is shared amongst a dominant coalition of the board chair, executive, and a small group of senior board members. While evaluation systems for board performance are still relatively simplistic, they do cover a wide range of board activities. Evaluation of individual board member performance is more problematic and is the subject of ongoing research.

Finally, VSOs are increasingly under pressure from funding agencies to improve the delivery of their core programs and services. The threat of litigation against sport organizations and their members or board members has forced sport organizations to address issues such as risk management, fiduciary compliance, incorporation, directors' liability insurance, and board training and evaluation. The heightened awareness of the implications of governance failure due to high-profile corporate cases worldwide has also forced sport organizations to improve their governance systems.

REVIEW QUESTIONS

1 Explain the difference between corporate and nonprofit governance.

2 What theory would you apply to the study of negligence on the part of a board of directors of a sport organization?

3 Explain the role played by boards, staff, volunteers, members, and stakeholder groups in governing sport organizations.

4 What criteria would you apply to gauge the performance of a nonprofit VSO? How would these criteria differ for a professional sport club?

5 What are the important elements in developing good relationships between boards and paid staff in VSOs?

6 Compare the governance structures of a multi-disciplinary sport (e.g. gymnastics, canoeing, athletics) with a single discipline sport (e.g., field hockey, netball, rugby league). How do they differ? What impact does this have on volunteers involved in governance roles?

7 Review the governance performance of a VSO of your choice using Henry and Lee's (2004) seven principles of governance presented in this chapter.

8 What issues does a potential amalgamation present for a VSO?

9 How are board performance and organizational performance linked?

10 Interview the CEO and the board chair of a small VSO. Whom do they perceive to be the leader of the organization?

DISCUSSION QUESTIONS

1 Why is sport governance such an important topic in sport?

2 What are some of the reasons it seems to be a struggle to govern sports well?

3 Why is it important to have boards with a mixture of elected and appointed directors?

4 Why do national sport agencies seek to intervene so regularly in the governance of national sport organizations?

5 Can a sport organization perform well if the board is dysfunctional?

FURTHER READING

Clarke, T. (Ed.). (2004). *Theories of corporate governance*. Oxon, UK: Routledge.
Ferkins, L. (2020). Strategy and the strategic function of sport boards. In D. Shilbury & L. Ferkins (Eds.), *Routledge handbook of sport governance* (pp. 285–295). Oxon: Routledge.

Ferkins, L., & Shilbury, D. (2015). Board strategic balance: An emerging sport governance theory. *Sport Management Review, 18*, 489–500.

Garcia, B., & Welford, J. (2015). Supporters and football governance, from customers to stakeholders: A literature review and agenda for research. *Sport Management Review, 18*, 517–528.

Geeraert, A., Alm, J., & Groll, M. (2014). Good governance in international sport organizations: An analysis of the 35 Olympic governing bodies. *International Journal of Sport Policy and Politics, 6*(3), 281–306.

Grix, J. (2009). The impact of UK sport policy on the governance of athletics. *International Journal of Sport Policy, 1*, 31–49.

Hamil, S., Morrow, S., Idle, C., Rossi, G., & Faccendini, S. (2010). The governance and regulation of Italian football. *Soccer & Society, 11*, 373–413.

Henry, I., & Lee, P. C. (2004). Governance and ethics in sport. In J. Beech & S. Chadwick (Eds.), *The business of sport management*. London: Prentice Hall.

Hoye, R. (2017). Sport governance. In R. Hoye & M. M. Parent (Eds.), *Handbook of sport management* (pp. 9–23). London: Sage.

Hoye, R., & Cuskelly, G. (2007). *Sport governance*. Oxford: Elsevier Butterworth-Heinemann.

Hoye, R., & Doherty, A. (2011). Nonprofit sport board performance: A review and directions for future research. *Journal of Sport Management, 25*(3), 272–285.

McLeod, J. (2020). Role of the board and directors: Board structure and composition. In D. Shilbury & L. Ferkins (Eds.), *Routledge handbook of sport governance* (pp. 243–253). Oxon: Routledge.

Parent, M. P., & Hoye, R. (2018). The impact of governance principles on sport organizations' governance practices and performance: A systematic review. *Cogent Social Sciences Sport, 4*(1), 1–24. https://doi.org/10.1080/23311886.2018.1503578

Sport Australia. (2020). *Sport governance principles*. Canberra: Sport Australia.

Sport New Zealand (2015). *Governance benchmarking review 2014*. Wellington, New Zealand: Sport New Zealand.

Walters, G., & Tacon, R. (2018). The 'codification' of governance in the non-profit sport sector in the UK. *European Sport Management Quarterly, 18*(1), 482–500.

RELEVANT WEBSITES

The following websites are useful starting points for further information on the governance of sport organizations:

Australian Sports Commission at www.ausport.gov.au

Sport Canada at www.pch.gc.ca/progs/sc/index_e.cfm

Sport England at www.sportengland.org

Sport Scotland at www.sportscotland.org.uk

CASE STUDY 5.1

Finding value in governance reform: football in Australia

The governance of football (soccer) in Australia has been problematic since the early 1980s. These issues came to a head in August 2002, when the then-federal minister for the arts and sport, Senator Rod Kemp, announced that Soccer Australia (SA) had agreed to a major structural review of soccer in Australia to be managed by the then-Australian Sports Commission. The review was undertaken after almost two decades of crises in the sport with the result that in mid-2002, SA was $2.6M AUD in debt, had reduced staffing levels at the national office, was racked by political infighting, had a lack of strategic direction, and had enjoyed mixed results in the international arena. The review commissioned by the minister examined the structure, governance, and management of soccer at all levels across Australia.

In all, the review (the Crawford Report) made 53 recommendations aimed at improving the structure, governance, and management of SA. The first three recommendations in the report illustrate the parlous state of affairs that existed in the organization in 2002. The review recommended that (1) the membership of SA be changed to recognize key interest groups and reduce the power of larger states and the National Soccer League (NSL), (2) a new constitution be developed, and (3) each state affiliate adopt a model constitution and membership agreements. These recommendations alone represent wholesale change in the governance system, but the review went on to recommend a further 50 changes to governance processes and structures throughout the sport.

The sweeping changes made to the governance systems of Soccer Australia as a result of the review, and the subsequent appointment as chief executive officer of John O'Neil (ex-CEO of the Australian Rugby Union), ushered in a new era for the sport. On 1 January 2005, Soccer Australia changed its name to Football Federation Australia (FFA) as part of the ongoing process of repositioning the sport. The new A League was launched to replace the NSL, and Australia famously re-entered the World Cup after qualifying in dramatic fashion in Stadium Australia on penalties against Uruguay on 16 November 2005. The next decade saw the introduction of a professional women's league, the expansion of the A League, continued qualification for World Cups, success in both men's and women's Asia Cups, and growth in player numbers across Australia.

Fast forward to 2017, and the power struggles within Australian football continued around two major issues. The first was the continued control of the A League by FFA, with all clubs struggling financially and claiming that FFA was unable to adequately operate as both the national governing body for the sport and run a commercial professional league. The second was the growing animosity amongst stakeholders such as the Member Federations, the players' association, and professional football clubs that they were inadequately represented by the FFA Congress, which at the time had only ten members – a representative from each of the nine Member Federations and one representing all the A League clubs. After much agitation by these stakeholders and pressure from the international governing body (FIFA) for FFA to get its house in order, a congress review working group (CRWG) was formed that involved all the stakeholders in football and in seven short weeks, from 12 June to 31 July 2018, produced a new blueprint for the governance of football in Australia.

The CRWG report makes for fascinating reading, especially the influence of FIFA in driving better governance outcomes as required in the mandate for the CRWG:

> The main objective of the CRWG is to propose a new composition for the FFA congress which ensures a broader and more balanced representation of stakeholders in line with the requirements of the FIFA Statutes, in particular its Article 15.j. Article 15.j of the FIFA Statutes states as follows: "Member associations' statutes must comply with the principles of good governance, and shall in particular contain, at a minimum, provisions relating to the following matters . . . legislative bodies must be constituted in accordance with the principles of representative democracy and taking into account the importance of gender equality in football".
>
> The CRWG's proposal shall also consider and take into account the following issues:
>
> * Alignment of the FFA statutes with the requirements of the FIFA Statutes, in particular art. 15.j;
> * The full participation of women at all levels of football governance;
> * FFA Board composition and independence;
> * Pathway for an alternative A-League governance model;
> * Pathway for other stakeholders to become FFA members, including the possibility of an associate membership;
> * Representation of NPL clubs in football governance structures.
>
> The CRWG shall seek input from the Association of Australian Football Clubs (AAFC) and other relevant stakeholders, including by inviting them to its meetings as observers when necessary. In particular, the AAFC is to be systematically included whenever the representation of NPL clubs in football governance structures is discussed.
>
> Furthermore, the CRWG shall seek input and regularly and systematically invite experts (such as Women Onside and female football officials and players) to provide input on how to best promote the full participation of women at all levels of football governance.

The CRWG membership included an independent chair and representatives from FFA (1), Member Federations (4), Australian Professional Football Club Association (2), and the Professional Footballers Australia (PFA) (1).

Each of these groups provided detailed submissions on their perspectives of how football should be governed in Australia. The PFA made two key points about the need for change that are highlighted by the CRWG in its report:

- The immediate task of the CRWG is to develop a Congress that satisfies FIFA; however the opportunity – nee responsibility – of the CRWG is to develop a governance model that aligns Australia's disparate stakeholders, incentivises Australia's stakeholders to organise meaningfully and ensure that those charged with governing the game are ultimately accountable to all stakeholders
- There is an asymmetrical relationship between political influence and economic contribution. Governance issues will inevitably arise when there is no equilibrium between these two fundamental principles.

In October 2018, the CRWG report was voted to be approved 8–2 by the FFA Congress, despite FFA and Sports Australia expressing reservations about the complexity of the new governance model and the increased decision-making rights and independence granted to the A League clubs, who would now operate their league under a new entity called the Australian Professional Leagues (APL), separate from FFA. The outgoing FFA chairman, Steven Lowy, was particularly concerned with power being ceded to A League clubs that were increasingly being owned in whole or in part by foreign entities. The CEO of Sport Australia, Kate Palmer, issued a statement on 14 September 2018 that noted the CRWG report went beyond the original remit and that some of the recommendations did not align with Sport Australia's view of best practice governance principles.

The new FFA Congress now comprises 28 members, exercising 100 votes: Member Federations (9 members with 55 votes); A League Clubs (now 8 members with 28 votes); PFA (1 member, 7 votes); and a new Women's Council made up of 10 members with 1 vote each comprising 1 chair appointed by a nominations committee, 3 individuals nominated by Member Federations, 3 individuals nominated by club, and 3 individuals nominated by the PFA. Stakeholders such as National Premier League clubs, any new A League entities, or other special interest groups can be added to the Congress upon completing a FFA New Member Pathway to Congress – detailed in Annexure 8 of the CRWG Report. This essentially forces these new groups to demonstrate their institutional integrity – a demonstration of (1) commitment; (2) capacity; and (3) capability to professionally represent, govern, and manage their constituents with regard and respect to integrity, transparency, accountability, and diversity. Over a five-year process, they would progress from having a voice at FFA Congress to having full voting rights.

The new APL now runs the A League, W League, and Y League and since its creation has worked with FA to secure a lucrative new broadcast deal. This follows the successful model in basketball when the National Basketball League split from Basketball Australia and, under the ownership of entrepreneur Larry Kestleman, has grown into a successful, viable commercial league. Football Australia will still have a role as competition regulator and thus oversee disciplinary and integrity issues; registration of clubs, players, and officials; the transfer system; and the draw. Football Australia will also retain the final say over expansion, contraction, or the long-desired creation of promotion/relegation and controls access to the Asian Champions League, FFA Cup, and other domestic and international competitions.

CASE STUDY QUESTIONS

1   Why does governance seem to be a perennial issue for football in Australia?

2   What seems to be at the heart of Sport Australia's concerns with this new Congress model?

3   Do you think separation of the elite professional leagues from the national governing body is a good thing for the overall development of football in Australia?

4   What does the second point in the quote from the PFA in relation to *political influence and economic contribution* mean? How is this related to governance?

Sources: The CRWG Report in full – http://pfa.net.au/wp-content/uploads/CRWG-Report-final-31-07–2018-For-Publication.pdf, Statement from Sport Australia on the CRWG report – www.sportaus.gov.au/media-centre/news/comment_on_ffa_governance_reform, FA website on current Congress – www.footballaustralia.com.au/about/football-australia-governance, and a news report on the issue – www.abc.net.au/news/2020-12-31/what-a-league-separation-from-football-australia-means-for-clubs/13023888.

CASE STUDY 5.2

Selling out the All Blacks?

Rugby is near enough to a religion in New Zealand, and New Zealand Rugby and its famous men's national team the All Blacks are the pride of New Zealand. New Zealand Rugby members comprise the 26 provincial unions (organized into three zones – Northern, Central, and Southern); the New Zealand Maori Ruby Board; and associate members such as school competitions, universities, or foundations, along with individual life members. On the face of it, New Zealand Rugby is a very conservative organization.

The impact of COVID on world sport in 2020 and 2021 has been enormous, and national governing bodies of all sports have been impacted by the downturn in international events, reduced ticketed games at domestic level, and greatly reduced broadcast revenues. The previous Super Rugby competition between South Africa,

Australia, and New Zealand ceased, and the five Super Rugby teams based in New Zealand formed a new domestic competition. International games were limited, and New Zealand Rugby had a drop in revenue of $40M NZD in 2020, or about a 26% reduction from 2019. Provincial unions have been struggling financially, and many emerging or leading rugby players are being lured to play professionally in overseas leagues. The sustainability of New Zealand Rugby was questionable under its current operating model in 2021.

Enter US global giant Silver Lake Partners, a global technology investment firm with more than $88 billion in combined assets under management and annual revenues on the order of $220 billion. Silver Lake has made investments in a number of global sport brands, notably a stake in City Football Group, the owners of Manchester City FC, and their network of clubs around the world. Silver Lake made an offer to purchase 12.5% of New Zealand Rugby's commercial rights portfolio (valued at over $3 billion) for $387 million in April 2021 after many months of negotiation. The deal would result in a revenue share model to benefit both New Zealand Rugby and Silver Lake over time. A new jointly owned entity (Commercial LP) would be set up from the sale proceeds and would control New Zealand Rugby's commercial interests. The premise is that if Silver Lake can help grow the annual revenue from those commercial interests, both parties win. In the short term, the cash received by New Zealand Rugby from the sale to Silver Lake would, in part, be passed on to its provincial unions to help clear debt and reinvest in the game across New Zealand.

In late September 2021, the deal had stalled, despite the New Zealand Rugby Board endorsing the deal and the national minister for sport also supporting the deal. Crucially, the New Zealand Rugby Players Association did not support the deal and wanted guarantees that the All Black jersey, silver fern, haka, and other Māori and Pasifika cultural values intrinsic to the All Blacks brand wouldn't be sold off or culturally misappropriated. They were also concerned about future pay. In 2021, they received about 36.5% of New Zealand Rugby revenue, and under the deal, that would be reduced to about 31% but theoretically 31% of a much bigger revenue pool, representing an actual increase in real dollars to players. Other stakeholders had concerns about who is represented on this new jointly owned entity – Commercial LP – how additional revenues will be distributed to stakeholders, whether the funds will be directed to help grow a future women's professional competition, and whether the risks of Silver Lake pulling out of the deal in later years would be adequately managed.

This case is more complicated than a private equity firm buying a professional sport franchise, as is the norm in the united States and increasingly prevalent in high-profile competitions such as the English Premier League. In an article by Matthew Brockett on Bloomberg in June 2021, he wrote:

> But the All Blacks aren't a franchise. They are the national team in the national sport, part of the country's past and present identity. The players' creed holds

that they don't own the black jersey, they are custodians of it, honoring its legacy before passing it on, said former captain David Kirk. "It's not ours to sell," said Kirk, now president of the New Zealand Rugby Players' Association. "How does this generation of administrators have the right to sell 130 years of custodianship? New Zealanders own it, that's what makes it so valuable."

The player's association suggested a better way might be to take the All Blacks public with a partial share offering and listing it on the local stock market to raise a similar amount of money and keep the ownership within New Zealand.

Other aspects of rugby have drawn strong interest from private equity. In March 2021, CVC Capital Partners purchased a 14.3% stake in Europe's Six Nations tournament for 365 million pounds ($516 million). As of September 2021, CVC was also in talks with the South African rugby union, and Rugby Australia is also considering raising capital through a deal with private equity. The dilemma facing national sport bodies is very real. Private equity firms clearly value those brands that they can leverage for profit, and with real financial pressure on national governing bodies to not only service their grassroots members and programs but look after their national teams, leveraging their brand equity may well be the solution. Time will tell if sports like New Zealand Rugby can navigate the sport governance challenges of getting all stakeholders on board, protecting their members from risk, and securing sustainable commercial deals.

CASE STUDY QUESTIONS

1   Why do private equity firms want to get involved in professional sport?

2   How might New Zealand Rugby satisfy the concerns of their players' association about the deal with Silver Lake?

3   What changes to the governance of rugby in New Zealand might occur as a consequence of this deal being approved by all stakeholders?

4   What risks does private equity involvement in national governing bodies of sport pose for the average person involved in grassroots sport as a player, coach, official, or club-level administrator?

Sources: The New Zealand Rugby website at www.nzrugby.co.nz and various media coverage of the story at www.theguardian.com/sport/2021/may/04/all-blacks-sale-could-prove-private-equity-intrusion-too-far-for-lovers-sport-rugby-union-new-zealand, www.bloomberg.com/news/articles/2021-06-01/all-blacks-players-fret-over-team-s-fate-if-silver-lake-buys-in#:~:text=Over%20more%20than%20100%20years,private%20equity%20firm%20Silver%20Lake, and www.foxsports.com.au/rugby/wallabies/rugby-championship-2021-wallabies-all-blacks-rugby-australia-new-zealand-rugby-hamish-mclennan-video/news-story/2c69f2b5ca5f771c1e17e8a52c47450d

CHAPTER 6

Legal issues and risk management

Written with Björn Hessert

OVERVIEW

The unique characteristics of sport, as highlighted throughout this book, have resulted in distinct legal developments. This chapter reviews some of the primary ways that the law intersects with sport. Beginning with the core principle of the "autonomy of sport",

DOI: 10.4324/9781003217947-8

it explains how sport rules coexist with domestic laws and international obligations. The chapter also provides a summary of principles for different ownership models and compares the federated (European) model with the private ownership (American) model of sport organizations and leagues. Competition and inequities between and within stakeholders throughout the sport eco-system inevitably lead to disputes and legal interventions. The concept of "natural justice" and the sport tribunal process to resolve those disputes are explored in this chapter. Last, the threats to the integrity of sport, including doping and match-fixing, are defined and the regulatory response summarized.

After completing this chapter, the reader should be able to:

- Identify what autonomy of sport means and understand the contexts in which this autonomy might be limited;
- Understand the contractual nature of sport membership agreements;
- Differentiate the federated and private ownership models;
- Explain the concept of "natural justice" and the legal principle of fair trial in the context of sports dispute resolutions; and
- Appreciate the threats to sport integrity, including doping and match-fixing.

SPORT AND THE LAW

While sport administrators do not need to be lawyers, they do need to have an awareness of the ways in which the law intersects with sport. It is especially important that sport managers proactively seek legal advice rather than waiting for issues to manifest into a full-blown crisis and public relations disaster. A general awareness of the types of legal matters that require the attention of sport managers is therefore important. There are obviously too many legal specialities to cover in one chapter. For example, employment law and taxation; intellectual property and ambush marketing; broadcasting rights; and personal injuries, whether caused by criminal behaviour or negligence, are beyond the scope of this chapter.

The starting position for managers is that sport organizations enjoy autonomy in regulating themselves, which means that they are free to make rules for their members. However, power comes with responsibility. As will be explained in the following chapter, the law places limits on that autonomy. The sport rules must comply with the general laws of the land and respect basic concepts of fairness in resolving sport disputes.

Sport managers also need to have a broad understanding of the legal structures underpinning the sport organizations they are working within and dealing with. The type of legal entity is likely to be different at the local, regional, state/provincial, national, and international levels for the same sport. The type of legal structure that the organization has been established under will further restrict the autonomy of the organization. The powers and scope of responsibility will primarily be set out in the organization's constitution but may be further detailed in its rules, regulations, by-laws, and policy documents.

The members of sport organizations are bound by the sport rules through contractual arrangements. It is, therefore, useful to have a basic understanding of contract law as every aspect of organizing sport events, from bidding for the event through to the procurement or licensing of goods and services, employment arrangements, entry conditions for competitors and spectators, and policing poor behaviour, is governed by the contracts in place.

Behaviour of members that threatens the integrity of sport is one area that sport organizations are recognized as having the incentive and expertise to address. This does not mean that sport organizations have the capability or the capacity to counter all threats, such as doping or match-fixing, alone. Instead, as set out in the following, a complex web of regulatory responses has been developed, from international and regional conventions to national legislation and sport policies.

THE AUTONOMY OF SPORT

Legal issues in the sports sector often test the so-called "autonomy of sport" and its limitations. The phrase "autonomy of sport" refers to the freedom enjoyed by most national and international sport organizations to decide on their internal matters without external interference. In most countries (and legal jurisdictions), this autonomy derives from the "freedom of association" guaranteed by the Universal Declaration of Human Rights (1948, Art 20), which is often also reflected in national constitutional law. For instance, the freedom of association is guaranteed under the First Amendment to the US Constitution as an essential part of the freedom of speech and in Article 23 of the Swiss Constitution.

The impact of Swiss law on the internal affairs of international sports federations is very important. Most international sports governing bodies, the International Olympic Committee, the World Anti-Doping Agency (WADA), and the Court of Arbitration for Sport (CAS) have their registered "seat", that is their legal place, in Switzerland and are established under Swiss law. For those sport organizations outside Switzerland – for example, the International Paralympic Committee has its seat in Germany, and the Badminton World Federation is registered under the International Organizations (Privileges and Immunities) Act 1992 in Malaysia – Swiss law may still have an impact on them if the sports include arbitration clauses in favour of CAS in their rules and regulations.

Within the member states of the Council of Europe, freedom of association is guaranteed under Art. 11(1) of the European Convention on Human Rights (ECHR): "Everybody has the right to freedom of peaceful assembly and to freedom of association with others, including the right to form and to join trade unions for the protection of his [their] interests" [bracket added]. In addition, the sports-related jurisdiction of the European Court of Justice (CJEU) and Article 165 of the Treaty on the Functioning of the European Union (TFEU) provide grounds for the recognition of a (conditional) autonomy of sport on the assumption that sport organizations are in a better position than national governments or other third parties to decide on how their association should be governed, regulated, and exercised. Upholding the ECHR is the European Court of Human Rights (ECtHR) in Strasbourg, France, which becomes relevant when considering the sport disputes appeals process. An example is set out in In Practice 6.1.

The autonomy of sport is a distinct feature that governs and regulates organized sport. More specifically, it enables sport organizations to decide on their internal organization and their statutes, rules, and regulations with minimal outside interference. To understand how sport organizations assert their position on autonomy, look to the IOC Olympic Charter (2020), for example, which states that the fifth Fundamental Principle of Olympism is:

> Recognising that sport occurs within the framework of society, sport organisations within the Olympic Movement shall apply political neutrality. They have the rights and obligations of autonomy, which include freely establishing and controlling the rules of sport, determining the structure and governance of their organisations, enjoying the right of elections free from any outside influence and the responsibility for ensuring that principles of good governance be applied.

Sports on the Olympic program include similar assertions of their autonomy in their own constitutions.

This wide discretionary power granted to sport organizations free from state interference is generally recognized through both the courts via common law and legislation. This remains the case even though sport organizations in common law jurisdictions, such as Australia, Canada, and the United Kingdom, are usually established as private organizations, whether companies limited by guarantee or unincorporated or incorporated associations under state/regional association law or national company law, such as the Corporations Act 2001 (Cth) (Australia) or the Companies Act 2006 (UK). In civil law jurisdictions, sport organizations are founded under national association law, for example, under the Swiss Civil Code (Art. 60–79). Swiss associations are not subject to the restrictions on companies and cooperatives, which, together with attractive tax benefits, is one of the reasons so many international federations are based in Switzerland. The legislation over company or association structures around the world has varying levels of reporting and other requirements, as referred to in the previous chapter on governance.

While sport organizations are relatively free from government interference in managing their internal business, that does not mean that sports do not often work cooperatively with the state and government agencies and in some cases establish public-private partnerships. As discussed in the section later on doping and match-fixing, cooperation between private sport organizations and state actors, particularly law enforcement agencies, is necessary at the domestic and international levels. Another example where sport organizations and governments at all levels work cooperatively together, ideally documented through detailed legal agreements (i.e. private-law contracts), is in the construction of sport infrastructure, such as football stadia, tennis courts, and golf courses. Similar cooperative agreements are also entered into when cities are bidding for major sporting events.

LIMITATIONS TO THE AUTONOMY OF SPORT

The "autonomy of sport" is also not without limits. All decisions of sport organizations must comply with the general law that applies to everyone in society. The fundamental rights of people enshrined in constitutional law may further limit the autonomy of sport, depending on the national legal system. For example, the German and Swiss constitutional values take priority in legal relationships between sport organizations and another private person (e.g. athletes). This means that all contractual clauses, regulations, and decisions of sport organizations that do not comply with these values are deemed null and void. An extreme example would be if a sport organization introduced the death penalty as a sanction for the breach of a sport rule. Compare the Swiss/German approach with US constitutional law, which may only limit decisions taken by private sport organizations if a link between the state government and the sport association can be established (the "state action doctrine"). For example, two of the judges in the case of *San Francisco Arts & Athletics, Inc. and Thomas F. Waddell, Petitions v. United States Olympic Committee [USOC] and IOC*, 483 US 522 (1987), found that the connection between the USOC and the US government was established and therefore the USOC is subject to US constitutional law. The main finding in that case was that the court agreed that the Amateur Sports Act of 1978 granting the USOC the exclusive commercial and promotional uses of the word "Olympic" and various Olympic symbols was not in contravention of the Constitutional right to free speech.

An example of where sport has been permitted to develop its own rules in contravention of standard legislation is in the area of anti-discrimination. As set out in Case Study 6.1 on the Blake Leeper case, sport has a complex relationship with anti-discrimination principles. Clearly, sport organizations are entitled to discriminate against people on the basis of performance criteria. Sport has also been primarily organized around gender binary sport categories, which can be considered from one perspective an affirmative action policy. (It should be noted that the definition of the gender binary category is being challenged by transgender and intersex or differences of sexual development [DSD] athletes). Age, weight, nationality, and para-athlete categories are accepted as legitimate inclusive reasons to discriminate in sport. Race discrimination is also permitted for the purposes of promoting the participation of minority indigenous or ethnic groups, such as the Maccabiah Games for Jewish athletes, World Indigenous Games, or annual Indigenous All Stars match against the Maori All Stars in the Australian rugby league. For the purpose of promoting equality and inclusion for LGBTQ+ people globally, the Gay Games and its international federation are permitted exclusions to the general position that people should not be discriminated against on the grounds of their gender or sexual orientation.

Outside of these permitted discriminatory provisions, controversy has frequently arisen over the extent to which the autonomy of sport could be limited in the direct or indirect application of international human rights law, which is addressed in more detail in the case studies at the end of this chapter. International sports federations particularly often choose to limit their autonomy by submitting to international human rights law. For example, sport organizations may voluntarily commit themselves to respect human rights conventions, such as the Convention on the Rights of Children or the Convention on the Elimination of All Forms of Discrimination Against Women. Sport organizations may also determine to bind themselves to a limited extent, such as including a provision in their statutes in line with Article 8(1) of the ECHR, which provides that "everyone has the right to respect for his [their] private and family life, his [their] home and his [their] correspondence" [brackets added].

Significant discussion and controversy have tested this autonomy, particularly in relation to freedom of speech. For example, the IOC restricts the ability of athletes to promote their own sponsors (Rule 40 of the Olympic Charter) and from podium protests (Rule 50 of the Olympic Charter). Rule 50 states that: "no kind of demonstration or political, religious or racial propaganda is permitted in any Olympic sites, venues or other areas". As a result of the international Black Lives Matter movement and prominent athletes involved in "take a knee" demonstrations intended to indicate the opposition to racism, the IOC had to revise its guidelines in relation to Rule 50. Adopting the IOC's Athlete Commission recommendations on 2 July 2021 (three weeks before the opening ceremony of the delayed 2020 Summer Olympic Games), the IOC published the "Rule 50.2 Guidelines for the Olympic Games Tokyo 2020" to balance the rights of those to freely voice their opinions while upholding the Olympic principles of tolerance and respect and the right of quiet enjoyment free of distractions for other participants and spectators during the Olympic Games.

Significantly, no IOC Guidelines on free speech have yet been published for what are expected to be controversial Olympic Winter Games in Beijing, China, in February 2022. The IOC was criticized for awarding the 2008 Olympic Games to Beijing when China was accused of both selling weapons worth many millions of dollars to the Sudanese government that were used against civilians in the Darfur region and for using its veto power on the UN Security Council to prevent timely action against the Sudanese government. Ahead of the 2022 Olympic Winter Games, the Chinese government was roundly criticized by human rights organizations and activists for the persecution, genocide, and slavery of the Uyghur people within China and its brutal repression of pro-democracy supporters in Hong Kong, Tibet, and Taiwan. The Chinese government has also been accused by the World Health Organisation and a number of major national governments for a lack of transparency and accountability in relation to its response to COVID-19, leading to a devastating pandemic. Any criticism against China has been met by displays of hard and sharp power, including crippling economic retribution. These allegations are enormously challenging for the international sport federations and the IOC to navigate while promoting a mandate of peace and harmony through sport.

Sport organizations may further decide to self-restrict the autonomy granted to them. A prime example in this regard is the acceptance of the WADA World Anti-Doping Code (WADA Code) by, among others, the IOC, the IPC, international federations, and national anti-doping organizations. By signing the declaration of acceptance of the WADA Code, the signatories commit to the implementation of the WADA Code and WADA's International Standards "without substantive change". In other words, signatories to the WADA Code agree to submit their regulatory autonomy in anti-doping matters to WADA. This effectively limits their discretionary power to a few clauses permitted in the code. This is further explored in Case Study 6.2 relating to WADA's "Whereabouts" requirements.

CONTRACTS, MEMBERSHIPS, AND LEGAL SPORT STRUCTURES

As set out previously, sport organizations have the right to create their own rules for their members. Members of sport organizations consent to be bound to their sport's rules and regulations through their membership agreements. The term "member" in this context may refer to direct members, meaning people or organizations that have entered into a membership contract with the respective sport organization. For example, national sport organizations are direct members of their international federations. However, professional athletes and other support personnel, including team doctors, technical officials, volunteers, or sport administrators, are rarely direct members of national and international sport governing bodies. Instead, they submit themselves to the international sport rules by signing employment contracts (often in team sports), athlete agreements, club memberships, or other event entry forms. The consequence is that sport organizations can apply and enforce their rules on these indirect members in the same way as upon their direct members.

All of these different types of contracts have the same basic legal requirements, namely offer, acceptance, and consideration. An offer may consist of club benefits such as access to competitions, coaching, and training facilities, while the acceptance of this offer will be indicated through signing a consent form (in paper form or electronically). The "consideration" to seal the legal deal is either the payment of entry or membership fees in community sport or salaries for participants in professional team sports. The consideration for unpaid volunteers might include the provision of uniforms, travel, or perhaps a title to enhance the reputation of the individual for future roles. For example, one of many sports not funded by Sport Australia is Handball Australia. The national men's and women's handball coaches are contracted for a period of two years to prepare the teams for the World Championships but do not receive a salary or per diem (compensation for out-of-pocket expenses such as transport). Instead, it is hoped that this experience will enable them to successfully apply for a paid role in the future while giving back to the next generation of players.

In recreational and professional sport, two main systems have an impact on national and international sporting activities worldwide: the European or federated system and the American or privatized model of sport. The legitimacy, authority, and operation of both systems are fundamentally different. Both systems have distinctive features which are formative for the respective model. In addition, the reference to the geographic areas of Europe and America is not necessarily an indicator of which model is used, as these terms are now only historical. In fact, some sports in the United States are structured according to the federated model, while some professional leagues in Europe, New Zealand, and Australia have closed leagues, which is one of the distinct features of the American model. The European model is largely community based and often reflects a national federated political system, whereas the fundamental nature of the American model is focused on commercialization opportunities.

The European model is governed by a pyramid structure from grassroots to the professional and/or elite level. The foundation of this sporting pyramid are the athletes and clubs, which are usually run by volunteers. The clubs provide access to anyone who wishes to participate in sport at a local level. In this way, the broader community is encouraged to play sport for health and social purposes. Sports people at the lowest level of the sporting pyramid are generally direct members, meaning that the club and the individual participant enter into some form of membership agreement, which is a contract. The next level of the pyramid are regional federations. For example, in Australia, these are usually state or territory federations. The members of the regional federations mostly consist of the community-level clubs. The authority of regional federations is generally limited to a specific area. They can also adopt sports rules and regulations for regional sports competitions, such as regional championships. Although individual participants are rarely direct members of regional federations, they are nevertheless eligible to participate in events sanctioned by the regional federations to which their clubs belong.

National sports federations form the next level in the federated model. One distinct feature of the European model is that only one national federation will be recognized by the funding body, and the international federation, in each sport. For example, the Football Association is the national governing body for the sport of football in England. Another example is Tennis Australia as the national sporting organization recognized by Sport Australia for the sport of tennis in Australia. National federations have the organizational and regulatory power to govern their sport on a national level. In general, the regional federations are members of national federations. Consequently, the clubs at the first level of the pyramid are usually indirect members of national sports federations. As set out in the governance chapter of this book, this can create challenges and power imbalances when some states are significantly bigger than others in terms of both participants, geographic spread, and financial resources. It is also the case in some sports, such as Australian Sailing, where some individual clubs are much larger and more powerful than other state bodies. For example, the Cruising Yacht Club of Australia in Sydney, New South Wales boasts more than 3000 members.

In many sports, continental federations form the next level of the pyramid, where national federations are the members of the umbrella continental federation. At the top of the pyramid are international sports federations that govern the respective sport on a global scale. For example, AusCycling is a member of the Oceania Cycling Confederation, which in turn is a member of the international federation, the Union Cycliste Internationale. An exception in this regard is, for example, the sport of ice hockey, for which, while an international sport and on the Olympic Winter Games program, no continental level exists. Continental federations have the national sports federations recognized by the international federation as their members. Similarly, there are continental Olympic Committees, such as the Olympic Council of Asia, which has recognized National Olympic Committees from its region as members. The IOC recognizes both National Olympic Committees and international sports federations in order to ensure that only one international sports federation governs the respective sport on the Olympic summer and winter program internationally.

In rare cases, athletes and other participants may also be direct members of the national sports governing body, as evidenced by Equestrian Australia. Equestrian Australia's legal structure is a company limited by guarantee. This is indicated by its full name: Equestrian Australia Limited. Companies limited by guarantee have members, not shareholders, under the Corporations Act, 2001. Prior to the 2020 amendment to the Equestrian Australia Constitution, the only members were known as "branches", which were the six state and territory bodies, for example, Equestrian Victoria. The individual equestrian athletes and officials participating in any of the nine disciplines were, therefore, members of the state or territory body where they lived. Under the Equestrian Australia Constitution, the individuals are referred to as "participating members" of Equestrian Australia. The 15 September 2020 constitution now provides participating members with voting and other substantive rights. Previously, they had no voting rights and were named in the constitution only to allow Equestrian Australia to have the ultimate disciplinary power over the individuals. The challenge now under this "unitary model" is that the number of people required to be present to make constitutional changes, known as a quorum, is 5%. This now means convening meetings for a minimum of approximately 900 of the approximately 18,000 members nationally. Conducting some of the core business, such as voting on new directors, only requires a quorum of 20 registered members to be present at the annual general meeting.

Members may only remain as members and have the right to compete in national sporting organization or other sport federation sanctioned events as long as they pay their annual registration fees. In practice, and is the case for many sports internationally, the payment of membership fees is processed nationally through a central membership database. In the Equestrian Australia example previously, participating members log on, choose their relevant state branch and club from drop-down menus, select their level of membership (such as junior or senior categories or as a technical official, etc.), and pay their annual fee. This process requires that, before the registration process is complete, the participating member click on a button agreeing that they consent to comply with the rules and regulations of Equestrian Australia. There is no ability for members to negotiate any of the terms of these policies under this process. This inability to meaningfully consent to the sport rules has been generally upheld by the courts under the "autonomy of sport" principle discussed previously, provided the rules are not patently unfair or in breach of general laws.

The traditional pyramid structure of the European or federated model, therefore, creates a chain of command to govern and regulate each sport from top to bottom, meaning that all members within the pyramid must generally accept the rules and regulations of the higher level(s). Therefore, the statutes of affiliated members generally refer to the statutes, rules, and regulations of the hierarchy. Particularly, affiliated members of the national and international sports federations recognize the exclusive authority to govern and regulate the respective sport nationally and internationally (so-called *Ein-Platz-Prinzip* or single-place principle). They further accept implementing and complying with their rules and regulations and applying them to their own members. Accordingly, this chain of references ensures that not only are the affiliated members bound by the rules and regulations of national and international sports federations but also that these rules bind clubs and participants at the grassroots level. This pyramidal structure is well summarized in the *SV Wilhelmshafen* case of the CAS, in which the panel held as follows:

> [T]he Appellant [SV Wilhelmshaven] is, as a member of the NFV [North German Football Federation], affiliated to the DFB and bound by the latter's rules and regulations (cf. para. 3 of the Statutes of the NFV). The DFB, in turn, is a member of FIFA and therefore bound by FIFA's rules and regulations (art. 13 para. 1 lit. a of the FIFA Statutes). In addition, as a member of FIFA, the DFB has the obligation to ensure that its own (direct or indirect) members, i.e., inter alia, the Appellant, comply with the Statutes, regulations directives and decisions of FIFA bodies (art. 13 para. 1 lit. d of the FIFA Statutes). Accordingly, pursuant to § 3 para. 1 of the Statutes of the DFB, the latter's members are bound by the regulatory provisions enacted by FIFA.

The pyramid structure of the European federated model closely intertwines the amateur and elite levels. In team sports, for example, a footballer could start their amateur career in an elite club as a child at a club such as Manchester United or Real Madrid and develop through the ranks to become a professional player and potentially represent not only their club in national and European competitions but also be chosen to represent their country at World Championships or the Olympic Summer Games.

The interplay between amateur and elite sports is a distinct characteristic of the European model that differs from the American model. In the American model, amateur sport is usually played in schools and at university (college). For example, the National Collegiate Athletics Association (NCAA) governs all college sport in the United States. The amateur status of college athletes has been the subject of considerable controversy, leading to a major development on 1 July 2021 to allow NCAA college athletes to profit from the use of their name, image, and likeness (known as NIL).

In the American model, there is no direct membership link between the NCAA and the professional sports leagues. Instead, anyone who wishes to become a professional athlete in one of the US major leagues, for example, the Women's National Basketball Association (WNBA) or National Basketball Association, the National Women's Soccer League (NWSL), or the National Football League (NFL), must be "drafted". The "draft" is the process by which teams in the league have the opportunity to select new talent. Taking the NFL as an example, players are "draft-eligible" only in the year after the end of their college eligibility period, or otherwise where undergraduates have received NFL approval to enter the draft early. There is, therefore, a contractual arrangement in place to ensure that only draft-eligible players participate in the college all-star games and to facilitate NFL player personnel staff working with NCAA compliance departments at the universities to conduct background checks and analyse performance statistics on draft prospects.

The professional leagues have a closed league system, where there is no promotion and relegation system, as is the case in the European model, such as English football. Consequently, the same teams, often called "franchises", will play in the league each year regardless of on-field performance. In the American model, these teams are often privately owned rather than having members. These teams will select the players who have declared for the draft in a certain draft order. In general terms, the idea is that the lowest-ranked team of the previous season should have the first "pick" in the draft, whereas the champion should have the last pick. The aim behind such draft order is the promotion of competitive balance within the league. The draft, in conjunction with a "salary cap" – another special characteristic of the American model that is rarely found in systems following the European model – are designed to avoid the accumulation of the leagues' best players in one team. A salary cap (or wage cap) is a rule imposed by a league on all club/franchises that limits either a maximum amount that can be paid for individual salaries and/or the total limit for the team. Teams have made attempts to circumvent both the draft and salary caps. For example the Australian National Rugby League team, Melbourne Storm, was found in 2010 to have created a dual contract system to circumvent the salary cap. Teams have taken advantage of the draft system by intentionally performing poorly in the second half of the season once it became clear they could not make the final rounds in order to select the best talent in the next draft. This is known as "tanking", and the leagues have introduced rules to discourage this unsportsmanlike practice, for example, a draft lottery in the NBA. The Australian Football League allows limited exemptions to the draft, including what is known as the "father-son" and "father-daughter" recruitment rule to give teams the prerogative to select the offspring of former AFL players to continue the family tradition in a particular AFL club. With the continuation of the AFL Women's Competition (AFLW), it can be presumed that this rule will become a "parent-child" rule in future.

As a side note, it should be mentioned that not all league systems in the sports industry follow either the European or American model in this respect. For example, in the Indian Premier League, the eight franchises bid for the players listed for the auctions to acquire their services. Marquee players, the franchises' star players, are generally not listed in this auction.

Finally, a difference between the European and American models is the way in which players under contract change clubs. In Europe, the transfer system provides that players can change their authorization to play for one specific team in exchange of a transfer fee, depending on the agreement between the releasing club, the engaging club, and the player. In the US major leagues, however, players can be traded against other players, draft picks, and monetary compensation with or against their will. The legitimacy of the trade system in the US major leagues derives from collective bargaining agreements between the owners of the franchises and the (powerful) players' unions. Such a system does not exist in Europe because the players unions generally lack bargaining power.

In Practice 6.1 How can athletes "voluntarily" consent to mandatory arbitration agreements?: the *Pechstein* case

Claudia Pechstein was an extremely successful long-track (speed) ice skater for Germany. Pechstein spent more than a decade challenging the premise of "voluntary consent" and the bias of the CAS in favour of sport organizations, particularly the International Skating Union (ISU) and the IOC.

It is increasingly important to ask whether it is reasonable to hold people accountable to "clickwrap" contracts and associated complex policies when they have no power or ability to negotiate the terms. For example, the Amazon Kindle app contract is over 72,000 words and reportedly took an actor nine hours to read aloud. If you printed out the aggregate Apple contract (single-sided Times New Roman 12), it would be 25 cm thick. Similarly, when an athlete pays their membership fee to join a sports club, then they are also agreeing to comply with a multitude of sport rules and policies, as set out previously in the Equestrian Australia example. These policies may apply at the local, state, national, and international levels. The athlete member may be completely unaware of the terms of these agreement, much less be able to negotiate.

The European Court of Human Rights had to deal with mandatory arbitration agreements in sport in the *Pechstein* part of its *Mutu and Pechstein* decision. In this case, the Court found that, if it is accepted that sports arbitration proceedings have specific advantages over ordinary legal proceedings in domestic courts, which are expensive and take a long time to be resolved, then the sport tribunals' proceedings are required to be fair and comply with the European Convention on Human Rights.

Accordingly, if athletes and other participants have no other choice than to use sport tribunals instead of domestic tribunals or courts, then the *Pechstein* decision sets out that the fair trial principle and the common law concept of natural justice that must be upheld. The "fair trial" principle and guaranteed procedural safeguards are set out under Article 6(1) of the ECHR. In the *Pechstein* case, in relation to the requirement under the relevant anti-doping policy that athletes must use CAS, the ECtHR held that:

> the acceptance of CAS jurisdiction by the second applicant must be regarded as "compulsory" arbitration within the meaning of its case-law. . . . The arbitration proceedings therefore had to afford the safeguards secured by Article 6 § 1 of the Convention.

As a consequence of this finding, athletes and other members of sport organizations may challenge a CAS decision on the grounds of a breach of natural justice before the Swiss Federal Tribunal (SFT). The grounds to challenge CAS awards before the SFT are set out in Article 190(2) of the Swiss Federal Act on Private International Law (PILA). Any shortcomings in the SFT's review of the case may then also be challenged before the ECtHR. This means that even where none of the parties are Swiss, the decisions appealing a CAS decision may go before the SFT and then on to the ECtHR. A recent example of this occurred in the case involving South African runner Caster Semenya and Athletics South Africa against World Athletics (with a legal seat in Monaco). It therefore remains to be seen whether the ECtHR will develop into a third level of appeal in sports matters.

Source: *Mutu and Pechstein v. Switzerland*, ECtHR, Application no. 40575/10 and no. 67474/10, 2 October 2018

FURTHER READING

Brown, A. (2019, February 6). Pechstein ruling represents a small victory for athletes. *The Sports Integrity Initiative*. Retrieved from www.sportsintegrityinitiative.com/pechstein-ruling-represents-a-small-victory-for-athletes/

Geeraets, V. (2018). Ideology, doping and the spirit of sport. *Sport, Ethics and Philosophy, 12*(3), 255–271.

Haas, U. (2016). The German federal court on treacherous ice – a final point in the Pechstein case. In C. Müller, S. Besson, & A. Rigozzi (Eds.), *New developments in international commercial arbitration 2016* (pp. 219–265). Geneva: Schulthess.

Podszun, R. (2018, September 6). *The Pechstein case: International sports arbitration versus competition law*. How the German Federal Supreme Court set standards for arbitration. http://dx.doi.org/10.2139/ssrn.3246922

Rigozzi, A. (2020). Sports arbitration and the European Convention of Human Rights – Pechstein and beyond. In C. Müller, S. Besson & A. Rigozzi (Eds), *New developments in international commercial arbitration* (pp. 77–130). Bern: Stämpfli.

SPORTS DISPUTE RESOLUTION

As part of the autonomy of sports described previously – deriving from the freedom of association – sport organizations are entitled to establish internal tribunals for the resolution of their disputes. Most international sports associations have made use of this by establishing one or more tribunals. Sport tribunals provide a form of alternative dispute resolution known as "arbitration", which is a procedure where parties agree to submit their dispute to an arbitrator (sitting solely or as a panel), who makes a binding decision. This is distinct from mediation, which is another form of alternative dispute resolution. In mediations, parties agree on an independent third party to assist them through negotiation and communication techniques to find a resolution to the dispute. As compared with arbitration, a mediator does not make a decision or impose a finding in favour of one party over the other.

In general, sport organizations can decide which internal tribunal has competence to deal with matters of, for example, disciplinary matters, unethical behaviour, selection and allocation cases, and field-of-play decisions. For example, Article 50(1) of the Fédération Internationale de Football Association Statutes (2021 edition) provides that the judicial bodies of FIFA are the Disciplinary Committee, the Ethics Committee, and the Appeals Committee. In addition, Article 54 of the FIFA Statutes refers to the Football Tribunal, which includes the FIFA Dispute Resolution Chamber, the Players' Statutes Chamber, and the Agents Chamber.

Many sport organizations have also established first-instance anti-doping hearing panels to determine whether an alleged anti-doping rule violation under their anti-doping rules has been committed. For the signatories to the WADA Code, under Article 8(1) of WADA Code, the signatories are mandated to "provide, at a minimum, a fair hearing within a reasonable time by a fair, impartial and Operationally Independent hearing panel in compliance with the *WADA International Standard for Results Management*". As set out previously in the *Pechstein* decision under In Practice 6.1, the procedure before the competent hearing panel must also comply with fair trial principles and natural justice.

The meaning and standard of "natural justice" for cases before sports tribunals is understood to include:

- Access to an independent and impartial tribunal
- Principle of equality of arms/equal treatment of the parties
- Right to have access to all files and evidence
- Right to be heard (which may be limited to documentation rather than in person/online)
- Right to a reasoned decision
- Right to a decision within reasonable time
- Right to a public hearing
- Legal aid, if legal representation is necessary based on the circumstances of the case.

Sport organizations can also decide – within their autonomy of sport – to delegate their power to adjudicate on internal matters to third parties. To satisfy requirements of independence and impartiality, sport organizations are increasingly making use of external tribunals. National and international organizations may delegate power to decide on internal first-instance matters to, for example, the National Sports Tribunal (Australia), Sport Resolutions (UK), Sport

Dispute Resolution Centre of Canada, The Sports Tribunal of New Zealand, and – in doping matters – the Anti-Doping Division of the Court of Arbitration for Sport. The rules of the sport organization must explicitly provide for a delegation of its first-instance authority to a third party. For example, Article 31.2.1 of the International Biathlon Union Constitution (2020 edition) provides that "where the alleged violation is of the anti-doping chapter of the IBU Integrity Code, the matter will be referred to the CAS Anti-Doping Division". In this context, it is also important to stress that the delegating sports organization remains accountable for, and responsible for implementing, the decision of the third party.

It is also a requirement that where there is an internal sports dispute mechanism provided under the rules, then that process must be followed before a decision can be challenged on appeal before a domestic court or sports arbitration tribunal, including CAS. In order to file an appeal with CAS, an arbitration agreement must exist between the parties naming CAS as the appeal tribunal and excluding the jurisdiction of the general domestic courts. These requirements are set out in Article R47 of the CAS Code of Sports-related Arbitration (2021). Evidence of the consent to arbitrate is usually provided in the sports rules, which has been described by the SFT as "arbitration by reference". As set out previously, participants consent by signing membership forms, employment agreements, athlete's agreements, or any other entry forms. The inclusion of arbitration agreements into the rules and regulations of international sports federations has become very common. The International Partnership against Corruption in Sport (IPACS) recommends the inclusion of an appeal mechanism to CAS as one of its good governance benchmarks.

Although, as noted in the *Pechstein* case previously, there is some discomfort with sport monopolies imposing compulsory arbitration clauses, on balance, the benefits are seen to outweigh the disadvantages. Sports arbitration proceedings are still perceived to be faster and cheaper than proceedings before ordinary courts. The speed of decisions is important for the eligibility of athletes in sports competitions and for the integrity of the competition itself. It is, therefore, in the interest of both sports federations and athletes that sports disputes be solved within a reasonable time, taking into account that sports careers are generally very short in comparison to other professions. Referring sport matters to national courts may result in different sporting sanctions for similar sports rule violations. For example, a German court may impose a two-year ineligibility sanction for the consumption of prohibited substances, while an Australian court may consider a four-year ban appropriate. To create a degree of harmonization in international sport, it is considered preferable to refer all sports-related disputes to independent and impartial sports arbitration tribunals composed of experts in sports law. However, as set out previously, if basic fairness requirements are not respected, these arbitration agreements may be found invalid and referred to the national courts for a decision.

In Practice 6.2 Natural justice: impartiality of tribunal members – the case of Sun Yang

A highly publicized example of demonstrable bias in a sports tribunal arose following the Court of Arbitration for Sport decision involving Chinese swimmer Sun Yang. The CAS panel determined on 28 February 2020 that – based on the evidence before them – two anti-doping rule violations had been committed by Yang. On 15 June 2020, Yang filed an application with the Swiss Federal Tribunal for the CAS decision to be annulled and for the chairman of the panel, Franco Frattini, to be disqualified.

Yang submitted evidence from Frattini's Twitter account from 2018 and 2019 which Yang alleged to be racist towards Chinese people. The posts were unrelated to sports competitions and dishonest athletes. Therefore, Frattini argued that he was exercising his right to free speech and that the context related to animal rights, not his capacity as an arbitrator. The Tribunal found the posts, including using the expression "yellow faced Chinese monster", raised legitimate doubts as to the impartiality of the arbitrator in determining Yang's case. With the CAS decision annulled, the matter was referred back to the CAS for a new hearing. The new hearing was conducted by a panel unrelated to the first procedure before the CAS. It remains to be seen whether this case, and this approach, inspires future appeals for CAS cases to be revised.

Source: Swiss Federal Tribunal Judgment 4A_318/2020 of 22 December 2020, Request for revision of the award CAS 2019/A/6148 at www.swissarbitrationdecisions.com/sites/default/files/584%20-%20SIAD%20-%204A_318-2020%20-%202020.12.22.pdf

FURTHER READING

Mavromati, D. (2021, January 21). Challenge of a CAS arbitrator for inappropriate tweets: The "duty of curiosity" revisited. *SportLegis*. Retrieved from www.sportlegis.com/2021/01/21/challenge-of-a-cas-arbitrator-for-inappropriate-tweet-messages-or-the-duty-of-curiosity-revisited/

Sterling, R. (2021, May 26). Court of arbitration for sport fails again in Sun Yang case. *Sport Integrity Initiative*. Retrieved from www.sportsintegrityinitiative.com/court-of-arbitration-for-sport-fails-again-in-sun-yang-case/

THREATS TO THE INTEGRITY OF SPORT: DOPING AND MATCH-FIXING

Wrongdoing in sport is widespread and includes criminal behaviour such as severe injury-causing foul play, fraud, fan violence, and sexual abuse all the way through to behaviour characterized as poor governance and/or causing reputational damage. There is not even an agreed-upon definition on what constitutes "sport integrity". The newly established body Sport Integrity Australia defines "sports integrity" as "the manifestation of the ethics and values that promote community confidence in sport" (Sport Integrity Australia Act 2020 s.4). It has been proposed that if there were an international equivalent to WADA responsible for sport integrity matters, this would be of assistance. It is not clear now where whistleblowers should refer threats to sport integrity, or other types of sport corruption, even if it involves event bidding, major games procurement, ticket scalping, or the mistreatment of athletes/officials and human rights abuses.

To date, sport organizations and governments have primarily focused on behaviour that directly impacts the uncertainty of on-field outcomes, that is, cheating to win (doping) and cheating to lose (match-fixing). The approaches to lowering the risks of these twin threats are fundamentally different. First, we consider doping.

Doping

The regulatory response to doping is supported by both an international convention ratified by national governments (states) – the UNESCO International Convention against Doping in Sport (UNESCO Anti-Doping Convention) – and a code of behaviour voluntary committed to by sport organizations – the World Anti-Doping Code drafted by the World Anti-Doping Agency. The UNESCO Anti-Doping Convention entered into force on 1 February 2007 and has been ratified by 191 states. The code first came into effect on 1 January 2004 and has been updated in 2009, 2015, and 2021. Approximately 700 sport organizations have accepted the code. The steps for full compliance are acceptance, implementation, and enforcement. The code works in conjunction with eight international standards, including:

*   International Standard for Testing and Investigations (ISTI)
*   International Standard for Results Management (ISRM)
*   International Standard for Laboratories (ISL)
*   International Standard for Therapeutic Use Exemptions (ISTUE)
*   International Standard for the Prohibited List (The List)

The cooperation between state governments and private sport organizations against doping had its historic beginnings in the so-called "Festina scandal" during the 1998 Tour de France. The Tour de France is an annual men's bicycle race. In 1998, police raids and arrests led to the exclusion of the Festina and TVM teams and the withdrawal of a number of other teams, shattering the race. The police discovered systematic and organized doping operations aimed at enhancing the riders' performance. This scandal led to the realization that doping could no longer be regulated individually by individual sports organizations but that universal and harmonized efforts were needed to fight doping in sport efficiently.

This development ultimately led to the establishment of the WADA. WADA is a Swiss foundation governed by the Swiss Civil Code with its headquarters in Montreal, Canada. The core responsibilities of WADA are to coordinate the fight against doping, to draft and amend the code, and to monitor the implementation and compliance with the code by its signatories, such as the IOC, the IPC, NOCs, NPCs, and international federations. These sport organizations become signatories to the code by signing a declaration of acceptance with WADA. The code explicitly mentions the purpose and fundamental values of the World Anti-Doping Program: protection of the health of athletes, protection and maintenance of the integrity of sport, fair competitions and clean sport, and sports competitions in the light of the spirit of sport. All signatories are obliged to implement, via "copy and paste", the most important provisions of the code – set forth under Article 23.2.2 of the code – into their own rules. In addition, Article 22 provides that the signatories must ensure that athletes and other participants are bound by these anti-doping rules. In other words, the code is not directly applicable to direct and indirect members of the signatories to the WADA Code. Instead, the anti-doping rules of the respective sports organization apply to the participants bound by them.

Article 2 of the WADA Code defines "doping" through what are referred to as anti-doping rule violations (ADRVs). It also stresses that "Athletes and other Persons shall be responsible for knowing what constitutes an anti-doping rule violation and the substances and methods which have been included on the Prohibited List" – the list that defines what substances and methods are prohibited. The code currently in force, the 2021 WADA Code, lists 11 different ADRVs. However, not all of them refer to the illicit consumption and use of prohibited substances and methods. Only Article 2.1 of the WADA Code ("Presence of a Prohibited Substance") and Article 2.2 of the WADA Code ("Use or Attempted Use of a Prohibited Method") deal with prohibited substances found in athletes' urine or blood specimens. Both provisions also contain the – controversial – strict liability principle, meaning that "it is not necessary that intent, Fault, Negligence or knowing Use on the Athlete's part be demonstrated in order to establish an anti-doping rule violation". Athletes then have to demonstrate, for example, how the substance has inadvertently been consumed in order to be able to reduce or absolve themselves of a sanction.

Other ADRVs defined under the code place the burden on the anti-doping organization alleging the breach of the rule to prove it, for example, tampering with doping control; possession or trafficking of prohibited substances; complicity; and the new ADRV, acts of discouraging or retaliating against – essentially – whistle-blowers. The code further covers the consequences of (alleged) ADRVs. The possible consequences under the code are:

1 disqualification of results;

2 ineligibility sanction;

3 provisional suspensions;

4 financial consequences (e.g., forfeiture of prize or appearance money); and

5 public disclosure ("name and shame").

The sanctioning regime of the code (from Articles 10.2) aims to ensure that all athletes are subject to the same sanction in similar cases. For example, Article 10.2 provides that the default sanction for the presence of a prohibited substance in the athlete's system will be a four-year ban, subject to aggravating and mitigating circumstances set out under the code.

The standard of proof to establish an ADRV is the standard of "comfortable satisfaction". This standard appears to be the common standard in sports-related disputes – not just in doping matters. Article 3.1 of the WADA Code requires arbitrations to consider the evidence in each case as proven: "greater than the mere balance of probability [i.e. more likely than not] but less than proof beyond reasonable doubt". In other words, the standard of comfortable satisfaction sits between the standards of proof generally applied in civil law (known as "balance of probability" or "preponderance of the evidence") and criminal law ("beyond reasonable doubt"). However, where the code puts the burden upon the athlete or other participant, the standard of proof is the one of balance of probability. In all cases, of course, it is a requirement that all parties have access to a fair hearing before an impartial hearing panel, as mentioned previously. In addition, Article 13.2.1 of the code provides that first-instance decisions relating to international events or involving international-level athletes may be appealed exclusively to CAS. The CAS panel can review the case afresh (*de novo*, i.e., from the beginning) and is not limited in its power of review (Code Art. 13.1.1). Generally, sport disciplinary decisions may only be reviewed by CAS when it can be demonstrated that "the sanction is evidently and grossly disproportionate to the offence", but in anti-doping, this additional hurdle is not required.

Match-fixing

The regulatory framework for combating match-fixing is fundamentally different. Each sports organization can decide within its regulatory autonomy what is to be understood by match-fixing within its organization. For example, FIFA may have a different understanding of match-fixing – and match manipulation – than the International Basketball Federation (FIBA) or the International Cricket Council (ICC). The Council of Europe Convention on the Manipulation of Sports Competitions, which is the first international convention to tackle all forms of sports competition manipulation at an international level, refers to match-fixing as:

> an intentional arrangement, act or omission aimed at an improper alteration of the result or the course of a sports competition in order to remove all or parts of the unpredictable nature of the aforementioned sports competition with a view to obtaining an advantage for oneself or for others.

Match-fixing poses a major threat to the integrity of sport that is arguably even more serious than the threat emanating from doping. This is because people who are involved in match-fixing operations are attacking two core values of sport: credibility and unpredictability. The perpetrators – usually consisting of a group of organized criminals or groups of criminals and sport participants – manipulate the matches based on an agreed-upon plot with the purpose to place large sums of money on the betting market. In other words, the group engineers a pre-arranged predictable result or aspect of the game that they use to their financial advantage. Either the result of the match (e.g., win/loss/draw, the number of goals scored, etc.) or aspects of the event (e.g. double faults in tennis, wides or no balls in cricket, or red cards in football, etc., known as spot-fixing) are fixed in advance. This has consequences for the credibility of sports competitions among sports fans and spectators. The more a sport is affected by match-fixing, the less interest the public has in that sport. The diminished interest impacts the commercial success of that sport. Fewer spectators means fewer tickets, less mechanizing, and less revenue. For the reasons mentioned, sport organizations have an interest in combating all forms of sports competition manipulation, including match-fixing.

The aim of a manipulation-free sport may only be achieved, if at all, in collaboration with national law enforcement agencies. Match-fixing requires the involvement of participants that fall within the disciplinary jurisdiction of sport organizations. These participants are bound by the rules and regulations, including provisions on match-fixing. The "puppet master" behind the fix, however, is rarely the participant. Instead, young and vulnerable athletes – who want to make it to the top of their sport – or athletes who are about to reach the end of their career are usually approached by organized crime groups. The members of organized crime groups – which fall outside of the disciplinary power of sport organizations – have an interest in earning a high sum on the betting market. Sometimes the intermediary is a retired athlete known to the current generation who has been recruited by the fixers. The player(s) or referee/ umpire is often offered money, drugs, and/ or prostitutes in exchange for information and/or the improper alteration of the result or parts of the game. For example, a tennis player may receive an offer to lose the first set of their match in exchange for $1000. These offers may be attractive for low-ranked players who are struggling to cover the expenses associated with the professional tour, such as accommodation, food, transport, and coaching. Participants who accept such offers and manipulate sports competitions commit a sports rule violation and can, therefore, be sanctioned and banned from the respective sport. However, it requires the support of national lawmakers and law enforcement agencies to prosecute organized crime gangs for their involvement in sports competition manipulation in protection of the legally protected interest of the integrity of sport. Therefore, match-fixing has been criminalized in various jurisdictions in recent years, for example, in Turkey, Australia, Germany, and Switzerland. Consequently, law enforcement agencies can investigate and prosecute organized crime groups for their involvement in illicit match manipulation. In addition, athletes may be subject to two parallel procedures: sports disciplinary procedures and criminal proceedings. It remains to be seen what consequences the parallel procedures will have on the fundamental procedural rights of athletes.

In Practice 6.3 How the anti-doping rules operate in practice: Maria Sharapova

While Maria Sharapova's anti-doping case study raised a number of complexities that do not need to be addressed in detail here, it illustrates how the anti-doping rules operate in practice. Sharapova was an elite-level tennis player from Russia. She was one of the most successful tennis players on the Women's Tennis Association (WTA) tour and won five Grand Slam titles. The WTA Tour comprises over 50 events and four Grand Slams, including the Australian Open. The Grand Slams are considered the most important tournaments in tennis.

The International Tennis Federation (ITF) is a signatory to the code. The ITF has implemented the code through its own Tennis Anti-Doping Programme (the "Programme"). By participating in Grand Slams and other events sanctioned by the ITF or WTA, Sharapova had agreed to be bound by the Programme. The Programme is managed and enforced by the ITF on behalf of the ATP, WTA, and Grand Slams.

As part of ITF's anti-doping program, Sharapova was required to undergo anti-doping tests in and out of competition on a regular basis. On 26 January 2016, Sharapova competed at the Australian Open in Melbourne, Australia. After her first-round match, Sharapova was asked by the responsible authorities to provide a urine sample. These samples were analyzed by a WADA accredited laboratory and returned an "adverse analytical finding" (AAF) for a substance on the Prohibited List.

The Prohibited List is one of the WADA international standards. It contains the prohibited substances and methods that have each been included where they have satisfied at least two of the three criteria: (1) the potential to enhance sport performance, (2) an actual or potential health risk to the athlete, and/or the catch-all (3) "violates the spirit of sport". The testing system therefore has the purpose of finding banned substances in athletes' specimens and eliminating "drug cheats" from professional sport.

In situations where athletes return an AAF, the responsible sport organization determines whether the International Standard for Testing and Investigations and the International Standard for Laboratories have been complied with before determining it is an alleged "positive" test, which is the ADRV for "Presence". As set out previously, "Presence" is a "strict liability" offence, so Sharapova had the burden of explaining how the prohibited substance "meldonium" was found in her specimen. The idea behind this principle is that it is very difficult for anti-doping organizations to determine the intention of the athlete to assess their denials and claims that they are not at fault or had no knowledge of the substance but may in any event have received an advantage over their competitors (ITF Art. 2.1.1).

In this case, Sharapova was advised to make a public admission that she had been taking the product on the advice of her doctor for ten years. Meldonium was only added to the 2016 Prohibited List on 1 January 2016. The Prohibited List is updated every year in October and provided to all the international federations and national anti-doping organizations, which in turn forwarded onto the athletes, including Sharapova, to review in advance. Sharapova admitted on 7 March 2016 that she had taken meldonium in January, having not checked the list, as she had delegated that task to her manager.

As athletes are personally responsible for the substances found in their systems, Sharapova, therefore, was unable to challenge the finding of the ADRV. The initial CAS decision on 6 June 2016 disqualified Sharapova's result from the Australian Open and banned her for two years. Under the 2021 code, the sanction would have been a four-year ban. Sharapova appealed, seeking to reduce the standard two-year sanction on the grounds of "No Significant Fault" (NSF). The CAS panel on appeal found that Sharapova's failure to properly monitor or supervise her manager and her failure to disclose the use of the prohibited substance on her anti-doping control forms meant that her fault was greater than the minimum degree of fault falling within NSF but less than Significant Fault. Considering the principle of proportionality, the CAS appeal panel determined on 30 September 2016 that a sanction of 15 months, backdated to 26 January, was appropriate for Sharapova's degree of fault. Proportionality requires a consideration in fairness to balance behaviour sought to be prevented against the severity of the wrongdoing in that particular case. In the criminal law, it is expressed as "the punishment should fit the crime". In this case study, the ban was upheld (although reduced), even though it was acknowledged that Sharapova did not intend to cheat. These types of cases, while legally correct under the code and sport anti-doping rules, attract criticism for being heavy handed and not prioritizing resources for preventing serious drug cheats.

Source: Arbitration CAS 2016/A/4643 Maria Sharapova v. International Tennis Federation (ITF), award of 30 September 2016 at https://jurisprudence.tas-cas.org/Shared%20Documents/4643.pdf

WTA Tour, *2021 Official Rulebook*, at https://photoresources.wtatennis.com/wta/document/2021/03/08/d6d2c650-e3b4-42e7-ab2b-e539d4586033/2021Rulebook.pdf

Tennis Anti-Doping Programme (2021 edition), at https://antidoping.ifftennis.com/media/317953/317953.pdf

FURTHER READING

David, P. (2017). *A guide to the world anti-doping code.* Cambridge: Cambridge University Press.
Haas, U., & Healey, D. (2016). *Doping in sport and the law.* Oxford: Hart Publishing.

SUMMARY

This chapter has provided a brief overview of the operation of amateur and professional sports on a national and international level. Sport organizations have the authority to decide on internal matters on their own without state interference. At a national level, sports can be governed by a federated (European) or private ownership (American) model. The American model is particularly used outside the organizational structure of national and international sports federations and is most common in sports league systems, such as the US major leagues, including basketball, baseball, football, and soccer. In both systems, the sport governing body can implement sports rules and regulations and apply and enforce them against the people under its authority. However, all decisions and regulations of sport organizations must comply with general law provisions. In this regard, the principle of proportionality is an important yardstick to measure the legitimacy of the decisions taken by sport organizations, considering the legal interests of their direct and indirect members. Sport organizations have an interest in the protection of the integrity of sport. Therefore, sport organizations have implemented rules and regulations aimed at preventing all forms of corruption in sport, including doping and match-fixing. The latter pose major threats to the fairness, equality, and unpredictability of sports competitions. This chapter has discussed that, on the one hand, athletes and other participants are subject to stringent sports regulations that have a severe impact on their personal and professional lives. On the other hand, such rules and regulations may be necessary to protect not only the values and ethics of sport but also the honest athletes who believe in those values of fair and equal sports competitions.

REVIEW QUESTIONS

1 Explain the concept of the "autonomy of sport".
2 How can the autonomy of sport organizations be limited?

3 Why do national and international sports federations seek to prevent any outside interference?

4 How does the European model of sport differ from the American model?

5 How does the draft system in the US major leagues work, and what is the purpose behind it?

6 What do we mean by "compulsory arbitration" in sports disputes?

7 What are the consequences of the *Pechstein* decision for national and international sports arbitration proceedings?

8 Why are doping and match-fixing argued to be the biggest threats to the integrity of sport?

9 How does match-fixing work?

10 How does the WADA Code ensure that the same definition of anti-doping rule violation and its consequences apply to all athletes and other participants at the elite level?

DISCUSSION QUESTIONS

1 Why do national and international federations have an interest in maintaining their autonomy over internal matters?

2 What are the main characteristics of the federated and private ownership models? Which model do you think is better, and why?

3 What are the reasons for the different approaches to combating doping and match-fixing in sport?

4 Why is it important to have sports dispute resolution mechanisms outside of general domestic tribunals/courts?

5 How can the individual rights of athletes be sufficiently protected in proceedings before sports arbitration tribunals?

FURTHER READING

Anderson, J., Parrish, R., & García, B. (Eds.). (2018). *Research handbook on EU sports law and policy*. Cheltenham: Edward Elgar Publishing.

Bowen, J., Katz, R. S., Mitchell, J. R., Polden, D. J., & Walden, R. (2017). *Sport, ethics and leadership*. Milton: Taylor & Francis.

Davis, T. (2011). What is sports law? *Marquette Sports Law Review, 11,* 211.

DeSensi, J. T., & Rosenberg, D. (2010). *Ethics and morality in sport management* (3rd ed.). Morgantown, VA: West Virginia University.

Epstein, A., & Osborne, B. (2017). Teaching ethics with sports: Recent developments. *Marquette Sports Law Review, 28,* 301.

Gardiner, S., O'Leary, J., Welch, R., Boyes, S., & Naidoo, U. (2012). *Sports law*. London: Routledge.

Haas, U., & Hessert, B. (2021a). The legal regime applicable to disciplinary measures by sports associations – one size does not fit all. In P. Jung, F. Krauskopf, & C. Cramer (Eds.), *Theorie und Praxis des Unternehmensrechts – Festschrift zu Ehren von Lukas Handshin*. Zürich: Schulthess Medien AG.

Haas, U., & Hessert, B. (2021b). Sports regulations on human rights – Applicability and self-commitment. In *Le sport au Carrefour des droits Mélanges en l'honneur de Gérald Simon*. Paris: LexisNexis.

Haynes, J., & Marcus, J. T. (2019). *Commonwealth Caribbean sports law*. London: Routledge.

James, M. (2017). *Sports law*. London: Macmillan International Higher Education.

Lewis, A., & Taylor, J. (2021). *Sport: Law and practice* (4th ed.). London: Bloomsbury.

Moorman, A. M. (Ed.). (2020). *Sport law: A managerial approach* (4th ed.). Abingdon, Oxon: Routledge.

Ordway, C. (Ed.). (2021). *Restoring trust in sport: Sports corruption case studies & solutions*. London: Routledge.

Ordway, C., & Opie, H. (2017). Integrity and corruption in sport. In N. Schulenkorf & S. Frawley (Eds.), *Critical issues in global sport management* (pp. 38–63). London: Taylor & Francis.

Thorpe, D., Buti, A., Davies, C., & Jonson, P. (2017). *Sports law* (3rd ed.). Oxford: Oxford University Press.

RELEVANT WEBSITES

The following websites are useful starting points for further information on legal and ethical issues in sport:

Australian & NZ Sports Law Association (students can join as members) at: www.anzsla.com.au/

Burn It All Down (podcast – human rights in sport) at: www.burnitalldownpod.com/

Council of Europe (CoE) HELP Course on Human Rights in Sport at: www.coe.int/en/web/help/-/new-versions-of-the-council-of-europe-help-course-on-human-rights-in-sports and http://help.elearning.ext.coe.int/

The Forward Line (podcast by The University of Melbourne sport law students) at: https://player.whooshkaa.com/shows/the-forward-line

Inside the Games (Olympic news) at: www.insidethegames.biz/subscribe

LawInSport (articles and podcasts) at: www.lawinsport.com/podcast/

Play the Game (investigative journalists) at: www.playthegame.org/

Siren Sport (Women's Sport) at: https://sirensport.com.au/

Sport Australia: Clearinghouse (database of resources) at: www.clearinghouseforsport.gov.au/

Sport Integrity Australia, Ethics and Integrity online courses at https://elearning.sportintegrity.gov.au/login/index.php

Sport Integrity Initiative at: www.sportsintegrityinitiative.com/

Sports Law India (international sport law resources) at: http://sportslaw.in/home/resources/

The Ticket, ABC Radio, hosted by Tracey Holmes (podcast) at: www.abc.net.au/radio/newsradio/podcasts/the-ticket/listen-again/

Tribunal Arbitral du Sport/Court of Arbitration for Sport at: www.tas-cas.org

CASE STUDY 6.1

Self-commitment to anti-discrimination in sport: the Blake Leeper case

The starting position under national and international law when considering sport regulations is that sport organizations are permitted to make their own rules to govern their sport under the "autonomy of sport" principle. This recognition of autonomy, however, is not absolute, as sport organizations can choose to limit their own autonomy through their rules, and, in some cases, national and international laws can override the rules of sport where fairness requires it. One area where the autonomy of sport has been challenged is when sports seek to be inclusive and undertake to act on a non-discriminatory basis, as in this case study featuring World Athletics.

Blake Leeper is an elite-level 400-metre runner from the United States of America. Leeper was born without both of his legs below the knee due to the congenital birth defect fibular hemimelia. To enable him to run, Leeper uses passive-elastic carbon-fibre running-specific prostheses (RSPs), or blades. In the beginning of his professional career, Leeper focused on participating in para-athletics events with great success. Leeper won the silver medal in the 400-m event at the 2012 London Paralympic Games and broke the 400-m Paralympic world record in 2017. In June 2017, Leeper started competing against able-bodied athletes in international 400-m World Athletics events (the governing body of the sport of athletics was formerly known as the International Association of Athletics Federations [IAAF]).

World Athletics is based in the Principality of Monaco and, therefore, has been permitted autonomy under Monegasque law. The IAAF Competition Rules 2018–2019 prevented:

> [t]he use of any mechanical aid, unless the athlete can establish on the balance of probabilities that the use of an aid would not provide him with an overall competitive advantage over an athlete not using such aid.
>
> (Art. 144.3(d))

This means that athletes who seek to use mechanical aids in World Athletics-sanctioned events must demonstrate that they do not have an "overall competitive advantage" over their competitors. The standard of proof is the balance of probabilities, which means that athletes who are using mechanical aids must prove that it is more likely than not that they do not have an overall competitive advantage when using mechanical aids.

World Athletics initially found that Leeper had not satisfied the burden of proving that he did not have a competitive advantage over his able-bodied peers and, therefore, was ineligible to compete in qualifying events for the 2020 Tokyo Olympic Games. Leeper challenged this decision before CAS. Leeper argued that Article

144.3(d) of the IAAF Rules is discriminatory against athletes with disabilities, even though the rule appears to be neutral. Leeper therefore argued that Article 144.3(d) should be declared invalid and unenforceable. This would then have had the effect that World Athletics would need to establish that Leeper did not have a competitive advantage over his opponents when using his RSPs.

As Leeper had made the allegation that the World Athletics provision was discriminatory, then, under the CAS rules, the burden was on Leeper to demonstrate that. If, on the balance of probabilities, any form of discrimination was established, then World Athletics would have the burden to provide compelling reasons for treating able-bodied athletes and para-athletes differently.

From an autonomy of sport perspective, Leeper argued that World Athletics had limited its autonomy by committing itself to be a non-discriminatory sport. The World Athletics Constitution states that it is: "the right of every individual to participate in Athletics as a sport, without unlawful discrimination of any kind undertaken in the spirit of friendship, solidarity and fair play" (Art 4.1(j)). The CAS panel considered whether the wording of Article 144.3(d) was directly discriminatory between able-bodied athletes and athletes with disabilities and found it was not.

However, as the World Athletics Constitution prevents "unlawful discrimination of any kind", then the CAS had to consider whether Article 144.3(d) amounted to indirect discrimination. "Indirect discrimination" refers to rules and regulations that appear to be neutral in their wording but, in practice, disadvantage a group of people who share certain protected characteristics, such as gender, race, sexual orientation, and – as in this case study – disability. Accordingly, the CAS panel had to determine whether by placing the burden on all athletes using mechanical aids might be indirectly discriminatory against athletes with disabilities. The panel concluded that mechanical aids are rarely used by able-bodied athletes but are necessary for athletes with limb deficiencies and leg length differences to participate in athletics. Therefore, the panel found that Article 144.3(d) has a greater practical impact on athletes with disabilities and is, therefore, indirectly discriminatory against them, including Leeper. The panel further found that World Athletics was unable to establish that this indirect discrimination was justified on the basis that it was necessary, reasonable, or proportionate.

The panel then amended Article 144.3(d) – in accordance with the World Athletics regulations – to remove the burden on the athlete and applied this new wording to the Leeper case, as follows:

> The use of any mechanical aid, unless on the balance of probabilities the use of an aid would not provide them with an overall competitive advantage over an athlete not using such an aid.

In placing the burden to prove "overall competitive advantage" on World Athletics, instead of the athlete, the panel took into account that proof requires scientific expertise that is generally very expensive and unaffordable for most athletes. From a legal perspective, it is also a reasonable expectation that sports federations declaring an interest in fair and equal competitions must then provide conclusive evidence demonstrating why an individual is ineligible. In the Leeper case, World Athletics had to establish that the athlete had an overall competitive advantage over the other competitors arising from the use of his chosen passive-elastic carbon-fibre running-specific prostheses.

The panel first had to examine the standard at which "overall competitive advantage" is measured. Rather than either comparing Leeper's performance against the performance of the best athletes in the world or comparing Leeper's performance with and without prostheses or the performance of a real or hypothetical para-athlete instead, the CAS panel considered it appropriate to compare:

> the athlete's likely performance when using the mechanical aid and their likely athletic performance had they not had the disability which necessitates the use of that aid. A disabled athlete who uses a mechanical aid which does no more than offset the disadvantages caused by their disability cannot be said to have an "overall advantage" over a non-disabled athlete who is not using such an aid. In such a case, the mechanical aid does no more than counteract a disadvantage which the able-bodied athlete does not share.

This formula set by the CAS panel will be the benchmark for similar cases in the future. World Athletics established that the athlete's height with his RSPs is 15cm different from his natural height which he would have with intact legs. Based on the scientific expertise before it, the panel ultimately concluded that this difference in height does more than offset the disadvantages caused by Leeper's bilateral transtibial amputation and therefore provides him with an overall competitive advantage over able-bodied athletes not using RSPs. Consequently, the panel found that the decision taken by World Athletics to exclude Leeper from qualifying competitions for the 2020 Tokyo Olympic Games against non-disabled athletes was legitimate.

NB: Leeper reportedly chose not to compete in the Tokyo 2020 Paralympic Games because his RSPs contravene the International Paralympic Committee's Maximum Allowable Standing Height (MASH) rule.

CASE STUDY QUESTIONS

1 How did World Athletics restrict its own autonomy to determine who is eligible to compete in World Athletics sanctioned events?

2 On what grounds did Leeper argue that the World Athletics Article 144.3(d) was discriminatory towards para-athletes?

3 What was the CAS panel's finding on Article 144.3(d) in relation to direct discrimination?

4 On what grounds did the CAS panel find that Article 144.3(d) was indirectly discriminatory towards athletes with a disability?

5   What test for determining "an overall competitive advantage" did the CAS panel use to determine the Leeper case?

Source: CAS 2020/A/6807 Blake Leeper v. International Association of Athletics Federations at: www.tas-cas.org/fileadmin/user_upload/Award__6807___for_publication_.pdf CAS Media Release (11 June 2021), The Court of Arbitration for Sport (CAS) Dismisses the 2nd Appeal of Blake Leeper, at: www.tas-cas.org/fileadmin/user_upload/CAS_Media_Release_7930.pdf

FURTHER READING

Marjolaine Viret. (2020, November 20). Pistorius revisited: A comment on the CAS award in Blake Leeper v. IAAF. *Asser Sports Law Blog.* Retrieved from www.asser.nl/SportsLaw/Blog/post/pistorius-revisited-a-comment-on-the-cas-award-in-blake-leeper-v-iaaf-by-marjolaine-viret

Mike Cook. (2021, July 23). Why Blake Leeper is not running at the Tokyo Olympic games – The 2nd CAS Award. *LawInSport.* Retrieved from www.lawinsport.com/topics/item/why-blake-leeper-is-not-running-at-the-tokyo-olympic-games-the-2nd-cas-award#references

Simon Watts-Morgan. (2021, March 3). The Blake Leeper case – CAS panel rejects double amputee's appeal to compete at the Olympics. *LawInSport.* Retrieved from www.lawinsport.com/topics/item/the-blake-leeper-case-why-cas-rejected-double-amputee-s-appeal-to-compete-at-the-olympics

CASE STUDY 6.2

Sport and human rights: WADA whereabouts

Case study 6.1 already touched upon the balancing process between the competing interests of sports federations and athletes. The aim of clean and doping-free sport competitions is in the interest of both sport organizations and honest athletes. However, the anti-doping obligations of athletes under the respective anti-doping rules and WADA's International Standards has a serious impact on the private life of all athletes. For example, unannounced testing has been identified as one of the key requirements for effective testing in the fight against doping in sport. This means that athletes can be subject to anti-doping sample collection sessions anytime and anywhere. Another stringent obligation that athletes who are included in "Registered Testing Pools" designated by the relevant anti-doping body is the provision of whereabouts information in order to enable the sports organization with testing authority to locate an athlete for the collection of urine and blood samples. Article 5.5 of the WADA Code (or its equivalent in the respective anti-doping rules of the signatories to the code) reads – in its pertinent parts – as follows:

> Athletes who have been included in a *Registered Testing Pool* by their International federation and/or *National Anti-Doping Organization* shall provide whereabouts information in the manner specified in the *International Standard for Testing and Investigations* and shall be subject to Consequences for Article 2.4 violations as provided in Article 10.3.2.

Based on this provision in conjunction with the International Standard for Testing and Investigations, athletes have the obligation to provide quarterly information on their whereabouts, including the location of their overnight stays, training, and sports competitions. They must further provide information on "one specific 60-minute time slot between 5 a.m. and 11 p.m. each day where the Athlete will be available and accessible for Testing at a specific location". Violations of this obligation may result in an ADRV and ultimately in an ineligibility sanction of up to two years (Article 10.3.2 of the WADA Code).

In a recent case, *National Federation of Participants' Association and Unions (FNASS) and Others v. France*, a group of French athletes challenged the whereabouts regulations of their national sports federation. National sports federations in France are public entities and therefore state actors. In addition, Articles L.232–13–1 onwards of the French statute *Code du sport* (Sports Code) contain a regulation on whereabouts that is similar to the one in the WADA Code. In the proceedings before the ECtHR, the athletes argued that the whereabouts obligations provided under the *Code du sport* constitute a severe violation of their privacy under Article 8(1) of the ECHR, that is, the right to respect for private and family life, home, and correspondence. The respondent state – the government of France – agreed that the whereabouts regulations interfere with the fundamental substantive rights of athletes guaranteed under Article 8(1) of the ECHR. However, the government argued that the statutory provisions on the whereabouts system in the *Code du sport* are justified to ensure fair and equal sports competitions. In addition, the government submitted that the interference with the athlete's private life is necessary, reasonable, and proportionate to prevent the misuse of medication for non-therapeutic purposes and ultimately to protect the welfare of athletes.

The dispute described here follows a path common in most regulatory and disciplinary matters, where the key to resolution, regardless whether the applicable legal standard is international human rights law or statutory law, often lies in the balancing process between the competing interests of sport organizations, on the one hand, and athletes and other participants, on the other hand. Therefore, national and international association tribunals, sports arbitral tribunals (CAS), and ordinary courts must generally refer to the well-established legal principle of proportionality.

For example, CAS applied this legal principle in the case of Caster Semenya in order to determine whether female athletes with a high level of testosterone should be eligible to compete in the binary female category. The same weighing may be applied in determining the appropriate consequences and sporting sanctions of a sports rule violation. In this regard, the term "appropriate" already indicates that all circumstances of the individual case must be considered in order to determine the reasonable and proportionate sanction in due consideration of both the interest of sport organizations in fair and equal sports competitions and the interest of the athlete concerned in their economic and occupational rights.

The principle of proportionality is also reflected in Article 8(2) of the ECHR, which states that interference with the right to respect for private and family life of individuals may not qualify as a violation if it:

> is in accordance with the law and is necessary in a democratic society in the interests of national security, public safety or the economic well-being of the country, for the prevention of disorder of crime, for the protection of health and morals, or for the protection of the rights and freedoms of others.

Accordingly, in the whereabouts case before the ECtHR, the Court first came to the conclusion that the athlete whereabouts obligations do interfere with the privacy rights of athletes under Article 8(1) of the ECHR. This point was, as mentioned previously, undisputed between the parties. Therefore, such an encroachment on the individual rights of athletes can only be justified under Article 8(2) of the ECHR. In this regard, the Court held that the fight against doping is a legitimate aim as permitted under Article 8(2) of the ECHR. More specifically, the Court stated that the objective of combating doping falls within the categories of the protection of health and morals and the protection of the rights and freedoms of others in the pursuit of fair and equal sports competitions. With regard to the protection of morals and the rights and freedom of others, the Court held that:

> [t]he use of doping agents in order to gain an advantage over other athletes unfairly eliminates competitors of the same level who do not have recourse to them, is a dangerous incitement to amateur athletes, and in particular young people, to follow suit in order to enhance their performance, and deprives spectators of the fair competition which they are entitled to expect.

Therefore, in the following, the ECtHR had to address the question of whether the whereabouts system is necessary and proportionate in order to achieve the pursued objective of doping-free sports competitions and the athletes' health or whether these regulations go beyond what is necessary, reasonable, and proportionate to achieve this aim. The Court concluded that, amongst other things, unannounced tests are a necessary requirement in anti-doping in the light of the UNESCO Doping Convention which France has ratified.

The last question to examine was, therefore, whether the whereabouts system strikes a fair balance between the interests of sport organizations, national governments, and clean and honest athletes in fair and equal sports competitions or whether the interests of athletes in their right to private and family life under Article 8(1) of the ECHR prevail. In this regard, the Court ruled that despite the interference with the private life of athletes, the whereabouts regulations contained in the *Code du Sport* are proportionate and, therefore, justified in order to effectively tackle doping in sport. More specifically, the Court concluded that it:

> does not underestimate the impact of the whereabouts requirements on the applicants' private lives. Nevertheless, the general-interest considerations that makes them necessary are particularly important and, in the Court's view, justify the restrictions on the applicants' rights under Article 8 of the Convention. Reducing or removing the requirements of which the applicants complain would be liable to increase the dangers of doping to their health and that of the entire sporting community, and would run counter to the European and the international consensus on the need for unannounced testing. The Court therefore finds that the respondent State struck a fair balance between the different interests at stake and that there has been no violation of Article 8 of the Convention. (para 191)

In summary, this case shows the interplay between the competing interests of the stakeholders involved in sports matters. Courts, arbitral tribunals, and practitioners are tasked with the difficult exercise of finding the right balance between the competing interests of the parties to the sports dispute. In this respect, sports disputes are not fundamentally different from legal disputes in other areas of law. However, sports disputes are special in the sense that the freedom of association grants sport organizations a margin of appreciation to deal with all internal matters on their own and which must, thus, be considered in the balancing process.

CASE STUDY QUESTIONS

1 What obligations do sport organizations take on when they become signatories to the WADA Code?

2 Why is unannounced testing so important for anti-doping in sport?

3 How do the WADA Code and the anti-doping rules of the respective sports organization affect the private and family life of participants?

4 How does the ECtHR determine whether whereabouts requirements of participants are necessary and proportionate to protect the integrity of sport?

5 What competing interests did the ECtHR take into consideration when determining the legitimacy of whereabouts requirements?

CHAPTER 7

Strategic management

OVERVIEW

This chapter explains the principles, processes, and techniques of strategic management and their relevance to sport. Specifically, it focuses on the analysis of an organization's position in the competitive environment, the determination of its direction and goals, the formulation of strategy, and the issues associated with implementation.

DOI: 10.4324/9781003217947-9

After completing this chapter, the reader should be able to:

- Understand the difference between strategy and planning;
- Understand the core concepts of strategic management;
- Identify a range of tools and techniques relevant to strategic management;
- Specify the steps involved in the documentation of a strategic plan; and
- Explain how the nature of sport affects the strategic management process;

PRINCIPLES OF STRATEGIC MANAGEMENT

In the simplest terms possible, strategy is the match or interface between an organization and its external environment. Shilbury (2012, p. 4) conceptualized strategy as "a pattern of actions employed by managers to position an organization for competitive advantage". Strategic management is the "process of formulating the pattern of actions and implementing them" (Shilbury, 2012, p. 4). It is important to note at the outset that both strategy development and strategic management involve choices being made between alternatives. Experienced managers, faced with similar information and resources, may make very different strategic choices, something that ultimately separates good managers from great managers.

Johnson, Whittington, Regner, Scholes, and Angwin (2017) noted several important features associated with strategic decision-making:

1   Strategy affects the direction and scope of an organization's activities;

2   Strategy involves matching an organization's activities with the environment;

3   Strategy requires the matching of an organization's activities with its resource capabilities;

4   The substance of strategy is influenced by the views and expectations of key stakeholders; and

5   Strategic decisions influence the long-term direction of the organization.

These points illustrate that management of strategy requires a keen understanding of the organization's capacity, culture and circumstances, and environment, as well as the consequences of decisions. The aim of strategy is to help an organization achieve a competitive advantage through better choices, better analysis, better understanding of the impact of the operating environment, better recruitment of talent, and a myriad of other choices involved in managing an organization.

Strategy and planning are not the same. Strategy can be defined as the process of determining the direction and scope of activities of a sport organization in light of its capabilities and the environment in which it operates. Planning is the process of documenting these decisions in a step-by-step manner indicating what has to be done, by whom, with what resources, and when. In short, strategy reflects a combination of analysis and innovation, of science and craft.

SPORT AND STRATEGIC MANAGEMENT

Somewhat surprisingly, Shilbury (2012) found that published research articles on strategic management in sport were only a very small portion of articles published in the leading sport management journals. Nevertheless, strategy is a key function of sport management practitioners and is an important process to understand. One of the biggest issues in sport strategy comes in finding the balance between two or more divergent obligations. For example, sport organizations such as national governing bodies of sport commonly seek both elite success as well as improved participation levels. Deploying resources to both of these commitments may be difficult from a strategic viewpoint because they are not necessarily compatible. International success for a particular sport is assumed to motivate people to participate. However, the retention of new participants in sport tends to be poor in the medium term and negligible in the longer term and rely on new capacity being available such as new facilities, coaches, and officials to meet any increase demand. Strategic management in sport also involves a lot of stakeholder engagement and communication to be successful, as this first In Practice example illustrates.

In Practice 7.1 Softball Canada

Formulating a strategic plan for any sport organization, let alone a complex national governing body for sport, requires a significant investment of time and political nous to ensure all the relevant stakeholders are "on board" with the overall direction of the sport. The latest strategy for Softball Canada covering 2019 to 2022 contains the usual details one would expect in such a plan around building participation in the sport, supporting elite performance, generating greater capacity from the member organizations that make up softball, and supporting greater stakeholder engagement. What is interesting is that the plan details the *process* that Softball Canada used to generate the plan – no doubt to illustrate its careful development but also to show stakeholders within the softball community that the plan was widely shared and that many people had the opportunity to shape its development. The following is an edited extract from that process description.

> Softball Canada's previous Strategic Plan took in the period of 2015 to 2018. That Plan utilized an extensive consultation process that generated input from a variety of constituents. Two elements were produced, the Strategic Plan and an associated Operational Plan which provided for specific actions to reach the Success Measures for the Quadrennial. The review at the end of 2018 showed that a significant majority of success measures had been achieved or had shown progression towards being fully accomplished.

> Looking towards the 2019–2022 process, the objective was once again to get as wide a consultation process as possible so that all interested stakeholders had the opportunity to be heard and be a part of the final product.

A Planning Facilitator, who had successfully guided us through the previous Planning process was again contracted to help us develop the new Plan. The process began with the development of an on-line survey which went out January 2018 to Provincial/Territorial Presidents, Executive Directors, and Softball Canada's Board and Staff. Responses came in from 41 of the 42 people canvassed. Those responses were tabulated and then presented at the Softball Canada Board meeting at the end of February. At that meeting the Board and Staff reviewed the responses and worked through framing a template of the new Plan. This process included reviewing and refining the Vision, Mission, Operating Principles, and Values from the previous Plan and incorporating feedback from the survey and comments from those in the meeting. At the meeting, it was decided to retain the 4 Pillar approach to the Plan but remove the word Enhanced from each Pillar – Participation, Excellence, Capacity and Excellence. A preliminary look at Success Measures for each Pillar was also undertaken. A summary document was then produced and reviewed.

The need to provide stakeholders with meaningful and authentic opportunities to engage with the process of developing a strategy also involved surveying stakeholders in the summer of 2018:

The survey was widely circulated through Softball Canada email lists, social media channels, and through those same avenues by our Provincial/Territorial members. The resulting 885 responses provided excellent feedback to the process and were summarized in a document which was shared with our Provincial/ Territorial partners, Board and Staff. As part of that sharing process and in order to continue to facilitate the feedback process, a series of small focus groups were held by phone with our Provincial/Territorial Presidents, Executive Directors, and any Technical Staff they wished to identify. The survey results were reviewed, and the opportunity was provided for any additional input on the Plan development. Seven Provincial/ Territorial Presidents and 11 Staff members took part, with 11 member associations represented.

In November at the Annual Meeting in Montreal, a full day session was held with Provincial/Territorial Presidents, Executive Directors and the Softball Canada Board and Staff to move the Plan to a more finished product. This was followed by a workshop that included the wider group of Annual Meeting delegates. Following these sessions, [the consultant] completed a template of the Plan for final refinement.

Softball Canada Staff met in December and provided some minor additions/ revisions to the Plan and began the process of developing a corresponding Operational Plan, with work continuing into the new year.

The final draft of the Strategic Plan and the Operational Plan were then reviewed at the March 1, 2019 Board meeting, with minor revisions being done prior to the acceptance of both documents.

Source: Softball Canada website at https://softball.ca/_uploads/5cc345388c2e0.pdf

THE STRATEGIC MANAGEMENT PROCESS

Strategic management involves four related stages – strategic analysis, making strategic choices, strategy formulation, and strategy implementation. In the first of these stages, the sport manager must first make an assessment of the operating environment and context of their organization. They do this by studying the capacities and deficiencies of their own organization, competing organizations, stakeholder groups, and the business environment.

Using the information obtained from the first stage, the sport manager must make some decisions about the future, weighing up various options as part of making strategic choices. These are typically articulated into a "mission" statement recording the purpose of the organization, a "vision" statement of the organization's long-term ambitions, and a set of objectives with measures to identify the essential achievements along the way to the vision. The examples throughout this chapter and in the case studies illustrate how pervasive this approach is within the sport industry around the world.

Choosing a direction determines what an organization wants to achieve. In the next step, strategy formulation, the sport manager must consider how the direction can be realized. This is the most creative part of the strategic management process and can involve many stakeholders to engage with each other to decide the best actions for the organization. At this time, sport manager's attempt to match the unique circumstances of the organization to its unique environmental conditions.

With a clear direction and plan for how that can be achieved, the task of the sport manager turns to implementation. This is where the resources, assets, and capability of the organization are actively managed to deliver the strategy.

STRATEGIC ANALYSIS

One of the biggest challenges facing sport managers lies with combating the desire to set strategy immediately and to take action without delay. While a call to action is a natural inclination for motivated managers, many strategies can fail because the preliminary work has not been done properly. This preliminary work entails a comprehensive review of the internal and external environments. The most common tools employed by organizations for this include: 1) SWOT analysis, 2) stakeholder and customer needs analysis, 3) competitor analysis, and 4) the five forces analysis.

SWOT analysis

One of the basic tools in the environmental analysis is called the SWOT analysis. This form of analysis helps to examine an organization's strategic position from the inside to the outside. The SWOT technique considers the strengths, weaknesses, opportunities, and threats that an organization possesses or faces. There are two parts to the SWOT analysis. The first part represents the internal analysis of an organization, which can be summarized by its *strengths* and *weaknesses*. It examines those things that an organization has control over, some of which are performed well and can be viewed as capabilities (strengths), while others are more difficult to do well and can be seen as deficiencies (weaknesses). The second part of the SWOT technique is concerned with external factors, those which the organization has little or no direct control over. These are divided into *opportunities* and *threats*. In other words, issues and environmental circumstances arise that can either be exploited or managed.

Given that the strengths and weaknesses part of the analysis concerns what goes on inside the organization, it has a time orientation in the present: what the organization does right now. Strengths can be defined as resources or capabilities that the organization can use to achieve its strategic direction. Common strengths may include committed coaching staff, a sound membership base, or a good junior development program. Weaknesses should be seen as limitations or inadequacies that will prevent or hinder the strategic direction from being achieved, such as poor training facilities, inadequate sponsorship, or a diminishing volunteer workforce.

In contrast, the opportunity and threats analysis has a future-thinking dimension because of the need to consider what is about to happen. Opportunities are favourable situations or events that can be exploited by the organization to enhance its circumstances or capabilities, such as new government grants, the identification of a new market or potential product, or the chance to appoint a new staff member with unique skills. Threats are unfavourable situations that could make it more difficult for the organization to achieve its strategic direction, such as new regulations that will add costs to an organization, new competitors, or shifts in consumer preferences.

Stakeholder and customer needs analysis

Before an analysis of the environment is complete, an assessment of the organization's stakeholders and customers remains essential. Stakeholders are all the people and groups that have an interest in an organization, including its employees, players, members, league or affiliated governing bodies, government agencies, facility owners, sponsors, media rights holders, or fans. Careful assessment and management of these possibly competing stakeholder interests is an important part of the process of making strategic choices and for the distribution of limited resources.

Competitor analysis

Opportunities and threats can encompass anything in the external environment, including the presence and activities of competitors. Because the actions of competitors can greatly affect the success of a strategic approach, *competitor analysis* ensures that an investigation

TABLE 7.1 Competitor analysis dimensions

Dimension	Description
Geographic Scope	Location and overlap
Vision and Intent	Ranges from survival to attempts at dominance
Objective	Short- to medium-term intentions
Market Share and Position	From small player to virtual monopolist
Strategy	Methods of gaining a competitive advantage
Resources	Volume and availability
Target Market	To whom the products and services are directed
Marketing Approach	The products and services and the promotions, pricing, and distribution behind them

is conducted systematically. There are many forms of competitor analysis; however, most competitor analyses consider the following dimensions, as summarized in Table 7.1. For each competitor, these eight dimensions should be considered.

Five forces analysis

An extension of the competitive environment analysis is the *five forces analysis*, which was developed by Michael Porter. It is the most commonly used tool for describing the competitive environment. The technique does this by focusing upon five competitive forces (Porter, 1980).

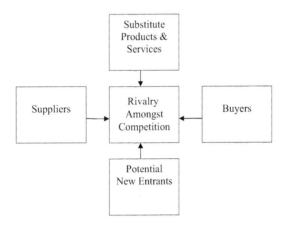

FIGURE 7.1 Five forces competitive analysis

The threat of new entrants: Most organizations are faced with the possibility that new competitors could enter their industry at any time. In some forms of professional sport, this is unlikely, as the barriers preventing entry are very high. For example, it would be extremely difficult for a private independent league to enter the market against any of the professional football leagues in Europe. On the other hand, new sport facilities, events, sport apparel companies, and equipment manufacturers are regular entrants in the sport industry.

The bargaining power of buyers: Buyers are those individuals, groups, and companies that purchase the products and services that sport organizations offer. The nature of the competitive environment is affected by the strength, or bargaining power, of buyers. For example, most football fans in the United Kingdom hold relatively little power in relation to the choices made by their clubs. Despite some extravagant sums paid by broadcasters and streaming services for the media rights of certain sports, the bargaining power of media buyers should be relatively strong. For most sport organizations, however, the chief buyers – fans – do not work together to leverage their power, and therefore the bargaining power of buyers is limited.

The bargaining power of suppliers: When suppliers of raw materials essential to sporting organizations threaten to raise prices or withdraw their products or services, they are attempting to improve their bargaining power. This may come from suppliers of the materials necessary in the building of a new facility or from sporting equipment suppliers. The most important supplier issue in sport has arguably come about with the unionization of professional players in an attempt to increase their salaries and thus the total salary pool paid by clubs. Where player groups have been well organized, their bargaining power has proven significant.

The threat of substitute products and services: Increasingly, the traditional sport industry sectors are expanding, and it is more common for different sports to compete against each other. When this threat is high, a sport organization is faced with the problem of being out-competed by other kinds of sports or, worse, by other forms of leisure activity.

The intensity of rivalry among competitors in an industry: The more sport organizations offering virtually identical products and services, the higher the intensity of rivalry. For example, in the sport shoe marketplace, the rivalry between Nike and Adidas is extremely intense. Rivalry is more ambiguous between sport clubs in the same league that share a general geographical region, for example, London football clubs, Melbourne Australian football clubs, and colleges in the same state in the United States. In these cases, it is unlikely that one club would be able to "steal" supporters from another local club. Nor is the alumnus of one college likely to start attending home games of another college team. However, these clubs do compete for media exposure, corporate sponsorship, players, coaches, managers, and management staff.

STRATEGIC CHOICES

Once the strategic analysis has been completed, strategic choices must be made. There are four conventional tools used to clarify and document these choices: 1) mission statement, 2) vision statement, 3) organizational objectives, and 4) performance measures.

Mission statements

A *mission statement* identifies the purpose of an organization. While it may seem strange to need to put this in writing, such a statement reduces the risk of strategic confusion. For example, players, members, spectators, staff, coaches, media, sponsors, and government representatives may all hold different interpretations of the purpose of a sport organization. The mission statement should define why an organization was established, what services and products it provides, and for whom it provides them. When reduced to a single statement, this mission is a powerful statement of intention and responsibility.

Vision statements

Making strategic choices, sometimes bold ones, literally can mean setting a vision for new direction for an organization. Thinking in this manner means being able to interpret the information collected during the analysis stage and determine the opportunities it presents. A *vision statement* captures the culmination of this kind of thinking. The statement is an expression of what the organization wants to achieve within a period of around three to five years.

Organizational objectives

Given that the vision statement is a reflection of the medium- to long-term ambitions of an organization, *organizational objectives* serve as markers on the way to this destination. Objectives reflect the achievements that must be accomplished in order to realize the vision. For example, if a club is situated at the bottom of the championship ladder, their vision might be to finish in the top three. However, achieving this vision inside a single season is unrealistic, so an objective might indicate the ambition to improve incrementally each season as a progression toward the overarching vision. Objectives are normally set in each of the major operational areas of an organization, such as on-field performance, youth development, finances, facilities, marketing, and human resources. However, it is essential that objectives stay measurable.

Performance measures

Key performance indicators (KPIs) are used in combination with organizational objectives in order to establish success or failure. KPIs are therefore inseparable from objectives and should be created at the same time. Each time a performance measure is used, care should be taken to ensure that it can indeed be measured in a concrete way. For example, a marketing objective of "improving the public image" of an organization is meaningless unless it is accompanied by something quantifiable. It is worth noting that measures do not have to focus exclusively on outputs like volumes, rankings, and trophies. They can also be used to measure efficiency; that is, doing the same with less or doing more with the same resources.

In Practice 7.2 British Equestrian Federation

The British Equestrian Federation is the national governing body for horse sports in the United Kingdom, affiliated with the Federation Equestre Internationale (FEI), the international governing body of equestrian sports. It exists to provide leadership, vision, and purpose in steering the direction of equestrianism. It is an umbrella organization representing the interests of 3 million riders, vaulters and carriage, drivers in Great Britain via 18 independent member bodies.

As a national governing body, British Equestrian works on policy issues with the FEI. It coordinates the British calendar of international events, disciplinary procedures, and doping control and oversees the training of British international judges, stewards, vets, and course designers. British Equestrian is responsible for distributing government funding to the equestrian sports. Funding from UK Sport and Sport England supports British Equestrian's work, from developing elite riders aiming to win medals for Great Britain to encouraging complete beginners from a range of backgrounds to get involved. Funding support is also provided by Sport Scotland for horsescotland, aligned with British Equestrian.

To organize these many disparate groups that make up British Equestrian, they created a national strategic plan for 2020–2024 that sets out seven strategic imperatives. As the chair noted in their introduction to the plan, these were:

> developed through a process of active dialogue and consultation with all key stakeholders and has the unanimous commitment of our Members through whom we will deliver these strategies. Our operational plans will provide more clarity on how our strategies will be delivered with clear measurements and timelines.

The seven strategic imperatives are:

- SPORT REPRESENTATION AND INSPIRATION – To be a leading nation in World Equestrian Sport.
- STANDARDS AND GOOD GOVERNANCE – To ensure that our sport delivers the highest ethical standards for all participants (both human and equine), enabling all – at all levels – to participate safely, fairly and be treated with dignity and respect. Ensuring that in all we do we are positively impacting on the lives of horses and people.
- WELFARE OF HORSE AND HUMAN – To ensure the highest standards of welfare are promoted and applied to both equines and humans, whatever their involvement in equestrianism.
- PARTICIPATION – To understand the benefits of equestrianism to people and use this to engage effectively with funders, partners and current and potential participants. To encourage new and continued involvement in equestrianism throughout peoples lives and to ensure a sustainable and thriving equestrian industry to support this.
- DEVELOPMENT AND PROMOTION OF EQUESTRIANISM – To communicate the benefits of equestrianism to a wide audience to deepen understanding of the value

that the sector provides in all forms. To engage effectively with Government, funders, media, current and potential partners and current and potential participants to encourage new and continued support for and involvement in equestrianism.

- COMMERCIALISM AND SUSTAINABILITY – We will support our Members to be – and ensure that we are – financially sustainable through economies of scale and leveraging additional sources of income.
- EQUINE DEVELOPMENT – Improved breeding and management of performance horses for all disciplines represented by Members; from Pony Club ponies to world-class competition horses

The seven imperatives act as the focus for effort and investment decisions, but the process of debate and dialogue to agree on them is equally important when establishing a strategy for a large and complex organization like British Equestrian.

Source: British Equestrian Strategic Plan at www.britishequestrian.org.uk/assets/About%20 the%20BEF/BEF_Strategy_Document_FINAL.pdf

STRATEGY FORMULATION

After making the big decisions about where to go, the next question is how to get there for an organization. In the strategy formulation stage of the strategic management process, sport managers must consider the implications of each potential approach. To help matters, however, from a strategic positioning viewpoint, there are a finite number of strategies available to the sport manager, especially in the strictly commercial context. Porter (1985) contended that there are only three fundamental or generic strategies that can be applied in any organization, irrespective of their industry, products and services, environmental circumstances, and resources. Sport organizations must take a position in the marketplace, preferably one that is both opportune *and* advantageous. As a result, some sport organizations choose to compete with cheaper prices; others compete on the basis of a unique product or service that is hard for others to replicate; others attempt to position themselves as the exclusive supplier in the marketplace. The key to making a decision between these three alternatives returns to the analysis and strategic choice stages of the strategic management process. Part of the choice is in determining what the sport organization is likely to be able to do better than others: their competitive advantage (like keeping costs low or delivering great customer service). The other part is in finding the opportunity in the environment that is worth exploring, perhaps where no other sport organization is offering a service, product, or unique experience.

STRATEGY IMPLEMENTATION

Strategy implementation represents the introduction of the organization's choice of competitive strategy. For example, if a differentiation strategy has been selected, the implementation stage considers how it can be brought about across the organization's products, services, and activities. There is an important distinction to be made here between the strategic level of decision-making and the implementation level.

Effective implementation of the strategy relies on each part of the organization being clear on its role; being adequately resourced to perform its role; and having the right organizational culture, leadership, and support systems in place. These concepts are covered in detail in other chapters.

In Practice 7.3 Resetting Australian hockey

Field hockey in Australia has struggled to increase participation and commercial sustainability despite more than 20 years of sustained international success of the iconic men's and women's national teams – the Kookaburras and Hockeyroos. Their 2019 to 2022 Strategic Plan was developed to not only improve the usual suspects you would find in plan for a national governing body for sport – increased participation and elite success – it also focused on revitalizing hockey as a united national organization along contemporary business principles. Their six strategic priorities were:

1 Address the inefficiencies in our sport
2 Improve participant recruitment and retention
3 Ensure sustained international success
4 Increase the visibility and commercial viability of hockey
5 Enhance the digital experience
6 Safeguard the integrity of our sport

It is telling that three of the six priorities are about improving the capability and capacity of the organization to serve its members. With regard to addressing the inefficiencies in hockey, the plan outlines some changes to fundamental business practices – using a common chart of accounts, reviewing policies and procedures, auditing capability among the member organizations, sorting procurement and supply arrangements, and developing a more efficient future operating model for the sport.

With regard to enhancing the digital experience, the plan provides the following commentary on the importance of delivering on that priority:

> Hockey Australia has some ground to make up in the digital space if we want to deliver the right products, services and content to the right people at the right time – but that is our plan. We recognise that we will have to make changes as a matter of urgency as our current systems do not meet the future requirements of the hockey community.

> The digital revolution has demanded that sports move with the times and address the way it engages with participant communities, volunteers, fans, clients and consumers. We recognise the need to generate a single view of our customers if we are to be better connected and improve our service offering.

We also appreciate the need to ensure our systems are streamlined and deliver efficiencies across the sport including players, club administrators and league managers. We want to deliver technology solutions to make it easier for all aspects of hockey, particularly to volunteer administrators.

Where hockey has traditionally focussed on communication, promotion and participation, we need to make a deliberate shift towards building contemporary models that embrace online communities, enhances fan engagement and delivers hockey as an entertainment product.

As a matter of urgency, Hockey Australia intend to overhaul our digital presence and practices including pursuing full data integration across our platforms to deliver a single customer view within a streamlined ecosystem.

To address these shortcomings, the plan calls out the need to develop a customer relationship management system and redesign their digital assets and interfaces with their members and customers, as well as investing in new digital solutions for coach and official education.

The plan also calls out some ambitious goals to increase the visibility and commercial viability of hockey by building the profile of the sport and diversifying revenue streams:

By celebrating our heroes from our best players to volunteers and tomorrow's stars, we plan to build the profile of our sport and tell our story for more people to enjoy. Our commercial and communications strategy will be underpinned by the strength of our storytelling so that hockey is positioned as a viable commercial partner capable of delivering real value. User generated content will feature more prominently in the future as we want to encourage more people to share their stories, including our high performance players, club participants, coaches, officials and fans.

Hockey Australia will endeavour to diversify our revenue streams and decrease the level of dependence on the traditional channel of government support. We will explore additional revenue generation opportunities including the reactivation of the 'hockey foundation' to assist the sport in pursuing the delivery of targeted projects.

Source: Hockey Australia website at www.hockey.org.au/about/governance/ and the Strategic Plan at https://cdn.revolutionise.com.au/cups/hockeyaus/files/9qjlapaps3necdvi.pdf

SUMMARY

This chapter is concerned with the principles, process, and intent of strategic management. Strategic management in sport organizations requires preparation, research and analysis, imagination, decision-making, and critical-thinking. It demands an equal balance of systematization and innovation and in the sport context, careful management, and engagement with a range of stakeholders.

REVIEW QUESTIONS

1 Why is strategic management important in the turbulent world of sport?

2 What is the basic principle that underpins strategic management?

3 Why would government funding agencies like to see sport organizations undertake strategic management?

4 What is the relationship between a SWOT analysis and competitor analysis?

5 Why are stakeholders influential in the making of strategic choices for sport organizations?

6 Explain the differences between the three generic strategies.

7 What are the common elements between the strategies of In Practice 7.2 and 7.3?

8 Select a sport organization that has a strategic plan on its website. Conduct an analysis of this plan and comment on its approach to each of the steps of strategic management explained in this chapter.

9 Select a sport organization that you know well that does not have a strategic plan available. Based on your background knowledge, make comments under the headings of the steps in strategic management to illustrate your approach to forming a plan.

10 Provide an example where a new kind of organizing method in a sport organization could impart a strategic effect.

DISCUSSION QUESTIONS

1 Discuss the relationship between the processes of strategy and of planning.

2 Some commentators argue that strategic plans are outdated tools given the rapid pace of today's sport business environment. Do you think this is a fair observation?

3 Sport enterprises tend to serve stakeholders with diverse, even contradictory, agendas. Discuss how balancing these divergent needs can be managed through the strategy process.

4 Is the structure-strategy relationship in sport organizations old fashioned? How could new, more innovative organizing forms be employed for strategic effect?

5 How are new developments in technology affecting sport strategy? Discuss examples.

FURTHER READING

Anagnostopoulos, C., Anagnostopoulos, C., Byers, T., Byers, T., Kolyperas, D., & Kolyperas, D. (2017). Understanding strategic decision-making through a multi-paradigm perspective: The case of charitable foundations in English football. *Sport, Business and Management: An International Journal, 7*(1), 2–20.

Heinze, K. L., & Lu, D. (2017). Shifting responses to institutional change: The National Football League and player concussions. *Journal of Sport Management,* 1–44. doi:10.1123/jsm.2016-0309

Johnson, G., Whittington, R., Regner, P., Scholes, K., & Angwin, E. (2017). *Exploring strategy* (11th ed.). London: Prentice-Hall.

Juravich, M., Salaga, S., & Babiak, K. (2017). Upper echelons in professional sport: The impact of NBA general managers on team performance. *Journal of Sport Management,* 1–38. doi.org/10.1123/jsm.2017-0044

Porter, M. (1985). *Competitive strategy: Creating and sustaining superior performance.* New York: Simon & Schuster.

Rodriguez-Pomeda, J., Casani, F., & Alonso-Almeida, M. D. M. (2017). Emotions' management within the real Madrid football club business model. *Soccer & Society, 18*(4), 431–444.

Szymanski, M., & Wolfe, R. A. (2017). Strategic management. In R. Hoye & M. M. Parent (Eds.), *Handbook of sport management* (pp. 24–38). London: Sage.

RELEVANT WEBSITES

European Sport Management Quarterly at www.tandfonline.com/loi/resm20

Journal of Sport Management at https://journals.humankinetics.com/view/journals/jsm/jsm-overview.xml

Sport Management Review at www.journals.elsevier.com/sport-management-review

CASE STUDY 7.1

City Football Group

The City Football Group has ownership stakes in football-related businesses around the world such as football clubs, academies, technical support services, and marketing companies. In 2021, the CFG fully owned three franchises across the globe: Manchester City FC in the United Kingdom, Melbourne City FC in Australia, and Major League Soccer team New York City FC. It also had investments in Yokohama F. Marinos in Japan, Montevideo City Torque in Uruguay, Girona in Spain, Sichuan Jiuniu in China, Mumbai City in India, Lommel SK in Belgium, and Espérance Sportive Troyes Aube Champagne (ESTAC) in France. In 2021, it also welcomed Club Boliva as a partner club that enables it to access the CFG intellectual property and expertise but without the CFG having an investment.

The CFG is owned by Abu Dhabi United Group (ADUG – a private investment and development company belonging to His Highness Sheikh Mansour bin Zayed Al Nahyan) (77%), and by two global investment firms – the China Media Capital (CMC) Consortium (13%) and Silver Lake (10%). The CFG operates a single board that oversees the CFG operations. CEOs of the fully owned clubs report to the board via the CFG CEO, Ferran Soriano. Soriano has an MBA and business degree and speaks five languages: Catalan, Spanish, English, French, and Portuguese. As one of the leading architects of Barcelona's dominance of European football in the 2000s, Soriano is considered one of the best sport CEOs in the world. He started with Manchester City FC in 2012 and has transformed that club, rolling out the CFG global strategy to lead the group to on-field and off-field success.

As an unlisted private company, the CFG is not obliged to publish a comprehensive annual report; however, the Manchester City FC Annual Report for 2019–2020 provides real insights into the strategy of not only Manchester City FC but the CFG and how the COVID pandemic impacted its strategy. Part of the chairman's statement:

> The 2019–20 season marked our entry into the second decade of His Highness Sheikh Mansour's stewardship of Manchester City. It was a season in which we brought home silverware in the form of the community shield and carabao cup, finished second in the premier league and scored more than 100 goals. It was also a season which saw us welcome new US investors, Silver Lake. Their incredible track record in sport, entertainment and technology investment together with their confidence in our business and ambition for the future, make them a perfect partner.
>
> Whilst the trophies secured during the 2019–20 season are now the expected football hallmarks of a normal Manchester City campaign, they hide the far from normal reality that the whole world was plunged into in the early months of 2020. The emergence of COVID-19 sent shockwaves around the world and rocked the foundations of many companies, especially those dependent on connecting directly with large numbers of people. Like most organisations, we did not have a business strategy for a global pandemic. What we had, and still have, is a business that is fundamentally strong, with committed shareholders and with significant assets, built carefully over a decade and upon more than a century of history.
>
> Over time, our income streams have been deliberately shifted and diversified – our fan base and audiences are global as well as local, our physical and digital infrastructure strategies are mature, and our commercial partnerships are diverse in terms of regions, industries and structures. Our long-term approach has meant that we are now not wholly dependent on those income streams that have been most vulnerable to the ongoing impact of COVID-19.
>
> From a City Football Group perspective, we did not shy away from delivering on our plans and were also able to realise opportunities that might otherwise not have existed in an 'ordinary' year. This approach saw us make the

geographically-significant deal to acquire Mumbai City FC and the strategic football acquisitions of clubs in Europe.

Whilst 2019–20 produced financial figures none of us expected, or wanted to see, the year needs to be viewed in the context of both of the seasons that will have ultimately been affected by the pandemic. The expectation of ourselves is that we will return to profitability in the second of those COVID seasons, the 2020–21 financial year.

The CEO's message provides further insights into how the strategy was impacted by COVID, but they still continued to pursue their overall goals:

Our vision is to continue to grow our global footprint, and to be faster, better and more efficient both on and off the pitch. The expansion of City Football Group with the addition of Lommel SK in Belgium, ESTAC (Troyes) in France, a partner club in Bolivar and the deal to acquire Mumbai City FC in India during this period is a clear example. We are privileged to have the unwavering backing of our shareholders, who continue to support and look to the long term with patience. This includes Silver Lake, a global leader in technology investing, who we welcomed as a new shareholder in City Football Group in November of 2019.

Following the outbreak of the COVID-19 pandemic, our overarching priority was to keep our people safe. We put measures in place to protect them and the livelihoods of their families by preserving jobs and personal incomes without seeking to access public funds to do so. We worked very hard to deliver football in a way the world had never seen; games were played, and seasons finished. We also helped our communities locally and globally, including but not limited to the provision of the Etihad Stadium as a base for the National Health Service, the creation of online resources for children's home-learning, and the launching of the Cityzens Giving for Recovery campaign.

We are very proud of the way the City family came together in this period. It has been a difficult and uncertain time for so many reasons, but throughout our organisation, we saw the ability to remain calm and focused, to never panic, to work extremely hard and to be able to find innovative solutions when needed. We were also pleased to have positively resolved almost two years of uncertainty with the conclusion of our successful appeal against UEFA's ruling.

Like so many businesses however, there have been difficult decisions to make and there is not yet clarity on some issues, not least when we will be able to welcome fans into our stadiums. COVID-19 has impacted our financial performance negatively, losing revenue and delaying some planned businesses. Clearly, the 2019–20 accounts in isolation are not the best representation of the reality of the season with delayed player trading and numerous games being played after June 30th 2020, the revenues from which will be accounted in the 2020–21 period.

CASE QUESTIONS

1 Take a tour of the Manchester City FC and City Football Group websites. What sort of benefits is their global strategy of growth delivering?

2 What are the advantages of creating a global network of clubs under such a strategy?

3 The media coverage of City Football Group at times seems to emphasize the huge investment being made by His Highness Sheikh Mansour bin Zayed Al Nahyan, the owner of CFG, in this global strategy, suggesting money buys success. Do you think this sort of coverage is warranted and does this diminish the contribution that good strategy and leadership by a CEO like Ferran Soriano can make to transforming a sport organization?

4 Aside from buying or investing in clubs around the world, what other key aspects of the CFG strategy are in place to leverage these very high-profile investments?

Sources: Manchester City FC website at www.mancity.com and the City Football Group website at www.cityfootballgroup.com

CASE STUDY 7.2

British Basketball League: club cartel?

The top men's professional basketball league in the United Kingdom is the British Basketball League (BBL), which has been in operation since 1987. The BBL is an independent company owned by its member clubs, each with an equal shareholding in BBL that operates under a licence agreement from the British Basketball Federation. Each club has a representative on the BBL Board of Directors, who oversee the operation of a central BBL office in Birmingham, which manages administration, marketing, and media functions. In 2021, the BBL franchises were:

- Bristol Flyers
- Cheshire Phoenix
- Glasgow Rocks
- Leicester Riders
- London Lions
- Manchester Giants
- Newcastle Eagles

- Plymouth City Patriots
- B. Braun Sheffield Sharks
- Surrey Scorchers

Unlike other sports, where second-division champions are promoted to replace the bottom-ranked team in the top league, the BBL operates independently of the second-tier competition, the English Basketball League (EBL). There is no promotion or relegation between the BBL and the EBL, and EBL clubs cannot join the BBL based on their performances in official competition alone. However, EBL clubs and any other organizations can apply for a franchise from the BBL. Indeed, new franchise development is a cornerstone of the BBL strategy.

The organizational structure or franchise system used by the BBL is used because of the significant costs of running a team in the BBL compared to running any other team in the United Kingdom. The structure attempts to provide financial security and protect investment in clubs by removing the threat that comes with relegation. A salary cap and income distribution policy amongst BBL clubs also assist with competitive balance and financial management.

One of the unique aspects of the BBL is that the clubs cooperate to make decisions in the interests of the BBL in areas such as competition rules, criteria for new franchises to join the BBL, and future strategy. The BBL clubs meet twice a year to make major decisions but utilize a management board with an independent chair, two independent directors, and two elected BBL club representatives to meet more regularly and oversee operational decisions in conjunction with the professional staff employed by the BBL.

The BBL licence agreement with the BBF allows up to 24 franchises to operate, and clubs from other leagues in England, Scotland, and Wales are eligible to apply. The interesting aspect of the strategy of the BBL is that each club operates as a franchise in designated areas across the United Kingdom in order to maximize commercial and media value within their local community. Clubs can apply to join the BBL by submitting a detailed business plan to the BBL Franchise Committee that specifies

- Complete details of the business and how it will function
- Full financial projections, including cash flow expectations and potential revenue targets
- Details of the proposed company structure, including information on shareholders
- Management structure, including CVs of all key staff
- Information on how the BBL's performance objectives (covering areas such as quality of venues, community programs, and player development) will be achieved
- Details of any history of running a basketball or professional sporting club
- Full details of the proposed home playing venue
- In-principle agreements with the venue and any potential sponsors
- Outline of PR plan and marketing initiatives to create a viable basketball club

Successful franchisees pay a franchise fee upon entry of approximately £150K, payable over seven years, and they are equal shareholders in the BBL with all the other clubs.

Because government funding for basketball goes to the BBF, the BBL receives no government financial support. Instead, it derives its income from sponsorship, media partnerships, merchandising, and ticket sales. Commercial and media rights generate the largest portion of income for the league and clubs.

The BBL has introduced player eligibility rules to provide more opportunities for British players, with each team allowed a maximum of five over-18 non-British players per game. There is no national draft system; players are recruited directly by clubs from their development programs or via direct application.

In 2014, the Women's British Basketball League (WBBL) was created along similar design principles. In 2021, there were 13 franchises in the WBBL, some operated by universities and three aligned with franchises in the BBL:

- Caledonia Pride
- Cardiff Met Archers
- Durham University Palatinates
- Essex Rebels
- Gloucester City Queens
- Leicester Riders
- London Lions
- Manchester Met Mystics
- Newcastle Eagles
- Team Northumbria
- Oaklands Wolves
- Sevenoaks Suns
- Sheffield Hatters

The challenge of organizing viable professional basketball leagues for men and women in a country dominated by football, rugby, and cricket is significant. Competition for sponsorship dollars, access to appropriate venues, securing media rights, and maintaining market share in a crowded professional sport market are all challenges for the directors of the BBL, WBBL, and the managers of their member clubs. The strategy adopted by the BBL and the WBBL in using the US-style franchise system without any relegation and promotion to other leagues is an attempt to combat these challenges. The strategy allows the league and clubs to plan for future expansion, manage income and costs across all elements of the organization, ensure equitable decision-making amongst the member clubs, and provide enough territory for clubs to carve out a membership and supporter base in their respective exclusive geographic areas to maximize commercial and media value.

CASE STUDY QUESTIONS

1   Access the BBL and WBBL websites at www.bbl.org.uk and www.wbbl.org.uk and read about the history of the leagues. Why do you think professional basketball has evolved to this structure in Britain?

2   Why is one of the key strategies for both leagues to increase the number of franchisees and, therefore, change the structure?

3   What are some of the economic and market forces that both leagues needs to be mindful of in order to ensure success?

4   Do you think the leagues would be able to quickly modify their strategy? Why or why not?

Source: British Basketball League website at www.bbl.org.uk and WBBL website at www.wbbl.org.uk

CHAPTER 8

Organizational design

OVERVIEW

Organizational structure or design is a phenomenon that receives a significant amount of attention from managers as they seek to organize their staff and volunteers to optimize their impact on organizational performance and meet their strategic goals. Rather than replicate the myriad of existing material on this topic, this chapter highlights the unique aspects of the design of sport organizations. Consequently, this chapter reviews the key concepts of organizational design, provides examples of the unique features of sport organization designs, and summarizes the key research findings on the structure of sport organizations. The chapter also provides a summary of principles for managing organizational designs within community, state, national, and professional sport organizations.

DOI: 10.4324/9781003217947-10

After completing this chapter, the reader should be able to:

- Describe the key dimensions of organizational design;
- Understand the unique features of the structure of sport organizations;
- Understand the various models of organization design that can be used for sports organizations;
- Identify the factors that influence the design of sport organizations; and
- Understand some of the challenges facing managers and volunteers involved in managing the design of sport organizations.

WHAT IS ORGANIZATIONAL STRUCTURE?

An organizational structure is "a primary aspect of the implementation of strategy and how the organization ultimately functions in terms of information flows, decision-making and power distribution" (O'Brien & Gowthorp, 2017, p. 39). Every sport organization has a structure that outlines the tasks to be performed by individuals and teams. Finding the right structure for an organization involves juggling requirements to formalize procedures and ensuring accountability for tasks is clear whilst fostering innovation and creativity. The "right" structure means one in which owners and managers can exert adequate control over employee activities without unduly affecting people's motivation and attitudes to work. It also provides clear reporting, accountability, and communication lines while trying to reduce unnecessary and costly layers of management.

An organization's structure is important because it defines where staff and volunteers "fit in" with each other in terms of work tasks, decision-making procedures, the need for collaboration, levels of responsibility, and reporting mechanisms. In other words, the structure of an organization provides a roadmap for how positions within an organization are related to each other and what tasks are performed by individuals and work teams within an organization.

DIMENSIONS OF ORGANIZATIONAL STRUCTURE

When designing any organization's structure, managers need to consider six elements: work specialization, departmentalization, chain of command, span of control, centralization, and formalization (O'Brien & Gowthorp, 2017).

Work specialization

Creating roles for individuals that enable them to specialize in performing a limited number of tasks is known as work specialization. This concept can easily be applied in organizations that manufacture things such as sporting goods or need to process a large volume of resources such as distributing uniforms and information to volunteers for a large sporting event. The advantage of breaking jobs down to a set of routine repetitive tasks is an increase in employee productivity and reduced costs through the use of a lower-skilled labour force. This advantage must be balanced against the risks of making work too boring or stressful for individuals, which can lead to accidents, poor quality, lower productivity, absenteeism, and high job turnover.

The majority of sports organizations employ small numbers of staff who are often required to perform a diverse range of tasks over a day, week, or year. In these cases, the structure of the organization will require a low level of work specialization. For example, a sport development officer within a state or provincial sporting organization would be involved in activities such as conducting skills clinics with junior athletes, designing coach education courses, managing a database of casual staff, or representing the organization to sponsors or funding agencies over the course of a season. These roles require very different skill sets, and in such an organization, the structure would benefit from a low level of work specialization.

Departmentalization

Departmentalization is the bringing together of individuals into groups so that common or related tasks can be coordinated. In essence, people are assigned to departments in order to achieve organizational goals. Organizations can departmentalize on the basis of functions, products or services, processes, geography, or customer type.

The most common form of departmentalizing is based on assigning people or positions to various departments according to the function a person may perform. For example, a state or provincial sporting organization might group its staff according to athlete development, competition management, special events, and corporate affairs departments, with each department having a very specific function to perform.

Alternatively, a sport organization that manufactures cricket equipment may group its staff according to the product line it produces, with groups of people handling the manufacturing, sales, and service for cricket apparel, cricket bats, and training aids. In this case, the functions of marketing, human resource management, financial management, and production are all replicated in each department. These criteria can also be applied to service-based sport organizations. For example, an athlete management firm may offer a range of services under financial planning, career development, life skills, and public relations training. Again, each department would manage its own marketing, human resource management, and financial management systems.

Sport organizations can also design departments on the basis of geography. For example, the operations for a sports law firm may be split into departments for capital city offices or regions. Each of the offices or regions would have responsibility with regard to its operations in a designated geographical region. Finally, sport organizations can arrange their departments on the basis of their various customer types. This approach could be used by an organization like the Australian Institute of Sport, which might create departments that support individual athletes or team sports.

It is important to note that organizations may choose to use more than one criterion to devise departments, and their choice will depend on organizational size, capabilities, and operational requirements.

Chain of command

The chain of command is the reporting trail that exists between the upper and lower levels of an organization. In essence, it is the line of authority that connects each position within an organization to the chief executive. It encompasses the notions of establishing clear authority and responsibility for each position within the organization. Authority refers to the rights managers have to give orders to other members in the organization and the expectation that the orders will be carried out. If managers at certain levels of an organization are provided with the authority to get things done, they are also assigned a corresponding level of responsibility. Having a single person to whom an employee is responsible is known as the unity of command. Having a single "boss" avoids employees having to deal with potential conflict when juggling the demands of two or more managers, and it helps achieve clear decision-making.

Arguably, the basic tenets of the chain of command are less relevant today due to the increase in the use of information technology and the corresponding ease with which most employees can communicate with each other at all levels of the organization and access information that was previously restricted to top-level managers. Nevertheless, managers of sports organizations should be cognizant of the basic principle of the chain of command when designing their organizational structure.

Span of control

Span of control refers to the number of staff any manager can directly supervise without becoming inefficient or ineffective. The exact number any manager can effectively control is determined by the level of expertise or experience of the staff – the logic being that more experienced and skilled staff require less supervision. The complexity of tasks, the location of staff, the reporting mechanisms in place, the degree to which tasks are standardized, the style of managers, and the culture of an organization also play a role in determining what the ideal span of control might be for an individual manager in an organization. The span of control impacts how many levels of management are required in any given organization. The wider the span of control, the more employees can be supervised by one manager, which leads to lower management costs. However, this reduced cost is a trade-off with effectiveness, as this single manager must devote more of his or her time to liaison and communication with a large number of staff.

The trend over the past ten years has been for organizations to introduce wider spans of control and a subsequent flattening of organizational structures. This must be done in conjunction with the provision of more employee training, a commitment to building strong work cultures, and assistance to ensure staff are more self sufficient in their roles.

Centralization and decentralization

Centralization refers to the degree to which decision-making is located at the top of an organization. An organization is deemed highly centralized when the majority of decisions are made by senior managers with little input from employees at lower levels. Alternatively, an organization is decentralized when decisions are able to be made by employees and lower-level managers who have been empowered to do so. It is important to understand that the concepts of centralization and decentralization are relative, in the sense that an organization is never exclusively one or the other. Organizations could not function if all decisions were made by a small group of top managers or if all decisions were delegated to lower-level staff.

Nonprofit sport organizations tend to be more centralized than decentralized due to the influence of their traditional structures. Decision-making is often concentrated at the board level, where volunteers make decisions related to strategy for paid staff to implement at an operational level. This can lead to problems of slow decision-making or politics. On the other hand, the nature of nonprofit sport organizations, which are often made up of disparate groups and spread over a wide geographical area, requires local-level decision-making for clubs, events, and sporting competitions to operate effectively.

Formalization

Formalization refers to the extent jobs are standardized and the degree to which employee behaviour is guided by rules and procedures. These rules and procedures might cover selection of new staff, training, general policies on how work is done, procedures for routine tasks, and the amount of detail that is provided in job descriptions. Formalizing an organization increases the control managers have over staff and the amount of decision-making discretion individual staff may have. An organization such as a local sport club may have very few procedures or rules for how things are done, but the tribunal for a professional sports league will have a very detailed set of procedures and policies with regard to how cases are reported, heard, and prosecuted.

In Practice 8.1 Victorian Institute of Sport

The Victorian Institute of Sport (VIS) is funded by the Victorian state government in Australia to "provide leadership that enables talented Victorian athletes to excel in sport and life". Its self-proclaimed core business is to select talented athletes and work to optimize all aspects of their preparation to achieve world-class performances by:

- Providing a daily training environment with world-class coaching, management, and support services;
- Enabling access to high-performance training facilities and equipment; and
- Supporting athletes to compete in national and international competitions.

The VIS's organizational structure is directly linked to its strategy. The entire organization is based on a simple structure, with the CEO having three direct reports (or a span of control of three): a performance director, a corporate manager, and an executive administrator to manage sponsor and stakeholder relations. The corporate manager works with a small team to provide finance, technology, and facility services to the organization and a communication and marketing coordinator. The performance director manages four teams led by four managers – a performance manager (podium), who works with team of specialists to support the provision of coaching specialists to deliver services to a range of sports; a performance manager (pathways), who works with a team of providers (i.e., doctors, physiotherapists, psychologists) to support athletes; a physical preparation/sport science manager who works with a range of sport science specialists to support athletes; and a data intelligence lead.

It is clear that each of the four contingency factors noted earlier in the chapter have impacted the structure of the organization. The VIS has a very clear mandate to deliver professional services and support for elite athletes in a number of targeted sports. Accordingly, the structure reflects these core functions or strategic foci. Any increase in the number of elite sports or athletes supported by the VIS would not necessarily lead to a change in structure; rather, each of the existing teams would simply expand to accommodate the increased service requirements. As a government-owned enterprise, its structure is in part determined by its mandate to deliver services to the Victorian sport industry and is unlikely to be unduly affected by environmental uncertainty. The drivers of change in structure would include any significant shifts in funding support, strategy, or government policy, such as a move to focus on a selected number of priority sports, which would perhaps require a redesign in organizational structure.

Source: Victorian Institute of Sport website at www.vis.org.au

STRUCTURAL MODELS

The types of structure adopted by sports organizations can be categorized into four common types: the simple structure, the bureaucracy, the matrix structure, and the team structure. Let's examine each of these briefly and explore their relevance for sport organizations.

The simple structure has a low degree of departmentalization and formalization and wide spans of control and would most likely have decisions centralized to few people. Such a structure would be used by a small sporting goods retail store that might have ten casual and full-time staff and an owner/manager. There would be no need for departments, as most decisions and administrative tasks would be performed by the owner/manager and all other staff on the sales floor. The majority of procedures would be executed according to a simple set of rules, and the owner/manager would have all staff reporting directly to him or her. The advantages of the structure in this case are obvious: decisions can be made quickly, it ensures a flexible workforce to cater to seasonal needs and busy periods, and accountability clearly rests with the owner/manager.

If the owner/manager wanted to expand the operation and open other stores in other locations, he or she would require a different structure to cope with the added demands of controlling staff in multiple locations, making decisions across a wider number of operational areas, and ensuring quality products and services are provided in each store or location. The owner/manager might consider adopting a bureaucratic structure.

The bureaucratic structure attempts to standardize the operation of an organization in order to maximize coordination and control of staff and activities. It relies on high

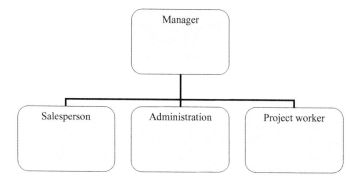

FIGURE 8.1 Simple structure

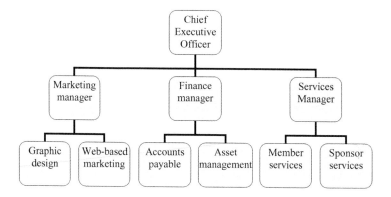

FIGURE 8.2 The bureaucratic structure

levels of formalization, the use of departments to group people into discrete work teams that deal with specific functions or tasks, highly centralized decision-making, and a clear chain of command. An organization such as Sport England, Netball New Zealand, or a state or provincial government department of sport would be structured along these lines. Obviously, as an organization expands in size, increases the number of locations it delivers services, or diversifies its range of activities, the more likely it is to reflect some elements of bureaucratization.

The matrix organization structure reflects the organization of groups of people into departments according to functions and products. For example, an elite institute for sport might group specialists such as sports psychologists, biomechanists, skill acquisition coaches, and exercise physiologists into discrete teams. At the same time, individuals in these teams might be involved in providing services to a range of different sporting groups or athletes, effectively creating two bosses for them. This breaks the unity of command principle but allows an organization to group specialists together to maximize sharing of expertise while facilitating their involvement in a number of projects or service delivery areas. The argument for this arrangement is that it is better to have the specialists work as a team than to appoint individuals to work in isolation to provide their services. While

TABLE 8.1 The matrix structure

	Football operations division	Corporate services division	Marketing division
Team 1	Manager 1	Project worker 1	Worker 1
Team 2	Manager 2	Project worker 2	Worker 2
Team 3	Manager 3	Project worker 3	Worker 3

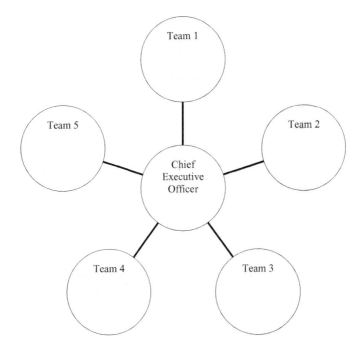

FIGURE 8.3 Team structure

this allows the organization to provide a range of services, it does increase the potential for confusion with regard to managing the demands from two bosses, which in turn may lead to an increase in stress.

A relatively new structural design option is the team structure. The team structure requires decision-making to be decentralized to work teams that are made up of people with skills to perform a variety of tasks. A football club franchise might employ such a structure with teams formed for club events or marketing campaigns, as it will allow quick decision-making with regard to finance, staffing, or impacts on players.

While these generic structures can be applied to all types of organizations, there has been some research that has attempted to categorize the various structures that exist within nonprofit sport organizations. Kikulis, Slack, Hinings, and Zimmermann (1989) developed a structural taxonomy for provincial (state) Canadian amateur sport organizations based on the organizational dimensions of specialization, standardization, and centralization. The evolution of Canadian sport organizations in the 1980s to a more professional and bureaucratized form prompted the researchers to attempt to establish exactly what form this evolution had taken. Kikulis et al. (1989) identified eight structural designs for voluntary sport organizations, varying in scale of complexity for the three structural dimensions. Theodoraki and Henry (1994), in a similar study, defined a typology of structures for British sport governing bodies. They too utilized the structural elements of specialization, standardization, and centralization to distinguish between various structural designs.

Identifying design types for national-level sport organizations was the focus of a study by Kikulis, Slack, and Hinings (1992) in which organizational values and organizational structure dimensions were used to identify three distinct designs – kitchen table, boardroom, and executive office. Each design represents a distinct mix of organizational values constituting their orientation toward private or public interests, the domain of activities conducted (ranging from broad participation based to a focus on high performance results), the degree of professional involvement in decision-making, and the criteria used to evaluate effectiveness. More recent work by Hoye, Parent et al. (2020) argued that these designs should now be developed using more contemporary criteria such as commitment to good governance, stakeholder involvement, and engagement as drivers of design. Parent et al. (2021) concluded that contemporary design archetypes for NSOs now included four types – board led, executive led, professional, and corporate.

Now that we have explored the elements of structure and the various ways they can be used, we can examine the factors that influence the structure adopted by a sport organization.

WHAT INFLUENCES THE STRUCTURE OF A SPORT ORGANIZATION?

There are generally four factors that influence the structure of an organization: strategy, size, technology, and environmental uncertainty. Each of these is briefly reviewed.

Strategy

In a perfect world, an organization's structure would be designed purely around the requirement to maximize the chances of an organization's strategic goals being achieved. This is rarely possible, but strategy does play an important part in determining the structure adopted by a sport organization. Whether an organization is pursuing an overall strategy of innovation, cost minimization, or imitation will necessitate the design of a specific organizational structure.

An important trend to note in the development of structure for nonprofit sport organizations has been the impact of the introduction of paid professional staff, a very deliberate strategy in response to increases in government funding in sport in most club-based sporting systems around the world. The impact of such a strategy on the structure of Canadian provincial VSOs was explored by Thibault, Slack, and Hinings (1991). They found that specialization and formalization increased after the introduction of professional staff but that centralization, after initially increasing, actually decreased over time. It was suggested that centralization increased because volunteer board members sought to retain control over decisions and then decreased as the relationship between board members and staff stabilized. Such resistance to changes in structure was noted by Kikulis, Slack, and Hinings (1995), who studied the changes in specialization, standardization, and centralization of Canadian NSOs over a four-year period. They found that incumbent volunteers resisted change across all three elements of organizational structure, highlighting the role of human agents and personal choice in determining organizational change outcomes.

Size

The size of an organization also plays an important part in the determination of what will be its best possible structure. Larger organizations tend to be more formalized, with more specialist roles and departments and more levels of management than smaller organizations. This makes sense, as managers need to implement greater control measures to manage the volume and communication of information in a large organization. Amis and Slack (1996) state that much of the research into the relationship between organizational size and degree of centralization suggest that as "organizations become larger, decision-making becomes more decentralised" (p. 83). In terms of nonprofit sport organizations, they also found that with an increase in size of the organization, control over organizational decision-making remains at the voluntary board level and concluded that a "central role of decision-making as a means of control and the desire for volunteers to retain this control" (Amis & Slack, 1996, p. 84) meant that the boards of many sport organizations were reluctant to relinquish control to professional staff.

Technology

Technology does have an impact on organizational structure. Robbins and Barnwell (2002) argue that if organizations predominantly undertake routine tasks, then there is a high degree of departmentalization and a high level of centralized decision-making. This appears logical, because non-routine tasks require decisions to be made at the level of organization where they actually happen. With regard to a sport organization such as a professional sport club, the increased use of information and communication technology means that it requires additional specialist staff such as video technicians, statisticians, and network programmers who may have replaced staff that used to perform tasks manually. The net effect is a higher level of departmentalization and specialization amongst the workforce.

Environmental uncertainty

Environmental uncertainty for sport organizations can be influenced by the actions of suppliers, service providers, customers, sponsors, athletes, volunteers, staff, stakeholder groups, and government regulatory agencies, as well as general changes in economic or market conditions. For example, if a group of professional athletes behave inappropriately, their actions can affect the ability of their club or team to maintain or develop sponsorships, which in turn may affect their ability to retain staff and hence require a structural adjustment. Similarly, a downturn in the economy can directly affect sales of sporting merchandise, and organizations may have to adjust their structure accordingly to reduce costs or change product lines.

There are some additional drivers of structural change in sport organizations that are worth noting. These include poor on-field performance; changes in personnel due to politics, competition, and market forces; government policy changes; and forced change via mergers and amalgamations. Poor on-field performance by professional sporting teams or clubs can lead to an end-of-season purge of playing or coaching personnel and may entail a review of how the group of staff involved in coaching, athlete support, or allied health services is organized. The political nature of some sport organizations that elect individuals to govern their activities can lead to structural change being implemented due to personal preferences of elected leaders or a mandate for change. Competition and market forces affect all organizations, but the interdependent nature of clubs operating within a league or competition necessitates them sharing information. Consequently, these organizations tend to be structured in similar ways, making structural change difficult. Governments may also change the way they fund high-performance programs or tie funding levels to the performances of international teams or individuals. Poor international performances may consequently reduce funding and therefore the capability of an organization to sustain its organizational structure. Finally, structural change may be forced upon sports organizations, either by economic conditions (such as population loss in rural areas, forcing clubs to merge) or government policy (such as forcing single-gender sport organizations to merge).

The earlier example of the Victorian Institute of Sport highlights how the four generic factors of strategy, size, technology, and environmental uncertainty can influence the structure of a sports organization.

In Practice 8.2 Netball New Zealand

Netball is the most popular women's sport in New Zealand and is governed by Netball New Zealand, which is responsible for developing and managing national programs for participation, coaches, umpires, and officials. Netball NZ is divided into five regional zones, with people playing at 83 netball centres across the country. In 2021, there were 140,000 registered members and over 300,000 people playing netball in New Zealand. As the national governing body for the sport, Netball New Zealand has a national board. However, the day-to-day running of netball is the responsibility of the professional staff, headed by the CEO and a team of five senior executives supported by approximately 30 staff, responsible for specific portfolios:

Chief executive officer

- Strategic leadership of Netball New Zealand and New Zealand's netball system

Head of commercial and business development

- Lead and drive commercial strategy
- Maximize growth of funding into the sport
- Managing commercial partnerships

Head of high performance

- Leadership, strategy, development, and management of NNZ's High Performance and Player Development Strategy and programs
- Direction to the zones and centres on player development
- Direction to the zones on their high-performance programs
- Monitoring and review of the Silver Ferns program

Head of communications and marketing

- Leadership and strategy for communications (all channels), media, marketing, and brand development
- Direction to zones on their communications, marketing, and brand strategy
- Development and protection of netball's legacy and heritage

Head of events and international

- International event and national competition leadership, strategy, development, and management
- ANZ Premiership delivery in NZ
- International relationships fostering international event and netball development, including Oceania

Head of community netball

- Lead the implementation of NNZ's community netball strategy to achieve growth and life-long participation in netball
- Responsible for the creation of all community netball programs, including umpiring, coaching, and bench officials that will lead to a strong and sustainable netball system throughout NZ
- Champion community netball in NZ in partnership with zones and centres

Netball NZ uses a very typical functional department structure, with managers responsible for specific functional teams aligned to the strategic priorities of Netball NZ.

Source: Netball New Zealand website at www.netballnz.co.nz

CHALLENGES FOR SPORT MANAGERS

An ongoing challenge facing sport managers is the need to strike a balance between lowering costs by using fewer staff and increasing productivity. This can be achieved through a greater use of technology for communication, data management and analysis, the appointment of skilled staff able to use technology, and the development of semi-autonomous work teams that are able to make operational decisions quickly. This requires the use of a more flexible organizational structure than perhaps is the norm for the majority of contemporary sport organizations.

A further challenge for sport managers is to ensure that their organizations are flexible enough to quickly react to opportunities in the market or to the demands of their stakeholders while at the same time maintaining adequate forms of control and accountability. Sport managers will need to establish clear guidelines for decision-making and acceptable levels of formalization for standard procedures without unduly constraining the flexibility to modify those guidelines and formal procedures.

An aspect of managing organizational structures that is relatively unique to sport is the presence of both paid staff and volunteers, often with volunteers directing the work of paid staff. Sport managers will need to be cognizant of the need to maintain close links between these two significant parts of their workforce and maintain a suitable structure that allows these groups to communicate effectively and work to achieve organizational outcomes.

Sport managers also need to ensure the structure can enable strategy to be realized. If strategic plans are devised, new markets identified, or new product and service offerings developed in the absence of concomitant changes to the organizational structure, then the ability of the organization to deliver such planned changes is questionable. It is imperative that sport managers pay attention to designing their structure to enable specific strategic directions to be achieved.

As illustrated in the previous chapters, organizations that work within the sport industry must work within a myriad of other organizations from the public, private, and non-profit sectors. Often, sport organizations have many stakeholders involved in setting the strategic direction of the organization. The organizational structure should therefore facilitate decision-making processes that engage all relevant stakeholders.

Finally, the interdependent relationships that exist between sports organizations that may be involved in a league, a collection of associations, a joint venture, or a funding agreement with multiple partners and sponsors necessitate organizational structures that reflect these connections. This may extend to establishing designated roles for external liaison within the structure or incorporating representation from members of external organizations on internal decision-making committees.

In Practice 8.3 Melbourne Cricket Club

The Melbourne Cricket Club (MCC) is a private club, incorporated under the Melbourne Cricket Club Act 1974, boasting by far the biggest membership of any sporting club in Australia at more than 132,000. In 2021, the MCC had 214,000 people on a waiting list to become a member, and while there is no definitive waiting period, the most recent intake of members had been on the waiting list for more than 23 years!

The Club also manages a range of diverse businesses, MCC Sporting Sections, where individuals represent the club in a range of community sports, cricket, the MCC Foundation, and the Australian Sports Museum.

The MCC has the public responsibility of managing the iconic sporting arena, the Melbourne Cricket Ground (MCG), home of many an Ashes defeat by Australia over the old enemy England and home to one of the world's great sporting events, the Australian Football League Grand Final, each September. It has also hosted the 1956 Olympic Games, the 2006 Commonwealth Games, Bledisloe Cup games between Australia and New Zealand, music events, and opera.

The MCG also houses the National Sports Museum within the Olympic Stand. The Museum has a number of exhibitions focused on Australian football, basketball, boxing, cricket, cycling, golf, netball, Olympic and Paralympic Games, rugby union, rugby league, soccer, and tennis. It also tells the MCG story and include an extensive interactive area that reinforces the MCG's traditional role as the spiritual home of Australian sport and curator of some of the finest sports-related memorabilia and interactive technology in the world.

The MCG is built on crown land and is a significant asset of the Victorian community. The Melbourne Cricket Ground Trust, established by the Melbourne Cricket Ground Act 1933, is responsible for the ground management of the MCG. Section 7(1) of the Act states "the function of the Trust is to manage and control and make improvements to the Ground at its discretion". In 2003, following the signing of the Management and Indemnity Deed between the Melbourne Cricket Club, the Melbourne Cricket Ground Trust, and the Treasurer of Victoria, the MCC is contracted to manage the MCG until 2042. Under the terms of the deed, the MCC has the exclusive rights to manage the MCG in accordance with the terms of the Management and Indemnity Deed.

The club's organizational structure is managed by the chief executive officer and consists of seven departments, with over 150 permanent employees and a pool of over 1000 casuals for event day operations:

- Club Services and Heritage – responsible for MCC membership services, functions, database management, rewards programs, and event services in the Members' Reserve. Also manages the Australian Sports Museum, MCC Museum, MCG Tours, and the MCC Library.
- Venue and Event Services – responsible for all events at the MG, including catering and hospitality, safety, security, ticketing, staffing, precinct operations, event operations, emergency management, and customer service delivery.
- Facilities – responsible for strategic and operational performance of the built assets at the MCG and MCC managed sites, including building services and turf management.
- Commercial Operations and Partnerships – responsible for enhancing reputation, branding, and commercial return at the MCG. This includes communications, publicity, marketing, community partnerships, brand and intellectual property management, corporate sales and commercial arrangements with sponsors, suppliers, advertising, and merchandise, as well as securing major events.

- Information Technology and Innovation – responsible for the delivery and management of information and communications technology, digital and broadcasting systems, network security, and operational integrity of systems.
- People and Culture – responsible for maximizing employee engagement and performance to assist with achievement of MCC business objectives, including employee support, organizational culture, recruitment and talent acquisition, learning and development, workforce capability, policy development, reward and remuneration, payroll, and employee relations.
- Finance and Business Performance – manages the finances of the Club's entities, including reporting, financial performance management, investment, compliance, financial integrity, and debt management. Also manages business intelligence, strategic and business planning, risk management, internal auditing, contract management, business resilience, and legislative compliance.

Source: MCC website at www.mcc.org.au

SUMMARY

Organizational structure was defined as the framework that outlines how tasks are divided, grouped, and coordinated within an organization. An organization's structure is important because it defines where staff and volunteers "fit in" with each other in terms of work tasks, decision-making procedures, the need for collaboration, levels of responsibility, and reporting mechanisms.

Six key elements of organizational structure were reviewed: work specialization, departmentalization, chain of command, the span of control, centralization, and formalization. In addition, four basic models for how an organization may use these six elements to design an appropriate structure were reviewed: the simple structure, the bureaucracy, the matrix structure, and the team structure.

The generic contingency factors that influence organizational design or structure – size, strategy, technology, and environmental uncertainty – were reviewed, as well as some unique drivers of change to the structure of sport organizations. Finally, a number of unique challenges for sport managers in dealing with organizational design were presented. Sport managers should be aware of these factors that drive structural change and the specific structural elements they can influence that are likely to deliver improved organizational outcomes and performance.

REVIEW QUESTIONS

1 Define organizational structure in your own words.
2 If you were to manipulate any of the six elements of structure, which do you think could have the most impact on the day-to-day role of the chief executive of a sports organization?

3 Do staff in small sports organizations have a low degree of work specialization? Why or why not?

4 Which structural model would suit a large sports event such as the Commonwealth or Olympic Games? Why?

5 How are organizational strategy and structure related?

6 How does a change in size affect the structure of a sports organization?

7 Compare the organizational structure of a sport manufacturing organization and a local community sports facility. How do each of the six elements of organizational structure differ? Which elements are similar?

8 Explain how environmental uncertainty can force change to the structure of a sports organization.

9 Interview the CEO of any sports organization. What is their most significant challenge in managing their organizational structure?

10 Explore the structure of a small community sport club. Are the principles of organizational structure outlined in this chapter directly applicable? Why or why not?

DISCUSSION QUESTIONS

1 What are some of the important issues that impact the structure adopted by a sport organization?

2 Why do sport organizations sometimes look to restructure themselves?

3 What are some of the common structural elements in place for national sport institutes across the world?

4 Should an organization's strategy drive its structure or the other way around?

5 Why do CEOs sometimes restructure an organization when they are appointed?

FURTHER READING

Amis, J., & Slack, T. (1996). The size-structure relationship in voluntary sport organizations. *Journal of Sport Management, 10,* 76–86.

Hoye, R., Parent, M. P., Taks, M., Naraine, M. L., Seguin, B., & Thomson, A. (2020). Design archetype utility for understanding and analyzing the governance of contemporary national sport organizations. *Sport Management Review, 23,* 576–587.

Kikulis, L. M., Slack, T., & Hinings, B. (1995). Toward an understanding of the role of agency and choice in the changing structure of Canada's national sport organizations. *Journal of Sport Management, 9,* 135–152.

O'Brien, D., & Gowthorp, L. (2017). Organizational structure. In R. Hoye & M. M. Parent (Eds.), *Handbook of sport management* (pp. 39–61). London: Sage.

Olson, E. M., Duray, R., Cooper, C., & Olson, K. M. (2016). Strategy, structure and culture within the English premier league: An examination of large clubs. *Sport, Business and Management: An International Journal, 6*(1), 55–75.

Parent, M. P., Hoye, R., Taks, M., Thomson, A., Naraine, M., Lachance, E., & Seguin, B. (2021). National sport organization governance design archetypes for the 21st century. *European Sport Management Quarterly*, 1–21. https://doi.org/10.1080/1618474 2.2021.1963801

Relvas, H., Littlewood, M., Nesti, M., Gilbourne, D., & Richardson, D. (2010). Organizational structures and working practices in elite European professional football clubs: Understanding the relationship between youth and professional domains. *European Sport Management Quarterly*, *10*(2), 165–187.

Theodoraki, E. I., & Henry, I. P. (1994). Organizational structures and contexts in British national governing bodies of sport. *International Review for the Sociology of Sport, 29*, 243–263.

Thibault, L., Slack, T., & Hinings, B. (1991). Professionalism, structures and systems: The impact of professional staff on voluntary sport organizations. *International Review for the Sociology of Sport, 26*, 83–97.

RELEVANT WEBSITES

The following websites are useful starting points for further information on the structure of sport organizations:

Australian Sports Commission at www.ausport.gov.au

Sport Canada at www.canada.ca/en/services/culture/sport.html

Sport England at www.sportengland.org

Sport New Zealand at www.sportnz.org.nz

Sport Scotland at www.sportscotland.org.uk

CASE STUDY 8.1

Hong Kong Jockey Club

Founded in 1884 as a membership club to promote racing, the Hong Kong Jockey Club is one of the world's leading sport organizations and one of the largest employers in Hong Kong. The Club operates a unique integrated business model of world-class racing and racecourse entertainment, a membership club, sports wagering, and lottery and donates the majority of its profits to charities and community causes, as well as being a major source of taxation for the Hong Kong government.

The Hong Kong Jockey Club is a company with liability limited by guarantee and has no shareholders. The Club operates horse racing in Hong Kong and, as authorized by the government, provides responsible sports wagering and lottery services. In 2020/21, after returning dividends to customers and paying betting duty and tax to the government, the Club donated 92% of its operating surplus to the

Hong Kong Jockey Club Charities Trust, which in turn donates money to charities and community projects.

The Club is governed by a board of stewards, all 12 of whom serve without remuneration. The stewards also serve as trustees of The Hong Kong Jockey Club Charities Trust. Responsibility for day-to-day operational matters is vested in the board of management led by the chief executive officer, who, in turn, has nine direct reports responsible for the varied departments or functions of the Club.

- Racing – all activities for horse racing, such as track management, equine welfare, regulations, veterinary services, handicapping, race program.
- Customer and International Business Development – betting control, lotteries, retail, and betting outlet services.
- Membership, Strategic Marketing and Branding – hospitality services, branding, marketing, membership services, and member experiences.
- Charities and Community – Tai Kwun Centre for Heritage and Arts and charities.
- Legal and Compliance – legal services, corporate services, and compliance.
- Finance – financial management, investments, procurement, commercial and contract management, and logistics and transport.
- People and Organizational Development – issues such as talent acquisition, talent management, learning and development, and analytics.
- Corporate Affairs – external affairs, government liaison, public and corporate communications.
- Information Technology and Sustainability – all issues related to information technology solutions, security, digital and social channels, information technology to support racing, wagering and lotteries, and sustainability.

The Club's website states that:

> The Hong Kong Jockey Club is authorised by the Government to provide wagering, via its subsidiaries, on horse racing and football and to operate the Mark Six lottery. This ensures that regulated channels are available to meet public demand for wagering and lottery services, thereby helping the Government to combat illegal gambling. It also ensures that any proceeds benefit the community as a whole, whether in the form of tax and duty to Government, proceeds to the Lotteries Fund, or through the Club's own charity donations. In 2020/21, this unique model of responsible wagering generated a total of HK$29.4 billion for the community. This included HK$24.9 billion to the Government in duty, profits tax and Lotteries Fund contributions and HK$4.5 billion in approved charity donations.
>
> In addition to the work of The Hong Kong Jockey Club Charities Trust, the Club reaches out to the community through events like The Riding High Together Festival, its flagship community event at Sha Tin Racecourse and Penfold Park, which seeks to educate and inspire Hong Kong people with a

positive can-do spirit. Drawing directly on its business design and sporting event management experience the Club also supports the development of equestrian sports and community football.

In support of the equestrian events of the Beijing 2008 Olympic and Paralympic Games, which were held in Hong Kong, the Club provided HK$1.2 billion to fund the construction of competition venues. It also provided equine services during the competition itself. The Club was subsequently named as an Outstanding Contributor. The Club was similarly recognised for its support for the equestrian events of the Guangzhou 2010 Asian Games. As a legacy it constructed Conghua Racecourse on the site. Building on this success the Club is now supporting the development of equestrian sport in Hong Kong and the region. This includes the Club's three public riding schools and its support for elite equestrian and para equestrian riders.

The business model of the Club has transformed enormously over the last 30 years, branching out from a racing-focused organization to now being one of the leading social institutions in Hong Kong. Through the Hong Kong Jockey Club Charities Trust, the Club contributes across ten areas of social need: arts, culture, and heritage; education and training; elderly services; emergency and poverty relief; environmental protection; family services; medical and health; rehabilitation services; sports and recreation; and youth development. Through its unique integrated business model and government-supported monopoly over racing, wagering and betting, the Club is able to make substantial charitable contributions. In 2020/21, the Club's Charities Trust approved a total of $4.5 billion HKD in donations to 528 charity and community projects, making it one of the world's top ten charity donors.

CASE STUDY QUESTIONS

1 Explore the website for the Hong Kong Jockey Club and it won't take long to get a sense of the enormous scale of the Club's operations. How does its current structure help it perform at such a high level?

2 How would you characterize the organizational structure of the Club?

3 Do you see any potential downsides to the Club operating so many diverse activities within a single organizational structure?

Source: The Hong Kong Jockey Club website at www.hkjc.com

CASE STUDY 8.2

Redesigning Sport New Zealand

Sport New Zealand (Sport NZ) and its wholly owned subsidiary, High Performance Sport New Zealand (HPSNZ), have a shared purpose – to contribute to the well-being of everyone in Aotearoa New Zealand. Sport NZ is the kaitiaki of the play, active recreation, and sport system in Aotearoa New Zealand, while HPSNZ leads the high-performance sport system supporting athletes and coaches to deliver performances on the world stage that inspire the nation and its communities, helping to build national identity and promote New Zealand internationally. As a crown agency, Sport NZ and HPSNZ promote and support quality experiences in play, active recreation, and sport, including elite sport, to improve levels of physical activity and, through this, ensure the greatest impact on wellbeing for all New Zealanders. Together, Sport NZ and High Performance Sport NZ provide end-to-end leadership of the system.

Sport NZ was established as a Crown entity on 1 January 2003 under the Sport and Recreation New Zealand Act 2002. Under the act, Sport NZ's purpose is to "promote, encourage and support physical recreation and sport in New Zealand". Sport NZ's statutory functions are set out in section 8 of the act and include investment, promotion of participation, support for capability development, and provision of policy advice.

HPSNZ was established as a Crown entity subsidiary by the board of Sport NZ in August 2011 with a mandate to lead the high-performance system. Its key objective is "making New Zealand the most successful sporting nation in the world by developing high performance sport". HPSNZ was established as a wholly owned subsidiary to enable it to dedicate its entire operational focus to high-performance sport, in particular to ensuring more New Zealand athletes win on the world stage. HPSNZ works in partnership with the targeted national sports organizations to deliver a high-performance system that enables athletes to excel on the world stage.

Both Sport NZ and HPSNZ have new strategies. Sport NZ has the Everybody Active 2032 and accompanying 2020–24 Strategic Plan, while HPSNZ has the 2032 High Performance System Strategy and accompanying 2024 Strategic Plan.

The Sport NZ Board is responsible to the minister for sport and recreation. The Sport NZ Board has accountability for the functions of the entire Sport NZ Group and oversight of the whole sporting pathway and ministerial engagement. To ensure group alignment, four Sport NZ board members also serve on the HPSNZ board. The chair of Sport NZ is also the chair of HPSNZ, the CEO of Sport NZ is an ex-officio board member of HPSNZ, and the CEO of HPSNZ is an ex-officio board member of Sport NZ.

As the "parent", the Sport NZ Board has accountability for the functions of the entire Sport NZ Group (including ratifying the key decisions of the HPSNZ Board) and oversight of the whole sporting pathway – from community sport through to high performance. The existing operating model was established in 2011 and is operated through a charter arrangement. The charter serves as a key link between the operating principles of Sport NZ and HPSNZ, where the relationship between the two organizations is based on partnership and collaboration.

Despite the creation of two separate entities and the rollout of two separate strategies by each organization, Sport NZ provides two types of services to HPSNZ: partnership services and shared services. Partnership services capture those services which are typically sector facing. The quality and value of these services is highly dependent on both Sport NZ and HPSNZ operating in partnership and collaborating where relevant. Shared services capture the provision of policy and corporate services to HPSNZ. They include policy advice, ministerial services, information technology, and human resources. Sport NZ and HPSNZ also enter into a number of joint procurement arrangements, including insurance brokerage, internal audit, stationery, motor vehicles, IT services, and so on. They also look to take advantage of all of government procurement arrangements where appropriate.

In April, 2021, a review to determine a new governance model and operational structure for these agencies was announced. The Terms of Reference for the review outlines the rationale for this decision:

> There are a number of reasons why a review is timely and appropriate:
>
> a) New strategic directions from both Sport NZ and HPSNZ promote an opportunity to ensure the best governance and leadership model is in place to deliver against the strategic plans that is cost effective and fit for purpose.
> b) Both the Boards of Sport NZ and HPSNZ are in full support of continuing to evolve the organization model to ensure its fit for purpose for the delivery of the new strategies, particularly in the context of strengthening and adapting the system, and doing things different and better.
> c) It has been ten years since the establishment of HPSNZ as a wholly owned subsidiary.
> d) The new strategies promote innovation which may lead to new investment approaches and engagement programmes.
>
> In addition to the above there is sustained pressure from the wider play, active recreation and sport sector to ensure that the model for the system is effective and efficient, and Sport New Zealand and HPSNZ's role within this continues to evolve. This is important to note as the Sport NZ Group cannot be successful alone. We work through and with others to achieve strategic

goals and outcomes. Working in partnership enables the Sport NZ Group to deliver more than it can on its own, it also ensures the system is strong and well connected.

The review has been tasked with reviewing

- Legislative and other obligations;
- Organizational visions and funding models;
- Key trends in areas such as participation and drivers of change – economic, social, and cultural trends;
- Structure – institutional and governance models for the play, sport, and recreation sector, and high-performance sector, to include learnings from Australia, United Kingdom, Denmark, and Norway as well as others that may be identified as part of the scoping; and
- Stakeholder engagement with an agreed-upon suite of stakeholders.

Key stakeholders identified in the terms of reference include what looks like half the New Zealand population:

- Minister for Sport and Recreation
- Ministry of Culture and Heritage
- SNZ and HPSNZ boards and staff
- NZ Olympic Committee (NZOC)
- Paralympics NZ
- National sporting organizations
- Regional sports trusts (RSTs)
- Active recreation organizations
- Māori representation, including national sporting organizations
- Young people
- Territorial local authorities
- Community funders
- Former CEOs of Sport NZ and HPSNZ
- Athletes and coaches, current and past
- The original authors of the 2011 model

The independent agency tasked by the advisory group overseeing the review will be required to produce an options analysis taking into account best practice of government-led institutional and governance models for the play, sport, and recreation sector, and high-performance sector, with particular focus on international models and the effectiveness and impact of Sport NZ and HPSNZ, including the parent-subsidiary operating model, since 2011, taking account of past reviews.

The review will provide a detailed current state analysis, including an assessment of the efficiency and effectiveness of the current model and the identification of strengths and opportunities for improvement and recommendations, including a proposed future state with cost estimations and implementation plan. The Sport NZ Board will approve a final position; depending on the nature of change recommended, further consultation may be needed.

CASE STUDY QUESTIONS

1 For a relatively small nation like New Zealand, what advantages were there in splitting off the responsibilities for high-performance sport to a subsidiary of Sport NZ back in 2011?

2 The terms of reference for the review are very comprehensive and point to the highly political nature of reforming national sport agencies. Given that each of the entities (Sport NZ and HPSNZ) have existing strategies in place, why does reviewing the structure matter?

3 Why do the terms of reference specifically require the review to address learnings from the national sport systems of Australia, United Kingdom, Denmark, and Norway? What relevance do they have for the New Zealand sport system?

4 What sort of criteria would you use to assess if an alternate structure put in place after the review is more successful than the current structure?

Sources: This case study has drawn extensively on content from the Sport New Zealand website at www.sportnz.org.nz, especially the Terms of Reference for the Review of Sport New Zealand and High-Performance Sport New Zealand Governance and Organisational Structure at https://sportnz.org.nz/media/3834/tor-final-for-review-16-april-2021.pdf

CHAPTER 9

Human resource management

OVERVIEW

This chapter reviews the key concepts of human resource management; explores examples of the unique features of human resource management within sport organizations, such as volunteer and paid staff management; and summarizes the key phases in the human resource management process. The chapter examines human resource management within commercial, nonprofit, and public sport organizations in order to illustrate core concepts and principles.

After completing this chapter, the reader should be able to:

- Identify the key concepts that underpin human resource management within sport organizations;
- Explain why human resource management in sport organizations differs across commercial, public, and nonprofit sport sectors;

DOI: 10.4324/9781003217947-11

- Understand each of the phases within the human resource management process; and
- Explain the ways in which each of the human resource management phases would be implemented in different sport organization contexts.

WHAT IS HUMAN RESOURCE MANAGEMENT?

Human resource management (HRM) refers to the decisions related to policies and practices that impact the relationship between the organization and people who are involved in the organization in some capacity (e.g. employee, volunteer) (Bach & Edwards, 2013). While the concepts that underpin human resource management are not particularly complex, the sheer size or unusual organizational structures of some organizations make human resource management a complex issue to deal with in practice. The sport industry encompasses an array of organizations that offer insights into the complexities of human resource management. From grassroots to elite sport, human resources are a necessity to achieve organizational objectives and offer sport participation and spectator opportunities and are critical for revenue generation. Without a dedicated and motivated group of individuals, sport organizations struggle to perform. People are drawn to work in the sport sector given its associated excitement, celebrity appeal, action, and passion, yet the culture of sport organizations is often fraught with stress, burnout, and extensive demands which compete with life-work balance (Weight, Taylor, Huml, & Dixon, 2021). Hence, the importance of human resources has been of interest to scholars and practitioners alike seeking to understand best practices of human resource management across various sport contexts.

Historically, the discipline of sport management has garnered credibility by drawing upon previously established management practices and theories from business. Business and management principles have shaped the broader sport system, as seen in the increased professionalization of human resource management strategies within sport organizations (Dowling, Edwards, & Washington, 2014). The transferability of these principles is especially applicable to professional sport organizations situated within the commercial sector that are profit-driven, such as the American National Basketball Association, Major League Baseball, or National Hockey League. Amongst professional sport organizations, successful human resource management is equated with profitability, long-term growth, and success (on and off the court, diamond, or rink). The public and nonprofit sectors increasingly draw upon similar principles. There are, however, significant differences between commercial, public, and nonprofit sport organizations, which can result in modifications to generic human resource management practices.

HUMAN RESOURCE MANAGEMENT PRACTICES ACROSS SPORT SECTORS

Commercial sector

The commercial sport sector (e.g., businesses, professional sport franchises, some major sport events) relies heavily on human resource management to attract and retain highly motivated paid employees. Professional sport organizations in North America such as the National Basketball Association, the National Hockey League, and the National Football League and sport organizations in Europe such as Formula 1 and Premier League require a wide range of staff (e.g., coaches, physical therapists, marketing professionals, accountants, managers, etc.) to function and grow their revenue. These for-profit organizations equate successful human resource management with profitability, long-term growth, and success. Achieving this is not necessarily done so at the expense of employees; however, human resource management focuses on enhancing the performance of employees in order to drive the business toward its goals and enhance profitability. One notable distinction in managing human resources in professional sport organizations in particular (versus other commercial non-sport organizations) is that within the staffing structure of a professional sport organization, the service producers (e.g., professional athletes) are amongst the highest-paid employees in the organization. In contrast, service producers within a non-sport organization (e.g., front line staff) would typically be paid much lower than senior management personnel. This is similarly true across entertainment industries such as film, where actors receive high compensation for their work and can create complex human resource dynamics.

In professional sport organizations, human resource management is changing to a more strategic approach centred on investing in holistic employee development and well-being because of its implications for employee commitment and retention at all levels of the staffing structure. Attracting, recruiting, and retaining highly talented individuals is an increasingly difficult task. Thus, offering perks such as flexible or remote work, generous overall benefit packages, and employee wellness programs or spending accounts are holistic human resource strategies that can aid in maintaining a strong workforce. Specific to the sport industry, player welfare and development programs that are designed to produce socially, morally, and ethically responsible citizens not only benefit athletes but are an intentional human resource strategy to produce better public relations and sponsor servicing. Athletes who behave well and demonstrate positive role modelling can enhance the reputation of professional sport teams and mean greater profitability for the franchises. Conversely, employers are now expected to invest in the personal well-being of their employees and take on a meaningful corporate social responsibility platform that aligns with the interests and values of the organization and its employees.

While the commercial sport sector heavily relies on paid employees, major sport events use a combination of both staff and volunteers. Events demand a small workforce of primarily paid staff for the rest of the year (events such as the Olympic Games or world championships require a permanent paid staff for many years prior to the event, but most staffing appointments conclude within six months of the event finishing). Volunteer contributions can help subsidize the amount of profit lost to paid labour and engage local citizens in the production of the event. In exchange, volunteers get access to a major event and can gain a diverse array of experiences. Major events such as the Olympics, Paralympics, PGA and LPGA, and Australian Open are, in large part, successful due to the contributions of volunteers. There is a large body of research in sport management examining event volunteers and their unique motives, barriers, and experiences. Given that different types of organizations will have varying capacity for volunteer management, it is essential to view volunteer management as a unique practice and tailor the experience to the needs and wants of the volunteer team. The rapid increase and decline in both staffing and volunteers within a one- or two-week period associated with a major sport event is complex and requires systematic recruitment, selection, and orientation programs in order to attract personnel and simple yet effective evaluation and reward schemes in order to retain them.

Public sector

The public sector provides public goods and governmental services that benefit society. The public sector is largely organized at three levels (federal or national, regional/state/provincial, and local/municipal/county). Public institutions offer sport and recreation opportunities for citizens and also require a human resource management function in order to support governmental services that impact the sport industry, including direct sport and recreation services, public infrastructure, education, and public transit. For example, in many countries, sport facilities are owned and operated by the public sector and leased or rented by other nonprofit or commercial sport organizations. These can range from local community-based facilities used by minor sport clubs to large stadia used by professional sport organizations. These facilities demand the expertise of specialized venue management staff (e.g., facility manager, ice operators scheduler, building maintenance, guest relations manager). Educational institutions provide sport participation opportunities at the elementary, high school, and collegiate level. Particularly in the United States, the collegiate sport system offers a large revenue source requiring a team of dedicated employees within their athletics department to boost ticket sales, facilitate game day operations, coach teams, provide student athlete academic support, and engage alumni. In addition, colleges in the United States that are regulated by the National Collegiate Athletic Association offer opportunities for student athletes to receive a fully funded education through substantial athletic scholarships raised by fundraising and advancement personnel.

In Practice 9.1 National Collegiate Athletic Association: the Fair Pay to Play Act

In 2021, the "Fair Pay to Play Act" overturned former amateurism rules to allow NCAA athletes to sell the right to their name, image, and likeness by accepting endorsements from brands and monetizing their social media presences. The desire for student-athletes to be able to earn alternative sources of income outside of their scholarship funding has been long fought for given that the NCAA is a multi-billion-dollar industry that makes its earnings off the talent of amateur athletes. Despite earning scholarship money, in some instances, the funding does not always provide a substantial enough income for cost of living, and their heavy training and academic commitment limits athletes from taking on part-time or summer student jobs.

From a human resource management perspective, this has implications for recruitment of athletes given the differences in NIL legislation across state lines. Some states have NIL legislation currently in place, whereas others do not. In instances where a state does not have NIL legislation, it becomes the responsibility of the individual college institution to develop a policy for athletes to follow. Without federal-level legislation, this leaves an ample grey area and confusion that may create inequities within the college system. In addition, this change in policy has implications for public relations and also presents potential difficulties for sponsorships to contribute to the whole team or athletics program in favour of sponsoring popular individual athletes with large followings. In conjunction with the athletics department, human resource management professionals will need to navigate how to manage the issues that may arise as NCAA student-athletes begin to capitalize on the opportunities the Fair Pay to Play Act allows.

In the public sector, human resource activities (orientation, recruitment, selection, etc.) do not vary as greatly as they may in other sectors, as staff are often used to operate diverse sports across all seasons. Depending on whether the sport is played indoor or outdoor, the sport might have a winter season (Australian rules football or ice hockey) or a summer season (cricket) or might be played all year (basketball). The regularity of the season and the competition, whether at the elite or community level, means that the paid and voluntary staffing requirements of sport organizations are predictable and remain relatively stable.

Yet, there are central differences across countries based on policies related to government funding allocation for public institutions. This can alter human resource functions, roles and responsibilities, partnerships, strategy, and organizational objectives. For example, the Canadian University sport system referred to as U SPORTS cannot offer full scholarships to varsity athletes. The government only allows a limited amount of funding to be allocated to students based on academic standing. At times, Canadian schools struggle to recruit talented athletes because of their lack of ability to offer the same scholarships as other universities internationally. This reward and recognition system may then have a significant impact on the relationship between athletes and their institutions, as they represent a key resource for public sector universities.

Nonprofit sector

The nonprofit sport sector (e.g., community sport, sport governing bodies) in countries like Canada, the United Kingdom, and Australia includes both paid staff and generally a large volunteer force of coaches, officials, board members, and sport administrators. As such, human resource management in the nonprofit sector requires an understanding of the specific needs of volunteers in comparison to paid employees (Hoye, Cuskelly, Auld, Kappelides, & Misener, 2020). Nonprofit community sport organizations have different organizational structures, some with paid employees, whilst others are entirely volunteer driven. In community sport organizations, a staff member responsible for general administration/registration is common. Depending on the size of the club, community sport clubs may have additional staff roles (e.g., executive director, technical director). State or regional associations may have more paid staff than community-level or even national-level organizations depending on the size and popularity of the sport, as these organizations are responsible for governance/strategic direction, insurance, club development, events, and so on. The differences in organizational structure often lead to diverse human resource management approaches, both formal and informal and, in some organizations, non-existent.

Staff-volunteer dynamics is one of the unique features of the nonprofit sport sector and requires unique management systems. In most cases, paid staff report to the board of directors, which is composed of volunteers (Hoye, Cuskelly et al., 2020). It is therefore crucial that the quality of relationships between volunteers and staff remain high in order to promote effective service delivery. Given their diverse roles and rewards, staff-volunteer conflict can occur based on communication problems, lack of trust, divergent attitudes, or perceptions of authority and vulnerability (Chelladurai & Kerwin, 2017). Managing these tensions through effective training and open communication is essential for enhancing staff-volunteer relations and a positive organizational culture (see a full discussion on culture in Chapter 11).

Volunteer management is a necessary function in nonprofit organizations to ensure volunteer well-being and satisfaction and to ensure safety precautions are followed during the selection process. Reference and vulnerable sector checks help to ensure that volunteers are safe to work with youth or vulnerable populations in minor sport or sport for development programs. Nonprofit organizations must invest in proper training for their volunteer managers as well as their volunteers in order to ensure they are maximizing volunteer engagement and creating a volunteer-friendly culture. Being mindful of the added commitment of training among volunteers is also important so that volunteers do not feel overburdened related to the demands of their role. These considerations are examples of the nuanced human resource management required in the nonprofit sport sector.

THE ESSENTIALS OF HUMAN RESOURCE MANAGEMENT

Human resource management in sport organizations aims to provide an effective, productive, sustainable, and satisfied workforce. Human resource management refers to the design, development, implementation, management, and evaluation of systems and practices used by employers use to recruit, select, orient, develop, evaluate, and reward their workforce. The core elements of the human resource management process are represented in Figure 9.1. It is important to keep in mind that these functions will differ significantly depending on the size, orientation, and context of the sport organization in which they are implemented.

Strategic human resource planning

Strategic human resource planning is a proactive approach to ensuring an organization is appropriately staffed with the right number and types of people needed to function efficiently and that these roles are integrated with the organization's strategic planning purposes (Trivedi & Srivastava, 2021) For sport businesses and organizations, the demand for

FIGURE 9.1 The human resource management process

a sport experience, product, or service needs to meet the supply. For example, Pickleball is a rapidly growing sport that has required an increase supply of facility space for courts as well as knowledgeable officials and league administrators. Intellectual or human capital is a critical asset that aids in the growth and strategic direction of an organization. Successful organizations incorporate human resource planning into their long-term and short-term plans as a way in which to forecast how human capital can contribute to the desired future direction and goals of the organization. This plan takes into account perceived rate of growth, new target markets, products, and services. Human resource planning then must match organizational objectives in order to operationalize the plan. In some instances, this may require organizations to develop entirely new jobs in order to accommodate growth, change, or new ventures within the organization.

In contrast, automation, computerization, and financial difficulties may lead to redundancy where there is no longer demand for certain skill sets or organizations need to recover from unprecedented financial impacts. The Football Association, English football's governing body, was set to make 142 positions redundant in 2020 due to the approximately 300 million euro revenue loss caused by the COVID-19 pandemic. Circumstances faced by the sport industry that resulted from the pandemic demonstrate the need to balance strategic thinking with flexible adjustments given present or contextual realities. Strategic human resource planning is truly a balancing act that is iterative in the management of human resources. Similar to preparing for a sport competition, human resource management requires a game plan; however, the plan does not necessarily always come to fruition when facing challenges such as gaining competitive advantage within the market. Successful strategic human resource planning should be done as a team process, not a single act, and will include support from senior management, involvement of all key stakeholders, alignment with organizational and department culture and vision, and creative thinking that can challenge the status quo and will address gaps and surpluses to meet future requirements.

Once an organization decides that a new staff member is required or a new position is to be created, the organization must undertake a job analysis in order to determine the job content (primary and implied tasks), requirements (skills, competencies, qualifications, and experience), and context (reporting relationships and job characteristics). Once the job analysis has been completed in as much detail as possible, the organization is ready to develop a job description (a document that covers the job content and context) and a job specification (a document that covers the job requirements, especially skills and knowledge base).

Recruitment and selection

Recruiting and selecting talented and well-suited individuals is a way in which sport organizations aim to create successful organizations. Human resource managers and recruiters take into account the requirements of the role, the cost valuation for paid employment or volunteer stipend, and the diversity of the individuals being recruited. In the sport industry, recruitment methods vary between sectors. Many nonprofit sport clubs reach out to parents of youth athletes to recruit their volunteer base. Public- and private-sector sport organizations often offer paid compensation, and professional recruiters reach out to individuals or use online sources to enhance the pool of job candidates. Some public institutions operate in a unionized environment, which requires them to offer the opportunity to qualified internal candidates prior to posting the job opportunity externally. Recruitment methods also include reaching out directly to an individual or human resource department in the organization, receiving employee referrals, advertising on social media, and utilizing online job listings.

Selecting and screening the right candidate for a position is at times a lengthier task and involves the process of condensing the candidates who applied for the position during the recruitment phase to a short-list and then selecting the best candidate for the role. The selection phase will usually include at least one interview of the short-listed candidates, which will supplement the application form and curricula vitae submitted by the applicants. These selection tools will be used to determine whether the applicant is appropriate in light of the job analysis and which of the applicants is the best person for the job.

An interview is the most common way of determining whether a prospective employee will be suited to the organization and the position. Depending on the geographic location of the applicants, the interview might be conducted in person, via telephone, via video conferencing, or via the Internet. Industrial relations/employment legislation covers a range of organizational and employment issues in most countries. It is important to comply with these laws and regulations throughout the human resource management processes, such as the recruitment and selection phase, so that people are treated fairly and the organization is not exposed to claims of discrimination or bias (on the basis of race, colour, country of birth, ethnicity, disability, religion, sex, age, marital status, pregnancy, or sexual preference). Other techniques, such as sophisticated personality and intelligence tests, are increasingly being used to determine whether the applicant has the job requirements identified in the planning phase (skills, competencies, qualifications, and experience).

Orientation

Orientation occurs after an employee or volunteer has successfully secured their role within an organization. Before they fulfil their primary job responsibilities, they need to be inducted into the organization and oriented to the organization's mission, culture, and practices. Strong orientation programs ensure that the individual feels welcome and empowered to perform their assigned duties. Starting a new role or advancing into a more senior role at a new organization can be intimidating. Orientation serves a different purpose from training (see Table 9.1) and allows supervisors to introduce the employee or

TABLE 9.1 The purposes of orientation and training

	Orientation	Training
Purpose	• Make employees/volunteers feel welcome	• Specific details of a role
	• Communicate the organization's history, values, mission, structure (organization chart)	• Learn about systems and processes related to the role
	• Explain basic policies and procedures to empower employees/volunteers to successfully navigate the organization	• Introduction to team members who will work closely with or support an employee/volunteer
	• Ensure employees/volunteers have access to a point person to speak with if they have questions	• Provide access to tools, technology, systems that will be needed in a role
	• Gather and file copies of qualifications and accreditation certificates from employee/volunteer	• Teach any specific skills or parameters that will help an employee/volunteer succeed in their role
	• Tour facilities and equipment, introduce clients/participants	• Familiarize employee/volunteer with the organization's day-to-day operations (safety and risk management, telephone, photocopier, keys, filing system, kitchen, office processes and expenditures)
Outcome	• Increase comfort with a potentially unfamiliar environment/organization • Foster excitement about the organization and its purpose	• Learn skills and responsibilities of a role • Foster excitement about an individual's role in the organization and contribution to the mission
Time Frame	• Typically three to six hours (half or full day)	• Range from two days to two weeks or longer, depending on how training is integrated into daily work routines and employee/volunteer proficiency

volunteer to the space, organizational culture, and operations of an organization. It also gives the individual an opportunity to feel comfortable asking questions, especially in instances where they may not have any direct supervision.

Orientation strategies that are used as part of the onboarding process may include a general overview, policies and procedures, occupational health and safety regulations, industrial relations issues, a physical tour of the organization's facilities, an overview of the training and development programs available to employees, or an explanation of the performance appraisal process. In addition to these topics, orientation for sport volunteers may also include an overview of the history of the organization, a social event so volunteers can meet one another, and a testimonial from a client or partic-ipant who has benefitted from the organization in order to demonstrate the impact that is possible from the volunteer's contribution and encourage excitement about their role.

Training and development

Training and development aids in the growth and improvement of an organization's human resources. Sport organizations that prioritize training and development help new and existing employees and volunteers learn skills necessary for them to be effective in their roles. These skills can vary from helping a novice employee learn how to operate and process payment at a ticketing counter to advancing an experienced employee's knowl-edge of branding in order to compete in a competitive marketplace. Training and devel-opment can be internal to the organization, or sport organizations can help to subsidize opportunities external to the organization such as paying part or all of the cost of higher education.

Sport governing bodies often require that staff and volunteers complete mandatory training modules or certifications. For example, Hockey Canada, the national governing body for ice hockey in Canada, has mandated volunteers and administrators complete a gender identity and expression training module to make a more inclusive sport envi-ronment for LGBTQ+ persons. Similarly, many organizations have training programs for effective leadership, communication, policy, or social media.

Dressler's (2003) five-step training and development process can be useful for sport organizations.

Step 1. Complete a "needs analysis"

- Identify the necessary skills for its employees or volunteers
- Analyse the current skill base
- Develop specific training objectives

Step 2. Develop an internal or external training program

- Internal training program may be difficult for smaller sport organizations that do not have sophisticated human resource management departments
- Building partnerships with universities or consultancy firms can help create tailored or standard programs

Step 3. Validate the training program

• Assess whether the program satisfies the needs analysis

Step 4. Implement the program

• Train individuals

Step 5. Evaluate the training program

• Expand, enhance, change, or discontinue the program as needed

---

In Practice 9.2 Ontario Soccer Match Official
Mentorship Program

Sport officials play an important role, ensuring that the rules of competition are followed and safety is prioritized (Cuskelly & Hoye, 2013; Sherry, Schulenkorf, & Phillips, 2016). Sport officials often face a high degree of pressure, criticism, and, at times, abuse. Training and developing resilient and highly knowledgeable officials is a priority for many sport organizations. One method of training and developing individuals is by instating formal mentorship programs. In fact, mentorship has been recognized by officials as fundamental to their success (Nordstrom, Warner, & Barnes, 2016). This is especially true for female officials, who are currently underrepresented at all levels of sport (Nordstrom et al., 2016; Baxter, Hoye, & Kappelides, 2021).

When mentorship and support are lacking, many officials choose not to return. For example, Ontario Soccer found that one of the primary reasons 40% of match officials did not return on an annual basis was due to lack of support or mentorship. In order to address this issue, the Ontario Soccer Match Official Mentorship Program, aimed at encouraging, supporting, and educating match officials during the first three years of their officiating career, was implemented. This program is led by accredited mentors who have undergone mentorship training. Mentors are required to meet specific requirements in order to advance within the four levels of mentorship based on player age groups. This type of training helps to standardize the guidance of soccer officials across Ontario so the correct educational material and information pertinent to development areas are passed on. Other institutional knowledge such as scouting and upgrading opportunities are also helpful in encouraging mentors to educate mentees on sport officials' pathways.

Performance appraisals

Performance appraisals are a difficult part of the human resource management process. On the one hand, positive performance appraisals can empower employees or volunteers, yet in contrast, negative appraisals can discourage individuals and cause them to feel unworthy and unmotivated. This can create a challenging power dynamic between management and employees or, in the case of entirely volunteer-led organizations, create tensions between fellow volunteer members.

Collaborative approaches to performance appraisals help the appraiser and the appraisee feel empowered. This allows leaders and managers to balance praise with suggested improvements while also allowing employees or volunteers to provide input on their performance as a part of their ongoing development. This process enables employees to feel comfortable identifying the things they did well as well as the things they could have done better as part of a process of ongoing professional and career development. In this way, performance appraisal fulfils both administrative and developmental purposes. The administrative purpose refers to the need within organizations to make judgements about performance that are directly related to rewards and recognition, such as promotions and salary increases. The administrative purpose often requires quantitative measures so that employees can be appraised based on similar criteria. The developmental purpose refers to developing and enhancing the capabilities of an employee, which often requires a mix of quantitative and qualitative measures and can be a catalyst for further training and development.

Appraisal differs depending on the type of sport organization and role of the individual within it. In professional sport, performance is often subject to public appraisal. Athletes and coaches are assessed by not only management but also fans and the media. Statistics allow for an in-depth analysis that goes beyond wins and losses to also include every point, assist, foul, penalty, and so on. Players are assessed on their own performance, and coaches are assessed on their team's performance in the form of win:loss ratio. This assessment is considered much more high stakes than other contexts, given that a negative assessment can lead to a player or coach losing their job, and other qualities of job performance are often not considered. In volunteer contexts, performance appraisal can be much more informal, where individuals may get feedback throughout the sport season from a variety of sources including parents, players, or club administrators. End-of-season evaluations are sometimes used to provide feedback to individuals in higher-profile roles (e.g., board chair, coaches) for developmental purposes.

Rewards and retention

Once a sport organization has planned for, recruited, selected, oriented, trained, and appraised its staff, it makes good sense that it would try to retain them. Retaining good-quality staff and/or volunteers is a crucial aspect of human resource management, as retention helps to reduce time and resources required for training new staff, and losing people often means losing knowledge. When turnover is high, teamwork is difficult to maintain and employees can have a harder time bonding and collaborating. This is draining on existing employees, who are often asked to help with onboarding and training new hires.

Organizational knowledge and intellectual property are lost when a sport organization fails to retain its staff. Constantly losing staff will mean that the organization may have the opportunity to encourage and develop new ways of thinking, but the more likely scenario is that it will lead to wasted resources, unnecessarily diverted to rudimentary induction programs. Given the service environment that many sport organizations work in, losing key people may also mean losing customers or participants if they are loyal to those individuals.

The other phases of the human resource management process all contribute to retaining quality staff and volunteers. Poor orientation, training, and performance appraisal programs in particular can all have a negative impact on retention. There are many strategies that can be used to increase employee retention, and organizations should seek to develop a well-rounded retention plan that will encourage people to stay. Factors to consider include work environment, culture, benefits, development opportunities, recognition, and monetary rewards. The strategies available will depend on the context, budget, talent needs, and goals of the organization. In a primarily voluntary organization, rewards may take the form of a letter of appreciation for being part of a successful event and an invitation to participate next year. In a commercial organization, a financial bonus or extra vacation days (e.g., Friday afternoons during summer months) can be highly satisfying to employees. In other words, the retention and reward strategy will depend greatly on the context in which it is being implemented and the existing level of job satisfaction. However, rewards and retention should not be an afterthought once people articulate a plan to leave or have left. These are key ingredients in a successful strategic human resource management plan and well worth the time and financial investment they require.

In Practice 9.3 Her Next Play

Her Next Play is a nonprofit organization based in Minnesota (US) that seeks to develop the next generation of women leaders through sports. The Her Next Play Rookie Career Accelerator works with current and former female, cis, trans, non-binary, gender non-conforming, and any women-identified athletes in their early years in the workplace to build professional skills, network, and build their career portfolio. For female athletes, this helps build confidence and gives them the opportunity to transfer many of the skills learnt in sport to a workplace setting.

The founders of this organization recognized that female college athletes are often limited by playing and training schedules that do not allow them to take on internships like other college students. Employers partner with Her Next Play as a strategic human resource recruitment strategy that can help diversify their staff and train women who can effectively take on leadership roles within their organization. Through mentorship programs, innovative retreats, monthly learning labs, and interactive development experiences, the Rookie Career Accelerator actively creates opportunities for career advancement. The program is funded entirely through grants and donations and is offered at no cost to participants. The program also entails a significant networking component, including a members-only LinkedIn site and a community of support. This is an essential part of breaking down barriers in business and encouraging more women to gain faster access to influential roles.

Her Next Play also provides workshops for girls in sport by teaming up with professional franchises to provide opportunities for girls to learn and develop skills both on and off the field. In 2021, they teamed up with the Minnesota Twins to put on a girls baseball workshop focused on leadership, resilience, and positive psychology in addition to baseball skills. This program offers an example of how the gender and racial gap in business can be closed through purposeful training and recruitment strategies.

HUMAN RESOURCES AND DIVERSITY IN SPORT ORGANIZATIONS

A paramount topic for human resource managers is diversity and inclusion amongst employees and volunteers in sport organizations. Many groups within society have been traditionally excluded or mistreated within the sport system and have faced systemic barriers to participation. This matter is of critical importance to human resource professionals who are responsible for ethical hiring practices, as well as the emotional and physical safety and well-being of current employees and volunteers of all backgrounds and identities. Traditionally, commercial, public, and nonprofit sport sectors alike have been dominated by white heterosexual males. Lack of diversity within the workforce can generate hegemonic thinking that may lead to policies and practices that do not promote an inclusive environment (Cunningham, 2019). Human resource management has an important function within the organization to ensure that different races, ethnicities, genders, ages, religions, abilities, social classes, and sexual orientations are represented, experience fair treatment, and have equitable access to all opportunities.

Diversity in sport organizations is important for a variety of reasons. Most centrally, everyone deserves the freedom to work in an environment free from discrimination and to experience well-being and full humanity. Research has also demonstrated that there are many benefits to organizations with a diverse workforce. Indeed, diversity in the workplace fosters a more creative and innovative workforce and is necessary to create a competitive economy in a globalized world (Cunningham, 2019). Sport organizations need to become more aware of how their positions, whether staff or volunteers, can be fulfilled by engaging with those they may not have previously engaged (Hoye, Cuskelly et al., 2020). For example, the Australian Human Rights Commission has developed a reflective practice framework to assist Sport Australia and their partners to monitor the implementation and impact of the guidelines for the inclusion of transgender and gender-diverse people in sport (Australian Human Rights Commission, 2019). This framework is designed for continuous improvement and short-, medium-, and long-term reflection in order to progress toward the objective of inclusion of transgender and gender-diverse people in sport. Cunningham and Hussain (2020) further suggest that multilevel efforts are needed to create and sustain a diverse environment and that organizations should focus on "individual interactions, leader behaviours, organizational policies, and the interaction with the broader environment in which the sport organization is situated" (p. 2). Diverse communities in sport can help to influence sport policy and resource distribution, thereby building new opportunities for more people to enjoy sport involvement.

HUMAN RESOURCE MANAGEMENT IN A DIGITAL ERA

In recent years, advancements in technology have changed the practice of human resource management in sport organizations in many ways. For example, e-recruitment is now a common practice, where organizations use web-based technology to attract, recruit, screen, select, and onboard candidates. E-recruitment offers the opportunity to reach a wider geographic area and pool of candidates than traditional local recruiting (e.g., in-person job fairs, university events). Technology also offers the chance for applicant tracking, online job boards, online testing, and social media reach. Downsides of e-recruitment include de-personalization, large volume of applicants who may not be suitable, lack of exposure to organizational culture to determine "fit", and technology issues that can come from online processes. Human resource management information systems are also a useful tool within the sport industry. These systems allow for efficient integration between various functions of the organization, data management, instant messaging, and streamlined payroll and benefits.

Online training methods are also being used as a cost-efficient and user-friendly method for onboarding new employees and volunteers. This allows for greater flexibility and accessibility for employees or volunteers working from home and can allow access to training programs that are not offered locally. Training can range from no-cost to modest cost depending on the course and provider. However, choosing the right training options can be complicated in the decentralized world of online learning and requires careful consideration.

SUMMARY

Effective human resource management in sport organizations relies on the implementation of an interdependent set of processes. This series of processes offers a blueprint for the successful management of people through a clearly delineated set of stages. Human resource management planning, recruitment, selection, orientation, training, performance appraisal, rewards, and retention strategies are essential for an organization to operate successfully in commercial, nonprofit, or public sport environments, because good people management is at the core of every successful sport organization, irrespective of the context.

However, applying processes without recognition of individual needs will be ineffective and potentially costly given that everyone has individual circumstances that shape their behaviour and attitudes and will undoubtedly influence their experience in a given organization. Thus, the characteristics of the employee, including traits, needs, and motivations, are important factors to consider when managing and investing in human resources. This includes offering different forms of support and flexibility at different career stages and levels of experience (Weight et al., 2021). Indeed, when people are managed with care, sport organizations can better deal with some of their unique and particular challenges, such as the place of athletes in professional sport organizations, the large casual and semi-permanent workforces required by major events (annual or periodic), and the large volunteer workforce within club-based sporting systems. On the other hand, poor human resource management can result in a workforce that is not only uncommitted but also subject to low levels of morale and job satisfaction (Chelladurai & Kerwin, 2017). Human resource management is an important function for all sport organizations and, when implemented well, delivers significant benefits for organizational success.

REVIEW QUESTIONS

1 Why is human resource management important for the effective management of sport organizations?

2 How does the place of athletes in professional sport organizations in relation to other employees influence human resource management practices?

3 Explain why the staff-volunteer dynamic is important in managing human resources in sport organizations.

4 Examine the human resource management processes of a local sport organization you are familiar with. Describe the activities used in each step of the process.

5 How are each of the human resource management processes linked to organizational performance?

6 Compare the orientation and training processes of a nonprofit sport/recreation organization and a commercial sport organization/business. How and why do they differ?

7 Should the human resource management role within sport organizations be combined with another functional division? Why?

8 How does the often-public appraisal of employees in sport organizations impact the integrity of the human resource management process?

9 How has technology changed human resource management practices in recent years?

DISCUSSION QUESTIONS

1 Does the pay structure of professional sporting teams, in which the players are paid more than the CEO and the senior managers, mean that these administrative staff have less or more job security than their colleagues in non-sport organizations? Take into account who is considered responsible for organizational performance in both arenas.

2 How and why should human resource practices differ between paid staff and volunteers? Develop examples across the sport sectors to illustrate how these practices differ. Consider the role of financial remuneration in your answer and how significant an influence you think it is on the ways in which people operate in the workplace. What other forms of rewards and recognition are important for volunteers?

3 Is asking candidates applying for a job in a sport organization to provide information about their marital status legal in the hiring process? Consult employment legislation in your region and create a list of questions that are allowable and those that are not permitted.

4 Nonprofit sport organizations often lack formal performance appraisal processes. What implications does this have for the practice of human resource management in sport organizations, and how could any negative effects be minimized?

5 Describe some of the key considerations for managing diversity in sport organizations. Research strategies that may assist in providing an inclusive environment and craft a letter to a sport club board of directors explaining why diversity is important for sport organizations.

RELEVANT WEBSITES

NCAA at https://d67oz7qfnvgpz.cloudfront.net/about/taking-action, www.theatlantic.com/politics/archive/2021/07/risks-supreme-court-ncaa-decision/619296/

Her Next Play at www.hernextplay.org/rookiecareeraccelerator

Ontario Soccer Match Official Mentorship Program at www.ontariosoccer.net/mentor

Australian Human Rights Commission at www.sportaus.gov.au/__data/assets/pdf_file/0007/707803/Reflective_Practice_Framework_for_TGD_Guidelines_2019_FINAL_1.pdf

FURTHER READING

Bach, S., & Edwards, M. (2013). *Managing human resources* (5th ed.). London: Wiley.

Chelladurai, P., & Kerwin, S. (2017). *Human resource management in sport and recreation* (3rd ed.). Champaign, IL: Human Kinetics.

Cunningham, G. (2019). *Diversity and inclusion in sport organizations: A multilevel perspective* (4th ed.). London: Routledge.

Cunningham, G., & Hussain, U. (2020). The case for LGBT diversity and inclusion in sport business. *Sport & Entertainment Review*, 5(1). Retrieved from https://serjournal.com/2020/01/15/the-case-for-lgbt-diversity-and-inclusion-in-sport-business/

Dowling, M., Edwards, J., & Washington, M. (2014). Understanding the concept of professionalism in sport management research. *Sport Management Review*, 17(4), 520–529.

Hoye, R., Cuskelly, G., Auld, C., Kappelides, P., & Misener, K. (2020). *Sport volunteering*. London: Routledge.

Trivedi, K., & Srivastava, K. B. L. (2021). A framework for integrating strategic HR and knowledge management for innovation performance. *Strategic HR Review*, 20(1), 11–16.

Weight, E., Taylor, E., Huml, M., & Dixon, M. (2021). Working in the sport industry: A classification of human capital archetypes. *Journal of Sport Management*, 35, 364–378.

CASE STUDY 9.1

Volunteer management during times of crisis: COVID-19 and the Tokyo Olympics and Paralympics

This case study explores volunteer involvement in the 2020 Tokyo Summer Olympic Games and Paralympic Games. Due to the global COVID-19 pandemic, the 2020 Tokyo Olympics were delayed by one year and occurred during July–August 2021. The Summer Olympics is arguably one of the most popular mega-events that occurs every four years and is largely possible because of many unpaid volunteers who contribute time and energy to ensuring the event takes place and the cost of running the event is minimized. For example, research conducted at the Sydney Olympics in 2000 revealed that 40,000 volunteers saved $60 million in costs (Chalip, 2000).

Volunteers undergo a lengthy selection process, and it is highly esteemed position to be selected for the Olympic games. While these positions are unpaid, volunteers usually receive a uniform, meals during their shift, and a stipend to cover daily commuting costs. In turn, volunteers are expected to cover the cost of their own lodging. Despite the Tokyo event being delayed a year, COVID-19 remained a major concern in 2021, as many countries faced high rates of virus infection and slow administration of vaccines. New variants of the virus were emerging at rapid rates with higher probability of infection and more adverse health outcomes. At the onset of the event in July 2021, a low percentage of Japan's population had been fully vaccinated (World Health Organization, 2021). The perceived lack of concern for the residents of Tokyo has led to heavy critique toward the International Olympic Committee's decision to move forward with the games during the ongoing pandemic, especially when, in many areas, borders were closed and global travel remained restricted.

With such heightened concern, many athletes chose to forgo competition for fear of the virus and concerns over their own health and safety as well as the health of the global community. Similarly, approximately 10,000 unpaid volunteers (of a total 80,000 planned volunteers) also decided to not partake in the games. Tokyo Olympics and Paralympics organizers claim that the dropout was due to several reasons, including the delayed start of the event, conflicting commitments, and worries about COVID-19. Volunteers themselves expressed the ethical dilemma of choosing to partake, some of whom felt that safety precautions would ensure a safe event, and others felt that the risks outweighed their desire to be part of such a spectacular event.

Despite losing 1/8 of the volunteer workforce, organizers claimed that the loss in human resources would not impede operations and that the Games would continue successfully. In early July, it was announced that the Tokyo venues would have no spectators and the Games would be held under a state of emergency. The announcement was made following a meeting of Olympic and Japanese government groups responsible for the Games. This was an unprecedented decision which restricted access to only those with accreditation to the venues. This change, driven by the high number of infected cases and severe impact of variants in the Tokyo area, came with specific health and safety measures. Considering the large number of volunteers who chose to remain involved, not all volunteers were able to be fully vaccinated prior to the start of the games.

Volunteers claimed that there was minimal information given to them about protection against COVID-19. Measures that were in place were cloth masks, sanitizer, and instructional pamphlets about maintaining social distancing. Volunteers were encouraged to take public transit to and from the venues. The IOC also produced a playbook, a written manual guiding volunteers to follow and learn about safety precautions that included information about travel, COVID-19 testing, and vaccinations. The playbook encouraged attendees, including volunteers, to get vaccinated; however, it was not mandated in order to participate in the Games.

COVID-19 presented an unprecedented human resource challenge for volunteer managers during the Tokyo Olympic Games. Volunteers claimed that testing for COVID-19 and control measures were not made clear despite the thousands of volunteers who flowed in and out of venues on a daily basis. However, per the written manual provided by the IOC, testing frequency for COVID-19 was outlined and varied, with daily testing for athletes or those working in closest proximity to athletes. Athletes willing to receive the vaccine were also prioritized over volunteers. Untested and unvaccinated volunteers created a risk for COVID-19 to spread within the supposed "Olympic bubble". Concerns over COVID-19 even led to strong disproval from Japanese and Tokyo-based doctors, who expressed significant concern in hosting a large-scale event considering the difficulties facing an already strained health care system. Media reported that volunteers who dropped out went so far as to claim that the choice to host the Olympics during a pandemic demonstrated a "belittling of human lives" (CTV news network, 2021).

On a world stage, this event has shown that volunteers should be managed in such a way to ensure their health and safety, alongside the safety of athletes, coaches, staff, and media personnel. Future events should ensure that volunteers are provided with information regarding safety precautions and that health measures are enforced. In addition, sport managers should consider their ethical role in protecting not only volunteers but also the general public in times of crisis when the very use of humans creates potential for unsafe outcomes.

COVID-19 presents a unique opportunity to understand volunteer management in a large-scale events and its impact on society as a whole. It also demonstrates that despite the crucial need for volunteers to run events such as the Olympic Games, volunteers do have agency and can choose not to partake for individual reasons. Future international events should consider the broader responsibility of managing human resources as it relates to local host cities as well as the broader global community.

CASE STUDY QUESTIONS

1   What are the implications from Tokyo 2021 for volunteer health and safety at future major events? Should the health and safety of athletes be prioritized over volunteers and staff? How can other major event organizers demonstrate greater concern for health and safety among staff and volunteers?

2   How can the IOC engage the 10,000 volunteers who withdrew from the Games to understand their experience and how volunteer management strategies can be improved in the future? What are the implications for human resource management when new volunteers must be recruited for each major games? What are the costs and benefits of volunteer turnover?

3   Which phases of the human resource management process are most important for staff and volunteers involved in major sport events? Given the unique circumstances around the Tokyo 2021 Olympic Games, provide a critical analysis of possible missed steps in the process of managing volunteers.

SOURCES

10,000 volunteers drop out with Tokyo Olympics set to open in 50 days. (2021, July 3). The Associate Press. Retrieved, July 20, from www.cbc.ca/sports/olympics/10000-volunteers-drop-out-with-olympics-opening-in-50-days-1.6051489

'Belittling human lives': How the pandemic pushed an Olympic volunteer to quit. 2021, June 2). CTV News Network. Retrieved, July 12, from www.ctvnews.ca/sports/belittling-human-lives-how-the-pandemic-pushed-an-olympic-volunteer-to-quit-1.5453110

Beset by coronavirus wave, Tokyo's doctors lead push against the Games. (2021, May 26). Reuters. com. Retrieved, July 10, from www.reuters.com/lifestyle/sports/beset-by-coronavirus-wave-tokyos-doctors-lead-push-against-games-2021–05–26/

Chalip, L. (2000). Sydney 2000: Volunteers and the organization of the Olympic games: Economic and formative aspects. In M. Moragas, A. B. de Moreno, & N. Puig (Eds.), *Volunteers, global society and the Olympic movement* (pp. 205–214). Lausanne: International Olympic Committee.

Olympic volunteers wanted to help at the Games. They didn't sign up for COVID. (2021, June 15). CNN.com. Retrieved, July 15, from www.cnn.com/2021/06/15/asia/japan-olympic-volunteers-intl-hnk-dst/index.html

The playbook workforce: Your guide to a safe and successful Games. Olympics.com. (2021). Retrieved, July 20, from https://gtimg.tokyo2020.org/image/upload/production/bhozjijlpvb-4pdsebpuf.pdf

World Health Organization. (2021). Retrieved July 30, from https://covid19.who.int/region/wpro/country/jp

CASE STUDY 9.2

Managing for the recruitment, training, and retention of female volunteer sport coaches, officials, and board members

In sport organizations, females are largely underrepresented in leadership positions, and volunteers are more likely to be male, white, and from a higher socioeconomic background (Sport England, 2016). Given that the majority of coaching, officiating, governance, and board positions are filled by males, managing for the recruitment, training, and retention of females in these roles is of concern to many sport organizations (Baxter et al., 2021). This case study explores initiatives related to increasing female representation amongst sport volunteer roles in amateur sport organizations.

In countries such as Canada, the United Kingdom, and Australia, the majority of sport coaching, officiating, and governance roles are voluntary in nature, given the nonprofit club structure within the sport system (Hoye, Cuskelly et al., 2020).

The majority of participants within sport are involved at the grassroots level, where the lack of female volunteers is highly visible, especially in front-facing leadership roles such as coaches and officials. Unlike male counterparts, females face additional barriers to sport volunteerism, including role conflicts, overarching patriarchal belief systems, not feeling empowered to articulate needs, perceived lack of interest in female volunteer development, exclusion from development opportunities, gender category sorting, and lack of support for new volunteers (Baxter et al., 2021). In community sport, where many volunteers are parents of youth athletes themselves, demands and expectations are high, but women often perceive their value to be low. In fact, "they often feel that they have to negotiate their right to be in their role and prove their leadership and coaching abilities more than men do" (Women In Sport, 2017, p. 2). When women feel that they need to adapt their behaviours to succeed and may have slower progression through levels of leadership, it can be discouraging and limit the impact that these leaders could have in the sport system.

Having a gender-diverse leadership team is crucial in community sport for a variety of reasons. A balanced number of women and men on sport boards can increase innovation by ensuring that diverse perspectives are considered, particularly when the organization is facing complex decisions. Sport leaders should reflect the diversity of the organization's stakeholders and wider community in order to ensure people see themselves as participants or volunteers. Having female coaches and leaders as decision-makers can increase networking opportunities and offer support as well as inspiring other women to pursue their goals. Having an inclusive environment that encourages all genders to be involved at any level demonstrates club values and can change the accepted norms and beliefs (LaVoi & Baeth, 2018). In addition, voluntary roles are often the gateway for females to progress to higher levels of sport involvement in various competitive structures and through paid roles (Baxter et al., 2021).

Several sport organizations have recognized the unique needs of female volunteers and are making intentional efforts to encourage more females to step into these sport volunteer roles. For example, the Tucker Centre for research on girls and women in sport has initiated a #SheCanCoach campaign to address the trend that most women consider coaching only after being invited or encouraged to try it (LaVoi & Baeth, 2018). This social media and poster campaign helps invite females to think about coaching and is intended to encourage women to become coaches themselves. Several national governing bodies and associations have also made headway in attempts to enhance the number of females represented across all levels of sport. In Australia, the Victorian government has employed the Change Our Game initiative in an attempt to increase the number of women and girls participating in sport and active recreation, from grassroots through to leadership roles through various grants, funding, development programs, and events.

The Coaching Association of Canada has incorporated a multifaceted program aimed at helping women coaches through mentorship, information about grants and partnerships, and recommendations on recruitment and retention. Similarly, Canadian Women and Sport offers gender equity consulting to help sport organizations understand how elements of their structure, including human resources, contribute to lack of diversity amongst staff and volunteers. International governing bodies such as World Rugby have provided an extensive toolkit and development plan to help guide strategy of international partners and local clubs toward increased gender equity in sport coaching roles.

On a more local scale, sport clubs are attempting to increase representation of female grassroots board members; however, this is not always achieved as easily as at the national and regional levels. Some national governing bodies such as the Norwegian Olympic and Paralympic Committee and Confederation of Sports (NIF) have mandated policies demanding a specific quota of volunteer positions to be filled by females. Research shows that while quota of female representation on NIF board or directors was made at the national executive level and the regional level, only 2/3 of sport clubs were able to make the quota (Sisjord, Fasting, & Sand, 2017). Additional support may be needed at the grassroots level of sport to aid in human resource recruitment strategy in order to enhance representation of females within the local sport club system.

Considering the declining volunteer force across the nonprofit sector, improving efforts to make a more inclusive environment for females, many of whom grow up participating in sport in similar numbers as their male counterparts, is an important endeavour to building capacity. From a volunteer management perspective, this requires human resource managers to look at what influences the volunteer experience, from policy and governance, coaching pathways, recruitment, retention, performance, stress and wellbeing, and support. Organizations need to consider improving their internal practices to see how they reflect traditional gender stereotypes, improving external communications to showcase both men and women in all volunteer roles, improving flexibility in roles to allow for shorter-term and shared roles, and encouraging progression through roles with greater responsibility (Women In Sport, 2017).

It is also important for human resource managers to recognize that we all have unconscious bias that causes us to make assumptions or create unintentional barriers. In sport organizations, structural level systemic bias is embedded within sport culture (LaVoi, McGarry, & Fisher, 2019). Human resources is not exempt from contributing to lack of diversity in hiring and management practices. Unconscious bias, often also referred to as implicit bias, refers to stereotypes about groups of people that have been formed when individuals are not conscious or fully aware of them (LaVoi et al., 2019). With regard to gender, gender stereotypes and gender ideologies dictate conscious and unconscious beliefs about the nature of males and females and their assumed roles (Wicker, Cunningham, & Fields, 2019). Unconscious bias is an important topic to discuss regarding human resource management, as it has the potential to affect the selection and promotion of female volunteers. Research has help shed light on how gender ideologies within patriarchal society have led to perceptions that sport coaching is a more masculine pursuit and that females are assumed to not have the physical nor mental strength to be successful (West, Green, Brackenridge, & Woodward, 2001). These unconscious assumptions are representative of a patriarchal culture that needs to be broken down to remove binary ways of thinking about gender. Human resource managers are responsible for creating awareness surrounding implicit assumptions about the capabilities of female volunteers. If they do not, sport clubs and organizations risk losing highly talented personnel who may help to contribute to their overall success.

A holistic approach to understanding the female as a unique human resource with life experiences and barriers different than what males may face is crucial to the development of a more inclusive sport culture.

CASE STUDY QUESTIONS

1   How might human resource management apply a gender equity lens in the phases of human resource management? What tools and learning modules are available in your country to help guide a sport organization towards continuous learning and effectively engage in gender equity work in the future?

2   What challenges might nonprofit community organizations face in comparison to for-profit professional sport organizations regarding the recruitment and retention of female coaches and board members? What strategies can be used to recruit female leaders in community sport?

3   What is unconscious bias and why is it important to recognize as part of human resource management? How does unconscious bias related to gender shape our behaviour and influence various human resource management processes? What steps can you take to identify and actively counter your unconscious bias?

SOURCES

Baxter, H., Hoye, R., & Kappelides, P. (2021). Female volunteer community sport coaches: A scoping review and research agenda. *Journal of Amateur Sport, 7*(1). https://doi.org/10.17161/jas.v7i1.13774

Canadian Women & Sport. (2021). *Winning plays: The gender equity playbook report.* Retrieved from https://womenandsport.ca/wp-content/uploads/2021/07/Gender-Equity-Playbook-Roll-Up-Report-Eng-Final.pdf

Gender Equity Consulting. Canadian Women & Sport. (n.d.). Retrieved from https://womenandsport.ca/learning-opportunities/consulting/

Hoye, R., Cuskelly, G., Auld, C., Kappelides, P., & Misener, K. (2020). *Sport volunteering.* London: Routledge.

LaVoi, N. M., & Baeth, A. (2018). Women and sports coaching. In L. Mansfield, J. Caudwell, B. Wheaton, & B. Watson (Eds.), *The Palgrave handbook of feminism and sport, leisure and physical education.* London: Palgrave Macmillan. https://doi.org/10.1057/978-1-137-53318-0_10

LaVoi, N. M., McGarry, J. E., & Fisher, L. A. (2019). Final thoughts on women in sport coaching: Fighting the war. *Women in Sport & Physical Activity Journal, 27*(2), 136–140. https://doi.org/10.1123/wspaj.2019-0030

#SheCanCoach Project. University of Minnesota, Tucker Center for Research on Girls & Women in Sport. (n.d.). Retrieved from www.cehd.umn.edu/tuckercenter/projects/shecancoach.html

Sisjord, M., Fasting, K., & Sand, T. (2017). The impact of gender quotas in leadership in Norwegian organised sport. *International Journal of Sport Policy and Politics, 9*(3), 505–519. doi:10.1080/19406940.2017.1287761

Sport England. (2016). *Towards an active nation. Strategy 2016–2021*. London: Sport England.

West, A., Green, E., Brackenridge, C. H., & Woodward, D. (2001). Leading the way: Women's experiences as sports coaches. *Women in Management Review, 16*(2), 85–92. https://doi.org/10.1108/09649420110386610

Wicker, P., Cunningham, G., & Fields, D. (2019). Head coach changes in women's college soccer: An investigation of women coaches through the lenses of gender stereotypes and the glass cliff. *Sex Roles, 81, 797–807*.

Women in Coaching. Coaching Association of Canada. (n.d.). Retrieved from https://coach.ca/women-coaching?gclid=CjwKCAjwr56IBhAvEiwA1fuqGq-ZSl2x4rlR93x66zhKIB9t_-D6Z0RPSCJPEDZMPO_tAuO2mGu1ZBoCO6YQAvD_BwE

Women in Rugby Toolkit. World Rugby. (n.d.). Retrieved from https://resources.world.rugby/worldrugby/document/2020/05/07/fcd591f0-f2dc-4c85-8ce9-822858e2eefa/21300_World_Rugby_Women_in_Rugby_Toolkit_DDv7.pdf

Women in Sport. (2017). *Good sports: Why sports need to engage female volunteers*. Retrieved from www.womeninsport.org/wp-content/uploads/2017/10/Good-Sports.pdf

CHAPTER 10

Leadership in sport

OVERVIEW

Leadership is arguably the most researched yet least understood topic in the context of management. What we define as excellent leadership and great leaders remain points of serious and widespread academic debate. In this chapter, we provide a broad outline of the different approaches that have been used to describe and analyse leadership. We will also use a number of examples and cases to explore leadership. Much of this discussion will take place in reference to the leadership challenges that confront sport organizations.

DOI: 10.4324/9781003217947-12

By the end of this chapter, the reader should be able to:

* Describe the need for leaders and for leadership;
* Distinguish between leadership and management;
* Outline the different levels (in the organization) that leaders can work at and how this impacts their approach to leadership; and
* Provide an overview of your personal leadership development needs.

WHAT IS LEADERSHIP?

It is not easy to find agreement among any group on a definition of leadership. Sometimes leadership is described as "getting things done through people". Others argue that leadership is about "exercising power in order to influence others" or that true leadership is about "envisioning a bright future and taking others by the hand towards it". In other words, leadership can be many things to different people. Cotton Fitzsimmons, former coach of the Kansas City Kings, argues that "if you're a positive person, you're an automatic motivator. You can get people to do things you don't think they're capable of" (Westerbeek & Smith, 2005). Vince Lombardi, the famous coach of the Green Bay Packers of the 1950s and 1960s, once said that "leaders are made, they are not born; and they are made just like anything else has been made in this country – by hard effort. And that's the price that we all have to pay to achieve that goal, or any goal" (Westerbeek & Smith, 2005). According to former US President Theodore Roosevelt, "the best executive is the one who has sense enough to pick good men to do what he wants done, and self-restraint enough to keep from meddling with them while the do it", and Lou Holts, a former coach of the Notre Dame football team, argued that "all winning teams are goal-oriented. Teams like these win consistently because everyone connected with them concentrates on specific objectives. They go about their business with blinders on; nothing will distract them from achieving their aims" (Westerbeek & Smith, 2005).

Harvard professor and leadership expert Linda Hill (2008) argues that fast-changing, multiple-stakeholder, decision-making business environments we may well have to "lead from behind" in order to let others take charge as leaders when it is most needed. According to these experienced but very different leaders and leadership experts, leadership is:

* goal-oriented;
* about influencing others;
* about empowering others;
* about seeing the big picture;
* about needing others; and
* about strength of character.

We can use these different components of leadership to construct a leadership definition. For the purposes of this book, we define leadership as "influencing and enabling others towards the attainment of aspirational goals". We appreciate that there are many other definitions of leadership, but as an introduction to the topic in this book, the previous definition will serve its purpose. In the next section of this chapter, we will further outline the ways that leadership can be viewed.

In Practice 10.1 Leading coach Craig Bellamy

Craig Bellamy, coach of the National Rugby League team, Melbourne Storm, has a winning percentage of 70% over his last 19 seasons in charge of the Storm. In 2021, he signed a five-year extension to his coaching contract that will see him through to the end of his 24th season as head coach in 2026 at the age of 66. He is widely acknowledged as the most successful coach in NRL history, having led the Storm to nine grand finals in 18 seasons, winning five of them.

Being a successful leader at the same organization for so long is a rarity in any industry and even rarer in the coaching ranks for professional sport. His success as a leader has been linked to his emotional intelligence, the ability to understand emotions and how they influence others' thoughts and behaviours. It has been widely reported that he never abuses his players for poor performance; instead, he focuses on instilling confidence in players and on the things people can control in sport – effort, preparation, intensity, understanding a game plan. Bellamy focuses on eliminating skill errors on the team, with players forced to perform push-ups at training if they drop the ball. Bellamy is also famous for seeking out new ideas, often visiting other teams such as the All Blacks, NFL teams, and NBA teams for coaching tips and ideas for innovation at the Storm.

Bellamy is also known for enforcing what many might consider "old school" values amongst the team – humility; honesty; good manners in all interactions of players with fans, on flights, and with support staff. He is also consistently described as an authentic leader, being consistent in his interactions with players whether they are winning or losing, and for being a straight talker. In 2017, one of the leading players at Storm, Will Chambers, was quoted as saying "He pushes you and drives you to be a better person and a better footballer but being a better person is the most important thing to him and that's the special thing about him and what he does". That authentic, caring nature as a leader engenders loyalty and commitment from his players.

Source: www.triplem.com.au/story/why-storm-players-love-playing-for-bellamy-58393

THEORIES OF LEADERSHIP

Northouse (2021) separates leadership theories into categories that relate to traits of leaders, their skills, their styles, the situation in which they have to lead, or the contingency that they face. He also lists theories such as the path-goal theory, the leader member exchange theory, the transformational approach, the authentic approach, team leadership, and the psychodynamic approach as separate categories. As this is an introduction to the concept of leadership, the dominant theories have been conflated into four approaches: trait or personality approaches, the behavioural approach, the contingency approach, and the transformational approach.

Trait or personality approaches

Although the personality and trait approaches to leadership stem from the earliest of leadership research times, popular leadership literature continues to stress the importance of personality and innate ability in the demonstration of leadership. Locke (1991) argues that trait theories (or great man theories, as they are also called) are incomplete theories of leadership, irrespective of traits and/or personality of the leaders being important contributors to, or detractors from, excellent leadership. Locke (1991) suggests that the possession of certain traits, such as energy and honesty, appears to be a vital for effective leadership. Basketball legend Michael Jordan, for example, has been credited with having an impressive range of innate leadership traits that will help him be an excellent leader in many different contexts. Leaders must use their traits to develop skills, formulate a vision, and implement this vision in reality. This being the case, it appears that traits only form part of the picture.

Although empirical evidence linking the personality of leaders with their success is weak, much of the popular literature still focuses on leadership traits as a way to better understand leadership. In general, the trait theories are based on the assumption that social background, physical features, and personality characteristics will distinguish good leaders from poor leaders.

Behavioural approach

When it became clear that good leadership could not simply be explained on the basis of the innate characteristics of the leaders, organizational research began to focus on discovering universal behaviours of effective leaders. Behaviourists argued that anyone could be taught to become a leader by simply learning the behaviours of other effective leaders.

Behavioural strategy takes behaviours as signs of learned responses to contingencies. If research shows that to behave in a certain manner results in success for a leader, then one can learn to discharge those behaviours in particular leadership situations. The behavioural approach to leadership was also a response to early approaches to management as a whole. Frederick Taylor was an early champion of the idea that managers should use science to improve efficiency. This approach became known as Taylorism or scientific management, a philosophy in which there was limited attention to the human side of the mass production movement. Rather, under Taylorism, humans were simply "part of the larger machines", and standardization of human labour would lead to great efficiency and higher profits. Managers, according to Taylor, should begin by studying the tasks workers perform and break jobs down by analyzing, measuring, and timing each separate element of the job in order to determine the most efficient manner of doing the job. The most efficient method for each job became both the standard method that workers were supposed to adopt and a means for measuring worker productivity.

In response to Taylor's ideas, behaviouralists demanded a new "human relations" approach to management of organizations involving an examination of the interaction between managers and workers. In the Hawthorne experiments, which were originally designed to study the effects of lighting upon factory workers, Elton Mayo discovered that human relations between workers and between workers and supervisors were most important in ensuring efficiency. In other words, by focusing on interaction between humans, and by studying the best ways of interacting, managers could better lead the people who worked for the organization. Another behavioural approach to the study of leadership is the so-called Theory X and Theory Y, developed by Douglas McGregor. The theories are formulated based on the assumptions that leaders have about individuals. Managers who have Theory X assumptions argue that the typical employee dislikes work and needs direction at all times. They also think that employees need to be coerced to perform their duties. Theory Y managers believe that employees are self-motivated and committed to work and to the company. They naturally seek responsibility for the work they perform. As a result, Theory Y leaders would behave in quite different ways from Theory X leaders.

Another behaviouralist approach was formulated by Blake and Mouton. They developed the managerial grid model along two dimensions, one with a concern for people and one with a concern for production. Blake and Mouton argued that differing levels of concern along those dimensions would lead to different styles of leadership. For example, managers with low levels of concern for people and production will have an impoverished style of leadership, whereas those leaders with high concern for people and production can be typified as having team-style leadership qualities. The Blake and Mouton approach has also been used to differentiate person-centred leaders from task-centred leaders. Ultimately, it is important to conclude that the behaviouralist approach to leadership leads to the identification of different styles that can be described as more or less successful.

Contingency approach

It became increasingly clear to those studying leadership that traits and behaviours of leaders were often observed in relation to the situation at hand or, in other words, according to situational contingencies. Isolated behavioural and trait approaches failed to take account of how situational variables, such as task structure, the characteristics of the environment, or subordinate characteristics, could impact and moderate the relationship between the behaviour of a leader and the different outcomes.

In contingency theories of leadership, the core argument is that different leadership styles and approaches will apply to a range of possible management situations. This is why, for example, the on-field leadership brilliance of Diego Maradona with the Argentinean team resulted in winning the 1986 World Cup, but when Diego was required to achieve similar results with club teams in different cultures (Napoli in Italy and Barcelona in Spain) or even as the national coach of the Argentinean side at the 2010 World Cup in South Africa, he failed dismally, also resulting in the exposure of a number of personal leadership flaws. The centrality of leader behaviour and/or personality needs to be de-emphasized, and in the contingency approach, we turn our attention to the leader in conjunction with circumstances that are specific to the situation at hand, including characteristics of the subordinates and the work setting. In the next section, we will present three situational theories of leadership that have influenced the ways in which leadership is understood and practiced. They are:

- Fieldler's least preferred co-worker approach
- Hersey and Blanchard's situational leadership theory
- Path goal theory

Fiedler's least preferred co-worker approach

Fiedler's (1967) model is based on the following three axioms:

1   The interaction between the leader's personal characteristics and some aspects of the situation determines the effectiveness of the leader,
2   Leaders are either "task-oriented" or "person-oriented", and
3   Effectiveness of the leader is determined by the leader's control of the situation.

Fiedler comes to his classification of task- or person-oriented leadership by the use of a measurement scale called the Least Preferred Co-worker (LPC) scale. The instrument asks leaders to assess co-workers on a series of bi-polar descriptors including pleasant-unpleasant, cold-warm, and supportive-hostile in order to assess to what degree they think they would not work well together with that co-worker. A leader who obtains a low LPC is more motivated by task achievements and will only be concerned about relationships with subordinates if the work unit is deemed to be performing well. A leader who obtains a high LPC score will be more motivated to develop close interpersonal relations with subordinates. Task-directed behaviour is of less concern and only becomes important once sound interpersonal relations have been developed. According to Fiedler, if the least preferred coworker still scores relatively high, it indicates that the leader derives a sense of satisfaction from "working on good relationships", indicating a person-oriented leadership style.

The model further suggests that control is dependent on three combined contingency variables:

1   The relations between the leader and the followers,
2   The degree of task structure (or the degree to which the followers' jobs can be specified clearly), and
3   The leader's position of power or amount of authority, yielding eight possible conditions, presented in Table 10.1.

Hersey and Blanchard's situational leadership theory

A theory claiming that as maturity of the group changes, leader behaviour should change as well is known as the situational theory of leadership. Hersey and Blanchard (1977) argued that as the technical skill level and psychological maturity of the group move from

TABLE 10.1 Fiedler's situational favourability factors and leadership effectiveness

| Condition | Situational favourability | | | Effective leadership |
	Leader-member relations	Task structure	Position power	
1	Good	High	Strong	Low LPC
2	Good	High	Weak	Low LPC
3	Good	Weak	Strong	Low LPC
4	Good	Weak	Weak	High LPC
5	Poor	High	Strong	High LPC
6	Poor	High	Weak	High LPC
7	Poor	Weak	Strong	High LPC
8	Poor	Weak	Weak	Low LPC

Source: Adapted from Fiedler, F. E. (1967). *A theory of leadership effectiveness* (p. 34). New York: McGraw Hill

low to moderate to high, the leader's behaviour will be most effective when it changes accordingly. When low levels of maturity are enacted in relation to the tasks being performed, a high task behaviour of the leader should be exhibited or, in other words, a "selling" and "telling" approach to communicating with the subordinates. At medium levels of maturity, leaders need to be more focused on relationship behaviours, and at the highest levels of subordinate maturity, the leader needs to offer little direction or task behaviour and allow the subordinate to assume responsibilities: in other words, a "supportive" and "delegation"-driven style of leadership communication.

According to sport organization theory researchers, there have been few attempts to empirically test the concepts and relationships that Hersey and Blanchard (1977) have outlined in their work, even in the management and organizational literature. Some attempts have been made to apply the theory directly in sport settings, but results have been inconsistent.

The path-goal theory

The path-goal theory (House, 1971) takes a behavioural and situational approach to leadership. There are many roads that lead to Rome, and therefore the path-goal theory suggests that a leader must select a style most appropriate to the particular situation. The theory in particular aims to explain how a leader's behaviour affects the motivation and satisfaction of subordinates.

House (1971) is cited in Wexley and Yukl, (1984) arguing that

> the motivational function of the leaders consists of increasing personal payoffs to subordinates for work-goal attainment, and making the path to these payoffs easier to travel by clarifying it, reducing roadblocks and pitfalls, and increasing the opportunities for personal satisfaction en route.
>
> (p. 176)

In other words, characteristics of the subordinates and the environment determine both the potential for increased motivation and the manner in which the leader must act to improve motivation. Subordinate preferences for a particular pattern of leadership behaviour may also depend on the actual situation in which they are placed (Wexley and Yukl, 1984). Taking those different perspectives into consideration, the path-goal theory proposes four styles of leadership behaviour that can be utilized to achieve goals (House and Mitchell, 1974). They are:

- Directive leadership (leader gives specific instructions, expectations, and guidance),
- Supportive leadership (leader shows concern and support for subordinates),
- Participative leadership (subordinates participate in the decision-making),
- Achievement-oriented leadership (leader sets challenges, emphasizes excellence and shows confidence that subordinates will attain high standards of performance).

The theory is principally aimed at examining how leaders affect subordinate expectations about likely outcomes of different courses of action. Directive leadership is predicted to have a positive effect on subordinates when the task is ambiguous and will have a negative impact when the task is clear. Supportive leadership is predicted to increase job satisfaction, particularly when conditions are adverse. Achievement-oriented leadership is predicted to encourage higher performance standards and increase expectancies that desired outcomes can be achieved. Participative leadership is predicted to promote satisfaction due to involvement (Schermerhorn, Hunt, and Osborne, 1994).

From transactional to transformational leadership

As already noted earlier in this chapter, the scientific approach to management (Taylorism) reduced the individual to performing machine-like functions. The human relations approach to management took into consideration the human part of the labour equation, appreciating that much better results can be achieved if people's individual needs are taken into consideration when leading them towards achieving certain work outputs.

One of the most recent thrusts in leadership research is that of transactional and transformational leadership. Transactional leadership encompasses many of the theories based on rational exchange between leader and subordinate, such as the theories presented previously, but transformational leaders, according to Bass (1985), are charismatic and develop followers into leaders through a process that transcends the existing organizational climate and culture. The transactional leader aims to create a cost-benefit economic exchange or, in other words, to meet the needs of followers in return for "contracted" services that are produced by the follower (Bass, 1985). To influence behaviour, the transactional leader may use the following approaches:

- Contingent reward (the leader uses rewards or incentives to achieve results),
- Active management by exception (the leader actively monitors the work performed and uses corrective methods to ensure the work meets accepted standards),
- Passive management by exception (the leader uses corrective methods as a response to unacceptable performance or deviation from the accepted standards), and
- Laissez-faire leadership (the leader is indifferent and has a "hands-off" approach toward the workers and their performance).

However, leadership theorists have argued that transactional leadership merely seeks to influence others by exchanging work for wages. It fails to build on the worker's need for meaningful work, and it does not actively tap into their sources of creativity. A more effective and beneficial leadership behaviour to achieve long-term success and improved performance, therefore, is transformational leadership. Sir Alex Ferguson, the longtime Manchester United manager, can be described as a transformational leader. He envisioned a future for the club, and the board has repaid him with the trust of keeping him at the helm at Manchester United since 1986 for more than 1400 games. Under his guidance and supervision, the club became the most successful team in the new English Premier League, and the team has also won multiple Champions League crowns. Sir Alex has prepared the likes of Eric Cantona, Ryan Giggs, Roy Keane, David Beckham, Ruud van Nistelrooy, Wayne Rooney, and Cristiano Ronaldo for the world stage of football leadership.

What is transformational leadership?

It has been argued by Bass and Avolio (1994) that transformational leadership is the new leadership that must accompany good management. In contrast to transactional models, transformational leadership goes beyond the exchange process. It not only aligns and elevates the needs and values of followers but also provides intellectual stimulation and increased follower confidence. Bass and Avolio (1994) identified four "I's" that transformational leaders employ in order to achieve superior results. These are:

- Idealized influence: Transformational leaders behave in ways that result in them being admired, respected, and trusted and ultimately becoming a role model. The transformational leader demonstrates high standards of ethical and moral conduct.
- Inspirational motivation: By demonstrating enthusiasm and optimism, the transformational leader actively arouses team spirit and motivates and inspires followers to share in and work towards a common goal.
- Intellectual stimulation: By being innovative, creative, and supportive; reframing problems; and questioning old assumptions, the transformational leader creates an intellectually stimulating and encouraging environment.
- Individualized consideration: Transformational leaders pay special attention to each individual's needs for achievement and growth by acting as a coach or mentor.

Looking more closely at the four, it can be argued that charisma (the ability to inspire enthusiasm, interest, or affection in others by means of personal charm or influence) is an important component of transformational leadership. Purely charismatic leaders may be limited in their ability to achieve successful outcomes due to their need to instil their beliefs in others, which may inhibit the individual growth of followers. However, transformational leaders are more than charismatic in that they generate awareness of the mission or vision of the team and the organization and then motivate colleagues and followers towards outcomes that benefit the team rather than merely serving the individual interest.

In Practice 10.2 NCAA leadership development

The National Collegiate Athletic Association invests in a leadership development program designed to provide education and training for college athletes, coaches, and administrators to assist with the transition to life after college sports. Their aim is also to foster the growth of the next generation of leaders and to encourage athletics administrators to translate lessons learned through competition. Their program offerings are comprehensive, including financial management, leadership training, and assistance in applying for graduate school entry.

One of their programs is focused on administrators, as their website attests:

> This programming is developed for the athletics professionals who work each day to serve student-athlete needs on campus and at the conference office. Administrators learn about emotional intelligence and student-athlete welfare and diversity initiatives, improve as public speakers, enhance leadership abilities and identify the skills related to specific coaching assignments. The opportunity is also there to build a close-knit network of advisors and engage the decision makers in college sports. In addition to exposure to university, conference and NCAA administrators, athletics professionals get real-time experience in budget management, strategic planning and fundraising, as well as university and NCAA compliance. Lessons include how to create comprehensive leadership curriculum for student-athletes and department staff; how to structure activities, facilitate discussions and build effective sessions; and create a leadership academy of your own on campus.

The Dr Charles Whitcomb Leadership Institute provides tailored programming to assist racial and ethnic minorities in strategically mapping and planning their careers in athletics administration. They also offer a Leadership Academy Workshop that educates and trains athletics administrators on the ins and outs of developing an effective, comprehensive leadership curriculum for student-athletes and department staff. Participants in the workshop learn how to structure activities, facilitate discussions, and structure effective sessions.

As an organization focused on athletes, the NCAA also offers an Athlete Development Professional Certification Program. The rationale on the website is:

As student-athlete development professionals grow in importance to college sports, it is critical that you possess not just a passion for sports, but consistent, applicable management and leadership skills and relevant business acumen. The Athlete Development Professional Certification Program will provide you with the business skills to work more effectively with college athletes, their families and campus constituents and become a well-respected and valued member of your school's team. During the program you will:

Develop essential management and leadership skills, including critical thinking and decision making, negotiation, influence and persuasion, finance for the college athlete, and crisis and media communications.

Hone your personal and professional leadership skills to motivate and engage peers, players, staff and league decision-makers.

This program is a joint venture between the NCAA, the Wharton Executive Education and the National Football League developed in conjunction with the Wharton Sports Business Initiative.

For more senior leaders, the NCAA also provides a pathway program designed to help people aspiring to reach the role of director of athletics. The summary from their website is as follows:

The Pathway Program is designed to elevate senior-level athletics administrators to the next step as directors of athletics or conference commissioners. This yearlong program is an intensive, experiential learning opportunity for selected participants who work at an NCAA school or conference in any division. Since its inception in 1997, the Pathway Program (formerly the Fellows Program) has produced more than 100 alumni. Nearly 25 percent of the participants have gone on to become directors of athletics, while more than 60 percent have received promotions in their careers. During the yearlong program, you will identify how values fit into your philosophy and execution of leadership within college athletics and higher education. You also develop knowledge in areas such as budgeting, strategic planning and fundraising for both your current job responsibilities and while you transition to the role of director of athletics.

The Pathway Program kicks off for all divisions during a weeklong session virtually with prominent guests, dedicated consultants, and an engaging curriculum. Throughout the year, program dates and locations will then cater to each division's needs, such as participating in governance meetings and media and interview training. Skill building will take place in the areas of values clarification, leadership, media training, diversity and inclusion, and you will get an in-depth look and introduction to search firms and the hiring process within college athletics. In addition to the in-person programming throughout the year, you will be paired with both a presidential and director of athletics mentor to assist you in navigating the year.

Source: NCAA website at www.ncaa.org/about/resources/leadership-development

LEADERSHIP AND MANAGEMENT

At this stage of the chapter, it will be useful to briefly consider the debate about the relationship between leadership and management and how to distinguish between the two. Kotter (1990) has conducted extensive research work in order to find how to differentiate managers from leaders. He concluded that management effectiveness rests in the ability to plan and budget, organize and staff, and control and solve problems. Leadership, however, is principally founded upon the ability to establish direction, align people, and motivate and inspire. According to Kotter, leaders achieve change, whilst managers succeed in maintaining the status quo. Bass (1990), however, states that "leaders manage and managers lead, but the two activities are not synonymous" (p. 383). It goes beyond the scope of this book to further elaborate on the distinction between leadership and management. Suffice it to say that in the context of discussing management principles in sport organizations, management without leadership is much less likely to be successful than a capable manager who can also provide excellent leadership. In the next section, we will therefore put forward what can be described as the five key functions of leadership:

- To create a vision
- To set out strategy
- To set objectives and lead towards performance
- To influence and motivate people
- To facilitate change and nurture culture

To create a vision

A vision can be described as "a state of the future that lies beyond the directly imaginable by most people". This view of the future, in the context of an organization, is a positive and bright state of being that only the "visionary" (one who is characterized by unusually acute foresight and imagination) can see at that time. In other words, the leader is responsible for envisioning a future for the organization that can become reality if the people working in the organization can be aligned towards achieving that envisioned state. It is often said that good leaders distinguish themselves from good managers because they have a vision, whereas managers do not. How to achieve the vision through strategy is the next function of the leader.

To set out strategy

The process of strategic planning is all about the different ways that a vision can be achieved. It constitutes two principal perspectives, that of the organization and that of the individuals making up the organization. Visionary leaders are not necessarily successful leaders if they are not capable of translating the vision into action strategies. The process of strategic management is, therefore, concerned with carefully managing the internal organization, including considering the individual needs of workers, and the external environment in which many opportunities and threats impact the ability of the leader to achieve the vision. To be better prepared for action, the leader needs to be involved in setting measurable objectives.

To set objectives and lead towards performance

Setting objectives is the next function of the leader. Once the broad strategies have been set out (and these strategies are never set in concrete; they need constant updating), it is time to link measurable outcomes to these strategies. In other words, what do we want to achieve in the short term in order to work towards our visionary objectives that lie ahead in the distant future? Stated differently, the leader often is involved in setting objectives at different levels of the organization, ranging from visionary and strategic objectives to mostly delegating the responsibility to set more operational objectives at lower levels of the organization. Only when SMART (specific, measurable, achievable, resources available, time bound) objectives are set will the leader be in a position to manage the performance of the organization and its employees effectively. An important part of the performance of an organization is achieved through the people management skills of the leader.

To influence and motivate people

In our overview of the different approaches to leadership, we have already commented on the different styles that leaders choose to develop (because they better fit their skill set) in order to influence groups of people and communicate with individuals or teams. Where setting objectives is important in making people aware of the targets of performance, the actual activation and application of people skills is critical when trying to steer people in a certain direction. This is where leaders with charismatic appeal will have an easier job. Their natural ability to inspire enthusiasm, interest, or affection in others by means of personal charm or influence will put these leaders in a favourable position with regard to achieving the objectives that were set.

To facilitate change and nurture culture

Finally it is important to acknowledge that in this day and age, change is constant. Leaders who are incapable of assisting others in understanding why change is needed and how this change can be achieved with minimal disruption and maximum outcomes will have a difficult time surviving in the organizations of the 21st century. Most organizations are required to keep close track of the market conditions that they are working under and the impact changes in market conditions will have on their structures and strategies. Often a rapid response to changing market conditions is needed, and this is where the interesting relationship with the organization's culture comes into play. Ironically, a strong and stable organizational culture can contribute to the need to constantly modify direction and change the systems and structures of the organization. It is the leaders' responsibility to create and nurture a culture in which change is accepted as part of the natural way of organizational life. A strong culture is the backbone of any successful organization, and the maintenance of culture is, therefore, one of the primary areas of leadership responsibility.

In Practice 10.3 UEFA Women in Football Program

The Union of European Football Associations has run an academy for many years that offers a range of professional development and education programs for people aspiring to work or currently working in football. Their programs include certificate, master, and specialist programs in general football management, governance, law, social responsibility, and communications, as well as programs for players in career transition and senior executive roles.

In 2019, UEFA launched a dedicated women's football strategy, committing UEFA to a five-year strategic framework with the aim of supporting, guiding, and lifting both women's football and the position of women in football across Europe by 2024. It focuses on building the foundations within UEFA and its member associations to give European women's football the best possible platform to thrive. This includes the further development of women who wish to work in football and the implementation of educational, leadership, and mentoring programs to achieve cultural gains and increase opportunities. The Women in Football Leadership Programme is one such program that UEFA has put in place to help double the number of women on UEFA governing bodies by 2024. The UEFA women's football strategy aims to reach the following goals by 2024:

- Double the number of women and girls playing football in UEFA's member associations to 2.5 million.
- Change the perceptions of women's football across Europe.
- Double the reach and value of the UEFA Women's EURO and the UEFA Women's Champions League.
- Improve player standards by reaching standard agreements for national team players and putting safeguarding policies in place in all 55 member associations.
- Double female representation on all UEFA bodies.

The Women in Football Leadership Programme aims to support the careers of women capable of influencing the football industry today and in the future and is designed for women in football who have the potential and motivation to progress into senior leadership positions within their organization or are already in such roles. Participants work on and discuss aspects of leadership while also focusing heavily on self-awareness and how this can support their career development. With the coaching included during the program, participants are challenged in both personal and professional aspects. Organized in collaboration with FIFA, the program also provides a platform for exchange and networking between participants with a rich variety of backgrounds.

The UEFA general secretary, Theodor Theodoridis, calls out UEFA's commitment and rationale for supporting women through this program:

> *Studies have shown that organisations with mixed senior management teams tend to outperform those with no women in positions of power. Football has*

traditionally been dominated by men, but gradually more women are moving into leadership roles. Still, more work needs to be done. UEFA understands that there is a real need for more balanced representation of women and men in key positions. Furthermore, UEFA acknowledges its responsibility to encourage and facilitate this shift. Through the Women in Football Leadership Programme, UEFA is committed to supporting and accelerating the process of placing more women in decision-making roles.

After completing the program, the aim is for participants to have:

- developed a clear understanding of what skills are needed for leadership and how these are reflected within their own professional characters;
- an increased level of self-awareness and an understanding of how this benefits their personal and professional goals;
- extended their network and created strong links with women working in positions of authority in football or ready to step into leadership roles; and
- built additional confidence to set and pursue ambitious career goals and fulfil their potential.

Source: The UEFA website at https://uefaacademy.com/courses/wflp/

SUMMARY

In this chapter, we described what it takes to be a leader. We argued that irrespective of leadership type or style, leaders are goal-oriented, they influence others, they empower others, they need to remain focused on the big picture, they need others to achieve their goals, and they have strong characters. Based on these components of leadership, we discussed a number of theoretical approaches to leadership, including the trait/personality, behavioural, and contingency approaches, ultimately resulting in a discussion about transactional versus transformational leadership. We also highlighted the differences between managers and leaders by outlining what the functions of leaders are: the creation of a vision, the setting out of strategy, setting objectives and measuring performance, influencing and motivating people, and finally, facilitating change and nurturing organizational culture.

REVIEW QUESTIONS

1 Are leaders born, or can they be made? Justify your answer by comparing the different leadership theories discussed in this chapter.

2 Does sport offer valuable leadership lessons to business? What are the specific characteristics of sport organizations that challenge leaders in sport organizations more than leaders in business, and how can this knowledge be transferred to a non-sport context?

3 "A good manager is also a good leader". Do you agree or disagree with this statement? Justify your answer.

4 Explain how leadership is important for the performance of a sport organization.

5 Interview the leader of a small sport organization. How would you describe their leadership style?

6 Is there any difference in the leadership skills required to be the CEO of a major professional sport franchise versus the leader of community sports club?

7 What criteria would you use to evaluate the leadership skills of a sport manager?

8 Is it possible to compare the performance of leaders of two different sport organizations? Why or why not?

9 Should leadership development programs focus on different skills for leaders of small, medium, or large sport organizations? Why or why not?

10 Should leaders of sport organizations look to learn from leaders in other sectors, or should they stay focused on what they can learn from other sport leaders? Justify your answer.

DISCUSSION QUESTIONS

1 Whom do you consider a good leader of a sport organization? What information have you used to form your view?

2 Whom do you consider a poor leader of a sport organization? What information have you used to form your view?

3 In professional sports, the CEO; coach; and sometimes chairman, president, or owner are seen as the leaders of the organization. Who is the most important and why?

4 What sort of support do middle managers need to make the transition from middle manager to CEO?

5 What sort of behaviours do you like to see exhibited by leaders in sport?

FURTHER READING

Bass, B. M. (1990). *Bass & Stogdill's handbook of leadership: Theory, research, and managerial applications* (3rd ed.). New York: Free Press.

Burton, L. J. (2015). Underrepresentation of women in sport leadership: A review of research. *Sport Management Review, 18*(2), 155–165.

Chelladurai, P., & Miller, J. M. (2017). Leadership in sport management. In R. Hoye & M. M. Parent (Eds.), *Handbook of sport management* (pp. 85–102). London: Sage.

Hill, L. A. (2008). Where will we find tomorrow's leaders? *Harvard Business Review, 86*(1), 123–129.

Kotter, J. P. (1990). *A force for change: How leadership differs from management*. New York: The Free Press.

Northouse, P. G. (2021). *Leadership: Theory and practice* (9th ed.). Thousand Oaks: Sage.

RELEVANT WEBSITES

Canadian Women and Sport website at www.womenandsport.ca

The Sport Australia website at www.sportaus.gov.au/grants_and_funding/wlis

Sport Leaders UK at www.sportsleaders.org/

UK Women in Sport website at www.womeninsport.org

Women Sport Australia at www.womensportaustralia.com.au/leadership

CASE STUDY 10.1

Leading Teams

Leading Teams is an Australian-based consulting firm specializing in facilitating change and improvement in organizations. Founded by Ray McLean and Kraig Grime, Leading Teams, according to its website, specializes in the delivery of culture change, leadership, and team development programs that create elite teams and improve performance in all industries. The Leading Teams model was first developed by co-founder Ray McLean during his days in the Royal Australian Air Force. He observed that all the teams he worked with received the same training, and yet some performed better than others. He realized there must be more to it than just training them on the mechanics of flying aeroplanes. So he started to explore the dynamics of the team – the behaviours and relationships between the members. Leading Teams shot to prominence through its work with a number of leading Australian Rules Football Clubs from 2002, including many that have subsequently had a sustained period of success, such as Geelong FC, Sydney Swans FC, and Hawthorn FC.

The Leading Teams website states there are three crucial elements to any high-performing team that create an environment of psychological safety in which team members can have genuine conversations about performance:

> Common purpose
> How do you define a team? We think that a team is any collection of people that have a common purpose; a group that is all trying to achieve the same thing. If you're not sure of yours, ask yourself, why does your team exist? What impact would there be on the organisation if your team didn't exist? You might be a sports team, all trying to win a premiership. Or you might be a sales team trying to win new business. Or you might be a working group drawn from lots of different areas of a business, all working together to deliver a project. Your team doesn't have to be formally defined, but it does have to share a common purpose if you are to achieve your objectives.

Agreed behavioural framework

What does it mean to be in your team? What behaviours do you expect? What behaviours do you accept that you know are counterproductive? Do you hear the language of responsibility of the language of blame and excuses? We ask every team we work with to create a set of behaviours – we call this a trademark – that define the team. And then we ask every member of the team to commit to living those behaviours, and to rewarding and challenging the behaviours they see from their colleagues according to that framework.

Strong professional relationships

Team dynamics are built on relationships. How much time do you spend working on your relationships in your team? We think it should be a priority, but often it's not. And to be clear, we're not referring to friendships – whilst it's great to be friends with your colleagues it's important to make sure you don't let friendship affect your ability to give and receive feedback. Building strong professional relationships, and an environment of trust and respect, takes time and effort but it pays dividends in performance.

The website for Leading Teams describes a key aspect of their approach:

Our Performance Improvement Program (PIP) is the cornerstone of our work at Leading Teams. It is a values-based approach to leadership, teamwork and culture change. For maximum impact the PIP is generally delivered over a sustained period and ideally encompasses an all-of-organisation approach. The program provides a structure that empowers team members to become leaders, be accountable, and participate in open and honest reviews of performance. We provide teams with the necessary tools to develop functional dynamics within the group and create shared vision, behaviours and expectations.

The specific aspect of the program that deals with leadership development includes:

Our leadership development activities are underpinned by our belief that true leaders need followers and it is these followers that empower the leader to actually lead. With this in mind, we have groups and individuals identify not only the tools required to lead, but also the leadership qualities and skills a good leader (in their environment) should display. Our focus, and the reason for our success, is the practical application of the tools, qualities and skills, not just the talking about them. We deliver these programs that not only do teams understand what it takes to be high performing, but also each individual knows what they need to commit to doing; in our world, everyone plays a role. This leads to the modelling, rewarding and challenging of the right behaviour in teams and a genuine commitment to help others in the team to do the same. We believe leaders are people that "see something, do something". We have had many success stories from our leadership programs – we believe that if there are high performing leaders, the team will be high performing.

Leading Teams has not only been involved in AFL; it was also engaged by the Australian Netball Diamonds Head Coach Lisa Alexander in their ultimately successful quest to secure a Commonwealth Games Gold Medal at the 2014 Glasgow Games. Players were asked to provide feedback on their own performances and their training sessions. In an article by Chris Barrett of The Age at www.theage.com.au, he cited the Diamonds captain, Laura Geitz, as saying

> It's about creating an honest environment. We've probably not had that in the Australian netball team before and it's speaking volumes. It was implemented at the beginning of last year [2013] and we went on to have our most successful series against New Zealand in 15 years. I think there's definitely something to be said for creating that environment where a lot of research goes into each individual, that's for sure. We've seen great things because of it.

The Leading Teams approach has not been without its critics, with some saying it can be too confrontational for some athletes and actually counterproductive to good performances. While this case study is not an endorsement of the Leading Teams approach, there does seem to be some merit in sport organizations engaging in a conscious attempt to develop their culture, their communication, and ultimately their leadership capacity at all levels of their organization.

CASE STUDY QUESTIONS

1   Is the Leading Teams model easier to implement in the context of sporting teams that strive for on-field success versus teams of people working in more off-field roles in sport? Justify your answer.

2   A detailed case study is provided by Leading Teams on its website based on its work with the Sydney Swans – www.leadingteams.net.au/wp-content/uploads/2018/03/Sydney-Swans-Success-Story.pdf. Do you think such an approach is viable over the long term in a football club with many players joining and leaving the group each year?

3   What challenges does this approach pose for leaders in organizations, given that they themselves are exposed to conversations about their own performance?

4   How well would this approach translate to other cultural settings where leaders and followers are not used to such "genuine conversations" and introspection on performance?

Sources: Leading Teams website www.leadingteams.net.au and the Chris Barrett article from July 23, 2014, at www.theage.com.au/commonwealth-games-glasgow-2014/commonwealth-games-news/lisa-alexander-has-some-homework-for-the-diamonds-20140723-zvw3y.html

CASE STUDY 10.2

Investing in women's leadership in sport

Australia, Canada, and the United Kingdom all have programs in place to address the lack of females serving in leadership roles in sport. This case explores the various programs across those three countries.

Australia has developed a national program conducted by Sport Australia to support the development of women as leaders in their respective sport systems. In Canada, a similar development program is conducted by the Canadian Women and Sport, formerly known as the Canadian Association for the Advancement of Women and Sport and Physical Activity (CAAWS).

The Women Leaders in Sport (WLIS) grant program (formerly Sport Leadership Grants and Scholarships for Women) is an Australian government initiative that is managed by the Sport Australia in partnership with the Australian Government Office for Women. The WLIS website claims it has supported more than 26,000 women with development opportunities since it started in 2002.

As part of the Women Leaders in Sport grant program, Sport Australia conducts a two-day residential sport leadership workshop for grant recipients, although during the COVID-19 pandemic, these were transitioned to an online format. The workshop aims to develop the participant's leadership capabilities to progress within sport as an administrator, coach, or official and to enable them to effectively manage the challenges within their sport and life in general.

Sport Australia also offers individual grants for women to undertake courses or training to support their professional development as leaders. Grant recipients can undertake courses or training in a wide range of areas, including leadership, governance, career coaching, coaching and officiating, media and communications, workforce and human relations, finance, integrity, and sport science and technology. Grants range from $4,000 to $10,000 depending on the experience of applicants.

Sport Australia also offers grants up to $20,000 to organizations that are committed to building leadership competencies for women and create more diverse and inclusive workplaces. The organization grant must go towards a project aimed at driving positive change in the workplace. Applications which outline how the grant will support their organization's gender equity policy/action plan or outline how female staff will continue to be supported following completion of the course will be prioritized. Applicants also need to demonstrate how the funding will improve either the leadership, capability, or culture of the organization in relation to supporting women.

Canadian Women and Sport, formerly CAAWS, was founded in 1981 to advocate for progressive change within Canada's sport system. Its goal was to see the enhanced presence of girls and women at all levels and in all areas – as athletes, participants, leaders, officials, coaches, and trainers. In 2020, the rebranded Canadian Women and Sport, stated that:

> our simple yet impactful new identity reinvigorates our platform as experts on gender equity and sport in the country. We are champions for girls and women in every arena and we are committed to building a better Canadian sport system – from the field of play to the boardroom.

Canadian Women and Sport is dedicated to creating an equitable and inclusive Canadian sport and physical activity system that empowers girls and women – as active participants and leaders – within and through sport. With a focus on systemic change, they partner with sport organizations, governments, and leaders to challenge the status quo and build better sport through gender equity. Their current strategic plan states:

> Canadian Women & Sport is committed to driving measurable impact that results in systemic change. Our goal by 2024 is to empower 10,000 leaders and 500 organizations to bring gender equity to life in their work. To achieve this, the new strategic plan focuses on the organization's three key priorities:
>
> * Deepening our gender equity work with sport organizations
> * Fostering ongoing relationships with our partners
> * Modernizing our current model
>
> This strategic plan responds in part to broader changes in the environment that place increasing value and priority on gender equity and inclusion. This is a unique moment in time when the benefits of building an equitable sport system for everyone are obvious and people are ready to act. Canadian Women and Sport seeks to leverage our position as the leading authority and voice on women and sport to advocate for gender equity and actively partner with organizations who share our goal of changing the game. Through our history collaborating with sport organizations to implement gender equity, our 40-year experience of leadership, impact programs and solutions, and our relationships at all levels of sport across Canada, Canadian Women & Sport is the right organization to help people get involved.

The UK charity Women in Sport was founded in 1984 and has a track record of success in securing change based on its deep understanding of the needs and aspirations of women and girls at each life stage and its determination to break down stubborn gender inequalities through its work within the sports sector and beyond. Its website provides the following summary of its role and work:

> Our expert and sector leading insight is driving innovation, our programmes are providing impactful solutions to tackle gender inequalities, and our campaigning

is empowering more women and girls to be active. Our purpose is to give every women and girl the opportunity to take part in sport and inspire her to do so.

By ensuring girls and women stay engaged in sport and physical activity, raising the profile of gender inequality, changing the culture of sport to eradicate sexism and discrimination, challenging gender stereotypes, and working with diverse communities to ensure all voices are heard, we can begin to breakdown these stubborn inequalities. Our expert and sector leading insight is driving innovation, our programmes are providing impactful solutions to tackle gendered inequalities, and our campaigning is empowering more women and girls to be active.

AIMS:

- Deeply understand the needs and aspirations of the full diversity of women and girls at each stage of their life
- Raise the profile of gender inequality in sport and the impact on women and girls
- Develop concepts, policy positions and identify solutions
- Campaign, collaborate and influence to inspire change
- Secure the future of the charity

CASE STUDY QUESTIONS

1   What are the differences between the programs offered by Sport Australia, Canadian Women and Sport, and the UK Women in Sport?

2   Why do we need these dedicated programs designed to support the role of women in sport and in particular within leadership roles in sport?

3   What other organizations exist to support women in sport leadership roles around the world, such as the UEFA Women in Football Leadership Program explained earlier in the chapter?

4   What other initiatives could be put in place by these agencies or others to support and improve the numbers of women in sport leadership roles?

Sources: The Sport Australia website at www.sportaus.gov.au/grants_and_funding/wlis, the Canadian Women and Sport website at www.womenandsport.ca, and the UK Women in Sport website at www.womeninsport.org

CHAPTER 11

Sport organizational culture

OVERVIEW

This chapter explores the basis for and influence of organizational culture in sport organizations. It examines what organization culture is and why organizational culture is important and explains how it can be understood and enhanced. This chapter is for readers who want to develop an understanding of organizational culture in sport and learn how to enact positive change in stagnant organizations where traditional values tend to dominate "how things are done". This chapter outlines how to discern

DOI: 10.4324/9781003217947-13

organizational culture and helps provide a guide for creating sport organizations with strong attachments and high performance. Various cases and examples will be used throughout the chapter to help explain the role of culture in a sport organization's ability to achieve its goals.

By the end of this chapter, the reader should be able to:

- Define organizational culture;
- Understand why culture is relevant to sport managers;
- Explain how different organizational contexts can influence culture;
- Connect organizational culture and organizational identity;
- Discuss various ways in which sport organizational cultures can be assessed; and
- Discuss how sport organizational culture can be changed or built.

DEFINING ORGANIZATIONAL CULTURE

Defining organizational culture presents a challenge; the idea itself has been conceptualized in different ways by researchers (Maitland et al., 2015). Another challenge presented in defining culture is that its mirror image, identity, can also be hard to define. Outlining what constitutes culture, and how it works, will help us to present the concept and its importance to those leading sport organizations. The general consensus among scholars is that organizational culture comprises the shared values, beliefs, assumptions, and standards for behaviour that influence the attitudes, habits, customs, and behaviour of an organization's members (Lussier & Kimball, n.d.). Sport managers need to be able to identify these shared ideas and determine how to use or modify them to make a positive impact within their organization.

Culture reflects the internal and external perceptions of an organization. Probing an organization's culture facilitates a better understanding of how groups, or subcultures, behave and work together and how others perceive them. The use of organizational culture in academic literature began to develop in the 1970s and beyond through scholars such as Pettigrew (1979) and Schein (1990) as researchers sought to understand the complexities of the phenomenon and the various ways that organizational culture is tied to organizational performance (Maitland et al., 2015). Since then, understanding culture became a key element of organizational theory and management practice given its central role in organizational functioning.

All organizations form their own distinctive culture(s); however, this does not prevent them from being dysfunctional or resistant to change. Typically, underperforming organizations utilize traditional values and customs as the underlying force which preserves old ways of doing things. Culture is embedded in the design, systems, and values of all aspects of the organization. Culture can serve as a backbone for unfounded beliefs retained under the premise of tradition and passed down through people who hold leadership roles in an organization for many years. It can be a formula for redundancy and chronic failure. While culture can be helpful to create synergy within an organization, not all cultures will lead to positive outcomes. In reality, some cultures are so embedded within an organization's identity that nothing can change them, and they can lead to poisonous attitudes and assumptions. For the outside observer, the effort that some organizations invest in preserving old identities does not make sense.

In contrast, appropriate cultures drive performance, leverage powerful histories, and adapt quickly in uncertain conditions. Organizations with great cultures find ways of succeeding because members agree upon and care about organizational values, which improves performance because people are motivated to work towards a shared vision and goals. Organizational culture provides an understanding of how and why an organization operates a certain way, the way the members behave, and the perceptions held by stakeholders. In other words, culture entails the way an organization's members interpret the expected behaviours, values, and beliefs.

THE RELEVANCE OF CULTURE TO THE SPORT MANAGER

All sport organizations possess cultures, but some are stronger than others. Strong cultures can exert a powerful influence on individual behaviour and organizational outcomes. Given the growth of sport management as a discipline of study, in combination with an increasing body of literature outlining sport's particular economies, sport cultures may be characterized by unique traits. As a result, the key to successful sport culture lies within understanding how it is conceived of, shared, preserved, and challenged within a specific context.

The idea of culture tends to receive only cursory attention from sport practitioners and educators alike. Part of this stems from culture's social and anthropological background, which does not instinctively hold any allure to the commercially minded, market-oriented, analytical sport executive. Sometimes, investigating culture can be seen as too intangible or removed from work-related outcomes or that too much "critiquing" of sport and organizations fails to accommodate the commercial realities of business. These arguments can then be easily linked to the belief that the assessment of culture may create a persistent tension within an organization about its identity, strategic management, and commercial outlook. For some, the critical analysis of culture will result in the organization being declared socially or culturally problematic. However, it is our view that the history and tradition associated with any sport organization needs to be recognized and interrogated to achieve any subsequent improvement in performance. Furthermore, any attempt to diagnose and improve sport culture must also acknowledge how sport is wielded as a tool for social benefit and shared understanding, yet this is not always the case.

Sport has both global and local relevance and is rarely best described in absolute terms. Indeed, the special features of sport organizations should be explored in order to understand their practices and environmental context. As a result, we caution against a view that limits the analysis of sport organizations to a single interpretive lens. Such a limited approach leaves little room for understanding the complexities in the relationships between sport fans, volunteers, employees, members, and the sport enterprise as a whole. If sport could be reduced to simple, one-dimensional cultural structures, then we would all be supporters of Manchester United and the Toronto Maple Leafs. We should also avoid dismissing the realities of sport's contextual factors, from its commodification to its media impact, which are discussed in detail in other chapters of this textbook.

DEFINING SPORT ORGANIZATIONAL CULTURE

Culture has been historically defined by anthropologists as the values and beliefs common to a group of people. Within academic literature, researchers are moving away from this traditional oversimplified definition of culture (Anderson-Levitt, 2012). Many current definitions explain culture as shared characteristics and social and behavioural practices (Edwards et al., 2013). While people in organizations do run the technology and invent the processes, they are also part of the process of shaping culture in their everyday actions. This means that much of their behaviour is determined by the systems they operate and how they enact various practices. In other words, there are underlying forces that impact behaviour of organizational members that shape shared meaning and coordinated action. The concept of culture is a way of putting a name to these forces.

While there is no single accepted definition of organizational culture (Edwards et al., 2013), most definitions typically include both intangible aspects (i.e., shared values, beliefs, and norms) as well as more tangible aspects (i.e., rituals and artefacts) that can be found in an organization (Odiakaose, 2018). Despite the lack of consensus surrounding definitions, several assumptions about organizational culture are widely accepted. These include:

1   Culture can be assumed to be inflexible and resistant to change.
2   Culture is created by an organization's history and its members.
3   Culture is learned and shared by organizational members and reflected in common understandings of beliefs and values.
4   Culture is often intangible and based on deep values and beliefs that drive behaviours that may not be easily identifiable.
5   Culture manifests in a variety of ways that impacts individual and organizational performance.

For the purposes of this chapter, we shall discuss organizational culture in a way that aligns with Schein (2016), which invokes a psycho-dynamic view of organizational culture. Essentially, this means that culture is an unconscious phenomenon, driven by deep level assumptions and beliefs, where conscious views are merely artefacts and symbolic representations (Schein, 2016). For example, most sport club members would report that on-field winning is important. Schein's (2016) interpretation of organizational culture suggests that we should ask questions about *why* winning is important. Does it relate to a need to belong to a successful group, the pressure of peers, or some other explanation? While many people involved in sport would think this question easy to answer, it is difficult to specify the underlying values that drive characteristics of culture, including rituals, ceremonies, myths, legends, stories, beliefs, artefacts, and attitudes.

Sports do have their own culture. Test cricket matches between countries can take up to five days to complete, often without a clear result. The various practices that members of cricket clubs and other stakeholders including fans engage in around cricket involve specific traditions and practices that become entrenched in how the game is played and in all forms of participation. Similarly, rugby can seem quite strange to anyone unfamiliar with the sport, as players are thrown to catch the ball and slide to score points. The practice associated with rugby off the field can be just as odd, with opposing teams gathering post-game for a "boat race", a drinking game that encourages a sense of camaraderie. In addition, many sport organizations are filled with memorabilia, performances of various kinds, and rituals. For example, the sport of curling often uses bagpipes and specific social rituals before and after games which have longstanding tradition in the Scottish heritage of the game and have carried to other countries outside of Scotland. Sport organizations are full of strong cultural symbols, which on the surface seem easy to interpret but sometimes are only superficial representations of deeper, more complex issues and can serve to enact culture in ways that signal inclusivity (or not).

Culture can be interrogated in order to understand both the superficial aspects of how things are done as well as the deeper, unconsciously held conceptions of why certain practices occur and the values that influence those practices. These values are the foundation of an organization's culture, but they do not exist or come into being in a vacuum. Instead, they are influenced by members of the organization who meticulously build them up as they learn to interact and achieve their collective and individual goals. An organization's past and present leaders are usually the most influential in developing and maintaining the culture. For this reason, it is important to examine the long-standing assumptions, beliefs, and practices of a sport organization.

For the purposes of this chapter, we define sport organizational culture as *the fundamental shared values, beliefs, and attitudes that are held by members of a sport organization and which subsequently establish the behavioural standards or norms for all members* (Lussier & Kimball, n.d.). This definition reflects the understanding that sport organizations have ways of operating those changes and develops over time. Based on this understanding, common phrases used to describe culture include how "things are done around here" and how "we think about things here".

THE IMPACT OF CULTURE IN DIFFERENT SPORT CONTEXTS

We can expect different sport organizations to possess different cultures. For example, professional clubs and major national leagues are more likely to emphasize dispassionate business values, while smaller, not-for-profit associations are more likely to value participation and fun. Indeed, there are many sports organizations which operate within the corporate commercial domain and exhibit the operational and structural characteristics of traditional business enterprises.

In some cases where profit is a significant driver of organizational values, sport organizations like the company Formula One Holdings manage the commercial rights to major events and have little interest other than to make money. While the Fédération Internationale de l'Automobile seeks to regulate motor sport, still others, like the International Olympic Committee, are interested in developing elite Olympic sports around the world and in so doing acquire vast sums of money and spend it liberally. Other organizations are less concerned with winning as long as they remain profitable and maintain a strong fan base associated with their brand.

Sport organizations within the nonprofit and public sectors hold values that are associated with civic participation, health, accessibility, fun, and inclusivity (e.g., Hemme et al., 2021). Here, sport organizations may demonstrate culture through particular stories and legends associated with those who have made a difference in their sport community rather than those who have been champions or built the organization's profit margin. Artefacts such as photographic displays, trophies, pieces of equipment, letters, and cards are particularly prominent in these types of sport organizations and can be an important material, sensory part of how an organization depicts culture (Mills & Hoeber, 2013).

One of the most important reasons for considering culture as a strategic tool in all sport organizations is that it can be very powerful in implementing (or resisting) change. Since culture can heavily influence how members behave and associate with the organization, the role of leaders in shaping culture can also determine whether changes in the organization are accepted or rejected and whether the process is smooth or laced with problems. In some sport contexts, it is common to have strong cultures that have been built by tradition and demonstrate a powerful connection to a sport's individual history. At the same time, some traditional cultural characteristics like excessive drinking and fighting may no longer suit the will of the expectations of stakeholders who question traditional elements and desire to see the culture of their sport evolve in different ways. Successful organizational change requires a change agent who can consistently implement, revisit, and communicate clearly in order to minimize concerns and maximize acceptance among key stakeholders (Hemme et al., 2021).

Discussions on organizational culture are highly diverse, and sport culture should not be seen as singular with no variability. Indeed, the nuances of each sport context and level should be examined, including various subcultures that can also exist within a singular organization. For example, each unit within an organization may have unique aims and objectives and may have differing traditions. Different stakeholder groups may also perceive the culture of an organization in unique ways based on their own motives and experiences. For example, a player may perform for a club because of loyalty or remuneration (or any number of other reasons), yet fans and supporters are usually passionately attached to a club's colours and traditions, expecting only on-field success in return. At the same time, some sport organizations are motivated by broader social and health agendas and values that relegate both winning and profit generation to secondary issues. Others still are held accountable to business returns by shareholders, owners, and sponsors. All of these motives help to shape the values that are reflected in an organization's culture and should not be dismissed or lumped into one singular effect.

In Practice 11.1 Culture as strategy: Arizona Diamondbacks, winning off the diamond

A key indicator of success in professional sport is on field performance. So, how can an organization be successful when they are losing on the field? The Arizona Diamondbacks of the MLB are a prime example. The D-backs have won numerous awards for their organizational culture, such as the Az Business Magazine and Best Companies Az Workplace Culture Award in 2013 (Goronkin, 2019). They have also been named one of the best places to work in Arizona for 12 consecutive years. Forbes has also recognized the D-backs as one of the best sports franchises to work for in the United States (Goronkin, 2019).

The D-backs use a core operating framework called the circle of success to describe the focus of the organization. The framework is made up of five areas: on-field performance, community, culture, financial efficiency, and fan experience (Temkin, 2015). It is easy to say you want to focus on culture and community, but these desires must be backed up by action. Since taking over as president of the D-backs in 2006 and then CEO in 2009, Derrick Hall has done just that. He has renamed their front office "The Culture and Innovation Centre" and has implemented several initiatives to ensure the organizational culture is strong and effective such as a president's council and round-table, quarterly outings, monthly health and wellness fairs, and arrival parties instead of going-away parties (Franks & O'Neill, 2014).

In sport organizations, it can be easy to focus on on-field performance and players while ignoring other organizational members. The D-backs have worked to integrate players into the wider organizational culture and encourage all employees to share the team's success. For example, when the team "sweeps" a series, there is a give-away of free housekeeping for a month; when a player makes the All-Star team, every employee gets an All-Star ring; players come shake hands with all the employees; and there are pictures of both players and staff on the walls of the organization's offices (Franks & O'Neill, 2014). Each of these examples contributes to a positive organizational culture through various manifestations of culture, including stories, symbols, and artefacts. Investing in a positive organizational culture makes employees feel valued, which leads to better performance and loyalty (Franks & O'Neill, 2014).

SPORT AND SUBCULTURES

Ideal business culture typically exemplifies the willingness of an organization's employees to accept a standard of performance that promotes quality in the production of goods and services in the attempt to generate a financial profit. It cannot be assumed that a single cohesive culture exists for all sports. Sport managers must be aware of the cultural nuances associated with their respective sports and the influence they have upon players, employees, members, fans, and the general public.

Culture is not a simple matter within a single sport either. Professional players, for example, have a different cultural attitude from most amateur participants, spectators, or sport parents. This variability of attitudes is indicative of a wider, more difficult area: the variety of cultures within sports. This is illustrated best at an international level, where players from different countries have been brought up with different ideologies of the game and how it should be played and represented. In the recent Tokyo 2021 Olympics, the German gymnastics team made a bold statement by wearing full-length unitards and challenging a long-held tradition of a leotard that revealed bare legs. Their action aimed to counter the sexualization of the sport and centred women's choice, showcasing how women should be able to wear what is comfortable and effective in their sport. Other gymnasts, coaches, and the media commended their actions, which have sparked movements in many countries to change uniform rules in sport clubs and schools. This is an example of the constantly evolving societal perspectives that can shift a sport culture.

Undeniably there is a need to study organizational cultures, accounting for the effect of the sport itself. For example, in the same way that we might expect that legal firms might share some cultural traits, so might we predict that curling clubs do as well. Similarly, the tradition and discipline central to a curling club might be expected to encourage cultural characteristics different to the youthful and eclectic philosophy found in a motocross club. Other sports, like field hockey and swimming, laud different values again, reinforcing perseverance, toughness, and power. These cultural attributes can even influence the behaviours of volunteers and employees of the clubs, especially since many sport organizations like to hire former/retired players. Since so many sporting organizations covet tradition and the accomplishments of the past, they tend to be resistant to change. However, before any change can occur, an organization's culture needs to be accurately diagnosed.

In Practice 11.2 Start-up culture breaks the mould of sport fandom with The Gist

The Gist is a Toronto (Canada)-based, women-founded and led sport media company. The Gist was founded in 2018 by a trio of college friends: Jacie deHoop, Ellen Hyslop, and Roslyn McLarty. The goal of the organization was to break the male-dominated mould of the sports media industry, where less than 14% of sports journalists are women (Oputu, 2014) and less than 4% of coverage is on women's sports (UNESCO, 2018). The Gist seeks to provide equal coverage of women's and men's sports with content designed particularly for fans who do not fit the standard traditional sport fan profile. While designed with women in mind, the content from The Gist is accessible for other groups marginalized in the sports industry. The bi-weekly email newsletters, social media posts, and podcast content provide updates on the latest in sports news and background information for newer fans and more diverse opinions than traditional sports media.

Culture is the essence of this company. It all started by recognizing that the male-dominated culture of sport fandom was problematic and exclusive. In response, they are building a successful enterprise that represents a fresh new sport culture focused on everyone being included and enjoying sport. Notably, 85% of their newsletter subscribers identify as female.

Developing a company that provides a fresh and fun perspective on sports was not easy. The team recognized and combined areas of expertise and shared values related to powerful storytelling, entrepreneurship, and challenging the status quo of sport fandom by making sport more accessible and inclusive to traditionally underserved audiences. They took part in various business-accelerator programs and received mentoring from successful entrepreneurs and sport media leaders.

Three years after the founding of The Gist, there are now 20 employees on the all-women team. Their weekly newsletters have grown to over 300K subscribers, and their social media following exceeds 110K on Instagram between their Canadian and US accounts. At the end of 2019, the founders of The Gist were featured on Forbes 30 under 30: Meet the Founders, Writers and Editors Shaping the Future of Media. Throughout their growth thus far, they have preserved their start-up culture by being flexible and recognizing employee preferences for working at home and developing specialized skills. This has enabled major new financing and the recruitment of top talent in different cities beyond Toronto and internationally.

The Gist is scaling up and hitting new milestones, but the founders remain passionate about their values; recognizing that female fandom is growing, women's sports are growing, and female purchasing power and control of wealth is increasing. By hiring people and covering athletes who are representative of a wider population, there is tremendous potential to shift sport media and culture moving forward.

SPORT ORGANIZATIONAL IDENTITY

Identity can be understood as an individual's self-definition (Ashforth & Schinoff, 2016). Previously, identity was thought of as stable and enduring, but it is now recognized that identity is fluid and can change over time, albeit slowly (Lawler, 2015). This fluidity is referred to as identity change, which occurs when the meanings of an individual's identity shift over time through a gradual and ongoing process (Stets & Serpe, 2013; Ashforth & Schinoff, 2016). Think of it this way: would you define yourself in the same way today as you did when you were 15 years old? Probably not.

Similarly, as social entities, sport organizations exhibit identities established by the adoption, reinforcement, and rejection of specific characteristics created by its members over time. The process operates as an extension of personal identity where individuals adopt or reinforce characteristics they perceive as advantageous while discarding those that are unappealing. For example, an organization might adopt team-based work practices if its members expect collaboration to be advantageous. An organization establishes its identity through the collective self-perceptions of insiders, which in turn complements how it performs (via culture), the way it expresses itself, and the way it is perceived by outsiders (via image). However, a sport organization might perceive itself in a manner incompatible with outside perceptions. It is difficult to bring these expressions and perceptions into alignment because identity reflects the views of insiders who may be unable to see issues present in the organization. Such beliefs determine not only an organization's understanding of itself but also how such statements are received and accepted (or rejected) by stakeholders.

In this way, culture and identity are highly related. Culture is about the way we do things, and identity is about how we perceive or are perceived. In this respect, organizational culture and identity work together in a reciprocal and synergistic manner. Culture is the deeper essence of the organization, often occurring at the unconscious or unseen levels, whereas identity is the visible and public dimension of an organization captured in public documents and forms of communication. Another way of looking at identity is as a manifestation and portrayal of culture. A metaphor of an iceberg is often used to describe the difference between and connection among these concepts. Organizational identity tends to be what we can see above the water, and culture is the deeper underlying dimensions of an organization that exist below the waterline. The two are completely connected, and leaders must be aware of the public identity of the organization and how it is connected to the actual organizational culture. There is danger when there is a gap between these and/or leaders are unaware of misalignment. In order to survive in a competitive environment, culture and identity must change together and remain aligned and relevant to their environment.

DIAGNOSING SPORT ORGANIZATIONAL CULTURE

There are many tools and methods to help a manager diagnose and manage organizational culture. It is dangerous to ignore culture until an organization becomes toxic and employees or volunteers leave. Negative culture can also cause reduced productivity and deterioration of people's well-being. Remember that sport organizations create meanings and atmospheres that influence behaviour, routines, practices, and the thinking of members. These systems and processes form patterns that are acquired primarily through socialization or learning over time from the reactions and behaviours of others.

Wise leaders take steps to understand culture all the time. In fact, individuals within a sport organization are exposed to what can be understood as "culture revealing" situations all the time. These can include the observable behaviour of other members, their organizational methods, "artefacts" – the photos, honour boards, and other memorabilia on show – and interactive communication, or the way in which individuals talk to each other. Some common intangible and tangible representations of organizational culture are outlined in Table 11.1. These are important to recognize because the underlying values and belief systems behind them are observable "symptoms".

These qualities include the physical environment, the public statements of officials, the way individuals communicate, the form of language used, what clothes are worn, and the memorabilia that fills the organization. Other important observable qualities in sporting organizations involve the place of sporting heroes. They represent highly visible indicators of the ideal culture. Heroes offer insight into the culture of an organization, because the members as well as power brokers select them. In addition, heroes exemplify the qualities in individuals respected and admired by the organization. The hero is a powerful figure in a sporting organization and may be simultaneously an employee and ex-player. The hero may also be charismatic, entrepreneurial, or just administrative, which often characterizes business enterprises. By understanding the orientation of hero figures, both past and present, it is possible to map trends of cultural change in the organization. Heroes can be both reactionary and progressive. For example, heroes who reinforce the dominant culture will not change the values and attitudes that the culture emphasizes. On the other hand, a hero who transcends and transforms the dominant culture will be a catalyst for change in the behaviours and values of a club. Often a hero is the most powerful medium for successful cultural change.

TABLE 11.1 Observable symptoms of sport organizational culture

Symptom	Explanation
Environment	The general surroundings of an organization, like the building it is housed in and the geographical location, like the city or in a grandstand.
Artefacts	Physical objects located in the organization such as photographs and trophies.
Language	The common words and phrases used by most organizational members, including gestures and body language.
Documents	Any literature, including reports, statements, promotional material, memos, and emails, produced for the purpose of communication.
Logos	Any symbolic visual imagery, including colours, fonts, and images, that convey meaning about the organization.
Heroes	Current or former organizational members who are considered exemplars or role models.
Stories	Narratives shared by organizational members based at least partly on true events.
Legends	Event with some historical basis but that have been embellished with fictional details.
Rituals	Standardized and repeated behaviours.
Rites	Elaborate, dramatic, planned sets of activities.

Tradition is another avenue for exploring the culture of an organization. Like heroes, traditions are observable through memorabilia. However, it is important to note the underlying values and assumptions that give meaning to heroes and traditions reside in the intangible aspects of a culture. Tradition may, on the one hand, be preserved by the present cultural identity, while, on the other hand, the sporting organization may have developed a contemporary cultural personality. For example, it may conduct business "the way it has always been done" while crafting a more modern public face through social media engagement. Thus, it is useful to acknowledge the importance of tradition and history to a sporting organization because it may be a cultural linchpin or a steppingstone from which the contemporary cultural character has been launched.

To avoid the obstacles (in the form of stereotypical views and superficial signs) that can impede an assessment of culture, it is essential to analyse and explore natural, observable aspects of culture: places where the cultural understandings can be revealed. By analyzing these areas, it is possible to gain practical insight into the deeper levels of culture in the organization. This level deals with organizational rites and rituals because their performance is readily apparent. By performing these rites and rituals, employees generally use other cultural forms of expression, such as customary language or jargon, gestures, and artefacts. These rites and rituals help disseminate values and beliefs (Smith & Stewart, 2011) and can be conveyed through stories associated with the occasion. Organizational rites and rituals may take the form of barbecues or presentations. To assess this level of culture, it is imperative that observational techniques be employed in collaboration with the meanings attached to them. This requires an in-depth analysis.

Although the surface level aspects of culture can be more easily observed, the difficulty comes in their interpretation because they are merely superficial representations of deeper held values. Schein (2016) recommends a layered approach to understanding organizational culture. In this approach, organizational norms stem from the values present in the artefacts and observable behaviour of an organization. Therefore, a valuable culture analysis will seek to comprehend what drives the observable behaviour. For example, what does it mean if an employee makes a mistake and is severely reprimanded by his or her boss? What does common jargon imply? Why are certain rituals typical, like the moment when a new player is allocated a number or jersey?

The key question remains as to how observable behaviours exemplify deeper values. Most research recommends some form of classification system that describes organizational culture in the form of "dimensions", each one a deeper, core value (Schein, 2016). These dimensions reflect on specific organizational characteristics as an aid to categorizing and understanding cultures. The summation of these characteristics may be used to describe an organization's culture, which allows for parallels to be drawn between organizations. For example, observable evidence in the form of a celebration event in a sporting club might be indicative of the nature of the organization's reward/motivation values. Enough observable evidence can lead a sport manager to make some tentative conclusions about each dimension.

Any analysis that captures the intricacy of organizational culture may struggle to separate the interwoven strands of organizational history and personal relationships. As a result, concrete conclusions may be difficult to establish. It is therefore important to take advantage of the symbolism created by sport's abundant myths, rituals, and ceremonies to gain a sense of the complete spectrum of human behaviour within a complex organization. The traditions, folklore, mythologies, dramas, successes, and traumas of the past are the threads that weave together the fabric of organizational culture.

In Practice 11.3 Embedding social responsibility into sport organizational cultures

Founded in 1950 by a group of 13 women, the LPGA is the oldest continuing women's professional sporting organization in the United States. The mission of the LPGA is to be a leader in sport by providing professionals the opportunity to chase their aspirations in the game of golf. While the LPGA's primary business operations revolve around the running of the tour, it also runs the LPGA Foundation, which was established in 1991. The mission of this foundation is to inspire and empower girls and women through golf. This mission is accomplished through four initiatives: LPGA-USGA

Girls Golf, LPGA Leadership Academies, Scholarship Programs, and the Dolores Hope LPGA Financial Assistance Initiative. In addition to the foundation, the LPGA Women's Network launched in 2017 to create an online space for women to connect, ignite their passion for golf, and inspire them. Currently, over 75% of the LPGA's management team is made up of women.

The LPGA is committed to increasing the diversity, accessibility, and inclusivity of golf. Part of this mission to make the game more approachable to under-represented girls and women as well as to increase the racial diversity of the association. The LPGA's diversity policy is built around a key principle, "act like a founder". The 13 founders were passionate about diversifying golf and making a difference and had the courage to stand up for their beliefs. In 1967, when a Black player was denied boarding with the rest of the tour, the other players responded with "We all stay, or we all go". The LPGA stands against racism, sexism, discrimination, and biases. This diversity policy extends to suppliers the LPGA partners with for tour events. The LPGA strives to support certified businesses owned or operated by underrepresented groups (i.e., minority, women, people of colour, LGBTQ+ individuals, veterans, people with disabilities, etc.).

While stating that the association does not tolerate racism, sexism, discrimination, and biases may seem like common sense, it is an important step to demonstrate how far the game has come. Golf has deeply racist and exclusionary roots, with many courses refusing to de-segregate. Golf remains a predominantly White sport, but the LPGA has been trying to grow diversity in the sport at a grassroots level through its actions and re-shaping traditions. The hope is that greater diversity at the grassroots level will translate to greater diversity on the tour in the future.

BUILDING SPORT ORGANIZATIONAL CULTURE

All possible data must be scrutinized to establish the most comprehensive image of the existing culture. For a culture to be created and bolstered, shared values and beliefs must be reinforced and transferred to organizational members through a tangible means. This can be achieved through cultural mapping. A cultural map typically identifies tangible aspects of organizational culture (Duxbury, 2015). Traditional forms of culture mapping do not adequately account for intangible aspects of organizational cultures. As part of culture mapping, there are some questions that a sport manager can ask and steps you can take to guide culture-building work.

Ask:

- What are the behaviours you want to encourage?
- What benchmarks show you're on the right path?
- What examples of positive culture are evident?
- How are our traditions holding us back?
- Who is/is not included in our cultural practices?

Steps:

- Review your stories: Examine the stories you tell and the people you exalt. These narratives are indicative of the culture you are building. Review whether these are the stories you believe reflect the culture you hope to achieve and whether these stories support your long-term goals.
- Review the connection between your words and actions: assess whether your language aligns with your own behaviour and find out whether others view this as congruent or not. Ask people you trust to be candid with you, or try an anonymous process (e.g., suggestion box) to determine this link.
- Observe the behaviours of other members: Observe how people act in meetings or celebrations and whether they attend willingly or with reservation. Assess whether quality relationships are built within the organization and whether people are welcome to express their views openly.
- Discuss organizational values on a regular basis: openly discuss the values of the organization in order to allow them to guide decisions and action and ensure they are embedded within culture. Develop a consensus on behavioural standards by ensuring that people know and are excited by the articulated values.
- Consider third-party assessments: don't shy away from getting help with culture-building activities when needed. These can include fun, team-building activities as well as focus groups and other in-depth evaluation practices to assess and build culture. Setting a tone that culture is valued and improvable is an important aspect of leadership.

Creating cultural change cannot be achieved without a clear understanding of an organization's primary cultural traits and how they present. Once an accurate analysis has been undertaken through some form of cultural mapping, elements of culture can be managed. For example, new rituals can be introduced to replace older, less desirable ones, like a club dinner instead of a drinking binge. Deep-rooted values and beliefs can be difficult to change, and even with the right implementation of new symbols, language, heroes, stories, employees, and so on, genuine cultural change in an organization can take a very long time to accomplish.

SUMMARY

As outlined at the beginning of this chapter, sport organizational culture can be defined as the collection of shared fundamental values and attitudes that are common to members of a sport organization and which subsequently set the behavioural standards or norms for all members. Although a challenging concept to define, culture shapes the combined conduct of all organizational members. It does this by instilling values and beliefs among organizational members. In turn, values, and beliefs convey and restrict ways of thinking. In short, culture shapes conduct and individual behaviour. For example, cultural values and beliefs might explain why profit should override environmental sensitivity or why winning and success are more important than participation. As a result, some cultures create socially valued outcomes, while others create dysfunctional cultures. Culture can be changed for the better, but it requires shrewd management, and it demands a deep understanding of how culture works. Remember to examine the tip of the cultural iceberg (the accessible aspects of culture like symbols and artefacts) as well as the iceberg's underwater composition (the deep values and beliefs of organizational members). Once a complete diagnosis has been achieved, sport managers can work toward creating cultural change.

REVIEW QUESTIONS

1   What are the key components of organizational culture?
2   Why is organization culture important to sport managers?
3   Describe the difference between tangible elements of culture and intangible elements of culture.
4   What is the difference between organizational culture and identity?
5   What symptoms of culture can be used to assess a sport organization?
6   How does mapping an organizational culture help to create change?
7   Select a sport organization you belong or have belonged to. Create a list of attributes or values that you believe embody its organizational culture. Which are the characteristics that distinguish it from other sport organizations in different contexts?
8   Select a sport organization you belong or have belonged to. Describe the stories, myths, artefacts, or rituals that are evident and explain how each illuminates aspects of organizational culture.

DISCUSSION QUESTIONS

1   Do all organizations that are affiliated with the same sport share cultural features?
2   Discuss the observable symptoms of culture and discuss some examples in a commercial sport organization and in a nonprofit sport organization.
3   Can an organizational member diagnose the culture objectively? If so, how do you think they could go about it? If not, what should they do instead?
4   Discuss the relationship between culture and change. As a sport leader, what considerations should you be mindful of when approaching an organizational change?
5   Identify a media story of a sport organization whose culture has influenced organizational performance (positive or negative). What aspects of culture were most powerful and could be enhanced or changed in the future to alter performance?

FURTHER READING

Anderson-Levitt, K. M. (2012). Complicating the concept of culture. *Comparative Education, 48*(4), 441–454. https://doi.org/10.1080/03050068.2011.634285

Ashforth, B. E., & Schinoff, B. S. (2016). Identity under construction: How individuals come to define themselves in organizations. *Annual Review of Organizational Psychology and Organizational Behavior*, 3(1), 111–137. https://doi.org/10.1146/annurev-orgpsych-041015-062322

Bailey, B., Benson, A. J., & Bruner, M. W. (2017). Investigating the organisational culture of CrossFit. *International Journal of Sport and Exercise Psychology*, 1–15. dx.doi.org/10.1080/1612197X.2017.1329223

Duxbury, N. (2015). Positioning cultural mapping in local planning and development contexts: An introduction. *Culture and Local Governance*, 5(1–2), 1–7. https://doi.org/10.18192/clg-cgl.v5i1-2.1437

Edwards, J. R. D., Davey, J., & Armstrong, K. (2013). Returning to the roots of culture: A review and re-conceptualisation of safety culture. *Safety Science*, 55, 70–80. https://doi.org/10.1016/j.ssci.2013.01.004

Eskiler, E., Geri, S., Sertbas, K., & Calik, F. (2016). The effects of organizational culture on organizational creativity and innovativeness in the sport businesses. *The Anthropologist*, 23, 590–597.

Hemme, F., Morais, D. G., Bowers, M. T., & Todd, J. S. (2021). Leading culture change in public recreation. *Journal of Sport Management*, 1(aop), 1–14. https://doi.org/10.1123/jsm.2020-0249

Lawler, S. (2015). *Identity: Sociological perspectives*. London: John Wiley & Sons.

Lussier, R., & Kimball, D. (n.d.). *Sport managers influence organizational culture*. Human Kinetics. Retrieved June 30, 2021, from https://us.humankinetics.com/blogs/excerpt/sport-managers-influence-organizational-culture

Maitland, A., Hills, L. A., & Rhind, D. J. (2015). Organisational culture in sport – A systematic review. *Sport Management Review*, 18(4), 501–516. https://doi.org/10.1016/j.smr.2014.11.004

Manley, A., Roderick, M., & Parker, A. (2016). Disciplinary mechanisms and the discourse of identity: The creation of 'silence' in an elite sports academy. *Culture and Organization*, 22(3), 221–244.

Mills, C., & Hoeber, L. (2013). Exploring organizational culture through artifacts in a community figure skating club. *Journal of Sport Management*, 27(6), 482–496. https://doi.org/10.1123/jsm.27.6.482

Odor, H. O. (2018). Organisational culture and dynamics. *Global Journal of Management and Business Research*. Retrieved from www.journalofbusiness.org/index.php/GJMBR/article/view/2406

Organizational Culture and Leadership – Edgar H. Schein – Google Books. (n.d.). Retrieved June 24, 2021, from https://books.google.ca/books?hl=en&lr=&id=Mnres2PlFLMC&oi=fnd&pg=PR9&dq=cultural+dimensions+in+organizations+schein&ots=opdsKe4wSl&sig=shBIHUAjtmZ3YKHx2HmWVBBPn4g#v=onepage&q=cultural%20dimensions%20in%20organizations%20schein&f=false

Pettigrew, A. M. (1979). On studying organizational cultures. *Administrative Science Quarterly*, 24, 570–581.

Schein, E. H. (1990). Organizational culture. *American Psychologist*, 45(2), 109–119. https://doi.org/10.1037/0003-066X.45.2.109

Schein, E. H. (2016). *Organizational culture and leadership* (5th ed.). San Francisco: Jossey-Bass.

Smith, A. C. T., & Stewart, B. (2011). Organizational rituals: Features, functions and mechanisms. *International Journal of Management Reviews, 13*(2), 113–133. https://doi.org/10.1111/j.1468-2370.2010.00288.x

Stets, J. E., & Serpe, R. T. (2013). Identity theory. In J. DeLamater & A. Ward (Eds.), *Handbook of social psychology* (pp. 31–60). Springer Netherlands. https://doi.org/10.1007/978-94-007-6772-0_2

Wagstaff, C. R., Martin, L. J., & Thelwell, R. C. (2017). Subgroups and cliques in sport: A longitudinal case study of a rugby union team. *Psychology of Sport and Exercise, 30,* 164–172.

RELEVANT WEBSITES

Arizona Diamondbacks at www.cxpa.org/blogs/tema-frank/2015/05/11/diamondbacks-customer-experience, www.linkedin.com/pulse/diamondbacks-winning-record-leadership-organizational-joleen-goronkin/, www.xminstitute.com/blog/diamondbacks-ceo-fan-culture/

The GIST at https://ca.thegistsports.com/about/, www.forbes.com/sites/jilliancanning/2019/11/05/the-gist-a-sports-community-for-women-by-women-launches-in-the-us-after-growing-subscribers-to-40k-in-canada/?sh=6573f5107661, https://techcrunch.com/2021/05/19/women-led-sports-media-startup-the-gist-raises-1m-to-challenge-sports-reporting-norms/

LPGA at www.lpga.com/diversity, www.theringer.com/2021/4/7/22370057/golf-diversity-issues-history-pga-lpga-the-masters

WNBA at https://globalsportmatters.com/culture/2021/04/09/its-in-our-dna-wnba-players-record-of-activism/, www.wnba.com/news/wnba-announces-a-2020-season-dedicated-to-social-justice/

CASE STUDY 11.1

Building research and evaluation into the culture of MLSE Launchpad

MLSE Launchpad is a living lab in Toronto where youth facing barriers can use sport to recognize and reach their full potential. The programming at MLSE Launchpad supports four key pillars: healthy body, healthy mind, ready for school, and ready for work. The Launchpad facility in downtown Toronto is made up of three sport courts, an adventure wall, classrooms, a wellness room, a nutrition lab, and several offices. Each of these areas contributes to the development of the four pillars and the organization's mission. Their programming is built around sport for development (SFD). UNICEF (n.d.) defines SFD as "the use of sport, or any a form of physical activity, to provide both children and adults with the opportunity to achieve their full potential through initiatives that promote personal and social development" (p. 3).

Launchpad partners with many community and corporate partners (including professional sport brands) to deliver programs that operate within a "sport plus" framework as well as a "plus sport" framework. For example, a sport plus program aims to increase participation in sport by providing resources, equipment, and coaching. Secondary benefits such as the development of life skills, education, and health are incorporated (e.g., a basketball program that incorporates tutoring or leadership development). A plus sport program is more focused on the non-sporting outcomes that can result from a given program, such as positive educational outcomes, mentorship, or reducing violence (e.g., an employment training session that incorporates a ball hockey activity). Among their programs, they provide free school programs like Fuel for Fun – an interactive physical and food literacy program for 5th-grade students; Homework Club, which provides tutoring support and educational activities for ages 6–16; and Sport and STEM, which is an interactive program where participants (7th- and 8th-grade students) explore STEM topics through sport. Launchpad also provides yoga and counselling through partner organizations.

To fulfil its mission, the organization demonstrates a clear commitment to anti-racism, equity, and inclusion by amplifying the lived experiences of Black, Indigenous, and other communities of colour. Given that many of the participants at Launchpad are racialized and marginalized individuals, there is strong sensitivity to understanding their perspectives in order to make decisions about programs and resource allocation. Given the variety of programs delivered, there is also a strong recognition that the success of each program should be measured in unique ways. These values are central drivers in "how things are done" and are the basis for a strong research arm of the organization. In fact, Launchpad is unique in that it is a program provider and a research centre. The research being conducted at Launchpad seeks to measure the programs' impact on educational and employment outcomes in addition to continued sports participation. Given that the organization is committed to achieving sustainable, wide-ranging social outcomes for youth facing barriers and that SFD uses specific methodologies to achieve impact, the organization is dedicated to extensive measurement and evaluation.

There are several staff among the Launchpad executive team whose primary roles connect to research and evaluation. This is an unusual and important asset to the overall mission and culture of the organization. By hiring experts in research, the entire organization is able to collect data and show specific results for a given program, thereby demonstrating impact for donors and other stakeholders. For example, the team recently conducted a pre- and post-assessment for a two-week youth day camp focused on physical literacy and was able to demonstrate significant increases in fundamental movement skills and self-perceptions of physical literacy (Warner et al., 2021). This is a unique capability given that 86% of Ontario nonprofits do not have staff with expertise in evaluation (Ontario Nonprofit Network, 2018).

In addition to measurement and evaluation projects using traditional tools and methods, Launchpad also engages in extensive program evaluation by engaging youth themselves in the process. But engaging youth in research is no easy task, as it is difficult to compete with their other priorities and preferences. In response, MLSE Launchpad has pioneered many creative approaches to engaging kids in the evaluation process. Rather than relying on survey techniques, it developed a "MISSION Measurement Model" that stands for minimal, I-statements, short, strengths-based, involve coaches, online, no neutrality (Warner & Heal, 2020). These principles have been applied to all of its research design and evaluation frameworks as well as research partnerships.

In addition to applying this model, Launchpad also uses "courtside" evaluation whenever possible to engage youth. By collecting data on portable tablets, it is able to value youths' time and conduct brief interviews to solicit feedback on program experiences. These processes combine digital and relational methods to ensure youth know that their voices and time are valued. As a result, it has seen increased youth and coach buy-in and generated better and more data (Warner & Heal, 2020). It has also incentivized participation by providing meals, draws for sport apparel or equipment, pizza parties, and outings. These efforts demonstrate to youth that they are an important part of making decisions and that they are valued in the Launchpad community.

Many nonprofit organizations struggle to collect meaningful data and demonstrate impact (Ontario Nonprofit Network, 2018). Engaging trained staff and youth in the evaluative process is one way in which an organization can reduce barriers and put its values into action, right in front of its key stakeholders.

CASE STUDY QUESTIONS

1   How can sport be used as a tool for improving social, educational, and employment outcomes for individuals? What makes SFD organizations unique compared to "traditional" sport organizations?

2   What are some strategies that can be used to engage youth in the evaluation of sport programs? Why is it important for their voice to be heard in decision-making?

3   What are some considerations for shaping a culture of research in sport organizations?

SOURCES

Engaging Youth in Evaluation Processes. (n.d.). *The sport information resource centre*. Retrieved July 30, 2021, from https://sirc.ca/blog/engaging-youth-in-evaluation-processes/

Getting into the game: Understanding the evidence for child-focused sport for development. (n.d.). Retrieved July 28, 2021, from www.unicef-irc.org/getting-into-the-game

Ontario Nonprofit Network. (2018). *The state of evaluation: Measurement and evaluation practices in Ontario's nonprofit sector*. Retrieved from https://theonn.ca/wp-content/uploads/2018/10/State-of-Evauation-October-2018.pdf

Warner, M., Robinson, J., Heal, B., et al. (2021). Increasing physical literacy in youth: A two-week sport for development program for children aged 6–10. *Prospects, 50*, 165–182. https://doi.org/10.1007/s11125-020-09519-5

CASE STUDY 11.2

WNBA and Black Lives Matter activism

In 2020, amid the COVID-19 global health pandemic, Black Lives Matter (BLM) protests occurred across the United States and Canada. The protests were in response to the police killings of George Floyd and Breonna Taylor and the shooting of 29-year-old Jacob Blake, who was left paralyzed by law enforcement. Following the shooting of Jacob Blake in August 2020, the WNBA and NBA teams that were scheduled to play that night postponed their games. After the postponements, most headlines detailed the leadership of the NBA while failing to acknowledge the consistent work on social justice done by the WNBA for years. This failure, while perhaps unsurprising, highlights the NBA as a leader in activism while painting the WNBA as followers of the NBA's example. While NBA players have been vocal about supporting the BLM movement, the women of the WNBA have led the charge for years with much more at stake. In the COVID-19 playing bubble, NBA players who opted out of the (playoff) bubble took a pay cut, while WNBA players who opted out for non-health-related issues (e.g., feeling unsafe) forfeited their entire salary.

While these postponements signalled a new era of social and racial justice in sport, it was only the most recent example of the WNBA activism. In 2016, shortly before Colin Kaepernick began kneeling during the national anthem before NFL games, players in the WNBA began protesting police brutality following the killings of Philando Castile and Alton Sterling. Four players from the Minnesota Lynx (Maya Moore, Seimone Augustus, Lindsay Whalen, and Rebekkah Brunson) held a pre-game press conference in which they wore black shirts emblazoned with "Change Starts with Us" and "Justice & Accountability". Following this press conference, the New York Liberty and the Phoenix Mercury wore BLM shirts during warmup. The league fined the players for violating WNBA rules governing approved warmup attire. These fines were rescinded after pushback from players, which included media blackouts post-game where players refused to answer questions about the game that had just finished. WNBA players also took to kneeling during the anthem to protest racial inequality. Several WNBA players opted out of the 2020 season to focus on social justice activism. Many players shared BLM content and encouraged people to vote on social media. They also started the Say Her Name campaign, which is dedicated to saying the names and fighting for justice for Black women, who are so often forgotten in the fight for justice.

The WNBA has engaged in collective action to raise awareness for social justice issues, especially the BLM movement. At the beginning of the 2020 season, the WNBA and WNBPA announced the launch of a Social Justice Council to address the United States' long history of inequality, implicit bias, and systemic racism that has targeted Black and Brown communities. This council will focus primarily on issues of race, voting rights, LGBTQ+ advocacy, and gun control, but other social issues will also be tackled. The Atlanta Dream were named the Sports Humanitarian Team of the Year for their activism. The Sports Humanitarian Team of the Year is awarded to a sports team that demonstrates how teamwork can create a measurable impact on a community or cause. Players of the Atlanta Dream protested US Senator Kelly Loeffler who, at the time, was part owner of the team and openly criticized the BLM movement. Loeffler has since sold her stake in team after pressure from the players and the league that her values didn't fit with the WNBA.

The WNBA's activism and other examples of protests and activism from athletes are ushering in a new era for sport organizations. Athletes are using their platform to advocate for social justice issues and shape tradition in a collective way that has not been seen before. Other professional sporting leagues must follow the example of the WNBA to remain relevant to younger, more diverse, and more civically engaged fans. With the prevalence of social media, athletes have a platform that extends beyond their sport, allowing them to engage with fans in new ways and draw public attention to their affiliated organizations' policies and values. Athletes can share content with their legions of follows from anywhere at any time, and this instantaneous media production and consumption can be incredibly influential.

The physical and mental health benefits of sport are widely known and claimed as values of sport organizations, but sport can stand for and improve more than health. Sport can also contribute to building awareness and support for social issues as a setting in which cultural and social barriers can be eliminated. Sport has even been used as a diplomatic tool on many occasions, which illuminates the power sport has to bring people together or to divide. The WNBA continues to demonstrate values related to racial equity, engaging in FIT month in July 2021 by engaging players, partners, and community organizations to focus on health inequities in communities of colour through All-Star events and pop-up collaborations focused on healthy lifestyles and nutrition. These actions represent a powerful way for organizations and leagues to ensure that their deeply held beliefs are evident through their public image and identity and to be accountable to their stakeholders for their actions. By continuing to profile athletes who are leading the fight against systemic racism and advocating for systemically disadvantaged people, the WNBA and the WNBA Social Justice Council can lead the movement to social reform through sport.

CASE STUDY QUESTIONS

1   What role did organizational culture play in the WNBA's ability to enact social change? Conduct internet research of your own to determine how various aspects of culture are evident through the WNBA's actions.

2   How can other leagues or sport organizations follow the WNBA's example and incorporate activism into their organization?

3   Where will activism in sport go from here? What does the future of sport look like? Has it impacted your perception of an organization or league's identity?

4   How can the WNBA better demonstrate its commitment to activism through its culture?

SOURCES

"It's in Our DNA": WNBA Players' Record of Activism. (2021, April 9). Global Sport Matters. Retrieved from https://globalsportmatters.com/culture/2021/04/09/its-in-our-dna-wnba-players-record-of-activism/

Black Lives Matter: WNBA players will continue to Say Her Name when season resumes | NBA News | Sky Sports. (2020). Retrieved July 30, 2021, from www.skysports.com/nba/news/36244/12058213/black-lives-matter-wnba-players-will-continue-to-say-her-name-when-season-resumes

How the power of sport can bring us together and drive social justice. (n.d.). World Economic Forum. Retrieved July 30, 2021, from www.weforum.org/agenda/2021/01/uniting-the-world-through-sport-what-can-we-learn-from-sport-in-enabling-social-cohesion/

Laurent Duvernay-Tardif, Atlanta Dream and Arthur Blank among Honorees at 2021 Sports Humanitarian Awards – ESPN Press Room U.S. (n.d.). Retrieved July 30, 2021, from https://espnpressroom.com/us/press-releases/2021/07/laurent-duvernay-tardiff-atlanta-dream-and-arthur-blank-among-honorees-at-2021-sports-humanitarian-awards/

The uniquely unifying power of sports, and why it matters. (n.d.). World Economic Forum. Retrieved July 30, 2021, from www.weforum.org/agenda/2018/02/north-and-south-korea-have-shown-us-the-unifying-power-of-sport/

WNBA Announces a 2020 Season Dedicated to Social Justice – WNBA.com – Official Site of the WNBA. (2020). Retrieved July 30, 2021, from www.wnba.com/news/wnba-announces-a-2020-season-dedicated-to-social-justice/

CHAPTER 12

Sport marketing

OVERVIEW

The principles and elements of sport marketing are essential knowledge for sport managers to be able to position their sport event, team, or athlete in the highly competitive sport market. This chapter examines the marketing of sport entities such as leagues, teams, athletes, sport equipment and merchandise manufacturers, and sporting events. The purpose of this chapter is to provide an overview of the key elements of sport marketing and demonstrate the value of sport marketing in this unique industry.

After completing this chapter, the reader should be able to:

- Understand the importance of sport marketing;
- Describe some of the unique aspects of sport marketing, including the core product and contemporary trends; and
- Recognize the role of branding and sponsorship as anchors for revenue generation.

DOI: 10.4324/9781003217947-14

UNDERSTANDING SPORT MARKETING

One of the biggest draws for students wanting to work in sport management or the business of sport is the marketing activities associated with the industry. Marketing, in all industries, generally refers to the process of planning and implementing activities and schemes designed to connect business entities with consumers, specifically meeting the needs and/or wants of the latter. But, at its core, the marketing process seeks to create an exchange, where, in the modern era, the customer relinquishes money (physical print money or through digital, virtual means) for the ability to consume a product or service.

Sport marketing draws on this general view of marketing and extends it further. Here, sport marketing is focused on satisfying the needs and/or wants of sport consumers, individuals seeking to buy sport-related goods and services such as equipment, apparel and merchandise, and autographed memorabilia but also playing, watching, or listening to sport. It is this latter piece which makes helps to make sport marketing unique. Unlike marketing computer tablets, a clothing brand, or vehicles, there are both tangible and intangible elements in the sport industry. Thus, whereas generalist marketers may be conditioned to consider the physical attributes and performance of a product (e.g., memory within a computer), sport marketers must recognize when to consider those physical attributes and when to consider non-physical attributes like the match day experience.

Given this dynamic, it is also important for students to understand that there are two key dimensions to sport marketing: the marketing *of* sports and marketing *through* sports. The first dimension is the marketing *of* sport products and services directly to consumers. This involves those tangible (e.g., sporting equipment) and intangible (e.g., sport events, club membership) elements mentioned previously. However, there is also a second dimension which involves the marketing of other non-sport products and services but which uses sport as a vehicle to get their message across. This is known as marketing *through* sport. Some examples might include an airliner providing travel to the team and its officials for away matches (e.g., Virgin Australia and the Australian Football League), a non-alcoholic drink manufacturer arranging to have exclusive "pouring" rights in a professional sport venue (e.g., PepsiCo and SoFi Stadium in Los Angeles), or even an electronics company providing smartphones for elite amateur athletes to utilize when resting after their competition (e.g., Samsung and Olympic and Paralympic athletes). In these examples, the prominence and high visibility of sport offers a unique proposition for non-sport businesses to market their traditional products and services. These two dimensions help to underscore the importance of sport marketing specifically in driving business development and revenue generation.

The sport industry is expansive in that it involves recreational, amateur, and professional sectors, but there is an important commercial function which highlights the importance of sport marketing. Perspectives will vary, but there is little doubt that business development and revenue generation is of critical importance to the sport industry. Without revenue, sport entities do not have the capacity to acquire human resources, business and athletic talent, and materials needed to create tangible sport

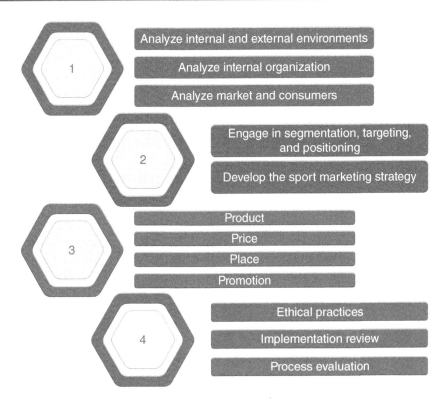

FIGURE 12.1 The sport marketing framework

products or intangible sport experiences. Revenue is the lifeblood of an organization, sport or otherwise, and is also an important source to draw from for innovation, research and development. Thus, irrespective of what sector a sport manager is operating within or their perspective of the commercialization of sport, generating revenue is critical to sustaining and growing organizations, and marketing aids in that revenue generation. Figure 12.1 presents a useful four-stage framework for sport management students who aspire to become marketers in the industry. While the process may seem complex, at its core, it is necessary to know what is being marketed: the sport product.

THE SPORT PRODUCT

Conceptually, sport marketing is built on a foundation of various dimensions known as "the Ps". Borrowing from traditional marketing literature, there are four Ps (product, price, place, and promotion), while contemporary literature has expanded to seven Ps, adding people, process, and physical evidence. Although these elements are important, they are incredibly nuanced, and whole courses are devoted to unpacking these intricate aspects.

However, whether from a traditional or modern view, there is one core P that deserves attention for students being exposed to the importance of the sport marketing function: product.

Products are goods and services that can bought, sold, and consumed. They are incredibly important, occupying the sport entity's ability to satisfy the needs and/or wants of consumers. For instance, a golfer wanting to stay dry during a rainy morning might *need* a product to prevent their person and their equipment from being drenched (i.e., a golf umbrella), while a child might *want* to see Australian global footballer Sam Kerr and ask their parents to purchase tickets to a Matildas match. In both of these examples, there is a product present that is central to the transactional exchange process in which marketing concentrates its efforts. Consequently, products have different forms. They can be 1) a physical good, 2) a service, 3) an idea, or 4) a combination of any of these. In a non-sport context, a physical good could refer to a coffee mug, a service could manifest in the form of second language tutoring, and an idea could be a new model or platform to buy and sell gift cards. These three types of products are abundant, and, as the globe has moved from an agricultural economy to an industrial economy to now a knowledge-based economy, there are more products that exist as combinations of these three, coinciding with the rise of innovation and entrepreneurship (Bessant & Tidd, 2015).

But what makes the sport product unique? This has been the underlying dilemma for marketers as the sport industry has evolved over the last 40 years in particular. Certainly, sport is made up of goods, services, ideas, and combinations of the three, but there exists significant variance in the sport product versus the non-sport product. Although there are physical goods in the sport industry, the core sport product is the production of an athletic event such as a match between two teams at a venue with large seating capacity. Using the notion of a "core" sport product, the differences between sport and non-sport products becomes clearer. In fact, there are eight key distinctions that separate the core sport product from non-sport products (O'Reilly et al., 2022).

First, the sport product is tangible and subjective. When a consumer purchases a ticket to a sporting event, what do they receive? The answer is a promise. That might shock students initially, but give the concept greater thought. When a ticket is purchased, the consumer receives a physical ticket stub or, in the modern era, a QR barcode or digital image with the seating information. If the sport product were conceptualized using a traditional marketing view, that would be a very expensive piece of paper or digital image! Instead, view the purchase of a ticket as a promise to experience sport. This experience is intangible; it cannot be physical touched. Instead, consumers attend the event and derive entertainment from their experience. Additionally, that experience can differ from person to person. Imagine attending the Manchester derby between United and City in global football. Depending on the outcome of the match, the experience might be highly enjoyable or highly disappointing. Furthermore, one fan sitting in a particular area of the facility might have had shaded, enjoyable sightlines, whereas another fan might have been upset because of the blistering sunshine and obstructed views.

The subjectivity of the sport product is also connected to its inconsistency and unpredictability. Fans attending a match on a Friday night might have a completely different experience the next night with the same teams playing. Furthermore, the outcome of the event is unknown. When the New York Jets in American football play the Buffalo Bills, there is a strong likelihood that the latter will win, but there are no guarantees. Conversely, if a consumer were to buy an iPhone on two consecutive nights, not only would there be consistency in the transaction process, but the outcome (i.e., obtaining a new phone and setting it up) would be predictable. It is this inconsistency and unpredictability that also highlight the ability of the sport product to be simultaneously produced and consumed. Fans in the crowd, athletes on the field, and all other elements in between work to "put on the show" and "take it in" at the same time. When the match is over, the crowd and players exist, and the product perishes (i.e., tickets cannot be sold for a game that has ended).

The core sport product is also strongly influenced by group dynamics and less likely to be manipulated by sport managers. While it is possible for a consumer to attend a sporting event alone, the atmosphere is created and consumed by those around them. Family, friends, venue security and ushers, media personnel, and athletes can all contribute to the positive or negative experience for the consumer. Concurrently, sport managers do not really have much influence over the group dynamic or what happens on the field. The players play, but whether that results in an elite, memorable performance or one to forget is out of their purview. So, it's important that sport marketers work on the extensions of the core product such as giveaways, contests, food and beverage, and concessions.

Finally, the core sport product represents both an industrial and consumer product, a pervasive product, and one that has strong emotional ties, incomparable to other sectors. As an industrial product, sport is manufactured to create other products such as a television broadcast or sport apparel store. As a consumer product, sport is manufactured as an entertainment product, offering more choice for consumers alongside movies, musicals, and concerts. But sport is also unique in that it has nearly universal appeal. Consumers across age, gender, nationality, and religion all enjoy sport, and that is difficult to find in other sectors. Finally, and arguably above all else, the core sport product invokes an emotional attachment and level of identification unheard of for non-sport products. In the modern era, there has been a stronger push by companies such as Apple, Google, and Tesla to stimulate consumers' emotional attachment to their products, but sport operations reign supreme. Consumers laugh, cry, yell, and punch their fists in the air in triumph when the outcome is favourable, and that just does not happen elsewhere; it is highly unlikely for a consumer to sit outside a Ford dealership, wearing Ford-branded clothing, cheering on salespeople as they sell more vehicles. But that is exactly what happens with the core sport product: groups of tribes settling in, cheering the performance of athletes on the pitch, wearing team colours and marks, and basking in the team's glory and revelling in the failure of the defeated.

These eight elements of the core sport product are indicative of why sport marketing is not just traditional marketing applied to sport. Sport marketing requires embracing those traditional elements but also appreciating and integrating the uniqueness of sport to meet the needs and/or wants of consumers. By doing so, sport organizations are able to modify or enhance the experience for consumers (as best they can) or even innovate to create new sport products, too. This dynamic is represented in Figure 12.2, where the sport product has its core benefit, features, and add-ons which can entice consumers with different intentions and behaviours.

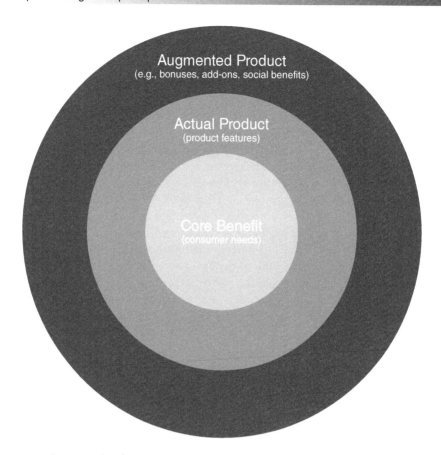

FIGURE 12.2 Sport product features

In Practice 12.1 Sport product innovation: Topgolf

Perhaps no sport grasps so firmly its history and tradition as golf. From the endless hills at St. Andrews (Scotland) to the ocean views of Pebble Beach (United States), golf embraces a scenic majesty laced with a mild-mannered, conservative aesthetic. Besides the incremental equipment innovations to golf clubs like hybrids and carbon graphite shafts, golf has remained relatively untouched; players are often seen with polos, skirts, and trousers; a high degree of sportspersonship is displayed amongst competitors; and speaking is often kept minimal, an almost library-esque atmosphere. Yet even this most venerable sporting institution has capitulated to the fickle nature of shifting fandom and a cramped competitive environment with the introduction of Topgolf, a revolutionary product innovation that has drawn the ire of new consumers to the sport.

In 2000, two twin brothers, Steve and Dave Joliffe, avid golfers, sought to revolutionize golf, and created Topgolf, a redesigned golf range just outside London, England. Born out of the time required to play a full round of golf and the poor experience provided by driving ranges, Topgolf was a different driving range experience, allowing players to see where their balls were going due to microchip technology. Initial reaction from the market was mixed: some consumers liked the idea, but many were still sceptical and preferred traditional golf. Consequently, golf equipment companies and even the Pro Golfers Association tour failed to endorse this new sport product.

However, the innovation intrigued investors from the United States who saw the potential in the product. These new investors went even further, shifting Topgolf from simple a new golf product to a new sport experience, adding event space and commercial restaurants and expanding the play offering with LED lighting. Instead of a horizontally linear golf range, Topgolf facilities were focused on horizontal and vertical integration, with driving bays that kept parties close yet far enough apart not to interfere with their conversation and ball strikes. Additionally, consumers were not just randomly hitting balls but could play "games" that the facility created, such as hitting it closer to certain pins for points, hitting coloured targets, or even a chipping challenge where short-distance targets were required. With the microchip golf ball technology, points could be given out in real-time, allowing for more hits and more fun.

Ultimately, Topgolf became a unique product, offering families, friends, and colleagues an opportunity to hang out, enjoy some time with one another, and add some competition into the mix. In this way, Topgolf occupied a space similar to (lawn) bowling or arcades, bringing people together with an active purpose. Its relaxed atmosphere also welcomed different groups who might have been intimidated by traditional golf attire and customs, as customers could wear whatever they felt comfortable in, including jeans, athletic shorts, and casual tops, and could use clubs provided by the facility. By 2013, there were ten locations in the United States, and sales were in the hundreds of millions. By 2018, there were millions of Topgolf customers in the United States, United Kingdom, and Australia, and the product continues to expand.

Although the COVID-19 pandemic slowed down some of the global expansion plans in places like Canada, Topgolf continues to grow, with 70 locations, including those in Mexico and the United Arab Emirates. In October 2020, Callaway, one of the major manufacturers in golf, agreed to purchase Topgolf for $2B USD, allowing customers to get acquainted with Callaway clubs in a relaxed atmosphere. So, a new sport product that was not initially well received has become a growing phenomenon and continues to bring more consumers into the sport of golf.

In order to develop a new product in sport, marketers must consider the uniqueness of sport and the process of innovation. Developing a new sport product can be risky given its expense, finance- and time-wise, and there are handfuls of new sport products that are introduced each year with few successes. Thus, it is critical to ensure that marketers are taking appropriate steps to ensure their innovation is positioned to be one of those success stories. The first step is to consider the goals and context for the innovation. To do so, practitioners can perform a SWOT (strengths, weaknesses, opportunities, and threats), five-forces, or PESTLE (political, economic, social, technological, legal, and ecological) analysis. Through this action, gaps and opportunities will arise, requiring the selection of the most appropriate to pursue. With a chosen innovation, then it is important to support the idea with adequate resources, specifically on the financial side. Innovative sport products require significant cash investments to pay for expenditures and ongoing research and development. Finally, once the product is nearly complete, it is critical to create a model where it can be exported and consumed and where it can create value for the consumers. In sport, there have been some amazing core product innovations such as the emergence of three-on-three basketball or limited over cricket, as well as completely new offerings like esports and drone racing. These sport product innovations stimulate new or renewed interest from consumers, generating revenue to sustain operations through ticket sales and product extensions (e.g., parking, concessions).

SPORT CONSUMER BEHAVIOUR TRENDS

Having a sport product, something to meet the needs and/or wants of the consumer, is certainly important, but the consumer should not be omitted from the marketing narrative. Understanding consumers is imperative to unpack their needs and wants to refine the sport product offering. To do so, sport marketers have traditionally viewed consumers as patrons who consume all aspects of the sport product from the time they purchase a ticket, encounter the sport facility grounds, and walk through a gate to the end when they egress and leave the facility's vicinity. However, modern consumers have unique behaviours and are not simply patrons inside the sport facility. Consumers are unique in that they play different roles (e.g., parents, employees), have varying interests beyond sport (e.g., music, reading), and also consume sport differently (e.g., live spectatorship, television viewing) with fluctuating frequency. So it is important to reveal some of these trends and how they can impact the marketing *of* and *through* sport.

One of the biggest consumer trends in sport is the increased function and usage of digital technology to augment or enhance their experience. It is highly probably that consumers own or have access to a smart device such as a smartphone or tablet and utilize various functions on those devices such as calendars, e-mail, and web browsing. Consequently, there have been an increased number of digital sport products such as over-the-top functions, team apps, and social media (more on those in Chapter 13). There also exists a general acceptance to using digital capabilities to improve past processes. Instead of going into a retailer to purchase new sport apparel, consumers are making their purchase online and never have to leave their home (especially critical during the COVID-19 pandemic). That same consumer can videotape their shots and kicks, upload them, and have a private coaching session through Zoom and Microsoft Teams. This trend of increased digital engagement offers sport marketers new avenues to market the core sport product and develop innovations to meet consumers' needs and wants.

Another pertinent trend is the focus on increased flexibility. Alongside the increasing digitization of society, consumers are more prone to wanting more access to information and the ability to customize and select the option that best suits their needs. In a traditional dynamic, consumers do not have much input or opportunity to explain their individual needs and wants; marketers often break down their entire consumer base into segments, then target their approach to each single, but still large, grouping. But within each segment lie consumers who yearn for more choices and, with increased competition in and outside of sport, consumer behaviour began to shift towards more convenient, less restricted options. For instance, take the season ticket holder (STH) model (also known as membership in other parts of the world). STH has always been the gold standard for sport organizations, as it presents recurring revenue, ensures there will be attendance at sporting events (which impacts the production and consumption of the core sport product), and can also facilitate additional spend in-venue through concessions and other elements. But STH can be very costly. For some sport properties, being an STH can range from the low four figures to high five figures (and even more depending on luxurious tiered offerings). Additionally, consumers have limited bandwidth; in considering the multitude of roles, responsibilities, and lifestyles, asking a consumer to commit to a full season of attendance can pose a challenge. This has been one of the reasons the sport industry has shifted to adopt more flexible or "flex" ticket packages, bundling smaller numbers of games and pricing them to target key segments. The industry has also introduced dynamic pricing, raising or lowering the price of tickets depending on market demand, the marquee athletes involved, and the context (e.g., weather, poor team performance).

In Practice 12.2 StubHub: ticket sales in the digital era

Ticket sales are one of the most important sources of revenue for sport organizations, particularly those at the minor or developing professional levels. But the distribution of tickets was, for a very long time, very regimental. To purchase tickets to a sporting event, consumers would typically visit the sport facility's ticket sales window area the day of or during business hours in advance of the event. However, that model of ticket purchasing slightly shifted with changing consumer needs. When a fan goes to buy a ticket, they are often looking for more than just a ticket. They want convenience, fast and friendly service, questions answered, and a reasonable price. Consequently, new ways of selling tickets were developed, including box office kiosks located away from the stadium or arena and online web sales. But consumers still wanted more convenience.

Traditionally, with ticket sales, consumers bought them from official distribution sites, but they could not re-sell to recoup some or all of the costs of the ticket if something prevented them from going. This practice, often referred to as "scalping", was deemed illegal for many reasons, including ties to hooliganism and gang/cartel-like behaviour. Many scalpers were still present outside stadia and arenas reselling tickets to marquee events at higher costs, despite its being an unauthorized, illegal practice, and for some consumers, it was challenging to trust a scalper, as the price could be too high or the tickets might even be counterfeit! But the convenience of accessing in-demand sport events and re-selling unusable tickets was valued, creating an opportunity for a new model.

Enter StubHub. In 2000, Eric Baker and Jeff Fluhr started a ticket exchange and resale platform that would allow fans to "trade" tickets to one another or access tickets to sport events that were sold out or highly sought after. At the beginning, many sport teams and leagues were not thrilled by StubHub's arrival. But, over time, the company signed agreements with premier leagues in North America and gained increased credibility with consumers by expanding beyond sport into concerts and festivals. In 2011, the company accelerated the experience for consumers by offering a mobile application to interactively search for tickets within a venue and identify parking nearby, as well as locating restaurants and bars. Ultimately, StubHub created an authorized, convenient way for consumers to not only purchase tickets but exchange or resell them, all at the click of a button or a swipe of a smartphone screen.

Today, StubHub is a multi-billion-dollar company, with over 16 million unique visitors to its platform each month. Just before the COVID-19 pandemic struck, StubHub was acquired by Viagogo, a similar company operating in the European and Australian markets, for $4.05B USD. Despite its growth, other companies were created to offer fans a similar experience, including Ticketmaster, Vivid Seats, and SeatGeek. So, whenever there's an event or sport and fans are looking to get tickets, purchasing from the facility box office or team's website comes after a quick search on the StubHub mobile application for cheap tickets and access to high-profile matchups.

Ultimately, sport consumer behaviour in the modern era is predicated on increased digitization and flexibility, providing instantaneous access and feedback, along with greater options and customization. For sport marketers, yielding to these trends requires an intuitive understanding of the sport consumer. It is useful to continue the practice of segmentation, but this practice should also be extended to consumers who exist in part or wholly online (Naraine, 2019). It is also not enough to consider consumers only when they are in the team's venue, but holistically. This requires considering sport consumers' entire journey from the time they wake on gameday, the entire process of getting to the facility with their family and friends, to the experience at the game, the activities and opportunities post-game, and, perhaps most importantly, what activities and engagements they partake in from one game to the next. Understanding each step in the consumers' journey can be incredibly useful to optimize features of the core sport product and, in some cases, identify new opportunities to generate revenue. For instance, in Ottawa, Canada, the Canadian football team Ottawa REDBLACKS renovated their facility but also worked with the city to develop the surrounding precinct to include a grocery store, fitness centre, pet store, cinema, and several restaurants, promoting the idea of a full-day experience instead of consumers having to travel here, there, and everywhere before the game.

BRANDING AND SPONSORSHIP

In order for a sport organization or entity to be successful, it must mean something to sport consumers. In practice, this demands that a consumer be aware of the entity and its products or services and respond in a positive way. The process of cultivating such a response is known as branding, and the name, colours, and other symbols associated with a brand can facilitate increased trust and loyalty from consumers, which ultimately leads to more revenue generation.

In sport, there are some iconic brands around the globe. The Leafs, Cowboys, Demons, and All-Blacks all conjure up feelings and emotions amongst consumers and associations with their historic (and current) on-field performances. These and other well-established brands are known to consumers for their brand associations, even if they don't hoist the trophy or raise a banner/flag every season. Those associations generally consist of the name, logo, place (e.g., city), fight songs, and uniforms and can create what is known as brand equity, or the value consumers perceive a brand to be worth. Brands with higher equity are able to market to many segments and generate more revenue. Moreover, when sport brands are able to build significant equity, they also becoming appealing prospects to non-sport brands who can harness consumer loyalty and perceived quality to sell their products and services.

In Practice 12.3 Leveraging sport brand equity: Google and the Toronto Raptors

Over the last 20 years, sport has seen a major shift in the number of sponsorship categories or types of sponsors that are involved. Traditional categories like automotive (e.g., Ford, Toyota), financial (e.g., Barclays, Royal Bank of Canada), and energy (e.g., Shell, Exxon-Mobil) have remained but are also now joined by cloud computing (e.g., Alibaba), food delivery, (e.g., DoorDash), and ride-sharing services (e.g., Uber). These new players have created even more competition for limited sport property sponsorship inventory, raising the costs of sponsoring a team, league, or athlete, but also provide a unique opportunity to gain more visibility in the marketplace through affiliation.

With one of the most well-recognized brands in the world, Google does not typically struggle with exposure and visibility in the market. Consumers seeking information for products and services online often use Google's search engine, and a whole suite of products and services have been developed for work and productivity (e.g., Google Docs, Google Sheets, Google Slides), email (e.g., Gmail), cloud storage (e.g., Google Cloud), maps and navigation (e.g., Google Maps, Google Earth), and even video and photo sharing and organizing (e.g., YouTube, Google Photos). Google has also even ventured into hardware products, including a line of computers known as Chromebooks and a smartphone known as the Google Pixel. The breadth of the Google ecosystem has resulted in hundreds of billions in annual revenue, making it one of the most successful companies of all time. But there is one product category where Google was well behind its competition: smart speakers. Smart speakers are voice-command devices with integrated virtual assistants, and Google's Home smart speaker lagged behind market leader Amazon and its Alexa product. So, to help alleviate this challenge, Google leveraged the brand equity in a popular sport brand.

Google teamed up with the Toronto Raptors in 2017. The sport brand had been building significant equity, with successful seasons and playoff appearances and a strong connection to urban centres across the country. As Canada's only team in the National Basketball Association, Google wanted to leverage the sport brand's fanbase of over 11 million to drive awareness, engage consumers, and overtake Amazon Alexa in the Canadian market.

To do so, Google and the Raptors developed a series of televisions advertisements where players would endorse the Google Home by association, including using the product to set timers (for baking a pie), repeating reminders (for practice and game-play), and watching Netflix (relaxing with teammates). For instance, one spot featured two players, Jakob Poeltl and Pascal Siakim, rooming together watching Gilmore Girls on Netflix. Overall, the campaign was a major success. Social media engagement targets of 4 million were eclipsed by the end total of 53 million, and Google Home became the #1 smart speaker in Canada, surpassing its initial target of 50.1% with a final result of 63%.

In the aftermath of the campaign, Google's team reviewed their approach and was comfortable renewing its relationship with the Raptors, beginning another similar campaign in 2019. Furthermore, Google's marketing team was so thrilled that they employed this sport leverage internationally, such as their campaign in Australia with Australian Football League players. For instance, Google used Max Gawn of the Melbourne Demons to mimic Poeltl and Siakim's commercial, as he lay in bed asking Google Home to play Gilmore Girls on Netflix. Therefore, even for well-known brands like Google, the brand equity that exists for sport brands has significant value and can be leveraged to market through sport.

Building the sport brand can result in increased partnerships with other sport and non-sport entities known as sponsorships. Sport sponsorship is a business agreement where an organization or individual provides financial or in-kind assistance to a sport property (any entity that includes the sport organization or person being sponsored such as an athlete, event, association, or competition) in exchange for the right to associate itself with the sport property. Traditionally, sport sponsorship involved non-sport entities seeking to engage in marketing *through* sport, but there are increasing instances of sport properties sponsoring other entities to gain the associative benefits. A prominent example is the Florida Panthers in the National Hockey League, who are sponsoring the star quarterback of the University of Miami American football team. There, the hockey team seeks to draw fans of American football and the Miami community, specifically, to become more aware of their product and consume accordingly. The objectives of sponsorship can vary greatly, depending on the size of the partners, the type of sponsorship, and the type of sport property being supported. But, typically, sponsors seek to promote their public image, increase customer awareness (like the Panthers are doing), and cultivate new relationships with consumers and other business entities.

Sponsorship works through an image transfer from the sport property to the sponsor. This image transfer works best when there is a strong sponsorship affinity or a good fit or match between the sponsor and the sport property. This is also known as congruence. Congruence occurs when two elements are met: 1) there is an overlap in the target consumer market between the sponsor and sponsee, and 2) there is a similar approach to branding and marketing strategies. If a sponsor targets an older audience but partners with a sport entity in esports, it is likely that there exists a lack of congruence. Conversely, if a financial institution presents an edgy approach to market to younger consumers, similar to the esports entity, then there is a higher likelihood of congruence. Once the sponsor and sponsee agree to establish a partnership, set out by term length and price, it is then critical that marketers activate the relationship, undertaking other promotional activities to draw consumer attention. Activation costs can be high and, given the competitive nature of the sport industry, it is highly likely that brands will overspend on the sponsorship agreement cost and underspend on activation. Along this vein, valuing a sport sponsorship agreement often poses a challenge for marketers on both sides but can certainly be impacted by the equity which exists for the sport brand; the higher the equity, the more costly the arrangement will be for the sponsor.

Branding and sponsorship are two important anchors in sport marketing, as they help facilitate revenue generation. The greater the brand equity, through branding activities and positive associations, the greater the likelihood of increased sponsorship deals and higher figures for those deals. Furthermore, strong branding facilitates other important revenue-generating activities such as licensing and merchandise sales; when brand equity is high, consumers are more likely to spend on apparel, merchandise, and memorabilia related to the brand. In turn, manufacturers may pay the sport entity for the right to use their name, image, and likeness. Furthermore, the greater the brand equity, the more sponsorships from non-sport entities in traditional (e.g., alcohol, automotive, airline, financial) and non-traditional (e.g., cannabis, cryptocurrency, smartphone) categories. This is especially the case when sport brands land a major sponsor; the likelihood of being perceived as cool, unique, and offering a high-value proposition for brands increases, and other major and minor non-sport brands may wish to associate with the sport entity, driving revenue forward.

SUMMARY

Sport marketing revolves around the premise of satisfying the needs and wants of sport consumers, in so doing cultivating a relationship that leads to increased revenue generation and sustenance for the sport organization. Sport marketing is not just traditional marketing applied to sport. The marketing of non-sport products and services omits critical, unique features such as its intangibility, unpredictability, group dynamic, simultaneous production and consumption, and the emotion element tying consumers to the product. However, there are important trends that sport marketers need to consider, specifically the need for instantaneous access and increased flexibility and choice. Finally, in order to ensure sport marketers are securing revenue for the organization, it is important to develop the brand and accrue lucrative sponsorship arrangements with sport and non-sport entities.

REVIEW QUESTIONS

1 Explain the difference between the marketing of sport, and marketing through sport.
2 What is the most important P in sport marketing?

3   What separates sport marketing from marketing non-sport products?

4   What steps constitute the sport product innovation process?

5   What are the two pertinent trends in sport consumer behaviour?

6   What is brand equity?

7   What is congruence, and why is it important in sport marketing?

DISCUSSION QUESTIONS

1   Do you think that marketing sport is truly different to marketing any other type of product or service?

2   Assuming that sport fans are generally loyal to their teams (and clubs), what do you think that team marketers should focus on?

3   Which sports have successfully introduced product innovations in the form of new game formats or versions? Which sports tried but failed? Discuss why some worked while others did not.

4   How has the nature of sport sponsorship changed much over the last decade? What trends seem to be foreshadowing change in the future? Provide examples of "new" or "novel" sponsorship arrangements and discuss their importance to cutting-edge sport marketing.

5   With the COVID-19 global health pandemic impacting live attendance, what strategies should sport marketers focus on to instil trust and regain fans once it is safe to resume play? What have we learned from the pandemic that will remain in our sport marketing strategies? What COVID-19-related strategies will sport marketers relinquish?

FURTHER READING

Bessant, J., & Tidd, J. (2015). *Innovation and entrepreneurship* (3rd ed.). West Sussex: Wiley.

Funk, D. C., Alexandris, K., & McDonald, H. (2016). *Sport consumer behaviour: Marketing strategies*. London: Routledge.

Greenhalgh, G., Dwyer, B., & LeCrom, C. (2017). A case of multiple (brand) personalities: Expanding the methods of brand personality measurement in sport team contexts. *Sport Marketing Quarterly, 26*, 20–30.

Jensen, J. A., Wakefield, L., Cobbs, J. B., & Turner, B. A. (2016). Forecasting sponsorship costs: Marketing intelligence in the athletic apparel industry. *Marketing Intelligence & Planning, 34*, 281–298.

Kelly, S. J., Ireland, M., Mangan, J., & Williamson, H. (2016). It works two ways: Impacts of sponsorship alliance upon sport and sponsor image. *Sport Marketing Quarterly, 25*, 242–259.

Kunkel, T., Doyle, J. P., & Berlin, A. (2017). Consumers' perceived value of sport team games – A multidimensional approach. *Journal of Sport Management, 31*, 80–95.

Naraine, M. L. (2019). Follower segments within and across the social media networks of major professional sport organizations. *Sport Marketing Quarterly*, *28*, 222–233.

O'Reilly, N., Séguin, B., Abeza, G., & Naraine, M. L. (2022). *Canadian sport marketing* (3rd ed.). Champaign, IL: Human Kinetics.

Pedersen, P. M., Laucella, P., Kian, E., & Geurin, A. (2017). *Strategic sport communication* (2nd ed.). Champaign, IL: Human Kinetics.

Shilbury, D., Quick, S., Funk, D., Westerbeek, H., & Karg, A. (2014). *Strategic sport marketing*. London: Routledge.

Taks, M., Séguin, B., Naraine, M. L., Thompson, A., Parent, M. M., & Hoye, R. (2020). Brand governance practices in Canadian national sport organizations: An exploratory study. *European Sport Management Quarterly*, *20*, 10–29.

Yuksel, M., McDonald, M. A., & Joo, S. (2016). Cause-related sport marketing: An organizing framework and knowledge development opportunities. *European Sport Management Quarterly*, *16*, 58–85.

RELEVANT WEBSITES

American Marketing Association at www.ama.org/
Australian Marketing Institute at https://ami.org.au/
Chartered Institute of Marketing at www.cim.co.uk/
Google at www.google.com/
Toronto Raptors at www.nba.com/raptors/
StubHub at www.stubhub.com
Sport Marketing Association at www.sportmarketingassociation.com/
Canadian Marketing Association at www.thecma.ca/
Topgolf at www.topgolf.com

CASE STUDY 12.1

Building brand equity in hockey

In December 2017, the National Hockey League announced it would consider an application for a new franchise in Seattle. The bid was highly regarded by famed Hollywood producer, Jerry Bruckheimer, and sport business executive, Tim Leiweike, as part of the ownership group. A year later, the official word was given: the Seattle franchise was a go, and the team would begin play in October 2021 at a remodelled KeyArena, the former home of the Seattle Supersonics of the National Basketball Association. Seattle was not a brand-new hockey market; in fact, the Seattle Metropolitans were the first US-based team to win the Stanley Cup (back in

1917), one of the most historic trophies in all of sport. But, after years of not having a professional team, hockey was returning to the Pacific Northwest.

Ice hockey has a strong foundation in North America. In Canada, organized hockey dates back to 1875, while in the United States, formal games were recorded in 1893, with one of the first being an intercollegiate match between Yale University and Johns Hopkins University. Although other sports dominate market share in this jurisdiction, notably American and Canadian football, as well as basketball, professional ice hockey embarked on a significant expansion path beginning in the 1960s. After keeping a original group of six teams, the NHL began to expand into non-traditional hockey markets such as Oakland and Los Angeles, as well as traditional hockey markets (i.e., Minnesota, Pittsburgh). In the 1970s, the league added more teams with Buffalo, Washington, D.C., and New Jersey, with more focus on Canada with Vancouver and Edmonton. Then, in the 1990s, there was a big shift away from the north towards shoring up the Sun Belt. Teams in Tampa Bay, Miami, Anaheim, and Nashville came into existence, and now the "coolest game on earth" is played in Arizona and Texas.

Particularly in these latter instances, teams have had to work extra to build brand equity in their markets. In North Carolina, the sport with the most market share is easily basketball. Just consider two of the big brands in that marketplace: Duke and the University of North Carolina (UNC). Even though they are not professional sport focused, intercollegiate athletes in the United States operates on a similar model, with significant commercial investment into revenue generation. Additionally, both of these schools have built significant equity in their respective brands. For Duke, their "Blue Devil" mascot and their colours, white and a trademark "Duke blue", are easily identifiable, and consumers, fans, students, and alumni all have a strong emotion and personal relationship with the school. Duke's brand is also well known through the team's men's basketball head coach, affectionately known as "Coach K". Similarly, the UNC basketball program has a storied history, including several men's and women's successes. On the men's side, major names such as Michael Jordan, Vince Carter, and Kenny "The Jet" Smith have all-suited up for the Tarheels, and the "Carolina Blue" and white are also well known. On the women's side, the team won the 1994 championship and involved multi-sport athletes like Marion Jones. With these two entrenched brands, how was an ice hockey team supposed to survive? In 1996, the Hartford Whalers were relocated to Raleigh, North Carolina. After being hit by Hurricanes Bertha and Fran, the owner of the team felt this would be an appropriate name. Their logo featured a black oblong circle with a larger red circle surrounding it (mimicking the "eye of the hurricane"), while secondary logos have included hurricane warning flags and an alternative version in the shape of the state flag. Although North Carolina loves its blue, the Hurricanes opted for a red-and-black colour scheme, matching those of the North Carolina State University athletic teams, with whom they share facilities. And, taking it a step further, the Hurricanes introduced a mascot known as Stormy the Pig, an ode to the high number of pig farmers in the region. The Hurricanes have not usurped

Duke or UNC in that market, but they have remained in existence and maintained a considerable fan base, a remarkable feat for a non-traditional market.

Beyond the Hurricanes, there have also been two other recent instances where teams have entered a new market: Winnipeg, Canada, and Las Vegas, United States. Unlike Carolina, Winnipeg is a known hockey market. For a long time, it did have a professional ice hockey team known as the Winnipeg Jets. However, in 1996, after the Canadian economy declined and the Canadian dollar was worth far less than the American dollar, the team relocated to Arizona. Fifteen years later, a failed attempt at a franchise in Atlanta relocated to Winnipeg. At the time, the team's new ownership considered multiple names, logos, colours, and other elements of branding in sport. However, the strength of the "Jets" brand made the team name a no-brainer. Except, instead of reusing the old logo, a modern, stylized logo could create equity in the new iteration of the team. So, rather than starting completely from scratch or rehashing all the same entities from the old team, this 50/50 compromise of same name; new logo; and updated, similar colour scheme seemed appropriate. The Jets also made sure to integrate their brand in the community. The jet image was taken from a McDonnell Douglas CF-18 Hornet, a nod to the planes located at Winnipeg's nearby military base. The team also donned a special shade of blue used by the Royal Canadian Airforce. But not everything was completely new: the Jets brought back two key pieces of their city's hockey history. First, their mascot, Mick E. Moose, was a known commodity in Winnipeg, serving as the mascot for a minor league team in the city for 15 years, and was now promoted to the big leagues. Second, the team reintroduced the "Winnipeg White Out", a cult event where, during the team's first playoff appearance in 1987, fans wore all white and waved white towels in the air. In 2015, when the new incarnation of the Jets made the playoffs, the White Out reappeared, with the team handing out free white t-shirts and towels. In Las Vegas, the situation was a bit different. Their expansion franchise was a blank slate, with no discernible hockey history and only the culture of debauchery from which to potentially draw. Instead, naming the team was driven by owner Bill Foley's homage to his military training. Originally wanting to call the team Black Knights, the franchise ran into legal troubles, but settled on Golden Knights, given the State of Nevada is the largest gold-producing state in the United States. However, in a shrewd move, the team dropped the "Las" part of the city's name, opting for Vegas Golden Knights instead of Las Vegas. Local residents felt betrayed and that the team was more interested in being associated with the infamous Vegas Strip, the mile-long precinct known for casinos, convention centres, and venues. Nevertheless, the team persisted with some unique brand elements, including a logo which utilized a knight's mask with dark space to present a giant V (for Vegas), as well as incorporating colours from the Vegas skyline: red from the canyons, black from the streets, gold from the mines, and grey from the towering buildings. Moreover, the Golden Knights introduced a mascot known as Chance, the lone connection to the region's gambling history, but chose a less threatening anthropomorphic animal (in lieu of a knight), going with a gila monster, a lizard that is native to that part of the United States.

These examples provide a basis to look introspectively into the new Seattle franchise. After being awarded the team, the franchise worked tirelessly to develop the name and colours prior to the October 2021 start date. Although some names seemed obvious, such as the Metropolitans or Totems, the latter an ode to the indigenous culture of the Pacific Northwest, the team opted for a name that was a particular fan favourite: the Kraken. On July 23, 2020, the team revealed its name and logo, the latter using a stylized "S" with a single tentacle emerging through the dark space. To wit, the "S" was a nod to the Metropolitans logo, which also featured a lone "S". For the colour scheme, the Kraken embraced their nautical theme, incorporating "deep sea navy", "ice blue", "boundless blue", "shadow blue", and "red alert", where the red symbolized the eye of the beast, fixed on its prey. Thus far, the choices have been successful: the Kraken have been one of the top-selling teams across all major sports leagues and surpassed the merchandise sales record that the Golden Knights set back in 2017. But, as the team awaits play, there are still many unknowns to be revealed, including what a mascot would be like (and be named) and what other traditions, actions, music, or artefacts might be used to raise the brand's equity. As more franchises are developed, especially in hockey, where women's hockey is especially deficient, increasing the amount of equity in the brand can be incredibly lucrative and ensure the team remains in the city for the long haul.

(This case study is adapted from Davies et al. (2019) in *Case Studies in Sport Management*. For review, please see https://doi.org/10.1123/cssm.2018-0035.)

CASE STUDY QUESTIONS

1 What are some of the important branding pieces in professional hockey? What elements were not mentioned that would also be useful for a team to consider?

2 Explain the brand-building similarities and differences between the Carolina Hurricanes, Winnipeg Jets, and Vegas Golden Knights. Were their choices appropriate, or should they have been different? Why?

3 How do you determine success for brand building? What elements do the Seattle Kraken need to incorporate, and how should they tie into the city and/or the team and its history and traditions?

CASE STUDY 12.2

Marketing women's sport: AFLW in Australia

If you are a resident of Australia or you have visited the country, then you will be intimately familiar with Australians' love of "footy" or, to give it the correct name,

Australian rules football. First started under the auspices of the Victorian Football League in 1897, and then the Australian Football League in 1990, footy has grown to be arguably the leading sport in Australia. There are now 18 teams in the AFL competition spread across five states. Each week during the season, over 33,000 fans on average gather to watch each of the games, giving the AFL the fourth-highest live attendance figures of any professional sport in the world (prior to COVID-19, of course). Since its first formal game, footy's speed, aerial leaping, kicking, and combative nature have made the sport a favourite in most of the country's regions. Despite the sport's popularity and professionalism, it has remained almost exclusively a male-dominated sport. That is, until recently.

The idea to have a professional women's Aussie Rules League was born several years ago. Interestingly, the initial thrust for the development of the game came from women players rather than from the men's sport or from any marketer who might have considered the implications of introducing what was, at that time, considered a novelty. In 2010, an AFL-sponsored report recommended that the AFL Commission – its independent board of management – begin working toward the establishment of a national women's league. This was followed in 2013 by an exhibition match. Two years later, another exhibition game was played, this time shown on free-to-air television, attracting extremely strong ratings, with over 1 million viewers.

The marketing problems inherent in forming the AFLW were, however, quite formidable. Three in particular were of obvious concern. First and foremost was the question of how the league, and thus the players, were to be funded. Second was the simple fact that there existed only a small coterie of female players already playing the sport at an elite, premier level. And third was the vexatious question of how to sell a women's league to an audience staunchly fixated on the men's league.

Despite a certain amount of initial controversy concerning whether the men's competition should financially subsidize the women's competition, the AFL, together with a major sponsor, the National Australia Bank, ultimately came to an interim agreement to financially support the league known as AFLW. The pay deal struck for the founding 2017 seven-match season and finals (playoff) gave marquee players a financial package of $27,000 AUD, which included allowances for marketing and ambassadorial roles, priority players $12,000 AUD, and other rostered players $8,500 AUD. For 2018, pay was increased by between 3% and 16%. Some ancillary costs for travel, insurance, out-of-pocket expenses, and carer's allowance were also included. By comparison, the average salary of female Australian cricketers in 2021 is approximately $52,000 AUD, while the pay for elite female cricketers has reached over $200,000 AUD. Furthermore, there was a significant gender wage gap, as the average pay of men's footy players was $300,000 AUD, albeit for a much longer season.

The issue of finding sufficient players for the proposed eight-team AFLW posed a separate conundrum. Almost without exception, the marquee players were self selected. All were playing or had played in recognized women's amateur leagues.

Most had played the game since early youth. A few priority players had some experience of the game but, for the most part, all the remaining players were junior or elite athletes from other sports (e.g., basketball). Of course, the idea of transferring skills from one sport to another is not new but has rarely been undertaken on such a vast scale. Women from numerous different sports, together with Olympic-level athletes tried out for the AFLW and, in the main, were given strong support to do so.

Marketing the sport to a sceptical audience was another matter. Under the auspices of the AFL, the league was branded the "AFL Women's League", with a stylized rendition of an Australian Football goal square and goal posts drawn from a perspective which shows a "W" as the official logo. The National Australia Bank was named the league's naming rights sponsor, with a number of smaller sponsors, including tertiary education institutions, backing individual clubs.

Rather cleverly, the AFLW marketing team revamped an old advertisement taken from a 1994 campaign for the men's competition. This saw some of the world's foremost athletes viewing scenes showcasing the skills of AFL players with the tag line, "I'd like to see that". The advertisement, drawing on the historical legacy of the game, portrayed black-and-white footage of the AFLW and ended with Moana Hope, probably the foremost female exponent of the sport, commenting: "Women making a name for themselves in Aussie Rules Football? We'll show you that".

Jemma Wong, AFL campaign lead and marketing manager, argued that the promotional campaign would be "bold, empowering and inclusive" and would "rally a generation of young girls". Aimed directly at a younger female population, showcasing women in a combative mode was considered advantageous. This, of course, simply reflected the way in which the male sport was marketed. The advertisements were pivotal to the marketing of the game and were deemed largely successful.

In the inaugural AFLW season, a deal was struck which saw one selected Saturday night game per week being shown on free-to-air television, specifically on Channel 7, the AFL website, and the league's "mobile app", while all season games were shown on pay (cable) TV network, Fox Sports. Costs were borne by the television channels and, in return, no licensing fees were paid to the league. Ensuring total professionalism, Channel 7 engaged a previous best and fairest Brownlow medallist, Patrick Dangerfield, as an on-air commentator. He was supported by other recognized AFL superstars. With the exception of some double-headed matches, nearly all league games had free entry. Now, after proving the viability of the concept, fans appeared far more likely to be prepared to pay for entry in subsequent seasons.

How successful has the AFL Women's League been? The initial week saw over 50,000 people attend the four matches, with one stadium locking out over a thousand fans because of the at-capacity crowd, while the Grand Final was watched by a gate of 16,000 exuberant fans.

This initial interest in the AFLW, together with its influential media coverage, has offered the AFL an opportunity to market itself to a different social demographic. While many of the initial games were held in smaller grounds, this resounding support was now a signal to potentially expand and connect with women and girls looking to support their own gender. There are some 350,000 women and girls playing footy at the grassroots level, and having an elite competition created a new pathway of ongoing sport development. These numbers provide a compelling explanation for why the sport attracted so much attention. Add to the number of players all the parents, families, partners, and friends of the participants, and the market becomes significant. Indeed, one wonders why women's football never progressed beyond the amateur level before.

Indeed, in the aftermath of the first season, two more teams were added for the 2019 season (Geelong Cats and North Melbourne Kangaroos), and four more teams started play during the COVID-19-impacted 2020 season (Gold Coast Suns, Richmond Tigers, St. Kilda Saints, and West Coast Eagles). For the 2022–2023 season, there will be 18 teams in the AFLW competition, each representing clubs on the men's side, sharing the same brand identities. Unlike other women's sport leagues elsewhere in the world, like the WNBA in the United States, where men's teams and women's teams are unique brand identities, one of the ways the AFLW has been able to grow is by capturing the brand allegiance that traditional fans hold for their clubs. Thus, a man who would traditionally barrack for the Collingwood Magpies in the AFL would also be inclined to support the Magpies in the AFLW. Additionally, AFLW player salaries have increased. With the commercial success of the league, average salaries are now well over $20,000 AUD.

The success of the AFLW should not come at the critical expense of the AFL. Despite many lost opportunities for promoting the women's game, their support for the successful marketing strategy proved instrumental. Their ability to get free-to-air television as well as pay TV coverage without cost was close to genius. With games on TV every week, a ready-made audience was assured. Additionally, many of the traditional AFL audience were fed up with the off-field behaviour of male players in all codes and probably thought that there was far less chance of such behaviour in the women's league. Many of the female players were already well known in their own sports and brought with them an established fan base interested to see how their skills would translate to a new environment. And one should never discount Australian's love of sport. Now, the AFL must persist in ensuring that TV provides higher-quality coverage and higher-quality commentary that includes female presenters.

Nonetheless, the AFLW needs to find a way to overcome the traditionally limited concept that views women's sport as less interesting to watch than men's sports. Quoted in the US *The Nation* magazine, Dr Marie Hardin, Dean of Penn State University's Donald P. Bellisario College of Communications and a long-time student of sport marketing, suggests that simply providing greater access to female sports or promoting women to more sports journalist or editorial positions will not suffice. "If that were true" she observed,

> media outlets would be doing it. Nobody does more audience research and understands consumers of women's sports better than ESPN. If they thought they could make massive amounts of money from coverage of women's sports, they would be doing it.

Today, ESPN operates ESPNW for women's coverage and has started to show more women's events globally, including intercollegiate athletics in the US and women's tennis. But AFLW is not shown abroad, despite the fact that the AFL is telecast (usually on delay) in the United States and Canada (on Fox Sports and TSN, respectively).

With the expansion to a full 18-team offering, there is an expectation that Australian's love affair with women's footy will continue, but will it thrive in the aftermath of COVID-19? Realistically, the pandemic has created a wealth of uncertainty for the commercial viability of many leagues around the world, men's and women's. However, it is especially challenging for women's sport, which has traditionally been given less airtime and opportunity relative to men's sport. However, the AFLW is expected to bring in thousands of additional fans, and 27% of footy participation in Australia is now female, with the junior AFL Auskick program also having thousands of young girls taking up the sport. Regardless, the inauguration and continued investment into the AFLW is a significant step in the progress of women's sport and its marketing to greater audiences.

CASE STUDY QUESTIONS

1   Women in sport is often seen as second class in comparison to men's sport despite the fact that almost 40% of all sport participants are female and provide about a third of the fan base. This is generally given as a reason that TV coverage of women's sport rates far below that of men's sport. Do you consider this a true statement and, if so, why?

2   What do you perceive to be the strengths and weaknesses of the original AFLW marketing campaign? Can you suggest any improvements?

3   Traditionally, sponsorship for female sport receives less than 15% of that given to male sport. Is this a failure of the corporate world, or are there more valid reasons? Should sponsorship be provided based on the gender of the participants?

CHAPTER 13

Sport media and digital technology

OVERVIEW

This chapter examines the key features of the sport media complex. It provides an examination of the traditional and modern media that connect consumers with the core, intangible sport product, specifically print, radio, and television in the former and social media and digital streaming in the latter. The chapter also discusses the importance of broadcast rights in the sport industry and the ways in which governments

DOI: 10.4324/9781003217947-15

regulate the sport media relationship. It concludes with an acknowledgement of the new array of digital technology impacting the modern sport manager in the professional sport industry.

After completing this chapter, the reader should be able to:

- Explain the sport media complex;
- Understand the difference between traditional and modern sport media platforms;
- Identify the importance of broadcast rights in linear and digital media and the role of government in terms of regulating broadcasting; and
- Comment on the advancement in digital technology and its impact on the modern sport manager.

WHAT IS THE MEDIA?

The word "media" has a diverse set of meanings. It can refer to the entire media industry, composed of organizations and journalists whose role is to cover and report on sport issues and topics for which consumers are likely to engage. However, media can also refer to the plural of mediums, specific platforms, channels, or stations that provide an opportunity for consumers to access coverage of and reports on teams, leagues, and athletes. In either case, media in sport provides three basic functions: information, education, and entertainment. Consumers need to know when their favourite teams are playing, which players are injured, and if there are any other roster transactions (just to name a few). These are examples of informational coverage that media can provide. However, media reports can also focus on educating fans, providing in-depth histories on athlete training regimens and childhood upbringing, analytics insights on team performance, and stories uncovering coach selection strategies and decision-making. Yet it has become increasingly clear that the entertainment value media can provide, particularly through professional sport, is also quite captivating. This has resulted in "news"-style programming where media organizations report on sport much the same way they report on politics and global issues, as well as prominent, energetic sport commentators offering their sporting insights and opinions. For instance, Mina Kimes in the United States, Jennifer Botterill in Canada, and Lisa Sthalekar in Australia are all well-known sport media personalities, as are Skip Bayless, Donovan Bennett, and Brian Taylor in those same respective jurisdictions. Fans often schedule their consumption around these personalities, and programming featuring these personalities can sometimes be bigger than the match or event itself! Ultimately, this mixture of information, education, and, of course, entertainment provides a unique opportunity to package and deliver sport.

THE SPORT MEDIA COMPLEX

The growing importance and role the media plays between sport entities and consumers can be unpacked further in what is known as the "sport media complex" (see Figure 13.1).

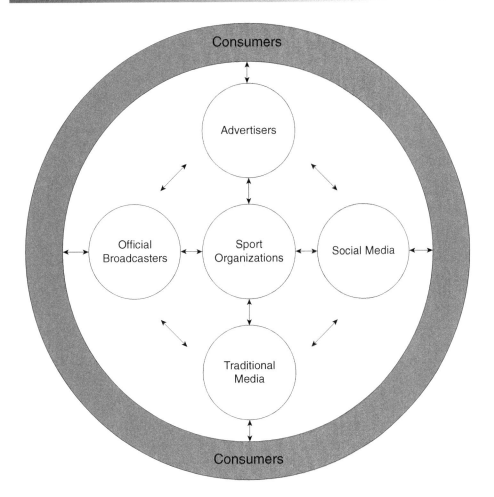

FIGURE 13.1 The sport media complex

At the core, there are sport organizations wanting to get their products and services to consumers. But, in this complex web, there are multiple media-related stakeholders that are connected, whether through airing sport matches on specific stations, creating digital content, or advertising through sport. For instance, consumers looking to watch their favourite team on television are filtered to the sport product through official rights broadcasters, those stations who pay for the exclusive right to air that sport content. At the same time, brands wanting to showcase their products and services to consumers may jump into the picture, advertising on official broadcasts, with the sport organization itself, and on social media. It is also possible for advertisers to reach consumers via traditional media through the sport organization and other sport entities the media cover. In the previous chapter, we discussed the marketing element of sport, including promotion and public relations, concepts that are linked with advertising and advertisers. Here, we will spend a bit more time on traditional media, social media, and broadcast rights.

The three most common forms of traditional media are print, radio, and television. Print media typically consist of newspapers and magazines (such as *La Gazzetta dello Sport*, the Italian sport newspaper published since 1896), typically reporting on sport affairs from a public interest capacity, as opposed to holding exclusive rights for a sport team or league. It is not uncommon for newspapers to post statistics and standings from major professional leagues, as well as articles featuring in-depth accounts of athletes' upbringings or deviance (e.g., doping, criminal behaviour). Print media platforms are also notable for their columns and opinion pieces offered by sport journalists and commentators, discussing thoughts and attitudes towards coaching strategies, player transactions, and management decisions. This form of media had been "analog", requiring companies to physically print their publications and sell them in stores and through boxes on the side of the road after major sport events took place. Some outlets were published daily but some well after major events, such as *Sports Illustrated*, which had a biweekly printing run. Today, print media has shrunk its analogue footprint and has increased its digital footprint. Companies have built websites and mobile apps that connect consumers with stories and columns much quicker than the conventional day-after time frame.

Radio is another common platform. Instead of reading material, consumers would tune in to a station that would orally present sport information, education, and entertainment. Sports radio gained a lot of traction in the mid-20th century, airing baseball games in North America, global football in Europe, and Australian football down under. Consequently, these radio stations became known brands, such as WFAN 660 in New York City and SEN 1116 in Melbourne, Australia. One of the major appeals of radio was the ease of access; consumers can listen to radio programming in their home, in their car, and on the go (through their mobile phone) to get their information, education, and entertainment. More recently, an evolution of sports radio has been the podcast, digestible audio clips of sports radio programming delivered on demand to consumers when they want to receive it, bypassing traditional scheduled time slots.

Finally, there is television. With the growing popularity of sport, dedicated television stations were created such as Star Sports in India, TyC Sports in Argentina, and SuperSport in South Africa. Fans may tune in to watch live sport, view commentators arguing about sport strategy, and visually connect with athlete and team interest stories. Over time, these three traditional forms of sport media have provided an opportunity for the creation of networks, typically composed of a multi-platform strategy. For instance, Rogers Sportsnet in Canada offers Sportsnet radio (in multiple cities across the country), Sportsnet TV channels (Pacific, West, Ontario, East, 360, One, and World), and Sportsnet Magazine. This convergence has also led to the creation of major network brands composed of individual stations and platforms on a global scale, so the fan watching their favourite global football team in England on Sky Sports and the fan watching lacrosse on NBC Sports Network are actually both connected to the same major network: Comcast. This is also the case for major networks like ViacomCBS, AT&T, Discover, Sony, Vivendi, Liberty Global, and Disney, just to name a few. Over time, these major networks have had to modify how they have delivered their television programming, embracing more digital technology to connect with consumers.

In Practice 13.1 ESPN: from linear to digital

On 7 September, 1979, a new type of sport television program was launched in the United States: SportsCenter. The telecast featured a recap of the top stories in the world of sports which consumers could find on the Entertainment and Sports Programming Network, commonly known today as ESPN. Back in the 1970s, ESPN was a novel creation; most sports news existed in a smaller window on the nightly general news, but the idea behind ESPN and its flagship program, SportsCenter, was that a visual, dedicated channel for sport news would captivate audiences. And so it did. That first broadcast in 1979 reached 1.4 million viewers in the United States. In the decades after, consumers kept regularly tuning in to SportsCenter to get their daily sport news fix, and the station expanded its offering to incorporate live telecasts of sport, everything from college basketball to American football and baseball and, by the 1990s, even poker. In 1996, ESPN was sold to the Walt Disney Company, a major media conglomerate with a storied history of high-value entertainment properties. Consequently, ESPN began to expand its offering, securing exclusive rights for additional North American sports such as ice hockey and little league (youth) baseball and growing its brand via print and radio media. The self-proclaimed "worldwide leader in sports" had built a massive empire, primarily on the shoulders of its television stations (which had grown from one to multiple), which hit over 100 million paid cable subscribers by 2011.

Not even the worldwide leader in sports could avoid changes in the environment and consumer behaviours. Although ESPN diversified beyond the United States with "sister stations" or part ownership of channels in Canada, Latin America, Europe, and Asia, the Great Recession in 2008 and its fallout in the years following began to put a strain on linear television viewership. Linear television refers to programming that is aired at certain specified times, which consumers can access through their television sets in their own homes. With the growth of ESPN, the network has become one of the most expensive paid cable channels. In 2011, subscribers paid $4.69 USD/month to have ESPN in their cable or satellite television station package. However, the economic downturn caused some consumers to "cord cut", reducing the number of channels to which they subscribed or cancelling their paid cable service altogether. At the same time, consumers who enjoyed linear delivery of television programming were growing older, and their children, Millennials, and grandchildren, Generation Alphas, desired more flexibility for access to sport news and entertainment and embraced the cordcutting trend. Things at ESPN got so bad that linear television subscriber numbers fell to 83 million by 2019, and the company had to raise its rates to more than $7.21 USD/month per subscription.

To counter cordcutting, ESPN introduced a new service called ESPN+ in 2018. Instead of consumers subscribing to a linear television package with ESPN bundled alongside other sport and non-sport stations, they could opt to subscribe directly to the network itself, a method known as "over-the-top" or OTT. With OTT, ESPN could be watched by consumers on their home television sets but also on their mobile phones, tablets, and computers, so long as they had access to the internet. ESPN+ was reasonably priced at $6.99 USD/month, and subscribers could access shows they missed on demand and have the flexibility to cancel their service any time (instead of traditional cable or satellite, which may have had locked-in contracts). By 2021, ESPN+ had over 13 million subscribers, helping to offset the losses from their linear television numbers. Although cordcutting continues to dampen their linear numbers, embracing OTT and the shift towards digital technology has allowed ESPN to connect with younger consumers and expand the types of programming it can air; ESPN is now showing more diverse international sports programming, increasing coverage of women's sports, and classic matches that captivate audiences.

As traditional media platforms have become more digital in recent years, new platforms have been developed to expedite the information, education, and entertainment that media can provide to consumers. Fans want to know how their team performed, and newspapers, radio stations, and even television programs can be a bit slow and cumbersome. Today, fans can instantly obtain score updates, watch in-game highlights, and interact with other fans, all with just a few swipe gestures and button presses. The key here is about convenience, which typically means on the run and often comes with the expectation of updates from our favourite and most trusted sources of social networks for insight. In short, fans want to know what is going on and want to be able to find out "24/7" or instantaneously. After that, access to media pieces must be customized, or at least "customizable", in order to meet the specific (even fickle) preferences of each fan. Access must also arrive seamlessly. That means both a smooth download as well as through an integrated platform where the sport fan need only engage with a single or a few locations for their updates. Additionally, because sport consumers are so well educated about modern technology, they expect more than just garden-variety results. Rather, content must be accompanied by novelty, entertainment, and insight. Finally, attending sporting events can be prohibitively expensive, leading sport consumers to find alternative ways of engaging with game content as well as looking for new ways of generating the excitement and buzz of the contest. Enter social media.

Social media are digital platforms that enable individuals, media organizations, and sport entities (athletes, teams, and leagues) to create and share content amongst a network of users within an ecosystem. While social media is a mainstay in the contemporary period, it is not a new concept. In the late 1990s and early 2000s, social media sites like MySpace and Friendster, alongside messenger services like ICQ, MSN, and Yahoo! Messenger, provided an opportunity for individuals to connect with one another. It was not until the late 2000s that social media became truly accepted as a means to inform, educate, and entertain. Some sites have come and gone like Vine and Path, while others like Twitch and Discord have taken off.

Sport organizations were slow to embrace social media at first, but, by the mid-2010s, most major and minor professional sport entities had a social media presence. Part of the reason for this shift was the growing technological trends in the environment. For example, one of the first opportunities fans have to connect with sport entities is not at night, typically when matches and games are held, but first thing in the morning, when the fan awakes and checks their phone for sports news (Naraine et al., 2019). In the lead-up to a sporting event, fans can use social media to find out about roster decisions, last-minute changes, and even up-to-date information on traffic and transportation issues getting to and from the sport facility. At the game, fans are also known to jump onto social media to interact with their network, friends, and family, especially during lulls in gameplay (e.g., halftime) or to share a cool picture or video in the moment (Naraine et al., 2020). To seize this trend, sport entities have developed their own personas and profiles to amass large followings and engage fans. By doing so, traditional media stakeholders are bypassed in favour of a direct connection to the sport.

Although there are many different types of social media platforms, sport entities tend to rely on the "core four", also known as the FITS: Facebook, Instagram, Twitter, and Snapchat (Naraine & Karg, 2019). Facebook is the largest social media platform in the world, with nearly 3 billion users active each month. Once of the reasons Facebook is popular amongst sport entities is because it allows for long-form content: more in-depth posts from athletes, teams, and clubs, as well as other engaging features such as live streaming and instant messaging (Wymer et al., 2021). Facebook's reach has also led to greater Instagram integration, another common social media outlet (owned by Facebook). On "IG", the focus is on multimedia, where every post contains a photo or short video. Because of this focus, sport entities experience large amounts of engagement from fans in the form of "likes" and comments. Whereas Facebook takes a long-form approach, Twitter offers sport entities a short-form approach, with micro messages, allowing quicker, faster bursts of information. Finally, there's Snapchat, a more private focused multimedia sharing platform. Although sport brands were averse to Snapchat because of its less public, mass connectivity focus, more and more younger fans are connecting on that platform and nudging brands to live on there, too. FITS represent a unique opportunity for sport teams, leagues, and, of course, athletes, to push content out that is unmediated, unfiltered by traditional media outlets, with more stories and information, and create an active community of users who push out their own user-generated content that amplifies brand awareness. While each platform is different, a strategy using the core four can be an impactful way to inform, educate, and entertain fans and bring them close to the sport entity, which adds another piece to the sport media complex picture.

In Practice 13.2 Tick tock, Tik Tok

In the mid-2010s, there were several new social media platform launches attempting to capitalize on the growing consumer interest in Facebook, Instagram, Twitter, and Snapchat. One of those platforms was Tik Tok, though it was not always known by its current name. In 2016, ByteDance, a Chinese internet application developer, created Douyin, a video-sharing social media platform. The focus of Douyin was to create small, digestible video packets that users could quickly consume, ranging from 15 seconds to three minutes. While there were other sites that allowed for video sharing, Douyin took a different spin, integrating short lip-sync style musical snippets into videos, allowing users to create choreographed video clips. Within its first 200 days, Douyin had over 100 million users; its success in China sparked ByteDance, in 2017, to create a sister app for consumers outside the country's internet restrictions, which was branded as Tik Tok.

Tik Tok grew rapidly once it was released internationally. By 2018, it was available in over 150 countries and reached nearly a billion downloads by 2019. What helped grow the platform was its integration of music, as well as the humorous and comedic trends which younger users adopted. Suddenly, millions of users were creating videos set to their favourite songs, as well as reaction videos to things seen on the internet and even challenges or contests showing off unique skills or abilities. Tik Tok was also able to harness artificial intelligence technology to optimize its algorithms; when a user searches for specific topic, likes certain content, or follows other users with similar attributes, the algorithm recognizes the patterns and presents similar information, content, or people in future occurrences. So, if a fan viewed a Tik Tok post of Cristiano Ronaldo, the global football icon, performing a deke on a defender and liked that content, there's a strong likelihood of being presented with more Ronaldo, global football, or sports-related content.

As Tik Tok competes against other social media platforms for views and engagements, it has adopted an ambitious strategy with sport properties. In 2019, ByteDance signed a partnership agreement with the National Football League in the United States. Where many deals between a brand and sport property focus on exclusive rights and on-site activation, the goal for ByteDance was to encourage the NFL to launch an official Tik Tok account and develop online activations (e.g., challenges, hashtags). By doing so Tik Tok gains more legitimacy as a trusted, reliable, and worthy social media platform and persuades sport fans to jump into their ecosystem and engage with NFL content, as well as non-sport content, too. Tik Tok's sport entertainment strategy has also expanded, with partnerships with the Ultimate Fighting Championship (UFC), a US-based mixed martial arts promotion, and the UEFA Euro 2020 global football tournament. In both circumstances, the goal is friendly collaboration, working together to promote the sport organization and its athletes and clubs on the app and encouraging more views, engagement, and overall usage by fans – a perpetual cycle. The UFC launched its official Tik Tok page in 2019, and by 2021, it had gained 6.3 million followers, so don't be surprised to see more sport organizations partnering with Tik Tok – the clock is ticking!

BROADCAST RIGHTS

Another important part of the sport media complex is broadcast rights. The importance of sport is such that major domestic and international broadcasters almost always bid for the rights to high-profile sport events and properties (Fujak et al., 2017). These broadcast rights typically involve free-to-air television, pay (cable or satellite) television, radio, OTT/digital, and social media, with the two television forms traditionally serving as the most lucrative.

On free-to-air television, broadcasters seek the rights to sport events and properties to enhance the sale of commercial advertising space and timeslots. As the vast majority of sport events occur in a primetime television window (e.g., 7 a.m. – 10 p.m.), free-to-air broadcasters can charge more to advertisers during that window than they can during a rerun of a sitcom or a soap opera. In some jurisdictions like Australia, free-to-air broadcasters are still quite significant, as networks like Seven, Nine, and Ten play a major role in airing Australian football, rugby league, and global football (respectively) to the masses in both urban and rural spaces. However, in places like Canada, free-to-air broadcasters like the CBC have struggled to compete with pay television broadcasters for the rights to sport, specifically premier professional sport, losing out on Major League Baseball, National Basketball Association, and even the Canadian Football League. Yet the CBC has still remained an important outlet for sport in Canada, gravitating toward other minor and developing professional sport leagues like the Canadian Elite Basketball League and Canadian Premier League (global football), as well as elite amateur sports like rowing, snowboarding, and athletics.

On pay television, the goal is to secure rights to major properties that entice consumers to the point where they demand that network on their pay television programming. In a traditional pay television environment, consumers sign up for a pay television service provider (PTSP) and receive a slate of channels occupied by various networks airing their content. In order for a PTSP to have a network on their slate, the former must provide a fee to the latter known as a carriage fee. As some networks have more popularity and demand than others, they are able to secure greater carriage fee prices from the PTSPs, who might raise their rates on consumers who want access to those premium networks. This dynamic is an important part of the sport media complex, as if networks are able to secure in-demand sport events and matches, then they are more likely to be featured on a PTSP slate and, subsequently, charge the PTSP higher carriage fee rates. On top of that, the network carrying sport can also generate revenue from advertisers, similar to free-to-air television networks. For some exclusive, high-value events, consumers might only to contact their PTSP and pay a premium fee for the event airing on a particular channel or broadcaster for a limited period. This is referred to as "pay per view", and it is very common in combat sports like boxing and mixed martial arts. For instance, in 2017, the Conor McGregor versus Floyd Mayweather boxing exhibition resulted in 4.3 million pay per view buys, totalling $600 million USD. The rights to "premium" sports have become such an important commercial property that not having them can adversely impact a company's financial bottom line or, in extreme cases, lead to the demise of media organizations (which in some jurisdictions has led to the regulation of exclusive rights agreements with a single broadcaster).

While radio exhibits a similar process to free-to-air (i.e., audio broadcasting sport to entice advertisers to reach consumers), OTT and mobile broadcasting is more aligned with the pay television model, except, whereas pay television is more concerned with revenue from carriage fees and working with PTSPs, the OTT model is about networks attracting consumers directly: no slates, no carriage fees. Instead, the network creates its own platform, typically a website with live-streaming channels or a mobile app where a consumer signs up and pays a monthly subscription to the network to access content. Usually, OTT applications do not have major advertising, and so the networks generate revenue solely from consumers paying their monthly fees.

Finally, there has been growing momentum to broadcast sport on social media channels. With social media, consumers have significant access to content, and do not need to pay to sign up for sites like Facebook, Twitter, or YouTube (although there is a paid premium version of YouTube). Because of this, the social media giants who own these channels have begun to get involved with broadcasting, securing exclusivity to various sport properties on their "networks". For instance, in India, Facebook signed an agreement to be the "digital rights" broadcaster for the International Cricket Council, airing global cricket events in their digital spaces until 2023. This type of agreement allows cricket fans in India to watch exclusive highlights and behind-the-scenes content and engage with athletes on Facebook, Instagram, and WhatsApp, three major networks under the Facebook corporate banner. For these media organizations, the goal is not to charge consumers to watch sport content but instead build a large following and pre-empt content with a brief video advertisement. Given how successful social media has been in growing user bases, broadcasting sport on this medium is more likely to reach a wider audience than traditional television and radio broadcasts.

The value of sport broadcast rights is increased by the fact that it is also very difficult for consumers of sport to satisfactorily substitute one product for another. In other words, a viewer who wants to watch televised games of a football league has little option but to consume the product offered by the broadcaster who has secured the rights. It is unlikely that the viewer will consider watching tennis or golf on another network a viable substitute. By contrast, a viewer interested in watching a law enforcement/legal or medical drama is likely to be able to substitute a variety of products on a variety of networks and stations. In essence, each sport is a relatively irreplaceable product, which means that it is of more value than a product with multiple variants or imitations. Finally, unlike the multitude of news and drama that is available to television networks in particular, the amount of professional sport is finite (Fujak et al., 2017). Moreover, premier sport leagues and events are even more limited, which means that competition to acquire the rights is greater.

REGULATING THE SPORT MEDIA COMPLEX

The media industry's ever-changing complexity, diversity and adoption of new technologies make it difficult for governments to develop and apply appropriate regulations that meet their policy objectives, protect the interests of all stakeholders, and allow the market to function as efficiently as possible. The sport media landscape is also often regarded as a separate component of the much broader media landscape because of its unique features: significant audience appeal, vigorous competition between broadcasters, relatively cheap production costs, and a mutually reinforcing web containing various stakeholders. Governments seek to regulate the relationship between sport and broadcast media in four areas. First, in some jurisdictions such as Australia, government regulation attempts to prevent the broadcast rights to sport events migrating exclusively from free-to-air television to pay television, the idea being to protect the rights of consumers to have free access to major sport events. Second, governments in most

Westernized contexts have developed regulatory policy aimed at ensuring that sport and media organizations do not engage in anti-competitive behaviour in the buying and selling of these broadcast rights. Such behaviour can lead to monopolies being created that will necessarily restrict supply, which in turn will raise prices to a level that will exploit consumers (New & Le Grand, 1999). Third, governments in some jurisdictions, especially Australia, prohibit certain types of advertising being associated with sports broadcasting, such as tobacco advertising, and there has been an ongoing debate in relation to sports betting advertising being banned during sport broadcasts. Finally, government regulations sometimes attempt to limit or prevent any negative consequences of the vertical integration of the sport and media industries, such as the purchase of a sport team or league by a media organization.

Preventing the migration of premium sport content from free-to-air (network) television to pay (cable) television has been the area of most significant government regulation. Prior to the introduction of pay per view television, the general public were able to access sport via commercial free-to-air broadcasters and, in some instances, via public broadcasters funded by the state. Advocates for the continuation of this system, in which consumers have free access to major sporting competitions and events, have argued that sport has cultural and social significance that needs to be protected and that the migration of sports to pay television or OTT will result in fewer people having access to the product because the cost imposed on the consumer will be too great. The responses by governments have varied depending on national and regional contexts. In the United States, broadcasts of the NFL are spread amongst a core group of media organizations, all of whom are on PTSP slates but some, like ESPN, that only exist on pay television or OTT. NFL rights are so lucrative that segmenting the rights across free-to-air and television is financially beneficial for the league. In Europe, the European Commission has argued that events such as the FIFA World Cup, the UEFA European Football Championship (Euros), and the Olympic Games are of major importance to society and, as such, has regulated broadcast rights to prevent instances where these events are found exclusively on pay television. In smaller nations, such as Australia, with the risk of one or two pay television networks creating a monopoly and putting sport behind a paywall (e.g., Fox), the national government regulated in favour of commercial free-to-air networks. So called "anti-siphoning" laws ensure that free-to-air broadcasters essentially have first access to the rights to major sports and events, even though they might have to pay a premium. Take the recent agreement between ViacomCBS and the Australian Professional Leagues (global football). The broadcaster signed a five-year, $200M AUD deal, putting A-League and W-league games on its free-to-air channel, Ten Network, as well as a larger assortment of matches and highlights on its paid OTT platform, Paramount+. Prior to this agreement, broadcast rights were held by Fox, who were paying the APL $32M AUD per year, and there was little collaboration to air matches on free-to-air stations. With the new deal, the APL has access to a larger audience, and, more importantly, consumers living in rural areas can access marquee matchups that ViacomCBS puts on the Ten Network. This is particularly important for the women's league, which might have struggled to get large viewership being placed behind the Fox paywall but which is now more accessible to the masses.

THE GROWING IMPORTANCE OF DIGITAL TECHNOLOGY

As we have already seen in this chapter, the nature of the sport media complex has been shifted with OTT and social media, and this sentiment also underscores the growing importance of digital technology for the modern sport manager. Beyond new ways to broadcast sport and engage with fans in a two-way conversation, digital technology also provides an opportunity for sport organizations to simply enhance and augment services they already deliver or to grow their product and service offerings.

One of the most common uses of digital technology to enhance sport is the changes to the sport facility experience for consumers. Traditionally, fans consuming sport at a venue would purchase a paper-copy ticket, present that to a ticket taker at the facility gate, and then be ushered to their seat by attendants. Today, that entire process has been enhanced by digital technology. First, while the internet provided the consumer the ability to buy tickets online and print out their paper-copy tickets at home instead of having to visit a ticket sales office kiosk, consumers can now go further, buying tickets on their smartphone or mobile device using sport team apps or authorized ticket selling apps like Ticketmaster, StubHub, and SeatGeek. Instead of printing out the ticket, the consumer receives a "quick response" or QR code that can be scanned at the gate. So, instead of ripping a physical ticket, facility staff digitally scan the QR code on the consumer's phone, improving the flow of patrons entering. But it does not stop there! Using their smartphone, the fan can log on to the team app and find directions to their seat without having to flag an employee down for help. Sport facilities are large and often confusing, and having a visual map that moves along with the consumer's movements is incredibly helpful to maintain a positive experience. Another digital add-on to this process is the recent innovation allowing fans to purchase food and merchandise from the comfort of their seats! Using team apps, fans can order concessions and have them delivered by attendants to their seat instead of having to wait in line and miss gameplay. All of these elements are indicative of the power of digital to make the sport consumption experience quicker and more enjoyable, promoting future consumption.

In Practice 13.3 WaitTime Crowd Intelligence

With the COVID-19 global health pandemic, one of the most desired parts of the sport industry was restricted: live spectatorship. Going to competitions and watching sport stars perform at elite levels captivates fans young and old. But, even before the pandemic, going to a match was fraught with several issues. For instance, fans have to navigate traffic and public transportation congestion to get to a sport venue and deal with the uncertainties of weather and climate. On top of that, once fans are finally in the facility enjoying the match, they are inundated with crowds, queues, and lineups – everything from waiting in line for merchandise, food and beverage (F&B), and even the washroom! Fans often have to decide whether to wait in the queue and miss out on the gameplay action. Sometimes it's easier for fans to just stay in the comfort of their own home and watch sport on television or their mobile device.

However, with digital technology, optimizing the fan experience at sport venues has been dramatically shifted. In particular, the WaitTime Crowd Intelligence platform has helped to alleviate these challenges. First the sport facility works with WaitTime to install sensors and cameras all around its concourse where F&B and washrooms are located. The sensors are then connected back to a central server with the entire venue mapped for seating sections (e.g., 101, 102, 103, 201, 202), as well as the specific F&B and washroom locations. As crowds gather in these spots, the platform uses an algorithm to provide real-time feedback to the venue operator in a colour-coded system: green (short wait), yellow (medium wait), and red (long wait). This information is also relayed to fans via concourse monitors and the WaitTime mobile app. On each, fans can see the amenities closest to them but also how far away other amenities are and the estimated time in the queue, helping them to decide whether to stay close and wait long or walk to another amenity with a smaller crowd and get served much quicker, increasing sales but also positively impacting the fan experience.

WaitTime has been a marvellous addition to major sport facilities worldwide, including the American Airlines Arena in Miami and the iconic Melbourne Cricket Ground. At quarter time, half time, or when "nature calls", fans at these facilities no longer have to debate whether to go hungry or stay uncomfortable in their seat versus navigating the maze of fans on the concourse, sometimes missing critical junctures in the action. The WaitTime platform has also advanced to develop active messaging for fans, informing them of discounts and sales at specific F&B outlets and even using new algorithms to indicate specific wait times in minutes instead of the colour-coded system. For sport managers, the easing of queues is critical to spread out fans (for safety reasons) and to ensure consumption is maximized; the smaller the line, the greater the number of consumers and purchases. So, with a little help from digital technology, fans can get their F&B and use the washroom without having to sacrifice their sport viewing experience.

Advancements in digital technology are also providing an opportunity for sport entities to expand. In particular, artificial intelligence (AI), extended reality (XR), and blockchain are providing the foundation for increased programs and services. For instance, brands are deploying AI-powered chatbots to provide customer service to fans with issues. But AI is also being used to create new products like athlete performance tracking systems and even sport content creation. XR, which includes virtual and augmented reality, is also enabling sport consumers to try new sports in a virtual environment and create new companies that customize locker rooms, sport equipment, and shoes using their mobile phone. So, for a consumer looking to snowboard on the Swiss Alps, a plane ticket can be substituted for a virtual reality headset. And then there's blockchain, the decentralized and transparent recording system. Blockchain provides the foundational layer for some of the prominent revenue-generating advancements the sport industry is currently experiencing, such as non-fungible tokens (NFTs) and sport-based cryptocurrencies. NFTs are digital assets that are original, authenticated pieces instead of just unverified copies floating online. This technology has made it possible for fans to own a physical trading card of their favourite athlete, as well as a digital card, verified by the team or league, that has a limited run. The potential of NFTs in sport, using the secure blockchain foundation, is endless. There have already been a plethora of video snippets, digital trading cards, and digital trinkets designed to gamify and incentivize consumption. Recently, the Golden State Warriors created an NFT program where fans could purchase exclusive digital assets like virtual championship rings. There are also unique applications of NFTs like Zed Run, the virtual horse racing platform, and Chicken Derby, the virtual chicken racing platform. Zed Run, built by a studio in Australia, sells virtual horses of various breeds and attributes, verified by the blockchain system. Consumers can grow their stable (by purchase and by breeding virtual stallions and mares) and race these horses against other competitors for prize purses, akin to traditional horse racing. There are other digital applications using AI, XR, and blockchain that we have yet to encounter, but the possibilities for sport managers and organizations are limitless!

SUMMARY

This chapter has provided an outline of sport and media, with a look into the present and future with digital technology. It has explored the different types of media, notably traditional and newer forms. The chapter also examined broadcast rights, the most significant way in which sport and the media interact in the contemporary professional sport landscape, as well as the reasons governments seek to intervene in the sport media relationship through regulation, particularly in order to protect the interests of consumers via preventing the migration of premium sport content to pay television. Finally, the chapter concluded with a glimpse into the advancements in digital technology, how they are enhancing or augmenting current sport services, and how they are expanding the product and service offerings for sport consumers. Ultimately, this chapter serves to equip sport managers with the understanding of the importance and changing nature of the sport media complex and an overview of the modern tools available to make sport consumption more efficient and/or appealing to fans.

DISCUSSION QUESTIONS

1   Examine some of the largest media organizations in your nation. Do many of these large media companies have an interest in sport and sport organizations via broadcast rights or the ownership of sport teams? Are sport broadcast rights held by one or two media companies, or are they spread across free-to-air and pay television networks?

2   As sport broadcasting rights have grown, some commentators have speculated that the fees that sport broadcasters, such as television networks, are paying mean that achieving a return on investment is difficult, if not impossible, from the sale of advertising or subscriptions. What other ways does sport content assist broadcasters such as television networks, and is this enough to sustain a return on investment into the future?

3   How does the ability of smaller sport organizations to connect directly to fans and consumers via new media improve their ability to secure advertising and sponsorship revenue? What information or data is required to assist them to maximize the revenue gained through these sources?

4   Sport is often viewed as a product that is unable to be substituted. Does the move away from traditional broadcasting channels and towards a multitude of sport offerings mean that this is no longer the case and sport is now similar to other broadcast products such as news, drama, and reality television? Why?

5   The rise of digital technology is creating more unique opportunities, including crypto-currency. Do you think paying athletes, broadcast fees, sponsorships, and even for F&B using cryptocurrency is sustainable? What is the downside to the rapid advancement of digital technology in the sport industry?

FURTHER READING

Billings, A., & Hardin, M. (Eds.). (2014). *Routledge handbook of sport and new media*. London: Routledge.

Fujak, H., Frawley, S., & Bush, S. (2017). Quantifying the value of sport broadcast rights. *Media International Australia, 164*, 104–116. https://doi.org/10.1177%2F1329878X17698051

Goebert, C. (2020). Augmented reality in sport marketing. *Sport Innovation Journal, 1*, 134–151. https://doi.org/10.18060/24227

Naraine, M. L. (2019). The blockchain phenomenon: Conceptualizing decentralized networks and the value proposition to the sport industry. *International Journal of Sport Communication, 12*, 313–335. https://doi.org/10.1123/ijsc.2019-0051

Naraine, M. L., & Karg, A. J. (2019). Digital media in international sports: Engaging fans via social media and fantasy sports. In E. MacIntosh, G. Bravo, & M. Li (Eds.), *International sport management* (pp. 215–331). Champaign, IL: Human Kinetics.

Naraine, M. L., O'Reilly, N., Levallet, N., & Wanless, L. (2020). If you build it, will they log on? Wi-Fi usage and behavior while attending national basketball association games. *Sport, Business and Management: An International Journal, 10*, 207–226. https://doi.org/10.1108/SBM-02-2019-0016

Naraine, M. L., Wear, H. T., & Whitburn, D. J. (2019). User engagement from within the Twitter community of professional sport organizations. *Managing Sport and Leisure, 24*, 275–293. https://doi.org/10.1080/23750472.2019.1630665

Naraine, M. L., & Wanless, L. (2020). Going all in on AI: Examining the value proposition of and integration challenges with one branch of artificial intelligence in sport management. *Sport Innovation Journal, 1*, 49–61. https://doi.org/10.18060/23898

New, B., & Le Grand, J. (1999). Monopoly in sports broadcasting. *Policy Studies, 20*, 23–36.

Pedersen, P. M., Laucella, P. C., Kian, E., & Geurin, A. N. (2021). *Strategic sport communication* (3rd ed.). Champaign, IL: Human Kinetics.

Pederson, P. (2013). *Routledge handbook of sport communication*. London: Routledge.

Wymer, S., Naraine, M. L., Thompson, A. J., & Martin, A. (2021). Transforming the fan experience through live streaming: A conceptual model. *Journal of Interactive Advertising*. Advance online publication. https://doi.org/10.1080/15252019.2021.1910884

RELEVANT WEBSITES

ESPN at http://espn.go.com
Fox Sports at www.foxsports.com
Seven Sports Australia at https://7news.com.au/sport
Sports Illustrated at www.si.com
Star Sports at www.startv.com/about-us/sports/
Tik Tok at www.tiktok.com/en/
Twitter at https://twitter.com
WaitTime at http://thewaittimes.com/

CASE STUDY 13.1

Streaming wars: the battle for digital rights

With the global advancements in technology over the last decade, there has been a rapid shift in how sport is broadcast to the masses and who is bidding for those exclusive rights. Traditionally, television has been the dominant medium in terms of sport broadcasting, and evidence would suggest it is still the pinnacle of broadcasting, connecting to both urban and rural consumers. However, new digital platforms like social media (SM) and subscription streaming services (SSSs), coinciding with increased access to the internet and streaming-capable devices and younger consumers who are increasingly cordcutting, have created a "perfect storm" for sport broadcasting. In this case study, we unpack some of the recent trends with SM and SSSs, highlighting the new stakeholders that have entered the fray, adding to the already intricate sport media complex.

Micro-blogging service Twitter was launched in July 2006 and has grown to become one of the world's largest SM sites. The platform is full of dynamic conversations spanning arts, culture, entertainment, medicine, politics, and, of course, sport. Whether it is commenting in anticipation of a game, live tweeting during a competition, or commenting about performance post-game, Twitter has become one of the go-to places for sport, particularly amongst Millennials. One of the reasons for that is the site connects fans and teams but also journalists and sport media organizations, sponsors, and the athletes themselves. So, for fans wanting immediate news and exclusive access, Twitter unlocks a trove of discussion to consume and with which to engage.

Being home to sport conversation is one of the reasons the platform decided to expand into live streaming, keeping consumers on its site longer and facilitating access to content for ongoing, interactive discussion. In 2016, it purchased the rights to stream ten Thursday night National Football League games. The NFL announced that it had chosen Twitter to provide a live and free digital stream, which would be part of a "Tri-Cast" model in which television broadcasters NBC and CBS would still televise the games, in addition to the NFL Network channel and Twitter. As NFL Commissioner Roger Goodell indicated, "Twitter is where live events unfold and is the right partner for the NFL as we take the latest step in serving fans around the world live football". The NFL strategy was an important first step but not Twitter's only foray into streaming sport (i.e., digital broadcasting).

In 2016 and 2017, Twitter signed agreements with Major League Baseball, the Professional Golfers' Association (PGA) Tour, and the National Basketball Association. With MLB, Twitter planned to live stream one game per week, homing in on a less desirable day for traditional broadcasters: Tuesdays. Later, Twitter would find success again, live streaming the PGA Tour's FedExCup Playoffs, airing more than 70 hours of live competition across 31 tournaments. Its NBA partnership resulted in a weekly pregame show with integration elements to encourage conversation and engagement with players and coaches.

However, Twitter has not been the only SM platform to get in on the action, as Facebook has viewed sport streaming as a means of remaining the most relevant platform for consumers. Launched in 2004 as a way to digitally connect with individuals from the same educational institution, the platform has been come to be known for long-form content, as well as the storing of photos and videos and generally accessing updates from various social circles. Its original strategy was to be the home of the highlights and recaps, partnering with the NFL to digitally distribute highlight packages, as well as the International Cricket Council to distribute highlights in the Indian subcontinent. However, in 2018, the company shifted and secured streaming rights to the (UEFA) Champions League, Europe's elite global football tournament, across South America. The site has also been home to unique matches, such as USA Basketball men's and women's exhibition matches in the lead-up to the Olympic Games and World Surf League events.

Although streaming is important for Facebook, it maintains a mixed strategy. With its Facebook Watch and Facebook Live features, it has been able to find success with sport with behind-the-scenes features, question and answer, analysis programs, and press conferences alongside the live streaming of matches. One of the reasons for this approach is that Facebook often seeks to be "all things to all people", the one-stop SM platform for all audience demographics. But another reason is that the sport streaming space has become highly competitive with Twitter and SSS emergent players like Amazon.

One of growing trends in broadcasting has been the rise of SSS platforms. Netflix, Apple TV, and Disney+ have become household names, and it is not uncommon to find televisions, computers, and mobile devices equipped with potential access to these SSSs. What separates SSS from SM is that the former requires a paid monthly subscription, while the latter is free to join but accompanied by display advertisements sprinkled throughout the platform. SSSs have taken the media world by storm, with hit shows like Orange is the New Black, The Morning Show, and Loki, and have slowly started to gravitate towards sport programs. For instance, Netflix's Drive to Survive documents the Formula 1 motorsport season, unveiling the drama between teams and drivers, while The Last Dance documentary highlighted the Chicago Bulls' tumultuous quest for a sixth championship in 1998. However, it's been SSS platform Amazon Prime which has made significant investments in sport programming, including live streaming of sport. On the documentary side, Amazon Prime has worked with some major sport properties such as the Toronto Maple Leafs and Cricket Australia to showcase behind the scenes for fans. But Amazon Prime has also pursued a live streaming of sport agenda to entice consumers to subscribe to the platform. In 2018, Amazon Prime jumped into the NFL's tri-cast set up but took a step further in 2021 when it announced its partnership with the NFL was now an exclusive deal. In essence, the tri-cast model was finished and, starting in 2022, Amazon Prime would be the sole home for Thursday night NFL games.

At present, SM and SSS and streaming of live sport is still mixed and in flux. Twitter has moved on from some of those premier professional sport leagues toward more minor and developing leagues such as the National Lacrosse League and National Women's Soccer League. Facebook, too, has not fully committed to a live match strategy. After bidding for digital cricket rights in India, Facebook has remained on the sidelines as it reassesses the market and changing landscape. Similarly, while Amazon Prime has been able to make inroads, SSS players like Netflix are looking at adding a video game service to its platform, not necessarily live sport. Apple TV+ has been rumoured to engage with premier sport entities but has yet to commit on that frontier. At the same time, the competition for sport partnerships with SM and SSS has been heating up. SM players like Snapchat and Tik Tok have signed agreements with sport leagues for more content creation and use of their platforms, while sport-specific SSS have sprouted up. Names like DAZN, Kayo, Sportsnet Now, BEIN, and Fubo TV are eating up market share in various regions like Canada, Australia, and the Middle East. However, with more players, consumers have to make decisions about what SSS, sport-specific or general, they should subscribe to each month. Finally, if SM players spend large amounts of money to stream live sport, there's a risk that consumers will jump on and watch the games in this free model and then immediately jump off once the game is over, making it more difficult to monetize and grow engagement. Coming out of the COVID-19 pandemic with consumers re-examining their behaviours, it is unclear what live streaming will look like in a few years, but what is certain is that the streaming wars are just getting started.

CASE STUDY QUESTIONS

1 What was the benefit of "tri-casting" model? Did it benefit the media platform or the sport organization more? Why?

2 Twitter broadcasting of games and sport content has largely been limited to a single game, often also broadcast on another platform; content that is not available on television; or specially created content. Is this reflective of Twitter's

strategy, the greater resources of the television networks, or the fan's desire for non-traditional programming?

3   Explore Amazon Prime's broadcasting of sport content. Is its strategy successful? Why or Why not? What advantage would it have over Netflix or Apple TV+ if those competitors secured live streaming rights?

Sources: NFL website at www.nfl.com; PGA Tour website at www.pgatour.com; MLB website at www.mlb.com; Sports Illustrated website at www.si.com; NBA website at www.nba.com; Twitter website at www.twitter.com; Facebook website at www.facebook.com; Amazon Prime website at www.primevideo.com

CASE STUDY 13.2

Digital collectibles and the sport industry

This case study examines one of the most popular trends in the sport industry: digital collectibles. One of the challenges that sport managers encounter is what to do when revenue is high but stagnant and corporate executives demand growth for sport properties that are winning on the field or pitch. This is one of the benefits of digital technology to add new products and services that engage consumers and grow revenue.

Collectibles in sport are not a new phenomenon. Fans from all over the world are accustomed to buying, trading, and collecting physical cards, stamps, memorabilia, and even miniature trinkets. For example, Tim Horton's, the famous Canadian drip-coffee chain, has worked with marketing agency Frameworth to produce a series of collectible ice hockey sticks in a miniature locker, while Australian grocery chain Woolworths has produced a series of physical "Aussie Heroes" collectibles for the Tokyo 2020 Olympic Games. This gamification element, the desire to collect all pieces and trinkets, and the pursuit itself, offer an engaging experience for consumers (even if it might be expensive or frustrating/tedious at times). But not all consumers like physical things. What do you with all of the swag and merchandise that is collected? For some promotions, collectibles have cases or designated shelves, and fans showcase their collections with pride. In other situations, fans end up with dozens, if not hundreds, of pieces scattered throughout their living quarters. Especially in the modern era where "hoarding" is frowned upon and "minimalism" is trendy, collecting physical things is not always sought after by sport fans, especially younger ones who enjoy digital consumption. However, if there were a way to combine the fun and enjoyment of collecting and the digital trends of minimalism and online activity, perhaps sport fans would be more inclined to continue to spend. And that's where digital collectibles come into play.

Over the past half-decade, sport entities at the league, team, and athlete levels have worked with technology companies to embark upon this new path of digital collecting. For many sport organizations, the concept of digital collecting is hard to understand: if fans do not buy something and cannot physically touch and feel it, how does it work? The answer is the creation of non-fungible tokens or NFTs. NFTs live on the blockchain platform and allow sport organizations to develop digital assets that are unique, verified, and authenticated, so the consumer knows they are legitimate. NFTs can be anything: digital pictures, videos, or trinkets that fans can collect and "store" on a digital shelf, removing physical clutter from their home and allowing the assets to live in perpetuity online. To further explore digital collectibles, there are three prominent examples from North America at the league, team, and athlete level that showcase how NFTs are being implemented.

At the league level, there is no more prominent fixture in the NFT space than the NBA. In 2019, a joint venture between the league and a Vancouver, Canada-based technology company known as Dabber Labs produced a new digital collectible program: NBA Top Shot. Akin to physical NBA trading cards that would have a player's name, image, statistics, and biography, NBA Top Shot created licensed video highlights, packaged in similar fashion. The program begins with the league creating "moments", a video highlight of a particular player doing a particular thing. For instance, NBA star Giannis Antetokounmpo blocking a shot at a critical juncture in game could be deemed an important moment that the league would then capture and send off to Dapper Labs. There, the technology company considers how many "moments" it will create, numbering them from 1 through to the end number, and places them into digital packs, just like regular trading cards. Except, unlike regular trading cards where consumers can buy them almost any time at collectible shops, grocery and convenience stores, and big-box retailers, NBA Top Shop packs are sold in "drops", exclusive events that require consumers to meet certain thresholds (e.g., owning a certain number of moments, being a member for a certain period of time). Pack prices also vary from $9 to $230 USD depending on the type of highlights, the stardom of the athlete, and the exclusiveness of the moment. With the latter, Dapper Labs has created tiers, such as "common", "rare", and "legendary", with the value of each increasing with each tier. When a pack is purchased, all moments are encrypted to the consumer's account and stored on their digital shelf for viewing.

This process seems easy enough for the consumer – they create an account, wait for a drop, and collect moments – but the gamification of digital collectibles has made NBA Top Shot a hot commodity. Dapper Labs used the secure underlying blockchain technology to create a personal digital shelf for collector moments but also a marketplace where these verified, authentic, and limited moments could be bought and sold from fan to fan. So, even though a pack might only cost $230 USD on the high end, individual moments can sell for thousands. The most expensive moment sold in the marketplace to date was a LeBron James dunk which was classified in the "cosmic" tier and was one of only 49 ever made; the sale in February 2021 was for $208,000 USD. For some fans, pulling a valuable moment in a pack is worth hanging onto, but others have found great profit by reselling top elusive moments in the marketplace. As of mid-2021, Dabber Labs and the NBA have kept all moments controlled in-house, and fans are unable to take their moments off-site and sell them elsewhere. This controlled environment ensures the authenticity of the paradigm and retains the mystique and allure of the Top Shot brand, a brand which has generated over $500 million USD in revenue.

At the team level, digital collectibles are also proving fruitful to extend the brand's reach. Merchandise and products with team names and logos are abundant. Fans can easily find a Melbourne Demons scarf, a Manchester United sweater, even a dog food bowl with the New York Yankees logo affixed to its side. Everything from shoes and lanyards to keychains and cutlery can feature team identity, helping to create more allegiant fans. In 2021, the Toronto Raptors of the NBA jumped onto the digital collectible bandwagon, introducing a series of collectible digital keys. With a total of six types of keys, the idea is that owning a key would unlock a set of digital and/or physical experiences for the holder, except, instead of like NBA Top Shot, where there are multiple moments created every month, these six keys were finite, and only a limited number of each was created. And, instead of buying moments in a pack, keys would be auctioned off, with the highest bidders receiving the collectible and its perks. Some of those perks included exclusive, never-before-seen behind-the-scenes footage; signed team jerseys; sit-down meals with front office executives; and even a being a player for the day (with training, meals, and coaching included). So, similar to Top Shot, some keys are more abundant (and inexpensive), while others have only one or a few copies for sale, limiting the experiences and driving auction prices higher.

Finally, athletes have also begun to embrace the digital collectible trend. While leagues and teams are natural fits for collectibles, athletes' names, images, and likenesses are also befitting of items and trinkets, such as the ice hockey stick and Aussie Heroes programs mentioned earlier. In North America, one of the first athletes to create a digital collectible of their likeness was Taijuan Walker, a pitcher in MLB. His "art" collectible sold for 2.35 Ether, a cryptocurrency equivalent to roughly $4000 USD, proceeds of which were donated to his team's charity. Since that initial foray, other athletes have jumped into the game. Rob Gronkowski, a tight end in American football, is one of those athletes, creating a set of five collectibles featuring prominent "Gronk" in-game action shots. In total, Gronkowski's collectibles amassed a whopping $1.8 million USD. Another American football star, Patrick Mahomes, also has some NFT collectibles for sale, as do a slate of elite women athletes, including Megan Rapinoe (global football), Sue Bird (basketball), and Ibtihaj Muhammad (fencing). Particularly for women and athletes in sports that do not bear high salaries from broadcast and sponsorship deals, NFT collectibles are a unique way to profit off their likeness and cash in on a trend that fans are demanding.

Although digital collectibles are occupying a unique position in the market, their longevity is still a question mark. Are NFTs just a fad that was exacerbated by the COVID-19 pandemic and accompanying lockdowns? Or is there truly a market for digital collectibles over the long haul? As the Toronto Raptors example demonstrates, some sport organizations are still trying to blend digital collectibles with physical experiences, so there are still mixed strategies being employed to facilitate this new era of digital sport products.

CASE STUDY QUESTIONS

1   What are the fan motivations for digital collectibles, and how do they differ from traditional physical collectibles?

2   Which sport stakeholder discussed in the case study (i.e., league, team, and athlete) has the most to gain from the emergence of digital collectibles?

3   Examine the digital collectible/NFT space in your country. What sport entities have embraced these products, and which organizations have stayed away? Why would sport organizations not want to offer such products?

4   How can digital collectibles in sport be further enhanced for fans in the future?

Sources: National Basketball Association website at www.nba.com; Toronto Raptors website at www.raptors.com; NBA Top Shot website at www.nbatopshot.com; DropShop website at www.dropshop.io; Rob Gronkowski NFT website at www.gronknft.com; Tim Hortons website at www.timhortons.ca; Woolworths Supermarket website at www.woolworths.com.au

Bibliography

Amis, J., & Slack, T. (1996). The size-structure relationship in voluntary sport organizations. *Journal of Sport Management, 10,* 76–86.

Anagnostopoulos, C., Anagnostopoulos, C., Byers, T., Byers, T., Kolyperas, D., & Kolyperas, D. (2017). Understanding strategic decision-making through a multi-paradigm perspective: The case of charitable foundations in English football. *Sport, Business and Management: An International Journal, 7*(1), 2–20.

Anderson, J., Parrish, R., & García, B. (Eds.). (2018). *Research handbook on EU sports law and policy.* London: Edward Elgar Publishing.

Anderson-Levitt, K. M. (2012). Complicating the concept of culture. *Comparative Education, 48*(4), 441–454. https://doi.org/10.1080/03050068.2011.634285

Ashforth, B. E., & Schinoff, B. S. (2016). Identity under construction: How individuals come to define themselves in organizations. *Annual Review of Organizational Psychology and Organizational Behavior, 3*(1), 111–137. https://doi.org/10.1146/annurev-orgpsych-041015-062322

Australian Human Rights Commission. (2019). *Guidelines for the inclusion of transgender and gender diverse people in sport.* Sydney: Australian Human Rights Commission.

Australian Sports Commission. (2016). *Governance Reform in Sport.* Canberra: Australian Sports Commission.

Bach, S., & Edwards, M. (2013). *Managing human resources* (5th ed.). London: Wiley.

Bailey, B., Benson, A. J., & Bruner, M. W. (2017). Investigating the organisational culture of Cross-Fit. *International Journal of Sport and Exercise Psychology,* 1–15. dx.doi.org/10.1080/1612197X.2017.1329223

Baldwin, R., Cave, M., & Lodge, M. (2012). *Understanding regulation: Theory, strategy and practice* (2nd ed.). Oxford: Oxford University Press.

Bass, B. M. (1985). *Leadership and performance beyond expectations.* New York: The Free Press.

Bass, B. M. (1990). *Bass & Stogdill's handbook of leadership: Theory, research, and managerial applications* (3rd ed.). New York: Free Press.

Bass, B. M., & Avolio, B. J. (1994). *Improving organisational effectiveness through transformational leadership.* London: Sage Publications.

Baxter, H., Hoye, R., & Kappelides, P. (2021). Female volunteer community sport coaches: A scoping review and research agenda, *Journal of Amateur Sport, 7*(1). https://doi.org/10.17161/jas.v7i1.13774

Berger, P., & Luckmann, T. (1967). *The social construction of reality: A treatise on the sociology of knowledge.* London: Penguin.

Bessant, J., & Tidd, J. (2015). *Innovation and entrepreneurship* (3rd ed.). London: Wiley.

Billings, A., & Hardin, M. (Eds.). (2014). *Routledge handbook of sport and new media.* London: Routledge.

Bowen, J., Katz, R. S., Mitchell, J. R., Polden, D. J., & Walden, R. (2017). *Sport, ethics and leadership.* London: Taylor & Francis.

Boyle, R., & Haynes, R. (2000). *Power play: Sport, the media and popular culture.* Sydney: Longman.

Braithwaite, J. (2008). *Regulatory capitalism: How it works, ideas for making it work better.* Cheltenham, UK: Edward Elgar.

Braithwaite, J., & Drahos, P. (2000). *Global business regulation.* Cambridge, UK: Cambridge University Press.

Brown, A., & Walsh, A. (1999). *Not for sale: Manchester united.* Mainstream: Murdoch and the Defeat of BSkyB.

Burton, L. J. (2015). Underrepresentation of women in sport leadership: A review of research. *Sport Management Review, 18*(2), 155–165.

Canadian Women & Sport. (2021). *Winning plays: The gender equity playbook report.* Retrieved from https://womenandsport.ca/wp-content/uploads/2021/07/Gender-Equity-Playbook-Roll-Up-Report-Eng-Final.pdf

Chalip, L. (2000). Sydney 2000: Volunteers and the organization of the Olympic games: Economic and formative aspects. In M. Moragas, A. B. de Moreno, & N. Puig (Eds.), *Volunteers, global society and the Olympic movement* (pp. 205–214). Lausanne: International Olympic Committee.

Chalip, L., Johnson, A., & Stachura, L. (Eds.). (1996). *National sports policies: An international handbook.* Westport: Greenwood Press.

Chelladurai, P., & Miller, J. M. (2017). Leadership in sport management. In R. Hoye & M. M. Parent (Eds.), *Handbook of sport management* (pp. 85–102). London: Sage.

Chelladurai, P., & Kerwin, S. (2017). *Human resource management in sport and recreation* (3rd ed.). Champaign, IL: Human Kinetics.

Clarke, T. (Ed.). (2004). *Theories of corporate governance.* Oxon, UK: Routledge.

Coakley, J., et al. (2009). *Sport in society.* Sydney: McGraw Hill.

Cousens, L., & Slack, T. (2005). Field-level change: The case of north American major league professional sport. *Journal of Sport Management, 19*(1), 13–42.

Cunningham, G. (2019). *Diversity and inclusion in sport organizations: A multilevel perspective* (4th ed.). London: Routledge.

Cunningham, G., & Hussain, U. (2020). The case for LGBT diversity and inclusion in sport business. *Sport & Entertainment Review, 5*(1). Retrieved from https://serjournal.com/2020/01/15/the-case-for-lgbt-diversity-and-inclusion-in-sport-business/

Cuskelly, G., & Hoye, R. (2013). Sports officials' intention to continue: Results of a time-lagged intervention study. *Sport Management Review, 16*, 451–464.

Cuskelly, G. (2017). Volunteer management. In R. Hoye & M. M. Parent (Eds.), *Handbook of sport management* (pp. 442–462). London: Sage.

Davis, T. (2011). What is sports law? *Marquette Sports Law Review, 11*, 211.

Delaney, K., & Eckstein, R. (2003). *Public dollars, private stadiums: The battle over building sports stadiums.* New Brunswick: Rutgers University Press.

DeSensi, J. T., & Rosenberg, D. (2010). *Ethics and morality in sport management* (3rd ed.). Morgantown, VA: West Virginia University.

Dowling, M., Edwards, J., & Washington, M. (2014). Understanding the concept of professionalism in sport management research. *Sport Management Review, 17*(4), 520–529.

Downward, P., Frick, B., Humphreys, B. R., Pawlowski, T., Ruseski, J. E., & Soebbing, B. P. (2020). *The Sage handbook of sports economics.* Sage. http://dx.doi.org/10.4135/9781526470447

Dressler, G. (2003). *Human resource management.* New Jersey: Prentice Hall.

Duxbury, N. (2015). Positioning cultural mapping in local planning and development contexts: An introduction. *Culture and Local Governance, 5*(1–2), 1–7. https://doi.org/10.18192/clg-cgl.v5i1-2.1437

Edwards, J. R. D., Davey, J., & Armstrong, K. (2013). Returning to the roots of culture: A review and re-conceptualisation of safety culture. *Safety Science, 55*, 70–80. https://doi.org/10.1016/j.ssci.2013.01.004

Epstein, A., & Osborne, B. (2017). Teaching ethics with sports: Recent developments. *Marquette Sports Law Review, 28*, 301.

Eskiler, E., Geri, S., Sertbas, K., & Calik, F. (2016). *The effects of organizational culture on organizational creativity and innovativeness in the sport businesses.*

Ferkins, L. (2020). Strategy and the strategic function of sport boards. In D. Shilbury & L. Ferkins (Eds.), *Routledge handbook of sport governance* (pp. 285–295). Oxon: Routledge.

Ferkins, L., & Shilbury, D. (2012). Good boards are strategic: What does that mean for sport governance? *Journal of Sport Management, 26*, 67–80.

Ferkins, L., & Shilbury, D. (2015). Board strategic balance: An emerging sport governance theory. *Sport Management Review, 18*, 489–500.

Fiedler, F. E. (1967). *A theory of leadership effectiveness.* New York: McGraw-Hill.

Fielding, L, Miller, L., & Brown, J. (1999). Harlem Globetrotters International, Inc. *Journal of Sport Management, 13*(1), 45–77.

Foster, G., O'Reilly, N., & Dávila, A. (2016). *Sports business management: Decision making around the globe.* London: Routledge.

Franks, S., & O'Neill, D. (2014). Women reporting sport: Still a man's game? *Journalism, 17*(4), 474–492. https://doi.org/10.1177/1464884914561573

Frick, B. (2009). Globalization and factor mobility: The impact of the "Bosman-ruling" on player migration in professional soccer. *Journal of Sports Economics, 10*, 88–106. https://doi.org/10.1177%2F1527002508327399

Frosdick, S., & Walley, L. (Eds.). (1997). *Sport and safety management.* Oxford: Butterworth Heinemann.

Fujak, H., & Frawley, S. (2013). The Barassi line: Quantifying Australia's great sporting divide. *Sporting Traditions, 30*, 93–109.

Fujak, H., Frawley, S., & Bush, S. (2017). Quantifying the value of sport broadcast rights. *Media International Australia, 164*, 104–116. https://doi.org/10.1177%2F1329878X17698051

Funk, D. C., Alexandris, K., & McDonald, H. (2016). *Sport consumer behaviour: Marketing strategies.* London: Routledge.

Garcia, B., & Welford, J. (2015). Supporters and football governance, from customers to stakeholders: A literature review and agenda for research. *Sport Management Review, 18*, 517–528.

Gardiner, S., O'Leary, J., Welch, R., Boyes, S., & Naidoo, U. (2012). *Sports law.* London: Routledge.

Gardiner, S., Parrish, R., & Siekman, R. (2009). *EU, sport, law and policy.* The Hague, Netherlands: Asser Press.

Geeraert, A., Alm, J., & Groll, M. (2014). Good governance in international sport organizations: An analysis of the 35 Olympic governing bodies. *International Journal of Sport Policy and Politics, 6*(3), 281–306.

Gender Equity Consulting. Canadian Women & Sport. (n.d.). Retrieved from https://womenandsport.ca/learning-opportunities/consulting/

Goebert, C. (2020). Augmented reality in sport marketing. *Sport Innovation Journal, 1*, 134–151. https://doi.org/10.18060/24227

Goronkin, J. (2019). *Diamondbacks winning record in leadership and organizational excellence.* LinkedIn. Retrieved from www.linkedin.com/pulse/diamondbacks-winning-record-leadership-organizational-joleen-goronkin/

Gratton, C., & Taylor, P. (1991). *Government and the economics of sport.* London: Longman.

Grattton, C., & Taylor, P. (2000). *Economics of sport and recreation.* Milton Park, UK: Taylor & Francis.

Green, M., & Houlihan, B. (2005). *Elite sport development.* London: Routledge.

Greenfield, S., & Osborn, G. (2001). *Regulating football; commodification, consumption and the law.* London: Pluto Press.

Greenhalgh, G., Dwyer, B., & LeCrom, C. (2017). A case of multiple (brand) personalities: Expanding the methods of brand personality measurement in sport team contexts. *Sport Marketing Quarterly, 26,* 20–30.

Grix, J. (2009). The impact of UK sport policy on the governance of athletics. *International Journal of Sport Policy, 1,* 31–49.

Haas, U., & Hessert, B. (2021). Sports regulations on human rights – Applicability and self-commitment. In *Le sport au Carrefour des droits Mélanges en l'honneur de Gérald Simon.* Paris: LexisNexis.

Haas, U., & Hessert, B. (2021). The legal regime applicable to disciplinary measures by sports associations – one size does not fit all. In P. Jung, F. Krauskopf, & C. Cramer (Eds.), *Theorie und Praxis des Unternehmensrechts – Festschrift zu Ehren von Lukas Handshin.* Zurich: Schulthess Medien AG.

Hamil, S., Morrow, S., Idle, C., Rossi, G., & Faccendini, S. (2010). The governance and regulation of Italian football. *Soccer & Society, 11,* 373–413.

Haynes, J., & Marcus, J. T. (2019). *Commonwealth Caribbean sports law.* London: Routledge.

Heinze, K. L., & Lu, D. (2017). Shifting responses to institutional change: The National Football League and player concussions. *Journal of Sport Management, 1–44.* doi:10.1123/jsm.2016-0309

Hemme, F., Morais, D. G., Bowers, M. T., & Todd, J. S. (2021). Leading culture change in public recreation. *Journal of Sport Management, 1*(aop), 1–14. https://doi.org/10.1123/jsm.2020-0249

Henry, I., & Lee, P. C. (2004). Governance and ethics in sport. In J. Beech & S. Chadwick (Eds.), *The business of sport management.* London: Prentice Hall.

Herman, R. D., & Renz, D. O. (1997). Multiple constituencies and the social construction of nonprofit organizational effectiveness. *Nonprofit and Voluntary Sector Quarterly, 26,* 185–206.

Herman, R. D., & Renz, D. O. (1998). Nonprofit organizational effectiveness: Contrasts between especially effective and less effective organizations. *Nonprofit Management and Leadership, 9,* 23–38.

Herman, R. D., & Renz, D. O. (2000). Board practices of especially effective and less effective local nonprofit organizations. *American Review of Public Administration, 30,* 146–160.

Hersey, P., & Blanchard, K. (1977). *Management of organizational behaviour: Utilizing human resources.* Englewood Cliffs, NJ: Prentice-Hall.

Hill, L. A. (2008). Where will we find tomorrow's leaders? *Harvard Business Review, 86*(1), 123–129.

Houlihan, B. (2017). Sport policy and politics. In R. Hoye & M. M. Parent (Eds.), *Handbook of sport management* (pp. 183–200). London: Sage.

House, R. J. (1971). A path-goal theory of leader effectiveness. *Administrative Science Quarterly, 16,* 321–338.

House, R. J., & Mitchell, T. R. (1974, Fall). Path-goal theory of leadership. *Contemporary Business, 3,* 81–91.

Hoye, R. (2017). Sport governance. In R. Hoye & M. M. Parent (Eds.), *Handbook of sport management* (pp. 9–23). London: Sage.

Hoye, R., & Cuskelly, G. (2003). Board-executive relationships within voluntary sport organisations. *Sport Management Review, 6*(1), 53–73.

Hoye, R., & Cuskelly, G. (2007). *Sport governance.* Oxford: Elsevier Butterworth-Heinemann.

Hoye, R., Cuskelly, G., Auld, C., Kappelides, P., & Misener, K. (2020). *Sport volunteering.* London: Routledge.

Hoye, R., & Doherty, A. (2011). Nonprofit sport board performance: A review and directions for future research. *Journal of Sport Management, 25*(3), 272–285.

Hoye, R., Nicholson, M., & Houlihan, B. (2010). *Sport and policy.* Oxford: Elsevier Butterworth-Heinemann.

Hoye, R., & Parent, M. (Eds.). (2017). *Handbook of sport management.* London: Sage.

Hoye, R., Parent, M. P., Taks, M., Naraine, M. L., Seguin, B., & Thomson, A. (2020). Design archetype utility for understanding and analyzing the governance of contemporary national sport organizations, *Sport Management Review, 23,* 576–587.

Hylton, K. Bramham, P. Jackson, D., & Nesti, M. (2001). *Sports development: Policy, process and practice.* London: Routledge.

James, M. (2017). *Sports law.* London: Macmillan International Higher Education.

Jarvie, G. (2013). *Sport culture and society: An introduction* (2nd ed.). London: Routledge.

Jensen, J. A., Wakefield, L., Cobbs, J. B., & Turner, B. A. (2016). Forecasting sponsorship costs: Marketing intelligence in the athletic apparel industry. *Marketing Intelligence & Planning, 34,* 281–298.

John, G., & Sheard, R. (1997). *Stadia: A design and development guide.* Oxford: Architectural Press.

Johnson, G., Whittington, R., Regner, P., Scholes, K., & Angwin, E. (2017). *Exploring strategy* (11th ed.). London: Prentice-Hall.

Juravich, M., Salaga, S., & Babiak, K. (2017). Upper echelons in professional sport: The impact of NBA general managers on team performance. *Journal of Sport Management,* 1–38, doi.org/10.1123/jsm.2017-0044

Kelly, S. J., Ireland, M., Mangan, J., & Williamson, H. (2016). It works two ways: Impacts of sponsorship alliance upon sport and sponsor image. *Sport Marketing Quarterly, 25,* 242–259.

Kikulis, L. M., Slack, T., & Hinings, B. (1995). Toward an understanding of the role of agency and choice in the changing structure of Canada's national sport organizations. *Journal of Sport Management, 9,* 135–152.

Kikulis, L. M., Slack, T., & Hinings, B. (1992). Institutionally specific design archetypes: A framework for understanding change in national sport organizations. *International Review for the Sociology of Sport, 27,* 343–367.

Kikulis, L. M., Slack, T., Hinings, B., & Zimmermann, A. (1989). A structural taxonomy of amateur sport organizations. *Journal of Sport Management, 3,* 129–150.

Kotter, J. P. (1990). *A force for change: How leadership differs from management.* New York: The Free Press.

Kunkel, T., Doyle, J. P., & Berlin, A. (2017). Consumers' perceived value of sport team games – A multidimensional approach. *Journal of Sport Management, 31,* 80–95.

LaVoi, N. M., & Baeth, A. (2018). Women and sports coaching. In L. Mansfield, J. Caudwell, B. Wheaton, & B. Watson (Eds.), *The Palgrave handbook of feminism and sport, leisure and physical education.* London: Palgrave Macmillan. https://doi.org/10.1057/978-1-137-53318-0_10

LaVoi, N. M., McGarry, J. E., & Fisher, L. A. (2019). Final thoughts on women in sport coaching: Fighting the war. *Women in Sport & Physical Activity Journal, 27*(2), 136–140. https://doi.org/10.1123/wspaj.2019-0030

Lawler, S. (2015). *Identity: Sociological perspectives.* London: John Wiley & Sons.

Lewis, A., & Taylor, J. (2021). *Sport: Law and practice* (4th ed.). London and New York: Bloomsbury.

Li, M., Hofacre, S., & Mahony, D. (2001). *Economics of sport.* Morgantown: Fitness Information Technology.

Locke, E. A. (1991). *The essence of leadership: The four keys to leading successfully.* New York: Lexington Books.

Lussier, R., & Kimball, D. (n.d.). *Sport managers influence organizational culture.* Human Kinetics. Retrieved June 30, 2021, from https://us.humankinetics.com/blogs/excerpt/sport-managers-influence-organizational-culture

Lyras, A., & Welty Peachey, J. (2011). Integrating sport for development theory and praxis. *Sport Management Review, 14*(4), 311–326.

MacIntosh, E. W., Bravo, G. A., & Li, M. (2020). *International sport management.* Champaign, IL: Human Kinetics.

Mackintosh, C. (2021). *Foundations of sport development.* London: Routledge.

Maitland, A., Hills, L. A., & Rhind, D. J. (2015). Organisational culture in sport – A systematic review. *Sport Management Review, 18*(4), 501–516. https://doi.org/10.1016/j.smr.2014.11.004

Manley, A., Roderick, M., & Parker, A. (2016). Disciplinary mechanisms and the discourse of identity: The creation of 'silence' in an elite sports academy. *Culture and Organization, 22*(3), 221–244.

May, T., Harris, S., & Collins, M. (2013). Implementing community sport policy: Understanding the variety of voluntary club types and their attitudes to policy. *International Journal of Sport Policy and Politics, 5*(3), 397–419.

McLeod, J. (2020). Role of the board and directors: Board structure and composition. In D. Shilbury & L. Ferkins (Eds.), *Routledge handbook of sport governance* (pp. 243–253). Oxon: Routledge.

Mills, C., & Hoeber, L. (2013). Exploring organizational culture through artifacts in a community figure skating club. *Journal of Sport Management, 27*(6), 482–496. https://doi.org/10.1123/jsm.27.6.482

Misener, K., & Doherty, A. (2013). Understanding capacity through the processes and outcomes of inter-organizational relationships in nonprofit community sport organizations, *Sport Management Review, 16*(2), 135–147.

Moorman, A. M. (Ed.). (2020). *Sport law: A managerial approach* (4th ed.). London: Routledge.

Muller, C., Lammert, J., & Hovemann, G. (2012). The financial fair play regulations of EUFA: An adequate concept to ensure the long term viability and sustainability of European club football. *International Journal of Sport Finance, 7*, 117–140.

Naraine, M. L. (2019). Follower segments within and across the social media networks of major professional sport organizations. *Sport Marketing Quarterly, 28*, 222–233.

Naraine, M. L. (2019). The blockchain phenomenon: Conceptualizing decentralized networks and the value proposition to the sport industry. *International Journal of Sport Communication, 12*, 313–335. https://doi.org/10.1123/ijsc.2019-0051

Naraine, M. L., & Karg, A. J. (2019). Digital media in international sports: Engaging fans via social media and fantasy sports. In E. MacIntosh, G. Bravo, & M. Li (Eds.), *International sport management* (pp. 215–331). Champaign, IL: Human Kinetics.

Naraine, M. L., & Wanless, L. (2020). Going all in on AI: Examining the value proposition of and integration challenges with one branch of artificial intelligence in sport management. *Sport Innovation Journal, 1*, 49–61. https://doi.org/10.18060/23898

Naraine, M. L., O'Reilly, N., Levallet, N., & Wanless, L. (2020). If you build it, will they log on? Wi-Fi usage and behavior while attending National Basketball Association games. *Sport, Business and Management: An International Journal, 10*, 207–226. https://doi.org/10.1108/SBM-02-2019-0016

Naraine, M. L., Wear, H. T., & Whitburn, D. J. (2019). User engagement from within the Twitter community of professional sport organizations. *Managing Sport and Leisure, 24*, 275–293. https://doi.org/10.1080/23750472.2019.1630665

New, B., & Le Grand, J. (1999). Monopoly in sports broadcasting. *Policy Studies, 20*, 23–36.

Nicholson, M., Hoye, R., & Houlihan, B. (Eds.). (2011). *Participation in sport: International policy perspectives*. London: Routledge.

Nordstrom, H., Warner, S., & Barnes, J. C. (2016). Behind the stripes: Female football officials' experiences. *International Journal of Sport Management & Marketing, 16*, 259–279.

Northouse, P. G. (2021). *Leadership: Theory and practice* (9th ed.). Thousand Oaks: Sage.

O'Brien, D., & Gowthorp, L. (2017). Organizational structure. In R. Hoye & M. M. Parent (Eds.), *Handbook of sport management* (pp. 39–61). London: Sage.

O'Reilly, N., Séguin, B., Abeza, G., & Naraine, M. L. (2022). *Canadian sport marketing* (3rd ed.). Champaign, IL: Human Kinetics.

Odiakaose, H. (2018). Organizational culture and dynamics. *International Journal of Scientific Research and Management, 6*(1), 32–39.

Odor, H. O. (2018). Organisational culture and dynamics. *Global Journal of Management and Business Research*. Retrieved from www.journalofbusiness.org/index.php/GJMBR/article/view/2406

Olson, E. M., Duray, R., Cooper, C., & Olson, K. M. (2016). Strategy, structure and culture within the English premier league: An examination of large clubs. *Sport, Business and Management: An International Journal, 6*(1), 55–75.

Oputu, E. (2014). Women still underrepresented in US media. *Columbia Journalism Review*. Retrieved from https://archives.cjr.org/the_kicker/women_are_still_underrepresent.php

Ordway, C., & Opie, H. (2017). Integrity and corruption in sport. In N. Schulenkorf & S. Frawley (Eds.), *Critical issues in global sport management* (pp. 38–63). London: Taylor & Francis.

Ordway, C. (Ed.). (2021). *Restoring trust in sport: Sports corruption case studies & solutions*. London: Routledge.

Organisation for Economic Co-operation and Development. (2004). *Principles of corporate governance*. Paris: OECD.

Organizational Culture and Leadership – Edgar H. Schein – Google Books. (n.d.). Retrieved June 24, 2021, from https://books.google.ca/books?hl=en&lr=&id=Mnres2PlFLMC&oi=fnd&pg=PR9&dq=cultural+ dimensions+in+organizations+schein&ots=opdsKe4wSl&sig=shBIHUAjtmZ3YKHx2HmWVBBPn4g# v=onepage&q=cultural%20dimensions%20in%20organizations%20schein&f=false

Parent, M. P., & Hoye, R. (2018). The impact of governance principles on sport organizations' governance practices and performance: A systematic review. *Cogent Social Sciences Sport, 4*(1), 1–24. https:// doi.org/10.1080/23311886.2018.1503578

Parent, M. P., Hoye, R., Taks, M., Thomson, A., Naraine, M., Lachance, E., & Seguin, B. (2021). National sport organization governance design archetypes for the 21st century. *European Sport Management Quarterly*, 1–21. https://doi.org/10.1080/16184742.2021.1963801

Pedersen, P. M., Laucella, P. C., Kian, E., & Geurin, A. N. (2021). *Strategic sport communication* (3rd ed.). Champaign, IL: Human Kinetics.

Pedersen, P. M., Laucella, P., Kian, E., & Geurin, A. (2017). *Strategic sport communication* (2nd ed.). Champaign, IL: Human Kinetics.

Pederson, P. (2013). *Routledge handbook of sport communication*. London: Routledge.

Pettigrew, A. M. (1979). On studying organizational cultures. *Administrative Science Quarterly, 24*, 570–581.

Pfeffer, J., & Salancik, G. (1978). *The external control of organizations: A resource dependence perspective*. New York: Harper & Row.

Porter, M. (1980). *Competitive strategy*. New York: The Free Press.

Porter, M. (1985). *Competitive strategy: Creating and sustaining superior performance*. New York: Simon & Schuster.

Productivity Commission. (2003). *Social capital: Reviewing the concept and its policy implications*. Canberra: Commonwealth of Australia.

Putnam, R. (2000). *Bowling alone: The collapse and revival of American community*. New York: Simon & Schuster.

Quirk, J., & Fort, R. (1992). *Pay dirt: The business of professional team sports*. Princeton: Princeton University Press.

Relvas, H., Littlewood, M., Nesti, M., Gilbourne, D., & Richardson, D. (2010). Organizational structures and working practices in elite European professional football clubs: Understanding the relationship between youth and professional domains. *European Sport Management Quarterly, 10*(2), 165–187.

Rigauer, B. (1981). *Sport and work*. New York: Columbia University Press.

Robbins, S., & Barnwell, N. (2002). *Organisation theory*. Frenchs Forest: Pearson Education Australia.

Rodriguez-Pomeda, J., Casani, F., & Alonso-Almeida, M. D. M. (2017). Emotions' management within the Real Madrid football club business model. *Soccer & Society, 18*(4), 431–444.

Schein, E. (2016). *Organizational culture and leadership* (5th ed.). San Francisco: Jossey-Bass.

Schein, E. H. (1990). Organizational culture. *American Psychologist, 45*(2), 109–119. https://doi.org/ 10.1037/0003-066X.45.2.109

Schermerhorn, J. R., Hunt, J. G., & Osborne, R. N. (1994). *Managing organizational behaviour* (5th ed.). Brisbane: John Wiley & Sons, Inc.

Schulenkorf, N., Sherry, E., & Rowe, K. (2016). Sport for development: An integrated literature review. *Journal of Sport Management, 30*, 22–39.

Sherry, E., Schulenkorf, N., & Phillips, P. (2016). *Managing sport development: An international approach.* London: Routledge.

Shilbury, D. (2012). Competition: The heart and soul of sport management. *Journal of Sport Management, 26*, 1–10.

Shilbury, D., & Ferkins, L. (2011). Professionalisation, sport governance and strategic capability. *Managing Leisure, 16*(2), 108–127.

Shilbury, D., & Ferkins, K. (2019). *Routledge handbook of sport governance.* London: Routledge.

Shilbury, D., & Ferkins, L. (Eds.). (2020). *Routledge handbook of sport governance.* London: Routledge.

Shilbury, D., Quick, S., Funk, D., Westerbeek, H., & Karg, A. (2014). *Strategic sport marketing.* London: Routledge.

Shropshire, K. (1995). *The sports franchise game.* Philadelphia: University of Pennsylvania Press.

Sisjord, M., Fasting, K., & Sand, T. (2017). The impact of gender quotas in leadership in Norwegian organised sport. *International Journal of Sport Policy and Politics, 9*(3), 505–519. doi:10.1080/194 06940.2017.1287761

Slesinger, L. H. (1991). *Self-assessment for nonprofit governing boards.* Washington, DC: National Centre for Nonprofit Boards.

Smith, A. C. T., & Stewart, B. (2011). Organizational rituals: Features, functions and mechanisms. *International Journal of Management Reviews, 13*(2), 113–133. https://doi.org/10.1111/j.1468-2370. 2010.00288.x

Smith, A., & Stewart, B. (2010). The special features of sport revisited. *Sport Management Review, 10*(1), 1–11.

Sport Australia. (2020). *Sport governance principles.* Canberra: Sport Australia.

Sport England. (2016). *Towards an active nation. Strategy 2016–2021.* London: Sport England.

Sport New Zealand. (2015). *Governance benchmarking review 2014.* Wellington, New Zealand: Sport New Zealand.

Standing Committee on Recreation and Sport Working Party on Management Improvement. (1997). *Report to the standing committee on recreation and sport July 1997.* Canberra, Australia: Author.

Stebbins, R. (2007). *Serious leisure.* New Brunswick: Transactions Publications.

Stets, J. E., & Serpe, R. T. (2013). Identity theory. In J. DeLamater & A. Ward (Eds.), *Handbook of social psychology* (pp. 31–60). Springer Netherlands. https://doi.org/10.1007/978-94-007-6772-0_2

Stewart, R., Nicholson, M., Smith, A., & Westerbeek, H. (2004). *Australian sport: Better by design? The evolution of Australian sport policy.* London: Routledge.

Stiglitz. (2000). *Economics of the public sector* (3rd ed.). New York: W.W. Norton.

Szymanski, M., & Wolfe, R. A. (2017). Strategic management. In R. Hoye & M. M. Parent (Eds.), *Handbook of sport management* (pp. 24–38). London: Sage.

Taks, M., Séguin, B., Naraine, M. L., Thompson, A., Parent, M. M., & Hoye, R. (2020). Brand governance practices in Canadian national sport organizations: An exploratory study. *European Sport Management Quarterly, 20*, 10–29.

Temkin Group. (2015). *Business-to-business (B2B) customer experience best practices: 20 Ways to embed customer centricity across 5 key B2B processes.* Temkin Group Insight Report. Retrieved from www. temkingroup.com

Theodoraki, E. I., & Henry, I. P. (1994). Organizational structures and contexts in British national governing bodies of sport. *International Review for the Sociology of Sport, 29,* 243–263.

Thibault, L., Slack, T., & Hinings, B. (1991). Professionalism, structures and systems: The impact of professional staff on voluntary sport organizations. *International Review for the Sociology of Sport, 26,* 83–97.

Thorpe, D., Buti, A., Davies, C., & Jonson, P. (2017). *Sports law* (3rd ed.). London: Oxford University Press.

Tricker, R. I. (1984). *Corporate governance.* London: Gower.

Tricker, R. I. (1993). Corporate governance – The new focus of interest. *Corporate Governance, 1*(1), 1–3.

Trivedi, K., & Srivastava, K. B. L. (2021). A framework for integrating strategic HR and knowledge management for innovation performance. *Strategic HR Review, 20*(1), 11–16.

United Nations Educational, Scientific and Cultural Organization. (2018). *Gender equality in sports media.* UNESCO. Retrieved from https://en.unesco.org/themes/gender-equality-sports-media

Wagstaff, C. R., Martin, L. J., & Thelwell, R. C. (2017). Subgroups and cliques in sport: A longitudinal case study of a rugby union team. *Psychology of Sport and Exercise, 30,* 164–172.

Walters, G., & Tacon, R. (2018). The 'codification' of governance in the non-profit sport sector in the UK. *European Sport Management Quarterly, 18*(1), 482–500.

Weight, E., Taylor, E., Huml, M., & Dixon, M. (2021). Working in the sport industry: A classification of human capital archetypes. *Journal of Sport Management, 35,* 364–378.

West, A., Green, E., Brackenridge, C. H., & Woodward, D. (2001). Leading the way: Women's experiences as sports coaches. *Women in Management Review, 16*(2), 85–92. https://doi.org/10.1108/09649420110386610

Westerbeek, H., & Smith, A. (2005). *Business leadership and the lessons from sport.* London: Palgrave Macmillan.

Wexley, K. N., & Yukl, G. A. (1984). *Organizational behaviour and personnel psychology* (Rev. ed.). Homewood, IL: Richard D. Irwin, Inc.

Wicker, P., Cunningham, G., & Fields, D. (2019). Head coach changes in women's college soccer: An investigation of women coaches through the lenses of gender stereotypes and the glass cliff. *Sex Roles, 81,* 797–807.

Wymer, S., Naraine, M. L., Thompson, A. J., & Martin, A. (2021). Transforming the fan experience through live streaming: A conceptual model. *Journal of Interactive Advertising.* Advance online publication. https://doi.org/10.1080/15252019.2021.1910884

Yuksel, M., McDonald, M. A., & Joo, S. (2016). Cause-related sport marketing: An organizing framework and knowledge development opportunities. *European Sport Management Quarterly, 16,* 58–85.

Index

Note: Page numbers in *italics* refer to figures; those in **bold** refer to tables.